EXPERIENCES WITH LITERATURE

A THEMATIC WHOLE LANGUAGE MODEL FOR THE K - 3 BILINGUAL CLASSROOM

SANDRA NEVÁREZ
RAQUEL C. MIRELES
NORMA RAMÍREZ

Foreword by Stephen D. Krashen

Addison-Wesley Publishing Company

Reading, Massachusetts • Menlo Park California • New York
Don Mills, Ontario • Wokingham, England • Amsterdam
Bonn • Sydney • Singapore • Tokyo • Madrid • San Juan

A Publication of the World Language Division

Executive Editor: Lise B. Ragan
Consulting Editor: Stephen D. Krashen
Editorial: Angela M. Castro of Robert Ventre Associates, Inc., Nicole S. Cormen
Production/Manufacturing: James W. Gibbons
Design/Typesetting: Robert Ventre Associates, Inc., Newburyport, Massachusetts
Illustrations: Grace Meyer
Cover Photo: Ken Lax, George Mastellone

Acknowledgements:

Poetry reprinted by permission of Fort Worth Independent School District: Page 29, "Los juguetes," anonymous; page 29 "Las mariposas," anonymous; page 90, "La niñita hacendosa" by Rosario Roldán de Alvarado; page 100, "Tres veces al día," anonymous; page 127, "Mi escuelita," anonymous; page 138, "El ayudante," anonymous; page 155, "Hojitas de otoño," anonymous; page 155, "Cuadro de primavera," anonymous; page 156, "Frío," anonymous; page 156, "Invierno," anonymous; page 184, "La lluvia," anonymous; page 184, "Ya llueve" by V. Lozano; page 184, "El viento," anonymous; page 231, "El payasito," anonymous.

NOTE: The bibliographical listings throughout this work are complete and correct to the best of the authors' knowledge, at time of publication.

ISBN 0-201-09368-5
ABCDEFGHIJ-AL-99876543210-89

TABLE OF CONTENTS

Mi mundo / My World

Mis fantasías / My Fantasies

Mis cuentos favoritos / My Favorite Stories

Appendixes

ACKNOWLEDGEMENTS

This handbook has been possible through the support of family, friends, educators, and editors. Our sincere thanks to:

- Dr. Stephen Krashen, who provided us with the inspiration to develop this handbook.
- Numerous colleagues from the ABC Unified School District, Cerritos, California, including Carla B. de Herrera, who have been supportive since the handbook's inception.
- Lilia Stapleton from the ABC Unified School District, Cerritos, California, and Phyllis Ziegler, Bilingual/English as a Second Language consultant, New York, for all their input and support.
- Nancy Villareal de Adler from the New York City Board of Education, Dr. Maria Brisk from Boston University, and Graciela Rodríguez from the Los Angeles Unified School District for their constructive input as the manuscript was being developed.
- Linda Goodman from the Bilingual Publications Company, Dr. Bernard Hamel of Hamel Spanish Book Corporation, and Carlos Penichet of Bilingual Educational Services, for graciously furnishing the majority of the books suggested in the handbook.
- Dr. Dewey Mays from Fort Worth Independent School District, Fort Worth, Texas, for granting permission to print those poems from a bilingual curriculum development project.
- Angela Castro and the editorial staff from Addison-Wesley Publishing Company, for their professional guidance.
- Carmen Rangel Lizarraga, Art Nevárez and Thelma Díaz for their exceptional technical skills.
- And most importantly, our families, especially our husbands, Art Nevárez, Ramón Mireles and Richard Ramírez, for their patience and encouragement.

FOREWORD

Stephen D. Krashen

WHY LITERATURE?

Literature is a magnificent way of encouraging both language development and cognitive development. Through the study of literature, students will naturally engage in those activities that promote language acquisition and that stimulate thinking.

A *good literature program* is one that deals with topics and themes of both universal and local interest, themes that encourage students to think about basic ethical questions ("How should we live?" "How should we treat each other?") and basic metaphysical questions ("Why are we here?"). In a good literature program, students:

* **Read** novels, short stories, and poetry dealing with these topics.

* **Listen** to others telling stories and reading stories out loud.

* **Write** about their own ideas and reactions to others' ideas.

* **Discuss** these ideas.

Reading, according to research, makes enormous contributions to both language and cognitive growth. There is very strong evidence that reading texts of genuine interest to the reader is the source of reading comprehension ability, writing style, and much of our spelling competence. While we get our basic vocabulary and grammar from listening to speech, most of our vocabulary and grammatical development after we reach school-age comes from reading.

Reading helps thinking in two ways. First, reading is probably the major source of new ideas for many people. Second, we read to validate, or confirm our ideas.

Listening can perform many of these functions as well. It is well-established that reading out loud to children is very beneficial for language development; children who are read to are superior in reading comprehension, vocabulary, and in oral language ability. When children are read to, they begin to acquire the special language of writing, its particular grammar and vocabulary, as well as knowledge about how stories are put together (the "story grammar"); all this knowledge helps make their own reading much more comprehensible. And as anyone who has read to children knows, reading out loud gets children "hooked on books." It leads to an interest in free voluntary reading, a habit that ensures continued literacy development.

Writing makes a profound contribution to cognitive development. We write, obviously, to communicate with others. Perhaps more importantly, we write for ourselves. When we write our ideas down, we take thoughts that are vague and abstract and make them concrete; we can then work with these thoughts and come up with better thoughts. Writing, in other words, is a powerful intellectual tool that helps us clarify our thinking and helps us solve problems.

Discussion has the potential of helping some aspects of language acquisition, since it can result in hearing new vocabulary and grammar. Also, when teachers and students discuss stories, teachers are able to provide background information that makes texts more comprehensible, and can relate stories to children's experiences, which makes the text more meaningful. In addition, discussion can contribute to cognitive development. Just as is the case with reading, in discussion we encounter new ideas and confirm our old ideas. Just as is the case with writing, in discussion we often clarify our own ideas—in trying to express ourselves, our own thoughts become clearer.

The table on page ix summarizes what I have tried to say so far, and illustrates how *Experiences with Literature* fits in.

What should students read about, listen to, write about, and discuss? A good literature program, such as *Experiences with Literature,* supplies the answer: Ideas. Students read and hear stories that encourage them to reflect on their lives, they discuss and occasionally debate about these ideas, and they write about the ideas.

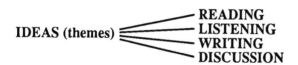

What is crucial is that language development and cognitive development are a **result** of students' "wrestling with" ideas, reading about them, listening to them, writing about them, and discussing them. We don't first learn language and learn facts, and then use them in the study of literature. Literature is the source of language and cognitive development. If teachers and students focus on the ideas, on the stories and their meanings, language and cognitive development will follow:

	READING	LISTENING	WRITING	DISCUSSION
LANGUAGE DEVELOPMENT				
reading comprehension	x	x		x
writing style	x	x		
spelling	x			
vocabulary	x	x		x
grammatical competence	x	x		x
COGNITIVE DEVELOPMENT				
finding new ideas	x	x		x
clarifying ideas			x	x
verifying ideas	x	x		x
COMPONENTS OF *EXPERIENCES WITH LITERATURE*				
Literature Input	x	x		x
Observation/Experience				x
Main Selection & Discussion	x	x		x
"What If" Story Stretcher		x	x	x
Integrating Other Disciplines	x	x	x	x

Table 1

WHY LITERATURE IN THE PRIMARY LANGUAGE?

Studying literature in the child's first language is not a luxury; there is good reason to believe it will help the child acquire English more rapidly, and provide him or her with the knowledge and abilities necessary for success in the English-language mainstream.

A good primary language literature program has these advantages:

Background Knowledge: Children who study literature in their primary language will gain knowledge of the world as well as an understanding of what literature is and how it is studied. Good books, and helpful, teacher-guided discussion can inform children about social studies and science. This knowledge will help make English input more comprehensible, and will thus accelerate English language development. In addition, a child who has participated in a good literature program in the primary language will understand how to discuss and write about the ideas in a story and will have developed an appreciation of good literature. This will make the study of literature in English more comprehensible and more meaningful.

Literacy Transfers: Gaining literacy through the first language is a short-cut to gaining literacy in English. Even if our goal were only English literacy, developing literacy in the primary language first is still the fastest route.

We can distinguish two different aspects of literacy that transfer. First, the mechanical aspects of literacy transfer. The mechanical aspects of literacy are easier for the child to acquire in the first language. We learn to read by reading, by making sense of print; this is much easier to do in a language we understand. Once we can read in one language, this ability transfers rapidly to any other language we acquire.

A second aspect of literacy that transfers is the ability to use language to solve problems. For example, students who have learned to use writing to aid thinking in one language will be able to do this in any other language they acquire.

Free Voluntary Reading: An indirect, but very powerful payoff of participating in a literature program in the first language is that well-taught literature programs instill in students a love of books and a desire to read on their own. If students become free readers in their first language, the chances are excellent that they will also become free readers in their second language. Since reading for meaning develops many literacy-related abilities, establishing a personal reading program makes a huge contribution to academic success.

I would like to finish this brief essay by mentioning a happy coincidence. It turns out that what happens to be best for children is also the most pleasant, both for children and teachers.

Experiences with Literature and other good literature programs allow children to hear and read entertaining stories, and encourage them to discuss and write about issues and topics that are of interest to them. Good literature programs allow teachers to do those things that attracted most teachers to teaching: Engage children in activities that stimulate their thinking and widen their intellectual horizons.

REFERENCES*

Reading is the source of language and literacy development: For a review of the research, see Krashen, S. *Inquiries and Insights*. Hayward, CA: Alemany Press, 1985.

Listening to stories and language development: Krashen 1985, op. cit.; Wells, G. *The Meaning Makers*. Portsmouth, NH: Heinemann, 1985.

Writing and cognitive development: Elbow, P. *Writing Without Teachers*. New York: Oxford University Press, 1972. For empirical evidence, see Langer, J. and Applebee, A. *How Writing Shapes Thinking*. NCTE Research Report No. 22. Urbana, IL: National Council of Teachers of English, 1987.

Discussion and cognitive development: Elbow 1972. op. cit.

Cognitive development is a result of wrestling with ideas: Smith, F. *Joining the Literacy Club*. Portsmouth, NH: Heinemann, 1988.

Why do literature in the primary language? Cummins, J. *Bilingualism and Special Education: Issues in Assessment and Pedagogy*. Clevedon, Avon, England: Multilingual Matters, 1984; Krashen, S. and Biber, D. *On Course: Bilingual Education's Success in California*. Sacramento, CA: California Association for Bilingual Education, 1988.

We learn to read by reading: Goodman, K. *Language and Literacy*. London: Routledge and Kegan Paul, 1982. Smith, F. *Understanding Reading*. Third Edition. Hillside, NJ: Erlbaum, 1982.

*Complete references cited by S. Krashen are found with References in Appendix E.

INTRODUCTION

EXPERIENCES WITH LITERATURE: A THEMATIC WHOLE LANGUAGE MODEL FOR THE K-3 BILINGUAL CLASSROOM serves as a tool for the whole language philosophy. It is an integrated, holistic literature guide that uses student-centered themes and quality Spanish books to foster children's love for reading through meaningful experiences with literature. When literature is used as a major source of language and cognitive input, it can be one of the most powerful educational tools for creating truly literate children.

We can make this become a reality in our classrooms by building on what our students know, their native language and culture, and their background of experiences. In this way, their own experiences are expanded and bridged with the vicarious experiences encountered in stories so that meaning and sensitivity are enhanced in new learning. Such an environment also contributes toward the development of literacy in a second language (Krashen 1985).

Through good Spanish books, we can capture our students' imaginations, stimulate their thinking about questions that are relevant to them, and expand their experiences so that they may develop a sense of mastery over life's many challenges.

This literature guide takes children deeply **into, through,** and **beyond** a story. It uses literature to help children look inward to seek answers to life's most important questions: "Who am I?" and "Why am I?" In other words, "What kind of person am I? Why am I here in this world? How is my own story going to turn out? What's my plot?" Children's literature gives some of the clues we need to answer these questions. (Trealease 1987: 11) In this manner, literature enriches their lives by releasing them from their immediate environment and placing them, through their imaginations, in other places, times, and situations which may not be accessible through first-hand experiences.

Furthermore, this guide provides carefully planned, **integrated literary experiences** that reflect the important values of literature: the development of the joy of reading, increased understanding of self and others, deeper compassion for one's fellow man, enhanced imagination, a greater flexibility of thought, and a greater appreciation for the richness and beauty of language and culture. These values, according to Charlotte Huck are " . . . the reward of a lifetime of reading, recognizable in the truly literate." (Huck 1975: 238)

Written for and dedicated to all teachers, who believe as we do that literature plays a vital role within the whole language classroom, we hope that this literature guide will serve as a valuable resource in helping teachers build meaningful learning experiences for Spanish-speaking students—truly literate students who value the joy, meaning, and imagination of literature.

The introduction to this handbook presents an overview of our literature model, describes the model and its five components, outlines supporting research for each of the components, and provides suggestions for classroom implementation and evaluation.

This handbook translates twenty-one thematic units into actual classroom practice. The thematic units are clustered within five general themes which focus on the child, the child's experiences, world, fantasies, and favorite stories. These thematic units, which have actually been used in the classroom, were chosen for their emotional appeal and relevance to young children. The diverse and universal themes about the family, self-esteem, friendship, adventure, and other relevant subjects, blend to foster children's emotional, social, cultural, moral, and creative development. Each thematic unit is built upon a literature model made up of five components—Literature Input, Observation/Experience, Read and Discuss the Main Selection, "What If" Story Stretcher, and Integrating Other Disciplines.

OVERVIEW OF THE LITERATURE MODEL

This thematic whole language literature guide describes a literature model that can serve as a valuable tool for your whole language program or that can complement a literature-based basal program such as *Hagamos caminos* (Ada, de Olave 1986). Our literature model incorporates several essential features of a well planned *whole language literature-based* program: teachers are encouraged to read regularly to children; to discuss stories through divergent questioning; to promote free voluntary reading; to integrate literature across the curriculum; to allow children the opportunity to share their response to books; to encourage the use of literature as a springboard for writing; and to create authentic, meaningful situations for real reading and writing.

Each of these features are carefully integrated within a theoretically-based five-component model:

     I. **Literature Input**
    II. **Observation/Experience**
  III. **Read and Discuss the Main Selection**
  IV. **"What If" Story Stretcher**
    V. **Integrating Other Disciplines**

This combination of components provides a meaningful program of learning experiences for children and a viable alternative to lock-step skill-building language arts programs. Instead, children are encouraged to explore themes via literature as a means to develop their language, literacy, and cognitive abilities; to expand their experiences; and to nurture their love for reading.

The model's five components actively involve and allow children to:

- select themes and activities of interest to them.
- listen to and read about theme-related stories.
- ponder and share their ideas.
- write about their feelings, ideas, and experiences.
- interact with others in creative and meaningful situations and experiences.

A practical feature of this literature model is that *flexibility* is built-in for the teacher. As you will differ in the selection of thematic units, choice of books, preference of experiences, and style of execution, each of the model's five components includes a range of questions or activities and experiences that allow you to have personal choice. Another valuable feature is that this model can easily be implemented in your English whole language program by using the wealth of books available in English for many of the thematic units.

A THEORETICALLY SUPPORTED LITERATURE MODEL

The five components in this literature model are consistent with current language and literacy theory (Krashen, this volume).

I. Literature Input. "Reading to a child can be the most important facet of his or her becoming literate." (Teale 1982: 152) This exposure to the most complex language available from reading " . . . does seem to go hand in hand with increased knowledge of the language." (Chomsky 1972: 33) Given time, voluntary selection, and accessibility of interesting books, students will not only read, but in fact, will become true readers (Huck, Hickman 1987; Smith 1979).

II. Observation/Experience. Motivational experiences that focus on a story's concepts help spark student interest, enhance comprehension, provide background knowledge to help students make predictions more accurately, and lead to a greater positive literary response (Burke and Goodman 1980; Purves 1975; Smith 1979).

III. Read and Discuss the Main Selection. Reading aloud in association with divergent discussion, in which personal involvement in imaginative exploration is encouraged, is one of the most effective ways of developing children's language and literacy (Krashen 1985; Snow 1983; Wells 1981).

IV. "What If" Story Stretcher. Reading a story again helps foster children's divergent responses. Divergent questioning, in which personal reflection is encouraged, promotes critical thinking necessary for creative and critical reading and writing (Martínez and Rosner 1985; Stewig 1984).

V. Integrating Other Disciplines. Providing relevant, meaningful, functional experiences for children expands and bridges their experiences; supports growth in literacy, language, and cognition; helps them explore the structure and art of literature; and supports growth in other areas of development (Goodman 1986; Goodman, Goodman, and Flores 1984; Huck 1979; Krashen this volume; Sloan 1984).

DESCRIPTION OF COMPONENTS

I. Literature Input

Recognizing that reading aloud is the single most important activity for building a foundation for literacy, Literature Input serves as the read-aloud component of the literature model. The central aim is to provide students with the experience of listening to good books and to expose them to as much language as possible.

Exposing children to daily listening experiences and allowing easy access to the unit's books may spark interest in a theme and may encourage more recreational voluntary reading and sustained silent reading (SSR). Prime-time reading practice, as is well known, will improve the development of children's reading fluency, comprehension, and writing; it is based on the principle that children learn to read and write by reading.

This handbook incorporates over 600 titles in Spanish—some originals in Spanish, others translations from English—representing a *range of literary genres* which includes folktales, fables, fiction, non-fiction, modern fantasy, and poetry. An annotated list of books clustering around a theme introduces each thematic unit. Key concepts or motifs central to each theme are listed or summarized at the beginning of each thematic unit. These are provided so that teachers can link the selected titles to the theme through informal discussion. Teachers should feel free to answer students' questions about the story as they come up and to comment on associated concepts before and during the reading to help make the story more meaningful.

We recommend that <u>five or more titles</u> be selected from the Literature Input Component for each unit. The titles vary in depth, length, and complexity; those having a plus symbol (+) are recommended for more proficient listeners; those with an asterisk (*) are Spanish translations of English books. Teachers are advised to preview each book's narrative, concepts, comprehensibility, length, and possibilities for positive response prior to reading it out loud.

The authors tried to select titles which are readily available for the Literature Input list, but these are subject to change as Spanish titles may go out of print. Every attempt was made to represent Caribbean children's books in the Literature Input although these are not as readily available as other Spanish books. However, Caribbean poetry references can be found in Appendix C.

RELATED TITLES IN ENGLISH FOR SECOND LANGUAGE ACQUISITION

This literature program builds upon the Spanish-speaking child's primary language and provides a literacy base from which knowledge can be drawn and transferred to a second language. Theme-related children's literature in English is a natural, stimulating choice for fostering second language acquisition.

It is advisable that teachers consider their students' proficiency and the English book's comprehensibility for them. Prior to reading a book out loud, preview it to check if the text needs to be adapted or retold for comprehensible listening. Additionally, we recommend that teachers add to the list of English titles and include books from which students can easily make predictions, repetitive-pattern books, and poetry. Each thematic unit includes at least three titles in English, related to each theme, listed at the end of the Literature Input Component. Additional English titles that are translations of Spanish books are indicated with an asterisk.

II. Observation/Experience

The Observation/Experience Component provides motivational experiences that sharpen students' observational skills through observing, doing, talking, or pretending; such engagement, extends and expands concepts and experiences from stories.

The Observation/Experience is aimed towards capturing children's interest and getting them to think; and to share feelings and ideas about a theme. It, in effect, serves as a point of focus that sets the stage for listening to and drawing meaning for an understanding of the story and theme's concepts; and uses background knowledge for helping students predict more accurately.

III. Read and Discuss the Main Selection

The Main Selection, chosen for its emotional and artistic appeal and for its possibilities for extended response, is the story that highlights the theme's concepts. Some units include two Main Selections, giving the teacher a choice for the thematic unit's main story. Unlike the suggested titles from the Literature Input, the Main Selection is more fully extended through response-oriented experiences. It is read aloud and followed by an informal discussion session which serves the following *purposes*:

- It is a catalyst for spontaneous oral response that provides an opportunity for teachers and children to discuss the effect the story has had on them, allowing children to reveal their personal understanding and feelings.
- It develops a concept of story and builds a natural awareness of literary elements— character, plot, setting, and mood.
- It encourages divergent thinking in which major concepts from the theme are clarified and personalized for children.

Four types of comprehension questions developed by Alma Flor Ada and María del Pilar de Olave as part of their Creative Reading Methodology (1986) are provided to help teachers stimulate children's thinking and discussion:

- *Descriptive* - These are recall questions at the knowledge and comprehension levels that include what, where, when, who, and how. These questions help confirm students' predictions about a story.

- *Personal Interpretative* - These are questions at the analysis and application levels that enable children to compare and contrast the stories in relation to their own personal experiences and feelings. These are personalized questions such as have you ever wished, felt, seen, and the like.

- *Critical* - These questions demand higher levels of cognitive processing to infer, synthesize, and evaluate. Children begin to weigh information from texts in light of their own experiences and feelings. Questions may include "What If" story stretchers, which place children in other places and situations; questions associated with exploring alternatives; and those associated with analyzing and making judgments about characters and situations.

- *Creative* - These questions stimulate children to stretch their imaginations and to creatively express themselves verbally through the arts and writing. Responses require a depth of feeling about characters, situations, and events in a story. By identifying with the characters and situations, children begin to understand that their actions have an effect on their lives and that they themselves play an important part in exploring creative alternatives for addressing life's many challenges.

The personal interpretative, creative, and critical questions, which are the most valuable, help to guide children in answering, "Who am I?" and "Why am I here?" In effect, children ponder and reflect upon stories and begin to understand themselves in light of the characters' experiences.

IV. "What If" Story Stretcher

The "What If" Story Stretcher Component provides open-ended, thought-provoking questions that afford another opportunity to stimulate students' *creative and critical thinking*. Unlike the discussion in Component III, children become engaged in an oral exchange of ideas in which creativity and enjoyment are enhanced by playing upon children's imaginations. Drawing students into a story by having them pretend that they are now the character(s), or are in the setting, or are faced with a given problem or situation provides a personal association for them. They relate stories to their own personal experiences and to that of others and begin to identify with characters' feelings and problems. An oral exchange of ideas coupled with creative dramatics and writing build an appreciation of literature which becomes a basis for their own oral and written narrations.

It is important to begin the "What If" Story Stretcher session with a second reading of the main story. Re-reading a story not only focuses children's attention on the richness and beauty of language but also aids children in internalizing the story's meaning and concepts related to the story theme.

The discussion questions from Component III (Main Selection and Discussion) and Component IV ("What If" Story Stretcher) are purposefully integrated to encourage questioning at all levels of comprehension and to heighten teacher's expectations for student response. This discourages the natural inclination to limit students according to their "expected" level of performance. However, though the extent of questioning should always be gauged by the maturity readiness of students, it is important not to "over-question" them as this may thwart their enjoyment of a story.

Some children may not display a readiness for responding to the divergent questioning in the "What If" Component until given prior exposure to direct and vicarious experiences. Therefore, this component is interchangeable with Integrating Other Disciplines, the fifth component of our model.

V. Integrating Other Disciplines

This component expands children's experiences and invites them to participate in the wider, creative application of literature within a whole language context. Moreover, it encourages them to respond to literature as an action or an event in drama, retelling stories, poetry, art, writing, and integrated content areas. Involving children in meaningful experiences allows them to practice a full repertoire of language functions in a natural context and for real purposes (Halliday 1981).

When children authentically respond to literature through experiences for real purposes, listening and discussion play an important part in encouraging them to talk about, to ask questions about, and to read and write about theme-related concepts. Each thematic unit includes experiences in *creative dramatics*, *art* and *writing*; other disciplines such as *science*, *social studies* and *health*; and *poetry*.

CREATIVE DRAMATICS

Drama and story retelling foster children's creative expression. Through personal involvement, children bring the story to life and gain an understanding of people, places, and life's happenings. Pretending and "acting out" allows them to identify with characters and situations and thus personalize the literary experience.

ART AND WRITING

Art, in association with literary experiences, is a medium by which children express their meaning of the story and theme. A variety of media are used as stimuli to motivate student writing and shared reading. A r*eproducible art activity master* accompanies each unit.

Using literature as a springboard for writing across the curriculum is an essential feature of this component. It is based on the assumption that in listening to quality literature, children will discover that reading and writing are closely linked and that these interrelated processes are a means of self-expression.

Children are motivated to write when they have something to express for a real purpose and when writing is an outgrowth of meaningful direct or vicarious experiences inspired by literature. The language and imaginative power of literature provide a catalogue of creative ideas that help spark children's imagination and interest in writing. As a daily feature of the whole language classroom, writing may be incorporated in association with "What If" story stretchers, story retelling, social studies, science, and the arts.

Writing experiences in this guide include *pre-writing*; *language experience writing*; *functional writing* (instructions, recipes, invitations, newspaper articles, science logs); *creative writing* (authoring books, stories, poems, songs); and *personal writing* (letters, diaries, literature logs, and journals). Personal journals in which children write about their experiences and interact with the teacher, literature logs in which they convey their interpretation of the story and theme, and science logs in which they record their observations and experiences about science related topics serve as books for children's cumulative writing. (Reproducible covers for the journals and logs are found in Appendix A beginning on page 329.) Many of these writing activities need not be daily, polished products but rather, on-going writing experiences for children to share with a reading audience.

INTEGRATING OTHER CONTENT AREAS

Science, social studies, health, math and other content areas are integrated with the language arts throughout the thematic units. Though many social science and science curriculum objectives can be satisfied through the use of our thematic units, they serve merely as an example of how literature can be integrated. When first-hand experiences are not feasible, literature can provide a *meaningful context* for learning about these disciplines.

A variety of functional and creative experiences are provided so that teachers and/or students may choose those most appealing and relevant. These may be modified to challenge students or to encourage them to tap their own creativity for authentic response.

POETRY

Extending a thematic unit through poetry fosters children's creative expression and exposes them to the rhythm of poetic language. When presented in association with creative dramatics, creative movement, music, or writing, it enhances their aesthetic experience. It is recommended that teachers add theme-related poems for each unit and include these as well as student poetry in a student poetry log. Additional theme-related poems can be found in books listed in the poetry reference section, Appendix C. Poetry references marked with an asterisk contain theme-related poems.

CLASSROOM IMPLEMENTATION

The literature model in *Experiences with Literature* may be implemented using one of two suggested approaches:

Approach One uses five or more selected stories from the Literature Input to **prepare** students for an understanding of the theme's concepts highlighted in the Main Selection. This approach takes students through the Literature Input and Observation/ Experience before the Main Selection.

Approach Two uses the Observation/Experience and the Main Selection to introduce the thematic unit. Selected stories from the Literature Input are used to **reinforce** the concepts already presented in the Main Selection.

In short, the basic difference between the two approaches is that in Approach One, Literature Input is used prior to the Main Selection to prepare students for the theme's concepts; and in Approach Two, the Main Selection is read first, then followed by Literature Input to reinforce the theme's concepts. Using either approach is a matter of personal choice; however, it is essential to implement all of the components (I - V) in the literature model in order to contribute to children's appreciation of literature and overall literacy development. The table on page xxi shows how Approaches One or Two may be implemented:

APPROACH ONE: Preparation for building a theme's concepts

Week One	Literature Input	Select five or more books to read aloud. Read at least one per day.
Week Two	1) Observation/Experience	Set the stage for the main story.*
	2) Read and Discuss the Main Selection	Read the main story. Select questions for a brief informal discussion.
	3) "What If" Story Stretcher Select questions for critical thinking.	Re-read the story.
	4) Integrating Other Disciplines	Select extended experiences for the theme and story.

APPROACH TWO: Reinforcement of a theme's concepts

Weeks One and Two	1) Observation/Experience	Set the stage for the main story.*
	2) Read and Discuss the Main Selection	Read the main story. Select questions for a brief informal discussion.
	3) Literature Input	Select five or more books to read aloud. Read at least one per day.
	4) "What If" Story Stretcher	Re-read the story. Select questions for critical thinking.
	5) Integrating Other Disciplines	Select extended experiences for the story and theme.

*When the unit contains more than one story, select one to develop the theme.

Table 2

Implementation Guidelines

As our aim is to provide primary grade (K-3) teachers with a flexible, adaptable whole language literature model upon which to build, the following considerations serve to assist teachers in the preparation and implementation of the model. These allow teachers to determine their individual needs and preferences with respect to their program objectives, teaching approach, feasibility of implementation, and preparation time.

1. Will this literature model help meet mandated curriculum goals?

   Certainly, this literature model builds the foundation for long-term developmental goals in language, cognition, and literacy which are naturally and meaningfully fostered through literature. Charlotte Huck (1979) outlines the long-term goals as follows:

   • *Language Goals* - Children will become skilled listeners in attending to and comprehending literature, understand and use the mature syntax of their language, enjoy the creative and aesthetic use of language, and effectively communicate oral and written language.

   • *Cognitive Goals* - Children will continue to acquire new concepts and to refine ones already held, develop skills in a variety of thinking processes, begin to utilize critical thinking skills, begin to expand their powers of logical reasoning, and engage successfully in problem solving.

   • *Literacy Goals* - Children will develop a sense of story, learn to read and write critically and creatively, communicate ideas effectively in response to books as a springboard for written composition, and, most importantly, will develop a life-long reading habit.

2. Is it feasible to implement this model and still meet curriculum requirements?

   When literature is used as an *integrative* vehicle, it naturally encompasses all aspects of language—listening, speaking, reading, writing—while incorporating other disciplines in a meaningful context. Whole language literary experiences that integrate social studies, science, health, and the arts allow for the most efficient use of time and the greatest efficiency in teaching.

3. To what extent should the literature model be incorporated?

   The model is a tool to be used to the extent that individual teachers wish. For example, it may be used as a comprehensive language arts curriculum, as an enhancement or complement to a quality literature-based basal program, or as a means of integrating content area instruction. Ideally, if teachers are already implementing a whole language program, the thematic unit literature model can be a useful tool. For all purposes, it is an at-the-finger-tips resource.

4. How will this literature model be implemented?

   It may be implemented using either of the two approaches: preparation for building a theme's concepts or reinforcement of a theme's concepts (See Table 1 on page ix).

Teachers also have the option of tailoring either approach to their individual preferences and needs.

5. Where does the teacher begin?

   The teacher begins by selecting the themes, units, and individual books that are most appropriate or that can best be adapted to the students' needs and purposes (or students may select themes that are appealing). The teacher should consider the availability of books and choose those activities that are most challenging and that lead to the most reading, writing, and integrative learning.

6. What are some management considerations when using the Integrating Other Disciplines Component?

   Extended theme-related experiences follow each main story, but any of the stories from the Literature Input list may prompt a follow-up activity. Story or theme-related experiences can be managed with the whole class or with cooperative/collaborative learning groups. Rotating theme-related activity centers may be used while guided, small group literacy-related experiences takes place.

7. How many class sessions will it take to implement each component of the model?

   - **Literature Input** will take several days to read the stories.
   - **Observation/Experience** and **Read and Discuss the Main Selection** can be delivered in one session.
   - **"What If" Story Stretcher** requires a session of its own since more time may be needed for creative extension.
   - **Integrating Other Disciplines** requires several sessions, depending on a teacher's desired extension.

INFORMAL EVALUATION GUIDE

Evaluating the literary growth of children is difficult to measure using formal assessment, but it can be informally assessed and recorded by observing the following behaviors:

- Do children appear attentive and involved when listening to stories? For example, are they requesting that favorites be re-read?

- Are children responding to books in a variety of ways: art, drama, writing, literature, and science logs?

- Are children responding to a wider range of literary genre?

- Are children relating literature to their own lives?

- Are children demonstrating, through discussion, a depth of understanding of a story's concepts or concepts relating to a theme?

- Are student predictions about stories becoming more accurate?

- Are unsolicited, authentic responses to literature evident, as seen in children's play, talk, art, sharing, or writing?

- Are children voluntarily reading independently at school?

- Do parents report increased home reading?

- Do an increasing percentage of students utilize the library more frequently?

- Are children beginning to adopt the conventions of language as modeled by literature?

- Are children becoming aware of their growth in literacy as evident in their writing: journals, literature, poetry, and science logs? (Throughout the year, collect writing samples, keep student writing folders, and make anecdotal records of their growth.)

UNIT ONE

PERTENEZCO A UNA FAMILIA

I BELONG TO A FAMILY

A family represents a unit of love and security. It establishes a foundation for a child's physical, emotional, intellectual, cultural, and spiritual whole-being. A child's experiences within the family unit affect his/her perception of self, the world, and the child's interaction with others.

Extended family members can play an important part in a child's life; they often serve as caretakers, role models and transmitters of cultural traditions. Most children enjoy interacting with grandparents, uncles, aunts, and cousins, but in today's mobile society a great number of families live away from extended family, leaving children little opportunity to socialize with them. Stories such as *Mamá ya no está enfadada* and *El abuelo Tomás* introduce characters with whom children can identify and characters as extended family members who relate the joy of being part of a family.

CONCEPTS AND VALUES

1. A family is a unit of love and security.
2. Families work and play together and share happy and sad times.
3. Family members need to cooperate and share responsibilities.
4. Family members can do nice or "not so nice" things for (or to) one another.
5. Families are different. There are small and large families, single-parent families, and step-families.
6. Grandparents, cousins, uncles, aunts, and godparents are extended family members who play a valuable part in a child's life.

CHOOSE THE MAIN SELECTION

Before reading the Main Selection aloud, take your students through the Literature Input and Observation/Experience phases which follow.

Nagasaki, Gennosuke, and Kozo Kakimoto.

Mamá ya no está enfadada.
Spain: Editorial Planeta, 1982.

This delightful story is about a fun-loving pig family. Mother does not think it amusing when she finds her three piglets and her husband playing in the mud. She cleans and hangs them on the clothesline to dry! While preparing bread, she plays with the dough and really enjoys herself. This helps her understand why her family had had so much fun in the mud.

If you choose *Mamá ya no está enfadada* as your selection, turn to page 5 to begin the Observation/Experience phase.

Zavrel, Stepan.

El abuelo Tomás.
Spain: Ediciones S. M., 1984.

Grandfather Tomás is his grandchildren's best friend. One day the city mayor decides to send all the elderly to a rest home because they are spending too much time with their grandchildren. Kept in captivity, the children devise the most hilarious plan to bring them home!

If you choose *El abuelo Tomás* as your selection, turn to page 10 to begin the Observation/Experience phase.

I. LITERATURE INPUT: *Both Selections*

Select five or more titles from the following list to read aloud. Read at least one selection per day to the students. Make available and incorporate the suggested titles for voluntary independent reading. Titles marked with * are Spanish translations of the original English story; titles marked with + are recommended for more proficient listeners.

* 1. Berenstain, Stan and Jan. *El bebé de los osos Berenstain.* New York: Scholastic, 1982. The family is preparing for the arrival of a new baby. When the baby arrives, big brother bear helps but is worried about his place in the family.

* 2. Carruth, Jane. *La hermanita.* Argentina: Editorial Sigmar, 1978. Tili is a little mouse who feels left out when his new baby sister arrives.

3. Claret, María. *Juegos de ayer y de hoy.* Spain: Editorial Juventud, 1983. This is an interesting book comparing games that grandparents played in past times and those that children play today.

4. D'Atri, Adriana. *Así son papá y mamá.* Spain: Editorial Altea, 1977. Clara and Enrique are siblings who relate the daily experiences and personal relationships of belonging to a family.

5. —. *Así es nuestro hermano pequeño.* Spain: Editorial Altea, 1977. Clara and Enrique enjoy having a new baby in the family.

6. —. *Así son los abuelos que viven cerca.* Spain: Editorial Altea, 1977. Clara and Enrique share their experiences with an attentive grandpa and grandma who live nearby.

7. —. *Así son los abuelos que viven lejos*. Spain: Editorial Altea, 1977. Clara and Enrique are happy to see their loving grandparents who live far away.

8. —. *Así son los tíos*. Spain: Editorial Altea, 1977. Clara and Enrique describe their relationship with their uncle.

9. Denou, Violeta. *Pepa. Tormenta en el bosque*. Spain: Editorial R.M., 1980. Pepa, who lives with her grandparents, loves animals, but her grandfather does not care for pets.

10. —. *Los tres y Tío Pek*. Spain: Ediciones Hymsa, 1980. Tío Pek takes his niece and nephews on an adventure in his hot air balloon.

11. —. *Teo y su hermana*. Spain: Editorial Timún Más, S.A., 1985. When a new baby sister arrives at Teo's home, he encounters new experiences.

12. Díaz, Oralia A. *Los conejitos de Don Julio*. Guatemala: Editorial Santa Piedra, 1984. Generous Don Julio takes pride in sharing his rabbits with his nieces.

*13. Eastman, Phillip D. *¿Eres tú mi mamá?* New York: Random House, 1967. A baby bird, born while mother bird is away, wanders through his new world trying to find her.

+14. García Sánchez, J. L. *El pueblo que se quedó sin niños*. Spain: Editorial Altea, 1978. Although parents and extended family members in this story already love their children, they learn how they can become better caretakers even in times of adversity.

15. —. *El niño y el robot*. Spain: Editorial Altea, 1978. Before grandfather dies, he creates a robot to care for his orphan grandson.

*16. Kraus, Robert. *¿De quién eres ratoncito?* New York: Scholastic, 1980. A little mouse, who thinks he has no one in the world, goes through his habitat trying to find his family.

*17. Lindgren, Astrid. *Yo también quiero tener un hermano*. Spain: Editorial Juventud, 1985. Having a new baby in the family is not as easy as it seems, especially for other siblings.

+18. Llimona, Merced. *Del tiempo de la abuela*. Spain: Editorial Hymsa, 1980. In this beautifully illustrated book, grandmother tells her grandchildren about her experiences as a child.

19. Lobato, Arcadio. *El valle de la niebla*. Spain: Ediciones S.M., 1986. This is a story about a boy who had faith in his grandfather's belief in the sun and learned that there is more to the world beyond a small village.

*20. Lobel, Arnold. *Tío Elefante*. Spain: Editorial Alfaguara, 1984. Uncle Elephant is a delightful character who would be every child's choice in uncles.

*21. Loof, Jan. *Mi abuelo es pirata*. Spain: Editorial Miñón, S.A., 1982. Grandfather loves to talk to his grandson about his past escapades. His storytelling takes them on an imaginative pirate adventure.

*22. Melsen, June. Adapted by Pat Almada. *¿Quién será mi mamá?* U.S.A.: Basic Plus, 1986. For beginning readers, this beautifully illustrated story portrays the concept of family in a simple way.

*23. —. *La familia de los tigres*. U.S.A.: Basic Plus, 1986. The tiger family is one of the busiest and funniest. Children readily identify with the characters.

*24. Minarik, Else Holmelund. *Osito*. Spain: Editorial Alfaguara, 1986. This is a popular book about a bear family. It is one of a series of stories about Osito and his family.

*25. —. *Papá Oso vuelve a casa*. Spain: Editorial Alfaguara, 1986. This is another book about Osito's family. In this story, father bear is away and returns home. A series of warm incidents develop between father and son.

26. Nagasaki, Gennosuke, and Kozo Kakimoto. *Mamá siempre está ocupada*. Spain: Editorial Planeta, 1982. In this story, mother is caught up in the chores of family living. When she becomes ill, father and children take over her "thankless" job.

27. —. *Mamá va de compras*. Spain: Editorial Planeta, 1982. The pig family takes a bus ride to their shopping destination. The adventures at the store and in the bus make this story fascinating for young readers.

28. —. *Mamá y el muñeco de nieve*. Spain: Editorial Planeta, 1982. The three little pigs and father have fun on the day of the first snowfall. When mother goes out to join them, she has an accident.

*29. Olson, Arielle North. *¡Ven de prisa, Abuela!* Spain: Editorial Altea, 1985. Melinda and Timoteo excitedly await the arrival of their adventurous grandmother.

*30. Oxenbury, Helen. *En casa de los abuelos*. Spain: Editorial Juventud, S.A., 1984. A little girl spends a wonderful, playful day at her grandparents' house as they give her all their time and affection.

*31. Parramón, José M. Illustrated by Carme Solé Vendrell. *Los padres*. New York: Barron's Educational Series, Inc., 1985. This is another beautifully illustrated book about family concepts.

*32. Parramón, José M. Illustrated by María Rius. *Los abuelos*. New York: Barron's Educational Series Inc., 1985. The typical, everyday experiences some grandparents have are beautifully portrayed in this book.

*33. Peavy, Linda. *El abuelo de Elisa*. Spain: Editorial Altea, 1985. In this story, Elisa and her grandfather have a wonderful relationship.

34. Perera, Hilda. *Pepín y el abuelo*. Spain: Editorial Everest, 1983. When Pepín takes a trip to the country to visit his grandfather, his life changes completely.

+35. Robles Boza, Eduardo (Tío Patota). *La cosquilla*. México: Editorial Trillas. S.A., 1985. Erika is a lucky girl, who has a wonderful relationship with her grandfather. She loves to be tickled by him and misses the tickles when grandfather becomes ill.

+*36. Stenson, Janet Sinberg. *Tengo un padrastro lo cual, a veces, me desconcierta*. México: La Prensa Médica Mexicana, S.A., 1983. A boy lives with his divorced mother and is used to getting all of her attention. When his mother remarries, things get confusing for him, but his new stepfather manages to gain his stepson's trust and respect.

+37. Turin, Adela. *Una feliz catástrofe*. Spain: Editorial Lumen, 1976. A flood at the *Casa Ratón* (Mouse House) changes family life into a series of adventures that causes father to become a less demanding mouse.

*38. Williams, Barbara. *El dolor de muelas de Alberto*. New York: E. P. Dutton, 1974. Poor Alberto is misunderstood by his family when he complains of a toothache. No one believes him except his grandma.

39. Zatón, Jesús. *Las adivinanzas*. Spain: Jucar Infantil, 1984. Veronica is bored and decides to make up riddles about anything that comes to her mind. She enjoys it so much that she includes all the family in the fun.

RELATED TITLES IN ENGLISH FOR SECOND LANGUAGE ACQUISITION

Borack, Barbara. *Grandpa*. New York: Harper and Row, 1967.

Flack, Marjorie. *Ask Mr. Bear*. New York: Macmillan, 1985.

Goldman, Susan. *Cousins Are Special*. Chicago: Albert Whitman and Company, 1978.

Hoban, Russell. *A Babysitter for Frances*. New York: Harper and Row, 1975.

Kalman, Bobbie. *People in My Family*. New York: Crabtree Publishing Company, 1985.

Kroll, Steven. *If I Could Be My Grandmother*. New York: Pantheon Books, 1977.

Rigby, Shirley Lincoln. *Smaller Than Most*. New York: Harper and Row, 1985.

Scott Ann Herbert, and Glow Coalson. *On Mother's Lap*. New York: McGraw-Hill, 1972.

+ Simon, Norma. *All Kinds of Families*. Chicago: Albert Whitman and Company, 1976.

Tax, Meredith. *Families*. New York: Little, Brown, and Company, 1981.

II. OBSERVATION/EXPERIENCE: *Mamá ya no está enfadada*
(Class Session One)

Guide students in the following observation/experience sequence to set the stage for reading the Main Selection.

Focus: Families are alike in many ways.

1. Have students bring in family pictures in advance.

2. Have each student introduce his/her family and state one thing that they all do together, e.g., eat, play, share, talk. (Record on chart).

3. Place pictures on a class bulletin board titled *«Mi familia y yo»* ("Me and My Family").

4. Tell students that in a story titled *Mamá ya no está enfadada* they will meet a family which, in some ways, may be like their own.

5. Show them the book cover and have them predict the types of things a pig family might do. Underline those previously recorded family activities that correspond to their predictions about the characters' experiences. Following the story, have children discuss whether their predictions were correct.

III. READ AND DISCUSS THE MAIN SELECTION: *Mamá ya no está enfadada*
(Class Session One)

Read the Main Selection from page 2 to the students. Highlight the unit's theme by relating this story to other selections from the Literature Input list on pages 2 - 5. Then, guide students in discussing some of the following questions.

1. *¿Qué trabajos tiene la mamá cerda en este cuento? ¿Tienen sus mamás algunos de estos trabajos?* (What chores does mother pig have in this story? Do your mothers have any of these jobs?)

2. *¿En qué se parece la familia del cuento a las de ustedes?* (In what way is the family in the story like yours?)

3. *Los cerditos se divertieron con su papá. Cuéntennos de algo divertido que ustedes han hecho con sus papás o sus mamás.* (The little pigs had fun with their father. Tell us about a fun time with your fathers or your mothers.)

4. *¿Fué el castigo de la mamá muy severo? ¿Qué les hubieran dicho sus mamás a ustedes?* (Was the mother's punishment too harsh? What would your mothers have said?)

5. *¿Por qué decidió la mamá bajar a la familia del tendedero?* (What made the mother decide to take her family off the clothesline?)

IV. "WHAT IF" STORY STRETCHER: *Mamá ya no está enfadada*
(Class Session Two)

Next, re-read the Main Selection and choose one or more of the following questions to develop students' critical thinking skills. Story stretchers may also prompt discussion, drama or writing activities.

1. *Si ustedes fueran cerditos, ¿cómo convencerían a sus mamás que jugar en el lodo es muy divertido?* (If you were piglets, how would you convince your moms that mud play is fun?)

2. *Si, en lugar del papá, la mamá cerda hubiera sido juguetona, ¿cómo habría cambiado el cuento?* (If, instead of father, mother pig had been the playful parent, how would the story have been different?)

3. *Si ustedes quisieran que sus mamás tuvieran más tiempo para divertirse, ¿cómo las ayudarían?* (If you wanted your moms to have more time to have fun, how would you help them?)

4. *Si ustedes y sus hermanos fueran castigados como los cerditos, ¿qué castigos chistosos les gustarían?* (If you and your brothers and sisters were punished as the piglets were, what silly punishments would you like?)

5. *Si ustedes y sus familias quisieran divertirse, ¿qué cosas harían juntos?* (If you and your families wanted to have fun, what things would you do together?)

V. INTEGRATING OTHER DISCIPLINES: *Mamá ya no está enfadada*
(Class Session Three and Ongoing)

The following activities are designed to enhance children's response to literature and expand *beyond* the story and its theme. The variety of activities gives teachers and students an opportunity to choose those most appropriate.

CREATIVE DRAMATICS

1. *Pig Mask Dramatization:* Have students make and use paper plate pig masks to dramatize an event that occurred in the story—mud playtime, worktime, punishment time, snack time.

2. *Fun-Loving Mischief:* Have several groups create and pantomime a new type of fun-loving mischief that the piglets might get into. Have a mother pig from each group choose a mood card—grouchy, happy-go-lucky, disappointed—that will instruct her to react to the group's spontaneous mischief.

3. *Imaginary Sensory Experiences:* Have students pretend that they are piglets knee-high in mud. Have them improvise how they would walk, play, roll in the mud. Have them pretend to be mother pig and a bag of flour has spilled. What might they do with the powdery substance? Have them imagine that they hose down the powder. Now what happens to it? Have them improvise what they might do in the sticky mess.

ART AND WRITING

1. *Illustrations:* To help children learn to appreciate the artistic value of illustrations and differentiate among different media used, talk about the book's illustrations. Have students use pastels to illustrate their favorite scenes in the story. Have students write their own descriptive captions.

2. *Paper Plate Books:* Have students select one member from the pig family that they would like to have in their own family. Have children draw and cut pig facial features out of construction paper and glue them on the backs of paper plates to represent the face of their chosen characters. Have students write explanations stating why the characters were chosen. Then have them imagine that they have adopted the characters. Have them tell about the homecoming. Have the students write the stories inside the front part of a second paper plate. Using yarn or fasteners have them attach the two plates together either on top or on the left side.

3. *Families at Work and Play (pre-writing activity):* Brainstorm ideas about how families work and play together. Record the children's ideas on the board around the word «*Familia.*» (This technique is called "clustering.") You can use the same clustering technique with non-readers by using pictures instead of words to surround the word «*Familia.*» Have children paint pictures showing the activities they enjoy doing with their families; e.g., trips, watching television, eating together, cleaning house, gardening, and so on. Have them write descriptive captions for their paintings. If needed, use the clustered words.

4. *Family Awards:* Furnish a teacher-prepared ditto sheet with six to eight family awards to have students acknowledge their family members. Have them write in the traits that are most admired.

¡Fantástico!

Mi _____ es _____
porque _____ .

Fantastic!

My _____ is _____
because _____ .

Have students draw portraits of these family members and frame them with bag frames. Have them trace around the edge of 8-1/2" x 11" sheets of paper placed on bags to form the outline of rectangular windows. Have them cut out the windows. Have them place glue around the borders of the portraits and place them on the inside windows. Have them pierce a hole through the center of the bottom of the bag and put a hanger hook through it so that it will hang.

5. *Straw Puppet Family:* Using Figure A (page 15), have students draw facial features. Have them color, cut out, and tape family figures on drinking straws. Then have students use construction paper to create dimensional designs for a living room setting inside a small box. Place the family straw puppets inside through slits made along the top of the box. Re-enact a typical scene at home. As a follow-up, have students write about «*Un día con mi familia*» ("A Day with My Family").

6. *Button Family:* Using Figure A (page 15), have each child make his/her family. Have them color and cut out people, using buttons for head and yarn for hair. Have the students use two long sheets of construction paper for the front and back of a house for the button family. Form and cut out a roof. Glue both parts together. Draw in windows and a door, and paste the family members in front. Staple a sheet of lined paper inside the house. Have children write about who lives there. Have them introduce family members and mention one thing about each of them. If needed, use the following fill-in sentence:

    Hay _____ personas en mi familia: mi (mamá) y (papá), _____ hermanos, _____ hermanas, y yo. (There are _____ people in my family: my (mother) and my (father), _____ brothers, _____ sisters, and myself.)

7. *Favorite Story Family:* From previous stories in the Literature Input, have children draw the family that they would like to visit. They should include themselves in the picture. Have the students pretend that they have been invited into the story as guests. The family really likes them and they like the family. Have them write about their experiences as characters in their favorite family stories.

SCIENCE

1. *Fictional Versus Real Animals:* The animals in the story are fictional characters; so that young children can make a distinction between real and story animals, have them compare and contrast the story pigs with real pigs. Discuss their behavior (e.g. playing,

eating, sleeping) in their real setting. Record their ideas on a two-column chart. If available, show a film about a farm or pictures displaying pigs. Have students record "pig facts" in their science logs.

2. *Animal Cookies:* As mother pig did in the story, guide students in a tactile experience such as baking cookies. Use a recipe such as the following:

Animal Sugar Cookies

1. Sift and measure: 4-1/2 cups flour.
2. In a separate bowl cream together: 1 cup shortening, 1-1/2 cups sugar, 3 eggs, 1 tsp. almond extract, and 2 tsp. vanilla extract.
3. Combine mixtures.
4. Roll in waxed paper and chill (can be used immediately but easier if chilled).
5. Cut with animal cookie cutters.
6. Bake at 325° for 6-8 minutes.

Have them write this special recipe in their science logs and record what happens to the ingredients when combined.

SOCIAL STUDIES

1. *Comparing Families:* Using picture books or books used in the Literature Input stage, present illustrations depicting all types of families in different situations. Guide students in a discussion by asking:

   ¿En qué se parecen estas familias? (How are these families the same?)

   ¿Cuáles dibujos les recuerdan a sus familias? ¿Por qué? (Which pictures remind you of your families? Why?)

   In personal journals, have students write about the illustration or story that most reminds them of their families, telling why.

2. *Family Album:* In advance, have children bring photographs of family members. Have them glue the photographs on 8-1/2" x 11" sheets of construction paper. Students may write their own descriptive captions or the following caption may be used:

   «Esta/e es mi _____.» ("This is my _____.")

   If recording student-dictated captions, type them or use a yellow or light pink marking pen, then have them trace their sentences and read them to you or to a partner. For a variation of this family album, have the students create a pop-up book.

3. *My Family "Team":* Discuss the concept of teamwork and the unique contributions that each family member makes to a family. Have the students write "thank you" cards to family members for their efforts in helping the family "team."

4. *Mother's Day Card:* Have children make Mother's Day cards. Have them write their own messages and use the poem *«Mi canastita»*. Have the students decorate them with their own illustrations.

5. *Father's Day Card:* Write a class language experience description on the theme *«Un papá es . . . .»* ("A father is . . . .")

   Each child volunteers his/her own idea and the teacher records it on a chart.

«Quien me lleva al parque,» dijó Ana. ("Someone who takes me to the park," said Ana.)

«Quien platica conmigo,» dijó David. ("Someone who talks with me," said David.)

Type the children's ideas and reproduce them. Then, have the children read their ideas and place them in Father's Day cards. Have the children decorate the cards with their own illustrations.

I. LITERATURE INPUT: *El abuelo Tomás*
See pages 2 - 5.

II. OBSERVATION/EXPERIENCE: *El abuelo Tomás*
(Class Session One)

Guide students in the following observation/experience sequence to set the stage for reading the Main Selection.

Focus: Grandparents can be very special.

1. Bring a picture of your grandparent(s). Tell students about the memorable times you had with your grandparent(s). Describe the special things you did together when you were a young child.

2. Have students share experiences they have had with their grandparents. (Record ideas on a chart.)

3. Tell them that in a story titled *El abuelo Tomás,* they will meet a special grandfather and his grandchildren who loved each other very much and who enjoyed being together. But one day, grandpa was taken away!

4. Show them the book cover and have them predict where grandpa will be taken and how the grandchildren will be able to get him back. Following the story, have children discuss whether their predictions were correct.

III. READ AND DISCUSS THE MAIN SELECTION: *El abuelo Tomás*
(Class Session One)

Read the Main Selection from page 2 to the students. Highlight the unit's theme by relating this story to other selections from the Literature Input list on pages 2 - 5. Then, guide students in discussing some of the following questions.

1. *¿Qué cosas hacía el abuelo Tomás que los niños se divertían tanto?* (What things did grandfather Tomás do that were so enjoyable to the children?)

2. *¿Qué cosas hacen ustedes con sus abuelitos? (Si los niños no tienen abuelitos, pregunte: «Si ustedes tuvieran abuelitos, ¿que les gustaría hacer con ellos?»)* (What do you do with your grandparents?) (If children do not have grandparents, ask: "If you had grandparents, what might you like to do together?")

3. *¿Por qué el alcalde de la ciudad mandó a los ancianos fuera del pueblo? ¿Están de acuerdo con esto? ¿Por qué? ¿Por qué no?* (Why did the mayor send the elderly away? Do you agree with his action? Why or why not?)

4. *¿Estaban los ancianos tristes en su nuevo hogar? ¿Cómo lo saben?* (Were the elderly unhappy in their new home? How do you know this?)

5. *¿Podría haber estado el abuelito escondido por mucho tiempo antes de ser descubierto? ¿Por qué? ¿Por qué no?* (Could the grandfather have remained hidden for a long time before being discovered? Why? Why not?)

IV. "WHAT IF" STORY STRETCHER: *El abuelo Tomás*
(Class Session Two)

Next, re-read the Main Selection and choose one or more of the following questions to develop students' critical thinking skills. Story stretchers may also prompt discussion, drama or writing activities.

1. *Si los ancianos se hubieran juntado a protestar contra el alcalde, ¿cómo habría cambiado el cuento?* (If the elderly had gotten together to protest the mayor's decision, how would the story have been different?)

2. *Si los ancianos tenían todo lo que necesitaban en su nuevo hogar, ¿por qué creen ustedes que ellos estaban tan tristes?* (If the elderly had everything they needed in their new home, why do you suppose they were so unhappy?)

3. *Si ustedes hubieran sido uno de los niños del cuento, ¿cómo habrían planeado rescatar a sus abuelitos?* (If you had been a child in the story, how would you have planned to rescue your grandparents?)

4. *¿Qué pasaría si todos los abuelitos tuvieran que vivir en una casa de ancianos? ¿Cómo cambiarían las familias de ustedes?* (What if all grandparents were forced to live in rest homes? What would change in your families?)

5. *Cuando ustedes sean abuelitos, ¿qué creen ustedes que van a recordar de cuando eran niños?* (When you become grandparents, what do you think you will remember about the time when you were children?)

V. INTEGRATING OTHER DISCIPLINES: *El abuelo Tomás*
(Class Session Three and Ongoing)

The following activities are designed to enhance children's response to literature and expand *beyond* the story and its theme. The variety of activities gives teachers and students an opportunity to choose those most appropriate.

CREATIVE DRAMATICS

1. *Welcome Home Party:* Have children plan and improvise a party to welcome the grandparents in the story when they return home.

2. *Family Interaction:* Have children, in pairs, plan and improvise a familiar situation in which extended-family members such as grandpa/grandma, cousin/cousin, uncle/niece interact. Provide cards having these names and distribute them among pairs of children. Encourage them to use dialogue.

3. *Good Times Together:* In cooperative groups, have students plan and improvise a good time when extended-family members get together.

ART AND WRITING

1. *Protest Letter:* Have students write letters of protest to the mayor (in the story) stating reasons why grandparents should stay with their grandchildren. Have them share the letters.

2. *Future Grandparents:* Have students draw themselves as grandparents. Then have them write descriptions of what they might be like as grandparents. If needed, use the following writing starter:

   «*Cuando yo sea abuelo/a, voy a . . . .*» ("When I become a grandparent, I will . . . .")

3. *Memories:* Have students think about a memorable time spent with a special grandparent(s), cousin, aunt, uncle, godparent. Then ask them to illustrate this occasion. Have them write descriptions of the event and tell why the person made it so memorable. Then they can mail the descriptions to that person.

4. *Special Card:* Have students create special cards for a grandparent(s) or for another extended-family member. Have them write a poem about this person or use the following example to write a grandparent "diamante" (diamond-shaped poem). Mount the poem on diamond-shaped colored paper. Directions:

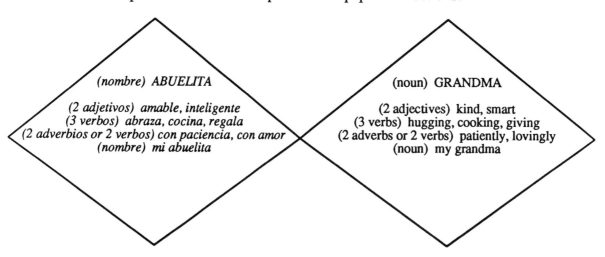

5. *Family Tree:* Have students draw large family trees. Let them take home their illustrations and, with their parents' help, have them write the names of their extended-family members on each branch. Have them share their family trees with the class.

6. *Interview:* As a homework assignment, provide a special interview booklet and have students interview an elderly extended-family member (or an elderly neighbor), surveying the following preferences during their childhood years:

Juego favorito	(Favorite game)
Deporte favorito	(Favorite sport)
Persona favorita	(Favorite person)
Cuento favorito	(Favorite folktale)
Libro favorito	(Favorite book)
Lugar favorito	(Favorite place)
Canción favorita	(Favorite song)
Comida favorita	(Favorite food)
Amiga/o favorita/o	(Favorite friend)
Momento familiar favorito	(Favorite family moment)

Ask them to include one thing that was passed on to them by their grandparents. To prompt writing, share and discuss what they might like to do for and with their own grandchildren.

7. *What We Value:* Have children list five things that they value right now. Then have them list five things that they think they will value when they are grown-up. Ask them to compare the lists. As an outside project, have them obtain the same information from a grandparent or any other elderly person. Have students compare their lists with those obtained from the adults. What was viewed as being most valued among children? Among elderly?

8. *Fantasy Picnic:* Have the students plan a family picnic in a fantasy land and invite all of their extended-family members. What is the occasion? Have them plan all the details and write invitations. The day of the picnic is here. Who came? What do they remember about the fantasy land? In cooperative groups, have them create big books describing the fantasy family picnic.

SOCIAL STUDIES

1. *Grandparents' Day:* With children, plan a "Grandparents' Day" in your classroom or, if possible, as a school-wide activity. If children do not have grandparents, they may bring any other special person. Have the children design and write creative invitations, bake cookies for guests, and perform for the grandparents—singing, dancing, reciting poems, presenting skits.

2. *Convalescent Home Visit:* Plan a class visit to a convalescent home and have children perform for the elderly—singing, dancing, reciting poems, skits, readers' theatre.

   "Sunshine" Letter: Follow up by having cooperative groups write "sunshine" letters to the elderly they met in the convalescent home. If a trip is not feasible, have students illustrate and write poems on cards to mail to the elderly in convalescent homes.

3. *Separation:* With children, talk about grandparents or other extended-family members or friends who have gone away for different reasons. Have children volunteer why this person was special to them. Have students write about special people in their personal journals.

4. *Reminiscing:* Have students reminisce with a grandparent or with an older adult about past stories, songs, customs, and memories. Encourage students to write about their shared experiences.

POETRY

When experienced in association with music, creative drama, creative movement or art, poetry may be used for children's recitations, choral reading, language experience writing or creative writing. Theme-related poems, like those below, may be compiled in a poetry log. Original student poems on each theme can be added.

Mi canastita

Ya se llegó el 10 de mayo
y comienzo a preparar
una linda canastita
para mi buena mamá.

Tiene rosas y claveles,
margaritas y crespón.
Te la entrego a tí mamita
con todo mi corazón.

*Folklore
(Poema del día de Mamá)*

Mensaje

En este mes de junio
un día especial he escogido
para agradecer a papá
lo bueno que él es conmigo.

Me guía por buen camino
Me escucha con atención
Por eso hoy Día del Padre
le envío un mensaje de amor.

*Raquel C. Mireles
(Poema del día de Papá)*

Amor filial

Yo adoro a mi madre querida,
yo adoro a mi padre también;
ninguno me quiere en la vida
como ellos me saben querer.

Si duermo, ellos velan mi sueño;
si lloro, están tristes los dos;
si río, su rostro es risueño:
mi risa es para ellos el sol.

Me enseñan los dos con inmensa
ternura a ser bueno y feliz.
Mi padre por mí lucha y piensa;
mi madre ora siempre por mí.

Yo adoro a mi madre querida,
yo adoro a mi padre también;
ninguno me quiere en la vida
como ellos me saben querer.

Amado Nervo

Mis abuelitos

Ya vienen mis abuelitos
como lo hacen cada año.
Vienen a vernos de lejos
ya sea invierno o sea verano.

A veces son regañones,
otras veces juguetones,
y les gusta mucho cantar
viejas y alegres canciones.

Se levantan muy temprano,
yo no sé ni para qué.
¡Ay pero que sabroso huelen
las tortillas y el café!

Papá y mamá están contentos,
mis hermanos y yo también.
¡Vamos por mis abuelitos
que ya mero llega el tren!

Raquel C. Mireles

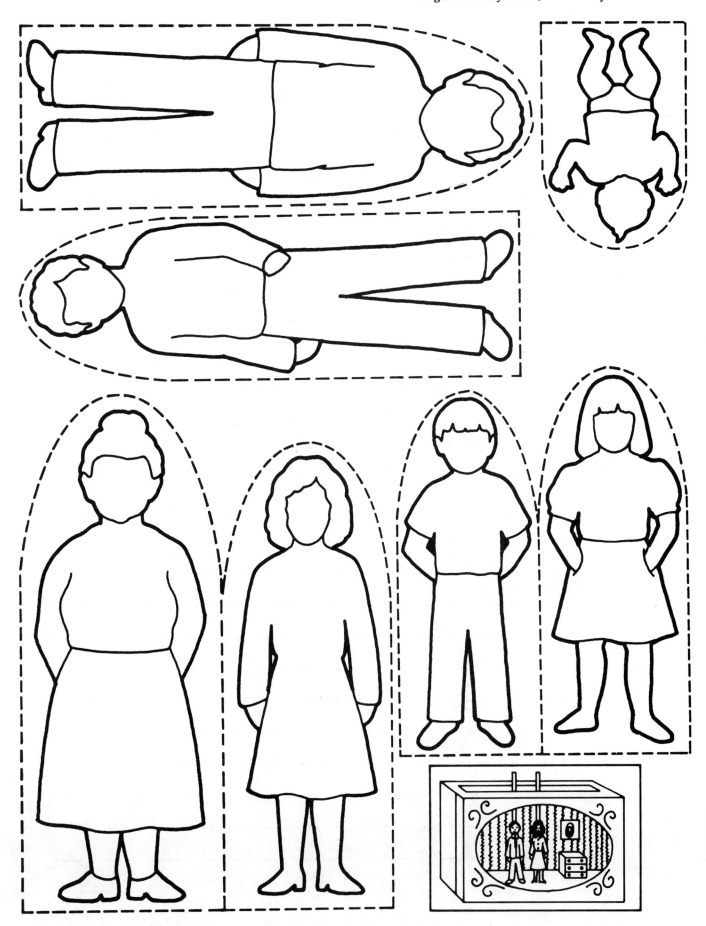

15

MY OWN CREATIVE TEACHING IDEAS FOR UNIT ONE

Books: _____

_____

_____

_____

_____

_____

Ideas: _____

_____

_____

_____

_____

_____

_____

_____

_____

_____

_____

_____

_____

_____

_____

_____

_____

UNIT TWO

LAS COSAS QUE YO AMO

THE THINGS THAT I LOVE

As children grow and experience their world outside of the family, they develop a fondness for other people, animals, places, and objects. These special attachments may symbolize security and love as portrayed in *César y Ernestina han perdido a Gedeón* and *Rollito*. Although with maturity these attachments may be outgrown or forgotten, the love and security they once provided live on.

CONCEPTS AND VALUES

1. People, objects and pets can be very special to us.
2. These special attachments can provide us with a sense of love and security.
3. When we outgrow or lose these special attachments, we realize the value we place on them.
4. Replacing special people, objects and pets may be difficult to accept, but we all need to make an effort to compensate.
5. Children have different interests and tastes: One child's discarded object can be another child's treasure.

CHOOSE THE MAIN SELECTION

Before reading the Main Selection aloud, take your students through the Literature Input and Observation/Experience phases which follow.

Vincent, Gabrielle.

César y Ernestina han perdido a Gedeón.
Spain: Editorial Timún Más, 1981.

Ernestina is frantic when she loses her dearest possession, her favorite stuffed penguin, Gedeón. Her good friend, César, finds it in the snow, too worn to repair. He tries to buy the exact penguin. When the attempt fails, he and Ernestina work together to create a new penguin. This occasion calls for a celebration!

If ·you choose ***César y Ernestina han perdido a Gedeón*** as your selection, turn to page 21 to begin the Observation/ Experience phase.

Robles Boza, Eduardo (Tío Patota).

Rollito.
México: Editorial Trillas, S.A., 1983.

Rollito is Xóchitl's precious pet caterpillar. She cares for him at home and takes him to school where the children feed and watch him. Much to their surprise, Rollito becomes a beautiful butterfly!

If you choose ***Rollito*** as your selection, turn to page 24 to begin the Observation/ Experience phase.

I.   LITERATURE INPUT: *Both Selections*

Select five or more titles from the following list to read aloud. Read at least one selection per day to the students. Make available and incorporate the suggested titles for voluntary independent reading. Titles marked with * are Spanish translations of the original English story; titles marked with + are recommended for more proficient listeners.

1.   Alberti/Wolfsgruber. *Simón y los animales*. Spain: Ediciones S.M., 1986. A beautifully illustrated story about Simón, a boy who loves animals and learns about the changing of the seasons.

+ 2.   Alcántara, Ricardo S. *Guaraçú*. Spain: Editorial La Galera, S.A., 1980. Guaraçú longs to become friends with a beautiful blue bird that guides him out of the jungle when he becomes lost.

3.   Alonso, Fernando. *El viejo reloj*. Spain: Editorial Alfaguara, 1983. When adventurous Ramón finds his grandfather's clock, interesting happenings occur.

4.   Altamirano, Francisca. *Elisa y Palín*. México: Editorial Trillas, S.A., 1986. Elisa loves her little bird enough to give him his freedom.

5.   Armijo, Consuelo. *Moné*. Spain: Editorial Miñón, S.A., 1981. This is the story of a little girl and her love for her teddy bear, Moné. Together they have many interesting experiences.

6.   Calders, Pere. *Cepillo*. Spain: Editorial Hymsa, 1981. This is a story about a boy whose dog is taken away and replaced with an ordinary brush. His "pet" brush helps the family in time of trouble and is rewarded for his deeds.

7. Caso, Katya, and Elena Climent. *Bety y su ratón*. México: Editorial Trillas, S.A., 1986. Bety is saddened when she discovers that her bedtime mouse is gone. Much to her surprise, the morning greets her with a well-groomed little mouse.

8. Cedar, Sally. *¡Cuidado, un dinosaurio!* Spain: Ediciones S. M., 1985. Dini is a dinosaur born fifty million years too late. He is adopted as a pet by a friendly family but finds it difficult to adapt to modern life.

9. Claret, María. *La sorpresa de la ratita Blasa*. Spain: Editorial Miñón, S.A., 1983. Blasa feels disappointed at her birthday party because she did not receive any gifts, but she is pleasantly surprised in the end.

*10. Cutts, David. *Como son las mariposas*. México: Sistemas Técnicas de Edición, S.A. de C.V., 1988. This beautifully illustrated book depicts the life of a butterfly during all of its stages.

11. Denou, Violeta. *Teo y su perro*. Spain: Editorial Timún Más, S.A., 1985. Teo and his pet, Puc, have many interesting experiences that strengthen their love for one another.

12. Fernández, Laura. *Pájaros en la cabeza*. México: Editorial Trillas, S.A., 1983. This is a charming story about a girl's fond attachment for a bird family. She treats them with love and care.

13. Fujikawa, Gyo. *Lanudo*. Argentina: Editorial Atlántida, 1981. Lanudo becomes a better pet as a result of a bad dream. He learns to have compassion for smaller creatures.

14. —. *El vuelo del barrilete*. Argentina: Editorial Atlántida, 1981. Nicolas borrows his best friend's special kite and loses it. He tries to cover up by telling a pack of wild stories.

+15. González de Tapia, Graciela. *El gato Cui*. México: Editorial Trillas, S.A., 1984. Cui is a very special stuffed cat that was given to Nani for Christmas. Their mutual love began the minute they saw each other, and many adventures quickly followed.

*16. —. *Las pantuflas de Alelú*. México: Editorial Trillas, S.A., 1984. Alelú receives a peculiar pair of slippers for her birthday. The slippers come to life every night in the most entertaining way.

*17. Koci, Marta. *Iván, Diván, and Zarimán*. Colombia: Editorial Kapelusz Colombiana, S.A., 1984. Iván, a boy who has a special attachment for an old couch and a mouse, is separated from his friends.

*18. Leclerg, Jean Paul. *Peluso y la cometa*. Spain: Editorial Miñón, S.A., 1979. This story tells about a child's fondness for a special kite.

19. Levert, Claude, and Carmé Sole Vendrell. *Pedro y su roble*. Spain: Editorial Miñón, S.A., 1981. Pedro has a special fondness for an oak tree. When fall arrives, the tree loses its leaves and Pedro learns a lesson about nature and love.

20. Lloyd, David, and Gill Tomblin. *El mejor de los perros*. Spain: Ediciones Altea, 1986. This simple but charming book is about three girls and their affection for dogs.

+21. Olaya de Fonstad, Carmen. Edited by Carla Inés Olaya. *Después de pasar la lluvia.* Colombia: UNICEF, 1977. This is a beautiful story about a shepherd boy and his special attachment for his flock of sheep.

+*22. Osorio, Marta. *La mariposa dorada.* Spain: Editorial Miñón, S.A., 1978. This is the story of a homely worm that becomes the world's first butterfly.

*23. Palmer, Helen Eastman, and Philip D. Eastman. *Un pez fuera del agua.* New York: Random House, 1976. A pet goldfish grows out of control when his friend overfeeds him. Interesting things happen until he is stopped.

24. Pecanins, Ana María. *El globo, la tortuga y yo.* México: Editorial Trillas, 1985. A sensitive girl is saddened when she loses a balloon, but a friendly turtle helps her find it and they become good friends.

+25. Pellicer López, Carlos. *Juan y sus zapatos.* México: Promociones Editoriales Mexicanas, 1982. This is an endearing story about a boy and a pair of shoes.

+26. Perera, Hilda. *La fuga de los juguetes.* Spain: Editorial Everest, 1983. All the toys decide to escape and search for something new. In the end, they realize that they can only be happy when the children are happy.

27. Puncel, María. *El perro perdido.* Spain: Editorial Altea, 1980. This is a delightful story about a pet dog. It is part of a series of stories about children and the experiences they have in their neighborhood.

28. Remolina López, María Teresa. *Un ciempiés descalzo.* México: Editorial Trillas, S.A., 1986. Ciempiesín is a pampered centipede, whose mother tries to please him by allowing him to wear shoes. This book won the 1986 *Antonio Robles Award* in México.

+29. Robles Boza, Eduardo (Tío Patota). *El cajón de los tiliches.* México: Editorial Everest Mexicana, S.A., 1985. The "catch all" box contains all sorts of discarded objects that come to life at night as the most fascinating characters.

+30. —. *Las letras de mi máquina de escribir.* México: Editorial Everest Mexicana, S.A., 1985. In this imaginative story, Tío Patota describes his first typewriter and its fanciful letters.

*31. Selsam, Millicent E. *Teresita y las orugas.* U.S.A.: Harper and Row, 1969. An interesting and true-to-life story of Teresa and the loving care she gives her silkworms as they go through metamorphosis.

32. Solé Serra, Luis, and Carme Solé Vendrell. *La pelota.* Spain: Editorial Hymsa, 1985. This is an interesting story about the adventures of a soccer ball and his friends.

*33. Ulf, Nilson. *Chancho, nuestro cerdito.* Spain: Editorial Juventud, 1983. Eva and Peter adopt a piglet. It brings them many worries but teaches them the meaning of caring and love.

34. Vanhalewijn, Mariette. *El gato sabio de Juanito.* Spain: Editorial Everest, 1980. Juanito loves his cat, but nobody else in his house does because the cat is mischievous. The cat must leave, but father later has a change of heart.

35. de Ybarra, Carmen. *El pájaro azul*. Spain: Editorial Everest, 1980. This is a tender story about a girl and her love for a beautiful blue bird. They love each other but one sad day the bird dies.

36. Zendrera, C. *Yaci y su muñeca*. Spain: Editorial Juventud, 1974. A corn doll is very special to a little girl. One day, when Yaci believes that the doll will be taken away, she buries it and something very unusual happens.

RELATED TITLES IN ENGLISH FOR SECOND LANGUAGE ACQUISITION

Asch, Frank. *Happy Birthday, Moon*. New York: Scholastic, 1982.

Freeman, Don. *Corduroy*. New York: Viking, 1968.

Havill, Juanita. *Jamaica's Find*. Boston: Houghton Mifflin, 1986.

Keller, Holly. *Geraldine's Blanket*. With illustrations by Holly Keller. New York: William Morrow and Company, 1984.

Koci, Marta. *Katie's Kitten*. Austria: Neugebauer Press, 1982.

Riddell, Chris. *Ben and the Bear*. New York: Harper and Row, 1986.

Shubert, Dieter. *Where's My Monkey?* New York: Dial Books for Young Readers, 1987.

Waber, Bernard. *Ira Sleeps Over*. New York: Houghton Mifflin, 1972.

II. OBSERVATION/EXPERIENCE: *César y Ernestina han perdido a Gedeón*
(Class Session One)

Guide students in the following observation/experience sequence to set the stage for reading the Main Selection.

Focus: We often form attachments to special things.

1. Have children (and teacher) share their favorite toy, stuffed animal, picture, or book. Discuss why these things have a special value.

2. Show them the book cover and tell students that in a story titled *César y Ernestina han perdido a Gedeón,* they will learn why a stuffed penguin was so special for Ernestina.

3. Have them predict what César and Ernestina will do when the penguin becomes lost. Following the story, have children check whether their predictions were correct.

III. READ AND DISCUSS THE MAIN SELECTION: *César y Ernestina han perdido a Gedeón*
(Class Session One)

Read the Main Selection from page 18 to the students. Highlight the unit's theme by relating this story to other selections from the Literature Input list on pages 18 - 21. Then, guide students in discussing some of the following questions.

1. *¿Por qué se sentía triste Ernestina? ¿Ustedes se han sentido así alguna vez? Platíquennos.* (Why is Ernestina saddened? Have you ever felt that way? Tell us about it.)

2. *¿Cómo saben que César ama y comprende a Ernestina?* (What tells you that César loves and understands Ernestina?)

3. *¿Han ayudado a alguien así como ayudó César a Ernestina? ¿Cómo?* (Have you ever helped someone as César did? How?)

4. *Qué hizo Ernestina para demostrar su gratitud a César? ¿Que habrían hecho ustedes?* (What did Ernestina do to show her appreciation to César? What would you have done?)

5. *Cuando ustedes crezcan, ¿qué cosas especiales recordarán siempre? ¿Por qué?* (When you grow up, what special things will you always remember? Why?)

IV. "WHAT IF" STORY STRETCHER: *César y Ernestina han perdido a Gedeón*
(Class Session Two)

Next, re-read the Main Selection and choose one or more of the following questions to develop students' critical thinking skills. Story stretchers may also prompt discussion, drama or writing activities.

1. *Si César no se hubiera preocupado por Ernestina, ¿cómo habría cambiado el cuento?* (If César had not cared about Ernestina, how would the story have been different?)

2. *Si ustedes perdieran un juguete, un animalito, o un amigo preferido, ¿qué dirían,y qué harían?* (If you lost your favorite toy, pet or friend, what would you say and do?)

3. *Si César hubiera traído a su casa a un pingüino de verdad, ¿que habría pasado?* (If César had brought home a real penguin, what would have happened?)

4. *Si ustedes vieran que a un niño se le cayera un juguete sin darse cuenta, ¿que harían? ¿Qué dirían? ¿Por qué?* (If you saw a small child drop a toy without noticing it, what would you do? What would you say? Why?)

5. *Si su mamá, su papá o su amigo les diera algo que ya no necesitaba ¿qué les gustaría que fuera? ¿Por qué?* (If your mom, your dad or your friend gave you something she/he no longer needed, what would you want it to be? Why?)

V. INTEGRATING OTHER DISCIPLINES: *César y Ernestina han perdido a Gedeón*
(Class Session Three and Ongoing)

The following activities are designed to enhance children's response to literature and expand *beyond* the story and its theme. The variety of activities gives teachers and students an opportunity to choose those most appropriate.

CREATIVE DRAMATICS

1. *"What If"* : Have children dramatize a previously discussed "What If" story twist; e.g. if César had brought a real penguin, what would have happened in the story?

2. *Lost and Found:* Have students pantomime César looking for Gedeón in the snow. Pantomime finding other things (animals, objects) while observers guess what is found.

3. *What's in the Bag?:* Have students bring in a favorite toy or object concealed in a paper bag. Have each child describe the special object, without naming it, while others guess the name of the object.

ART AND WRITING

1. *Stuffed Animals:* Provide appropriate materials for students to create paper-bag stuffed animals of their choice. Have them write adventure stories about the animals becoming lost. Have them share stories and compile them for a class book.

2. *Listening to Descriptions:* While working in pairs, have one child describe a hidden stuffed animal while another draws an illustration from the description without looking at the model. When the drawing is completed, let them compare the drawing and the stuffed animal. As an alternative, have each student write the description first and then read it to her/his partner.

3. *Mailgrams:* Provide mailgram forms and have students write mailgrams to thank César for being a caring friend. Have them enclose self-portraits to introduce themselves to César.

4. *Box Books:* Have students advertise ***César y Ernestina han perdido a Gedeón*** (or any other book from the Literature Input list) on cereal boxes. Have them draw illustrations of the book on paper and fold them around the boxes. Then have them write the title on the spine of the "box book." Display them in the class or school library. Have the students create flyers advertising their books.

5. *Stuffed Gedeón:* Duplicate Figure B (page 30). Have students cut and color penguin pattern and glue on body parts. Have students glue penguin figure onto a small paper bag. Next, have the children pretend that the coming of spring has uncovered Gedeón. Allow them to write in their literature logs about the sensory and emotional experience of finding Gedeón. What will they do with Gedeón?

6. *Animal Stories:* Provide a box of stuffed animals. Tell students that the animals have belonged to many children, have seen many things, and have been in many places. Show them an animal, and have them imagine the experiences the animal has had.

Allow them to share their ideas. Let them choose and place stuffed animals on their desks. Have them write stories about the experiences the animals have had. Compile the stories to make a class book.

7. *Patchwork Quilt:* Show students a real or illustrated patchwork quilt. Explain that each of the patches has a unique story because each patch was made by a special friend or family member. Have each student design one colorful 6" x 6" patch on a piece of paper or an appropriate cloth. Let them sew (or tie with yarn) all of the patches together. Have each of the students write a sentimental story about his/her special patch and about its uniqueness as part of the class quilt.

8. *Clay Sculptures:* Have students make a clay penguin, a mouse or a bear. Let them give their creations to a family member. Have the students write cards expressing that the sculpture was made especially for the receiver with love.

MATH

1. *Toy Sale:* Explain to children that they will have an opportunity to make toys which may be special for other children. Form several cooperative groups to organize a toy sale. Provide toy catalogs, construction paper, crayons, sheets of newsprint, small paper bags, and newspapers for students to make eight stuffed animals or dolls. Once all eight toys are ready, have them advertise and price each toy from one to ten cents (or make compatible with your class computation level) and display. Use pre-cut paper coins for making purchases. Provide each student with play money and let them shop at each toystand. Let groups decide what they would like to do with their "profits." (Their choices may generate creative ideas that can be expanded.)

SCIENCE

1. *Fictional Versus Real Animals:* The animals in the story are fictional characters; so that young children can make a distinction between real and story animals, have the students compare and contrast César and Ernestina with a real bear and mouse (habitat, hibernation, temperament, and social behavior). Record their ideas on a two-column chart. If available, show a film and present other resources about these animals. Have children record their observations in their science logs.

I. **LITERATURE INPUT:** *Rollito*
See pages 18 - 21.

II. **OBSERVATION/EXPERIENCE:** *Rollito*
(Class Session One)

Guide students in the following observation/experience sequence to set the stage for reading the Main Selection.

Focus: We become attached to pets and other things we love.

1. Share a pet with the children. Ask them if they have pets of their own. Have them draw an illustration of a pet they have or would like to have.

2. Have them tell why the pet is (or would be) special. Ask how they would feel if they were separated from their pets.

3. Tell students that in a story titled **Rollito,** they will learn about the special love that a little girl has for her pet caterpillar.

4. Show the book cover and have them predict whether the caterpillar will stay with the little girl or if it will leave. If so, why? Following the story, have children discuss whether their predictions were correct.

III. READ AND DISCUSS THE MAIN SELECTION: *Rollito*
(Class Session One)

Read the Main Selection from page 18 to the students. Highlight the unit's theme by relating this story to other selections from the Literature Input list on pages 18 - 21. Then, guide students in discussing some of the following questions.

1. *¿Cómo se sintió Xóchitl cuando ella vió a la oruga salir del huevecillo? ¿Han visto ustedes alguna vez a una oruga, un pollo, o algún otro animal salir de un huevecillo?* (How did Xóchitl feel when she saw the caterpillar hatch out of the egg? Have you ever seen a caterpillar, a chicken, or another animal hatch?)

2. *¿Qué hacía Xóchitl para cuidar a su oruga? ¿Qué harían ustedes para cuidar a un animalito (mascotita)?* (What did Xóchitl do to care for her caterpillar? How would you care for a pet?)

3. *¿Por qué estaban los papás tan contentos con el afecto que Xóchitl sentía por Rollito?* (Why were Xóchitl's parents so happy about her attachment for Rollito?)

4. *¿Por qué recordará siempre Xóchitl a su mascotita? ¿Por qué recordarían ustedes a las suyas si ustedes tuvieran mascotitas?* (Why will Xóchitl always remember her little pet? Why would you always remember yours if you had pets?)

5. *¿Podría haber sido verdadero este cuento? ¿Por qué? ¿Por qué no?* (Could this story really have happened? Why? Why not?)

IV. "WHAT IF" STORY STRETCHER: *Rollito*
(Class Session Two)

Next, re-read the Main Selection and choose one or more of the following questions to develop students' critical thinking skills. Story stretchers may also prompt discussion, drama or writing activities.

1. *Si el animalito de Xóchitl hubiera sido un renacuajo, ¿qué habría aprendido ella?* (If Xóchitl's pet had been a tadpole, what would she have learned?)

2. *La mamá comparó a Xóchitl con la mariposa. Cuando Xóchitl crezca, ¿en qué se parecerá a una mariposa? ¿En qué se parecerán ustedes a unas mariposas?* (Mother compared Xóchitl to the butterfly. When Xóchitl grows up, in what way will she be like a butterfly? In what way will you be like butterflies?)

3. *Si ustedes fueran la mamá de Xóchitl, ¿cómo le habrían hecho entender que a veces las cosas que amamos no permanecen con nosotros para siempre?* (If you were Xóchitl's mother, how would you have made her understand that sometimes the things we love do not stay with us forever?)

4. *Imagínense que ustedes son el autor del libro y díganme que quiere decir, «Desde entonces, la mariposa acompaña a Xóchitl en sus sueños.» Si ustedes pudieran escoger un animalito para sus sueños, ¿cúal sería? ¿Por qué?* (Pretend you are the author and tell me what you mean by, "From then on, the butterfly accompanies Xóchitl in her dreams." If you could choose an animal to accompany you in your dreams, what would it be? Why?)

5. *Si ustedes fueran la mariposa de Xóchitl, ¿a dónde la llevarían en sus sueños? Describan el lugar y platíquennos que harían.* (If you were Xóchitl's butterfly, where would you take Xóchitl in her dreams? Describe the place and tell us what you would do.)

V. INTEGRATING OTHER DISCIPLINES: *Rollito*
(Class Session Three and Ongoing)

The following activities are designed to enhance children's response to literature and expand *beyond* the story and its theme. The variety of activities gives teachers and students an opportunity to choose those most appropriate.

CREATIVE DRAMATICS

1. *Special Toy:* Have students pretend that they are at a yard sale where many interesting used toys are displayed. There is one toy that they want because it is special. Let students pantomime playing with the toy while observers guess what it is.

2. *Guess Which Pet:* Provide several boxes of varying lengths and sizes. Have students pantomime taking a pet out of a box, playing with it, and giving it to an observer. Have all the other observers guess what the pet is.

3. *Butterfly Movement:* Provide children with music that will awaken their imagination to fly as butterflies. Allow them to describe themselves and how they feel. As they fly around the room, have them describe what they see in flight.

   Metamorphosis Pantomime: Have cooperative groups pantomime the metamorphosis of butterflies while observers identify or describe the stages.

ART AND WRITING

1. *Do's and Don't's Chart:* Make a two-column chart listing things we should and should not do when caring for pets. Have children brainstorm ideas such as the following:

LO QUE SE DEBE HACER	*LO QUE NO SE DEBE HACER*
Darle comida a tu animalito	*Dejar a un animalito dentro del carro*
THINGS TO DO	THINGS **NOT** TO DO
Feed your pet	Leave a pet inside a car

2. *Favorite Pet:* Have children paint their favorite pet, real or imagined. Have them write a tribute to the pet to accompany their artwork. If needed, use the following writing starter:

   «*Tengo un . . . especial. Es muy especial porque. . . .*» ("I have a special. . . . It is special because . . . .")

3. *"Adopt" a Pet:* Let children "adopt" an imaginary pet of their choice, either a pet in a story from the Literature Input or any other pet they may choose. Using assorted teacher-prepared animal patterns, have students make an animal shape book. Allow the students to use ideas from the pet chart to include in their books. Have them write descriptions of special moments they imagine sharing together including why "adopting" the pet has been so worthwhile.

4. *Lost-Pet Poster:* Have students pretend that their pet is lost. Have them write a complete description for a lost-pet poster. Have them make a drawing of their pet on a poster, offer a reward and attach the description beneath the picture. Display posters in class and have students read them. For fun, have students respond to the pet owner.

5. *Butterfly Murals:* In cooperative groups, have students create murals illustrating imaginary places for Xóchitl and her butterfly to visit. Use children's handprints as butterflies. Have them think of all the things Xóchitl and the butterfly will do. Let them write their ideas in their literature logs.

6. *Imaginative Dialogue:* Pair students and have them dramatize dialogues between the following pairs of things: "What did the leaf say to the caterpillar?"

   • the twig to the cocoon?
   • the butterfly to the flower?
   • the butterfly to the net?

   Let them illustrate and write about these encounters. Have them share dialogues with the class.

7. *If I Were a Butterfly:* Have students complete the following open-ended statement orally:

   «*Si yo fuera tan libre como una mariposa, yo . . . .*» ("If I were as free as a butterfly, I would . . . .")

   Allow them to write ideas in their personal journals.

SCIENCE

1. *From Worm to Butterfly:* In preparation for observing the metamorphosis of silkworm moths, have cooperative groups prepare shoeboxes. Arrange for volunteers to bring mulberry leaves daily for the silkworms. Give each group four to six silkworm eggs to put in their box. Let them predict how many eggs will hatch, how many silkworms will become moths, and which cocoon will open first. Have the groups observe their projects and record their observations in science logs. Let them measure their worms every four days and create illustrations of the worms' development.

2. *Butterfly Shape Book:* Provide a butterfly-pattern ditto for cooperative groups to trace and cut out. Have them cut out front and back covers and four sheets of paper in the butterfly shape. Have each group describe the stages of metamorphosis for a butterfly,

one stage on each page (egg, caterpillar, chrysalis, butterfly). Let each child contribute to the book. One cuts while others draw illustrations; another writes while others dictate descriptive captions.

3. *Moths and Butterflies:* Show a film and display books about butterflies and moths to provide background information. With students, discuss the differences between moths and butterflies and record these on a two-column chart. Using assorted colors of tissue paper, construction paper, yarn and pipe cleaners, have students create their own butterflies or moths, referring to the chart.

SOCIAL STUDIES

1. *Special Attachments:* Have students share their most valued possession; e.g., pet, toy, book, photograph, or any other object. With students, discuss the importance of special attachments that can provide us with a sense of love and security. Allow the discussion to prompt the students to write in their personal journals.

2. *Pet-Sitting:* Have students pretend to be pet owners and write a letter to a friend asking if she/he can take care of their pet during a two-week vacation. Remind them to include instructions for providing love and care and for continuing any special routine to which the pet is accustomed.

3. *Pet Week:* Organize a school-wide pet week. Have students take turns bringing pets to share. With the students, discuss which animals make good pets and why. Small pets in cages or containers could be displayed in class, a library or a multipurpose room. Have the students select the pet of their choosing to observe and to record facts about in their science logs—physical characteristics, movement and eating habits.

4. *What I Learned:* Discuss how Xóchitl and her classmates are like the students in class. (All children have a natural curiosity to learn about things in their world.) Ask students what the caterpillar taught them (growth and development), what the butterfly taught them (freedom to explore the world), and what Xóchitl taught them (we can love pets and learn from them). Allow students to write about one of these concepts.

La ratita

Mi linda ratita
era planchadora
y al planchar su falda,
se quemó la cola.

Se puso pomada,
después un trapito
y a mi pobre ratita
le quedó un rabito.

Folklore

Los juguetes

Muchos juguetitos
me compró mamá
para que yo pueda
con ellos jugar.

Tengo una pelota
que sabe botar
y unos soldaditos
que pueden marchar.

Tengo una corneta
que hace tu tu tu
y una muñequita
vestida de tul.

Anónimo

La mariposa

Una oruga muy golosa
nació de un huevecillo
para comer y comer.

Por un tiempo, muy misteriosa,
se escondió en un capullo.
y no la podíamos ver.

¡Salió convertida en mariposa!
y en nuestro jardín de flores
vuela libre y salerosa,
pero no la podemos coger.

Raquel C. Mireles

Las mariposas

Las mariposas
llegando están
de mil colores
vestidos van.

Y entre las flores
volando irán
a despertarlas
para bailar.

Las flores con su perfume
y su mágico color
engalanan los jardines
se abren radiantes al sol.

Las alegres golondrinas
en parvadas llegan ya
y entre las hojas el viento
murmurando va al pasar
primavera, primavera
ha llegado ya.

Anónimo

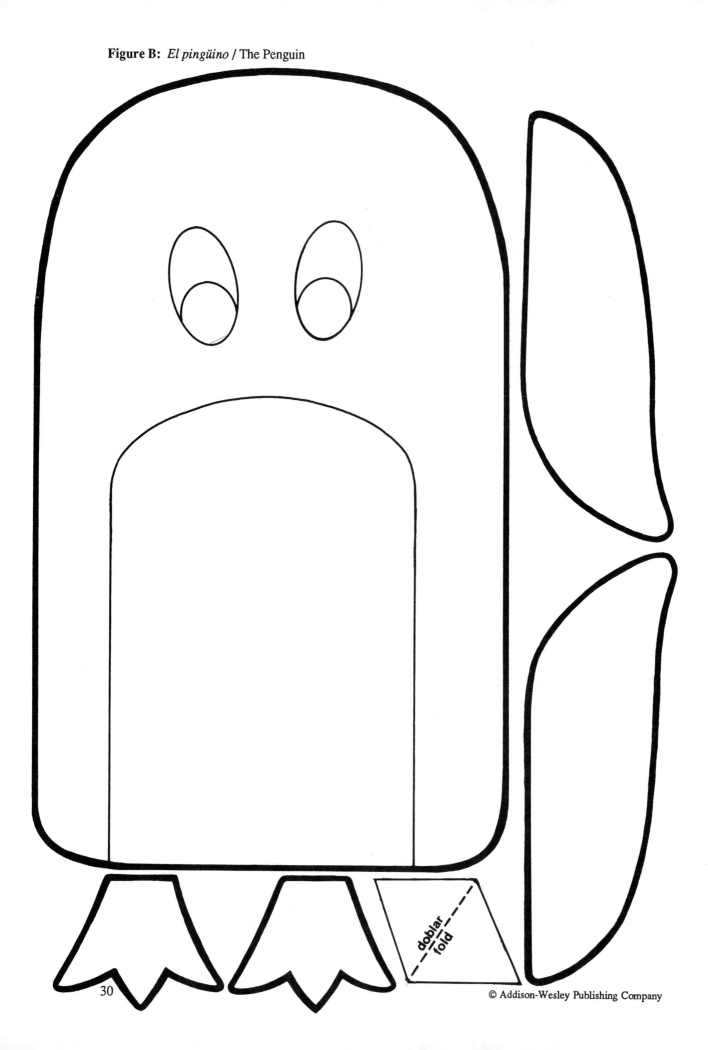

Figure B: *El pingüino* / The Penguin

doblar / fold

30

© Addison-Wesley Publishing Company

MY OWN CREATIVE TEACHING IDEAS FOR UNIT TWO

Books: _____

_____

_____

_____

_____

_____

Ideas: _____

_____

_____

_____

_____

_____

_____

_____

_____

_____

_____

_____

_____

_____

_____

_____

_____

_____

_____

UNIT THREE

MIS AMIGOS Y YO

MY FRIENDS AND I

From the time children are aware of other people, through childhood, adolescence, and adulthood, friendship plays an important part in their lives. As children interact with others in varied situations, they begin to understand important concepts about friendship and often raise questions such as: Will I have a friend? Who will be my friend? Who should be my friend? Who is and is not my friend? Stories such as *La noche después de Navidad* and *Mazapán* help children clarify many concepts relating to their social development.

CONCEPTS AND VALUES

1. Friends do nice things for each other—share possessions, share secrets and help in time of need.
2. True friends really care about their friends' feelings and well-being.
3. Friends share happy, sad, humorous, and mischievous moments.
4. Friends sometimes misunderstand one another, fight, and learn to forgive.
5. A friendship with an old friend has not ended when a new friend joins the play group.
6. Family members can also be friends.
7. Friendship does not have age limits.
8. A friendship can sometimes be difficult to develop. (Be sensitive to those children who need guidance in this area.)

CHOOSE THE MAIN SELECTION

Before reading the Main Selection aloud, take your students through the Literature Input and Observation/Experience phases which follow.

Stevenson, James.

La noche después de Navidad.
Spain: Ediciones Generales Anaya, 1982.

Cuqui, a friendly and hospitable dog, helps his new friends, Ana, a doll, and Panda, a stuffed bear. Both friends were replaced by new toys at Christmas, but Cuqui understands and helps them.

If you choose *La noche después de Navidad* as your selection, turn to page 36 to begin the Observation/Experience phase.

Osorio, Marta.

Mazapán.
Spain: Editorial Miñón, S.A., 1984.

Toñete encounters the most enjoyable friend when his father bakes him a marzipan bread boy. Toñete and his life-like friend, Mazapán, have fun with word play and with imaginative adventures.

If you choose *Mazapán* as your selection, turn to page 40 to begin the Observation/ Experience phase.

I. LITERATURE INPUT: *Both Selections*

Select five or more titles from the following list to read aloud. Read at least one selection per day to the students. Make available and incorporate the suggested titles for voluntary independent reading. Titles marked with * are Spanish translations of the original English story; titles marked with + are recommended for more proficient listeners.

+1. Alcántara, Ricardo S. *Guaraçú.* Spain: Editorial La Galera, S.A., 1980. Guaraçú, a native boy, yearns to have a friend. One day he sees the most beautiful blue bird and follows him into the jungle.

+2. Alonso, Fernando. *El hombrecillo de papel.* Spain: Editorial Miñón, S.A., 1983. An extraordinary friend comes to life from a cut out newspaper doll. At first he brings sad news to the children but later he makes them feel happy by bringing them cheerful stories.

+3. Ballesta, Juan. *Tomy y el elefante.* Spain: Editorial Lumen, 1983. This is a hilarious adventure about a bright boy named Tomy and his imaginary elephant friend.

4. Balzola, Asun. *Munia y la luna.* Spain: Editorial Destino, 1982. Munia has a special attraction to the moon. One night she takes part of the moon, but the moon comes to claim it.

5. Blanco, Cruz, and Lolo Rico. *Kalamito y dos amigos.* Spain: Editorial Altea, 1984. Kalamito is upset because he has to play with his sister when he would rather play with his best friend.

6. Brisville, Jean-Claude, and Danielle Bour. *Un invierno en la vida de Gran Oso.* Spain: Editorial Miñón, S.A., 1981. Great Bear, the king of the forest, and Pequeño Niño, a poor orphan boy, develop a warm friendship while working in a circus. Their friendship is truly confirmed when they encounter a dangerous enemy.

7. Broger, Achim. *Buenos días querida ballena*. Spain: Editorial Juventud, 1978. This charming story is about a friendship between a sailor and a whale that follows him home.

8. —. *Adiós, querida ballena*. Spain: Editorial Juventud, 1985. Children will truly enjoy this sequel to *Buenos días querida ballena*.

9. Cantieni, Benita, and Fred Gächter. *Elefantito y Gran Ratón*. México: Editorial Trillas, S.A., 1984. In this beautifully illustrated book, two friends discover the difference between the words "small and big" and "far and near."

10. D'Atri, Adriana. *Así son nuestros amigos*. Spain: Editorial Altea, 1977. Clara and Enrique love having friends. This book describes their daily experiences with friends.

11. —. *El amigo nuevo*. Spain: Editorial Altea, 1980. The neighborhood children welcome a new Japanese boy and become great friends.

12. Heuer, Margarita. *Chipil y Macanudo*. México: Editorial Trillas, S.A., 1984. This is a story of two friends who are very different when it comes to making new acquaintances. Together they learn the value of friendship.

*13. Hoff, Syd. *Danielito y el dinosaurio*. New York: Harper and Row, 1969. Danielito goes to the museum and meets a real dinosaur. Together they visit the city and have a wonderful time together.

14. Larreula, Enric. *Las dos nubes amigas*. Spain: Editorial Teide, 1984. Two friendly clouds spend their days together enjoying all the seasons of the year. They have a wonderful time until, one day, they are separated by a storm.

*15. Lobel, Arnold. *Sapo y Sepo son amigos*. Spain: Editorial Alfaguara, 1985. This is a delightful book about the friendship between a frog and a toad.

*16. —. *Sapo y Sepo son inseparables*. Spain: Editorial Alfaguara, 1985. Children will also enjoy this hilarious story about the friendship between the frog and the toad.

*17. —. *Sapo y Sepo un año entero*. Spain: Editorial Alfaguara, 1985. This is another one of Lobel's children's favorites.

*18. Minarik, Else Holmelund. *Los amigos de Osito*. Spain: Editorial Altea, 1986. This is one of a series of Minarik's stories about Osito. Osito meets a new friend who, together with other friends, explore the wonders of the forest.

19. Ruille, Bertrand. *Historia de la nube que era amiga de una niña*. Spain: Editorial Miñón, S.A., 1973. This is a story of friendship between a cloud and a girl. The cloud is generous in giving water to all the creatures until, one day, it begins to dissipate; but the girl and all the animals devise a plan to save it.

*20. Steadman, Ralph. *El puente*. Spain: Editorial Miñón, S.A., 1972. Teo and Dimitri are two boys separated not only by a wide river, but by the prejudice of the adults in both their hometowns. In spite of the differences among their elders, they remain good friends.

*21. Stevenson, James. *Howard*. Spain: Ediciones Generales Anaya, 1982. Howard, the duck, is left behind in a cold northern city when his family flies south. He meets a frog and a mouse who teach him how to survive.

+22. Uribe, María de la Luz. *La señorita Amelia*. Spain: Editorial Destino, 1983. La señorita Amelia is a lovely miniature lady who develops a beautiful friendship with birds and children.

+23. Varley, Susan. *Gracias Tejón*. Spain: Editorial Altea, 1985. When Tejón, a wise elderly friend of the community, dies, he is remembered by his friends because of the wonderful things he taught them.

24. Vásquez, Zoraida, and Julieta Montelongo. *El gavilán no quiere a las gallinas*. México: Editorial Trillas, S.A., 1984. In this folktale explaining the rivalry between hawks and hens, a friendly hawk's son, Laidu, becomes ill.

25. Vincent, Gabrielle. *César y Ernestina músicos callejeros*. Spain: Editorial Timún Más, 1981. In this story, our two friends give a musical performance to raise enough money to fix their house.

26. —. *César y Ernestina van de picnic*. Spain: Editorial Timún Más, 1981. This is one of several delightful stories about a special friendship between a bear and a little rat.

27. Williams, Leslie, and Carme Solé Vendrell. *Un oso nuboso*. Spain: Editorial Hymsa, 1979. While watching the clouds, an inquisitive boy finds a bear that has an interesting past. They become good friends and have a wonderful time with word play.

RELATED TITLES IN ENGLISH FOR SECOND LANGUAGE ACQUISITION

Carle, Eric. *Do You Want to Be My Friend?* New York: Thomas Crowell Co., 1971.

Cohen, Miriam. *Will I Have a Friend?* New York: Macmillan, 1967.

Heine, Helma. *Friends*. New York: Atheneum, 1982.

Hoff, Syd. *Who Will Be My Friend?* New York: Harper and Row, 1960.

Kraus, Robert. *Three Friends*. New York. Windmill Books, 1975.

Udry, Janice. *Let's Be Enemies*. New York: Harper and Row, 1961.

Zalben, Jane B. *Lyle and Humus*. New York: Macmillan, 1974.

II. OBSERVATION/EXPERIENCE: *La noche después de Navidad*
(Class Session One)

Guide students in the following observation/experience sequence to set the stage for reading the Main Selection.

Focus: Friends interact in many ways.

1. During recess, assign students to observe the social behavior among friends; e.g., friends talking in a group; the closeness between two friends; friends playing, sharing, fighting, helping, cooperating, being mischievous or being alone. Discuss their observations and have them record them. Encourage children to talk about their own social behavior among friends.

2. Tell them that in a story titled *La noche después de Navidad,* they will meet three friends who show us how special good friends can be.

3. Have them predict what these friends will do to teach us about friendship. Following the story, have children discuss whether their predictions were correct.

III. READ AND DISCUSS THE MAIN SELECTION: *La noche después de Navidad*
(Class Session One)

Read the Main Selection from page 34 to the students. Highlight the unit's theme by relating this story to other selections from the Literature Input list on pages 34 - 36. Then, guide students in discussing some of the following questions.

1. *¿Cómo se sintieron el osito y la muñeca después de Navidad? ¿Por qué?* (How did the teddy bear and the doll feel after Christmas? Why?)

2. *¿Por qué creen ustedes que la perra les ayudó? ¿Qué habrían hecho ustedes?* (Why do you think Cuqui helped them? What would you have done?)

3. *Cuando la muñeca y el osito se sentían tristes y rechazados ¿quién de los dos trataba de mejorar la situación? ¿Por qué creen esto?* (When the doll and the bear felt sad and unwanted, which one of the two tried to make the best of the situation? What makes you think that?)

4. *¿Cuál de los tres amigos fue el que pudo resolver el problema? ¿Cómo?* (Of the three friends, which was able to solve the problem? How?)

5. *¿A dónde creen ustedes que fueron la muñeca y el osito?* (Where do you suppose the doll and the bear went?)

IV. "WHAT IF" STORY STRETCHER: *La noche después de Navidad*
(Class Session Two)

Next, re-read the Main Selection and choose one or more of the following questions to develop students' critical thinking skills. Story stretchers may also prompt discussion, drama or writing activities.

1. *Si la perra no hubiera encontrado a la muñeca y al osito, ¿quién más les podría haber ayudado? ¿Cómo?* (If the dog had not found the doll and the teddy bear, who else could have helped them? How?)

2. *Qué habría pasado si la perra hubiera sido brava y no se hubiera preocupada por la muñeca y el osito? ¿Cómo habría cambiado el cuento?* (If the dog had been unfriendly and uncaring, how would the story have changed?)

3. *Si a ustedes les dieran o la muñeca o el osito, ¿qué cosas harían juntos?* (If you were given the doll or teddy bear, what things would you do together?)

4. *Si pudieran escoger a uno de los personajes para que fuera su amigo, ¿quien sería? ¿Por qué?* (If you could pick one of the characters to be your friend, who would you choose? Why?)

V. INTEGRATING OTHER DISCIPLINES: *La noche después de Navidad*
(Class Session Three and Ongoing)

The following activities are designed to enhance children's response to literature and expand *beyond* the story and its theme. The variety of activities gives teachers and students an opportunity to choose those most appropriate.

CREATIVE DRAMATICS

1. *Characters' Feelings:* Have groups dramatize the story, emphasizing the characters' feelings during the night after Christmas, at the dog's house, and when finding a new home.

2. *What Toy Is It?:* Form a circle. Have the students pretend to find a discarded toy, pantomime playing with the toy, and have the class guess what the toy is.

3. *Expressions of Friendship:* Friends display their friendship in many ways: sharing, arguing, being jealous, telling secrets, playing and working together, and going places together. Provide cards with these action words written on them and have cooperative groups improvise the actions labeled on chosen cards.

ART AND WRITING

1. *Book Media:* Discuss the illustrations in the book. Talk about the medium used (watercolors). Encourage children to use descriptive words. Provide watercolors and let them draw and then paint a different ending to the story. Have the students write new story endings and attach them to their illustrations. Compile them for a class book for the library corner.

2. *Rainbow:* As a class project, have students make a friendship rainbow. Let them select a color from the rainbow. Pair children to trace each other's half body from the waist up on colored paper. Draw facial features. Have them cut out the figure. On a separate lined paper, have each child write a positive message about his/her partner and attach to figure. On the bulletin board, display figures according to the order of the rainbow. With students, write a group poem titled *«El arco iris de la amistad»* ("The Friendship Rainbow").

3. *Friendship Mural:* Pair students to trace each other's body on a long strip of butcher paper. Have them trace the body using a pencil and then have them use colored markers, crayons and tissue paper to create body features and clothing. Cut it out. Have each student write something positive about the person he/she traced on the figure. Connect the figures by the hands and display them in the classroom to show the entire class.

4. *My Favorite Friend:* Have students brainstorm and make three charts, each one related to one of the following areas:

   • Things children like to share: books, toys, talk.
   • Qualities admired in other friends.
   • Games children play.

Friendship Portrait: Using Figure C (page 45), have students write about a favorite friend. If needed, students may use words from the charts or the following writing starter:

> *Mi amigo favorito es _____.*
> *El/ella es especial porque . . . .*
> *Nos gusta jugar . . . .*
>
> (My favorite friend is _____.
> He/she is special because . . . .
> We like to play . . . .)

Have them draw facial features and use yarn for hair. Then have them cut out and frame the figures for classroom display.

5. *Diorama:* Have students make a diorama of ***La noche después de Navidad.*** Using construction paper and marking pens, have them create the characters in the story. Using a shoebox for the background of the diorama, have them illustrate a winter scene. Then have them write about an adventure that the characters might experience in the diorama setting.

6. *"What If" Story:* Have students write a story using the following story starter: *«Si yo hubiera encontrado al oso y a la muñeca después de Navidad, yo habría . . . .»* ("If I had found the bear and the doll after Christmas, I would have . . . .") Have them illustrate their stories and compile to make a class book for the library corner.

7. *My Friend:* Supply a teacher-made boy or girl body pattern (6 inches tall) for each student. Have the students use construction paper, tissue paper, and yarn to design their friend's clothing. Have them glue it onto the body pattern and draw in the facial features.

Friendship Poem: Have them write a poem about friendship. If needed, use the following poem starter:

«Un amigo es alguien que . . . .» ("A friend is someone who . . . .")

Place artwork and poems on a bulletin board with the same title.

SOCIAL STUDIES

1. *Friendship:* Have the children talk about the meaning of true friendship; e.g., sharing, helping, caring. Highlight the concept: *«Tener un amigo significa ser un amigo.»* ("To have a friend is to be a friend.") Have the students use a large piece of construction paper folded in half. On one half, have them illustrate *«Yo soy un amigo cuando . . . .»* ("I am a friend when I . . . .") On the other half, have them illustrate *«Yo no tengo amigos cuando . . . .»* ("I do not have friends when I . . . .") Allow them to write about these concepts or copy and complete the writing starters on the bottom of their papers.

2. *Valentine's Day Letters:* Discuss how the thoughtful gesture of giving a friend a card or letter shows that we care about them. Within cooperative groups, have students write letters to other members. Let them write their own friendship letters or, if needed, use the following pattern:

Querido _____,
Me gusta como tú . . . (dibujas, lees, juegas).
Tu amigo, _____

(Dear _____,
I like the way you . . . (draw, read, play).
Your friend, _____)

Have the students place their letters in a classroom mailbox. Mailboxes may be decorated folders, shoeboxes or large envelopes displayed on a bulletin board. At a later time, have a student deliver individual letters. Have volunteers share their letters with the whole class or within their group.

3. *Friendship Circle:* As a group interaction activity, have children sit in a circle and have each child say something positive to the child sitting to his/her left. Have each student recall and write the positive thing that the other child said.

4. *Friendship Award:* Discuss what a nice gesture it is to occasionally tell our friends that we hold them in high esteem and that they are special. Have students write friendship awards using the following pattern:

Deseo anunciar que _____ *es un/a*   *gran amigo/a porque* _____ ,   _____ , *y* _____ .   *(mi nombre)*   *(fecha)*

I want to announce that _____ is a   great friend because _____ ,   _____ , and _____ .   (my name) (date)

I. LITERATURE INPUT: *Mazapán*
See pages 34 - 36.

II. OBSERVATION/EXPERIENCE: *Mazapán*
(Class Session One)

Guide students in the following observation/experience sequence to set the stage for reading the Main Selection.

Focus: The fun part of friendship is playtime, especially during imaginative play.

1. Have children form a circle. Place 30 interesting objects in the center; e.g., paper, pencil, pipe, old shoe, lever, ball, funnel. Have the children look at the objects and think of creative ways in which the objects could be used in imaginative play with a friend; e.g., a piece of pipe could be a rocket, and a ball, the moon.

2. Instruct one child to toss a small ball to another child as an invitation to help choose two objects for imaginative playtime. Cooperatively, let them choose two objects. Repeat with the entire class until all children are paired and each pair possesses two objects. Let each pair plan and then show how they would play with the two objects while observers guess what the imaginative play is. Have each pair give several hints until their idea can be guessed.

3. Tell them that in a story titled *Mazapán*, they will meet two friends who played together in imaginative play, in much the same way that they have played with their friends.

4. Have them predict the fun activities the two friends will have when they play together. Following the story, have children discuss whether their predictions were correct.

III. READ AND DISCUSS THE MAIN SELECTION: *Mazapán*
(Class Session One)

Read the Main Selection from page 34 to the students. Highlight the unit's theme by relating this story to other selections from the Literature Input list on pages 34 - 36. Then, guide students in discussing some of the following questions.

1. *¿Por qué les gustó Mazapán? ¿Han tenido un amigo chistoso como Mazapán? Platíquennos quien es.* (What was likeable about Mazapán? Have you ever had a funny friend like Mazapán? Tell us about him or her.)

2. *¿Hubiera podido guardar Toñete a Mazapán por mucho tiempo? ¿Por qué? ¿Por qué no?* (Could Toñete have kept Mazapán for a very long time? Why? Why not?)

3. *¿Que hizo Mazapán para que Toñete lo recordara? ¿Que harían ustedes para que un amigo les recordara?* (What did Mazapán do so that Toñete would remember him? What would you do so that a friend would remember you?)

4. *Toñete y Mazapán se divertían con adivinanzas; ¿saben algunas que quieren compartir?* (Toñete and Mazapán entertained themselves with riddles; do you know any that you would like to share?)

5. *Toñete y Mazapán compartieron cuentos; ¿saben algún cuento especial? Platíquennos cual es.* (Toñete and Mazapán shared bedtime stories; do you have a special bedtime story? Tell us about it.)

IV. "WHAT IF" STORY STRETCHER: *Mazapán*
(Class Session Two)

Next, re-read the Main Selection and choose one or more of the following questions to develop students' critical thinking skills. Story stretchers may also prompt discussion, drama or writing activities.

1. *¿Que habría pasado si los papás de Toñete hubieran descubierto el amigo nuevo de Toñete?* (What would have happened if Toñete's parents had discovered Toñete's new friend?)

2. *Si Toñete no hubiera sido tan amigable, ¿cómo habría cambiado el cuento?* (If Toñete had not been so friendly, how would the story have been different?)

3. *Si ustedes y Mazapán pudieran ir a la panadería, ¿qué cosas harían juntos?* (If you and Mazapán could go to the bakery, what would you do together?)

4. *Si ustedes pudieran darle algo a su mejor amigo para que los recordara siempre, ¿qué sería?* (If you could give something to your best friend so that she or he would always remember you, what would it be?)

V. INTEGRATING OTHER DISCIPLINES: *Mazapán*
(Class Session Three and Ongoing)

The following activities are designed to enhance children's response to literature and expand *beyond* the story and its theme. The variety of activities gives teachers and students an opportunity to choose those most appropriate.

CREATIVE DRAMATICS

1. *Freshly Baked Friend:* Have pairs of students pantomime the process that the baker used to bake Mazapán and the fun things they could do with a "freshly baked friend."

2. *Riddles:* Present story riddles on charts and have children chorally read the riddles. Have pairs of children pantomime riddles from the chart.

3. *What Game Is It?:* In cooperative groups, have students pantomime a special game or sport that can be played with their best friend. Have observers guess what it is.

ART AND WRITING

1. *Group Book:* Have the students make a group book. Allow cooperative groups to illustrate and write a story for a friend that Mazapán might write himself. Have them share their book in class or with other classes.

2. *Valentine's Day Special Friend:* Have students draw pictures of their best friend. Have them make frames for their drawings and frame them. Have the students brainstorm the qualities admired in friends. Cluster words on the board. Have the students use the word clusters to write a *"diamante"* (a diamond-shaped poem) about his/her best friend. (See Unit One on page 12.)

3. *Riddles:* Mazapán shared delightful riddles with Toñete; as a homework assignment, have students collect riddles *(adivinanzas)* from family and friends to share at school. Choose those that are most appealing and appropriate for students to write, memorize, and include in their riddle books.

4. *Class Riddle Book:* Have the children write original riddles to share with the class. Have them draw a picture of their riddle. Compile riddles for a class riddle book.

5. *Mazapán Friend:* Supply teacher-made Mazapán body patterns. Have the students cut them out and "transform" them into one of their friends. On the Mazapán figure, have them write a description of their friend's unique qualities and later give the figure to that special friend.

6. *Friendly Dialogue:* In cooperative groups, have students write dialogues that could take place between Mazapán and themselves; e.g., meeting each other for the first time; solving a problem such as finding a lost toy or a pet; asking for information about how to get to the bakery. Pair students to read their dialogues to the class, acting as Mazapán and themselves.

SCIENCE

1. *Bread Observation:* Discuss why Mazapán was getting dry. Discuss the effect that air has on bread. Bring bread to class and let it age. Have children observe every day and record how long it takes for bread to become completely dry. Allow them to record facts in their science logs.

   Discuss the effect that moisture has on bread. Place bread that has been slightly moistened in a plastic bag. Let it sit for several days. Have children observe and record the changes taking place in the bread and how long it takes for the bread to become moldy. Have them record their observations in their science logs.

2. *Cookies:* Using a sugar cookie recipe, (see Unit One page 9) have students make cookies that look like Mazapán. A gingerbread-boy cookie cutter may be used to represent Mazapán. Have children decorate the cookies with chocolate frosting for hair, two candies for eyes, strawberry jam or another red candy for mouth, and chocolate chips for buttons. Have children write advertisements describing their delicious cookies.

SOCIAL STUDIES

1. *Showing Kindness to My Friend:* Brainstorm and list the things friends can do to show kindness to another friend. Later, allow students to follow through on an idea and then write about the experience of expressing kindness to someone. Let them illustrate and write about their own experiences with friends and share with the class.

2. *Paper-Doll Chain:* Brainstorm and list admirable qualities found in good friends. Make three pleats in each 8-1/2" x 11" piece of white paper. Provide a small body pattern that can be traced on the first pleat. Have the students cut out the body without cutting into the fold at the hands. When unfolded, the three bodies will be linked. Have the students draw in the features and clothing of several friends. On the body of each "friend," have the students write the name and an admirable quality about each friend.

3. *Friendship-Link Chain:* Brainstorm and list positive qualities about this year's class friends. Prepare construction paper strips with each child's name on one of the strips. Have each student randomly draw a strip and write two positive qualities about the person whose name is on the strip. With the students sitting in a circle, have each student call out the name written on the strip, read the two positive qualities, and glue the link to his/her own link. Continue with this procedure until all the chains have been linked. Ask children, «¿Qué nombre le daremos a nuestra cadena?—la cadena de la amistad.» ("What should we call our chain?—the friendship chain.") Use the chain to decorate the classroom.

4. *All Kinds of Friends:* Guide students in a discussion about developing friendships among all age groups, sexes, family members, ethnic groups. Have them write personal journal entries using the following writing starter:

   «Un amigo puede ser . . . porque . . . .» ("A friend can be . . . because . . . .")

Friendship Collage: In cooperative groups, have students make a collage titled, *«Los amigos pueden ser de todos tamaños y formas.»* ("Friends come in all shapes and sizes.") Students can draw their own illustrations or cut out pictures from magazines.

5. *Friendship-Cake Book:* Have the students discuss qualities that make a strong friendship. As a class language experience activity, write a recipe for a friendship cake. For example:

Pastel de Amistad

4 tazas de amor	*2 tazas de cooperación*
1 taza de atención	*3 abrazos y saludos*
3 tazas de diversión	*2 cucharadas de voluntad para compartir*

Se deben mezclar los ingredientes con amor y respeto y hornear con paciencia. Se decora con risa y se rosea con humor. Se sirve con una sonrisa.

Friendship Cake

4 cups of love	2 cups of cooperation
1 cup of listening	3 hugs and handshakes
3 cups of fun	2 tablespoons of sharing

Mix these ingredients together with love and respect and bake with patience. Frost it with laughter and sprinkle with humor. Serve it with a happy smile.

Have students paint a big cake and cut it out to be used as the book cover. On a piece of lined paper, have students copy their friendship cake recipe (or you may wish to type it and duplicate for reading) and staple it inside the cake book.

POETRY

La amistad

Cultivo una rosa blanca,
en junio como en enero,
para el amigo sincero
que me da su mano franca.

Y para el cruel, que me arranca
el corazón con que vivo,
cardo ni ortiga cultivo:
¡cultivo una rosa blanca!

José Martí

Un amigo

Un amigo
es aquel que te busca
y te hace reir;
que comparte sus cosas
y siempre te invita a jugar.

Un buen amigo
es aquel que te quiere
y te acepta como eres;
que comparte sus secretos
y te hace gozar.

Pero el mejor amigo
es aquel que te da la mano
cuando tú lo necesitas;
que jamás te lleva por el mal camino
y siempre te sabe respetar.

Raquel C. Mireles

AMIGOS

MY OWN CREATIVE TEACHING IDEAS FOR UNIT THREE

Books: _____

_____

_____

_____

_____

_____

Ideas: _____

_____

_____

_____

_____

_____

_____

_____

_____

_____

_____

_____

_____

_____

_____

_____

_____

_____

UNIT FOUR

TENGO SENTIMIENTOS

I HAVE FEELINGS

Expressing and understanding our feelings is a natural learning process of our emotional development. Early on, children begin to recognize and to identify positive and negative feelings in themselves and in others. *Historia de un erizo* and other stories from this thematic unit help children relate to the characters' feelings. Stories such as these encourage children to talk about and to understand their own feelings and their right to express them in appropriate ways.

CONCEPTS AND VALUES

1. Everyone has personal feelings; we express these feelings verbally and nonverbally.
2. When we feel angry or frustrated, we need to express these feelings through words, rather than with our bodies.
3. We are sometimes misunderstood when our feelings are not clearly expressed.
4. We feel understood when our feelings are acknowledged.
5. Those who make an effort to understand our feelings are special to us.
6. We sometimes have a different outlook on life depending on how we feel.
7. Some experiences cause us to have mixed feelings.

MAIN SELECTION

Before reading the Main Selection aloud, take your students through the Literature Input and Observation/Experience phases which follow.

Balzola, Asun.

Historia de un erizo.
Spain: Editorial Miñón, S.A., 1982.

Erizo is a hedgehog saddened by those who shun him. No one will play with him because of his peculiar appearance. His outlook toward life becomes a lot brighter when a friendly turtle becomes his dear friend. This story won the Spanish *Premio Nacional de Literatura Infantil* in 1978.

I.   LITERATURE INPUT: *Historia de un erizo*

Select five or more titles from the following list to read aloud. Read at least one selection per day to the students. Make available and incorporate the suggested titles for voluntary independent reading. Titles marked with * are Spanish translations of the original English story; titles marked with + are recommended for more proficient listeners.

1.   Alonso, Fernando. *El hombrecillo de papel.* Spain: Editorial Miñón, S.A., 1983. An extraordinary friend comes to life from a cut-out newspaper doll. At first he brings sad news to the children, but he later decides to make them happy by bringing them cheerful stories.

+2.   Andersen, Hans Christian. Adapted by Rossana Guarnieri. *El patito feo.* México: Fernández Editores, S.A., 1980. This is an adaptation of Andersen's classical story, *The Ugly Duckling.*

3.   Balzola, Asun. *Munia y el cocolilo naranja.* Spain: Ediciones Destino, S.A., 1984. When Munia begins to lose her teeth, she dreams of enormous crocodiles with sharp teeth. She is afraid of crocodiles, but she meets one that has no teeth and helps her ease her fear.

4.   Blanco, Cruz and Lolo Rico. *Kalamito se equivoca.* Spain: Editorial Altea, 1983. Kalamito makes an accusation and has to apologize to his friend when he discovers his mistake.

5.   —. *Kalamito tiene miedo.* Spain: Editorial Altea, 1983. When Kalamito experiences loneliness and fear, he is ashamed of his natural feelings. His best friend helps him overcome and accept his mixed feelings.

*6.   Bornstain, Ruth. *Gorilita.* New York: Scholastic, 1978. This is a delightful story about a gorilla who is loved by all as a baby but who wonders whether he will still be loved when he grows up.

7.   Carbajal, A. Merino. *El niño que no sabía reir.* Spain: Editorial Everest, S.A., 1981. Edgar is a boy who does not like to laugh; in fact, he does not show any emotion at all. One day a strange cloud appears. The cloud proves to be the only thing that can make him laugh.

*8. Carruth, Jane. *Aventura en la oscuridad*. Argentina: Editorial Sigmar, 1978. Tipu, the little mouse, is afraid of the dark and imagines "monsters" one night when he becomes lost in the forest. His friend finds him and helps him.

*9. —. *La pierna lastimada*. Spain: Editorial Sigmar, 1978. Pinchita has an accident, hurts her leg and ends up in the hospital.

10. Flores, Rosa. *Caracolitos: ¿Sientes miedo algunas veces?* Oklahoma: Economy Co., 1979. A young boy talks about his fears but recognizes that they are natural.

+11. García, Richard. *Los espíritus de mi tía Otilia*. San Francisco: Children's Book Press, 1978. A boy's fears of the dark and the supernatural are explored in this hilarious story.

*12. González de Tapia, Graciela. *Medianito*. México: Editorial Trillas, S.A., 1984. In this story about a worm family, the middle son worries that his parents do not love him, especially when he stirs up mischief.

*13. Goss, Janet L., and Jerome C. Harste. *No me asustó a mí*. New York: School Book Fair, 1984. A boy is sent to bed and imagines all kinds of creatures that do not scare him a bit until a real owl that truly frightens him appears.

*14. Hazen, Nancy. *Los adultos también lloran*. Chapel Hill, NC: Lollipop Power, Inc., 1984. A little boy talks about the times when he has cried, and he becomes aware that his parents sometimes have a need to cry, too.

+15. Hiriart, Berta, and Claudia de Teresa. *Un día en la vida de Catalina*. México: CONAFE, CIDLI, S.C., 1984. Catalina's new sister has arrived, but Catalina feels confused, nervous and somewhat envious. She tries to ignore the situation but finally learns to accept her new sister.

+16. Kocy, Marta, and Edgar Breuss. *Negroscuro*. México: Editorial Trillas, S.A., 1985. María, an adventurous little girl, overcomes her fear of a strange-looking lady but not of the lady's fierce-looking dog.

17. Larreula, Enric. *El buho miedoso*. Spain: Editorial Teide, S.A., 1984. An owl has an unusual phobia. He is afraid of the dark! He tries several tricks to overcome his fear.

18. Levert, Claude, and Carme Solé Vendrell. *Pedro y su roble*. Spain: Editorial Miñón, S.A., 1981. This is a delightful story of a boy and his loving concern for an oak tree.

19. Martínez, María I. Vendrell. *Serie hablemos de como duele*. Spain: Ediciones Destino, S.A., 1986. Martin has an accident and is afraid of going to the hospital.

20. —. *Serie hablamos de uno más*. Spain: Ediciones Destino, S.A., 1986. Celia's family welcomes a new baby, but she feels apprehensive about the new addition in her family.

+21. —. *Yo las quería*. Spain: Ediciones Destino, 1984. Martha, a sensitive young girl, goes through a difficult time when her mother dies. Having no one to braid her hair, she must cut off her braids.

22. Pecanins, Ana María. *La bruja triste*. México: Editorial Trillas, S.A., 1985. An unhappy witch hid and cried because she felt ugly and scary looking. One day she finds a group of children who are not afraid of her.

+23. —. *El globo, la tortuga y yo*. México: Editorial Trillas, S.A., 1985. A girl is saddened when she loses her balloon. A friendly turtle helps her find it, and they become good friends.

+24. Robles Boza, Eduardo (Tío Patota). *La cosquilla*. México: Editorial Trillas, S.A., 1985. Erika is a lucky girl who has a wonderful relationship with her grandfather. She loves to be tickled by him and misses that when her grandfather becomes ill.

25. Schroeder, Binette. *Florian y el tractor Max*. Spain: Editorial Lumen, 1986. A horse feels obsolete after a new tractor arrives on the farm. When the tractor is in trouble, the horse comes to its aid and both become friends.

+26. Sennell, Joles. *Yuyo, el niño que no podía llorar*. Spain: Editorial Hymsa, 1981. The is the story of a boy who is saddened when he must leave his country. Sympathizing with his sorrow, a breeze takes his tears. After four years, the boy returns to his homeland.

*27. Simón, Norma. *Cuando me enojo*. Chicago: Albert Whitman and Company, 1976. This interesting book explores feelings as different children share the incidents that make them feel angry.

*+28. Stenson, Janet Sinberg. *Tengo un padrastro lo cual, a veces, me desconcierta*. México: La Prensa Médica Mexicana, S.A., 1983. A young boy feels confused about his mother's second marriage. He goes through a period of tribulation until his feelings are acknowledged by his stepfather.

*29. Stevenson, James. *¿Qué hay debajo de mi cama?* Spain: Ediciones S.M., 1986. The grandchildren are afraid there is something under their bed. Their grandfather tells of his youthful experiences with every monster imaginable.

*30. Szekeres, Cyndy. *La gatita miedosa*. Argentina: Ediciones Sigmar, S.A., 1986. Pimpollita was a scaredy cat who was afraid of loud sounds, insects and shadows until, one day, she overcomes her fears.

31. —. *La sorpresa del osito*. Argentina: Ediciones Sigmar, S.A., 1986. A little bear feels very confused about the commotion and secrecy in his family, but he is happily surprised in the end.

*32. Timlinson, Jim. *El buho que tenía miedo a la obscuridad*. Spain: Editorial Miñón, S.A., 1982. Plop is an owl who is afraid of the dark. Some friends help him discover how beautiful and how much fun the night can be.

*33. Wells, Rosemary. *¡Julieta, estate quieta!* Spain: Editorial Altea, 1981. Julieta, the mischievous middle child in a mouse family, feels left out when she sees her mother and father giving attention to her brother and sister.

+*34. Wilde, Oscar. *El gigante egoista*. Spain: Editorial Debate, 1985. This is Wilde's well-known story of a selfish giant who becomes more humane because of the beauty and innocence of a helpless little boy.

RELATED TITLES IN ENGLISH FOR SECOND LANGUAGE ACQUISITION

Carle, Eric. *The Grouchy Ladybug*. New York: Scholastic, 1977.

Heide, Florence. *Some Things Are Scary*. New York: Scholastic, 1975.

Lindbergh, Reeve. *The Midnight Farm*. New York: Dial Books for Young Readers, 1986.

Scott, Herbert. *Sam*. New York: McGraw-Hill, 1967.

Slate, Joseph. *How Little Porcupine Played Christmas*. New York: Thomas Y. Crowell, 1982.

Viorst, Judith. *Alexander and the Terrible, Horrible, No Good, Very Bad Day*. New York: Atheneum, 1972.

Wilhelm, Hans. *Let's Be Friends Again!* New York: Crown Publishers, 1986.

Winthrop, Elizabeth. *Sloppy Kisses*. New York: Penguin, 1983.

II. OBSERVATION/EXPERIENCE: *Historia de un erizo*
(Class Session One)

Guide students in the following observation/experience sequence to set the stage for reading the Main Selection.

Focus: Our feelings can change from moment to moment and seemingly negative experiences can have positive outcomes.

1. Plan a fun activity such as a popcorn party, parachute play or game time. In order to prepare the students for the focus of this session, do the following to elicit strong reactions from the students:

    • Without giving an explanation, tell students that they may not go out for recess (reaction: surprised and angry).
    • Eat a delicious treat for one minute while they watch (angry, envious).
    • Tell them that it is too bad that they cannot go outside to play (disappointed, angry).
    • Tell them that the reason is because you (teacher) decided to do something different (surprised, curious).
    • Tell them that instead of recess, they will have a fun activity (happy, relieved).

    Ask students to describe what their feelings were as you gave them first the bad and then the good news. Discuss the fact that our feelings are natural, and that they can change from moment to moment. Good things are possible even from seemingly terrible situations.

2. Tell them that in a story titled *Historia de un erizo,* they will meet a hedgehog that thought he would always feel sad because no one would play with him. Ask the students if they can tell you what a hedgehog is and what it looks like. Ask them why they think no one would play with him.

3. Show them the cover of the book and have them predict what will happen to change the hedgehog's feelings.

4. Following the story, have the students discuss whether their predictions were correct.

III. READ AND DISCUSS THE MAIN SELECTION: *Historia de un erizo*
(Class Session One)

Read the Main Selection from page 48 to the students. Highlight the unit's theme by relating this story to other selections from the Literature Input list on pages 48 - 51. Then, guide students in discussing some of the following questions.

1. *¿Por qué no querían los animales jugar con el erizo? ¿Puede pasar esto en la vida real? ¿Qué les parece a ustedes esto?* (Why didn't the animals want to play with the hedgehog? Can this happen to people in real life? How do you feel about this?)

2. *¿Creen ustedes que los animales deberían haber tratado de conocer mejor al erizo? ¿Qué habrían aprendido de él?* (Do you think that the animals should have tried to get to know the hedgehog better? What would they have learned from him?)

3. *¿Qué aprendieron ustedes de la tortuga?* (What did you learn from the turtle?)

4. *¿Cómo le parecía el mundo al erizo antes de conocer a su amiga? ¿Cómo le parecía después?* (How did the world seem to the hedgehog before he met his friend? How did it seem afterwards?)

5. *Piensen en alguna vez cuando el mundo a su alrededor parecía mas brillante y hermoso porque se sentían felices de si mismos. ¿Quién quiere platicarnos?* (Think of a time when the world seemed bright and beautiful because you felt good about yourselves. Who would like to tell us about it?)

IV. "WHAT IF" STORY STRETCHER: *Historia de un erizo*
(Class Session Two)

Next, re-read the Main Selection and choose one or more of the following questions to develop students' critical thinking skills. Story stretchers may also prompt discussion, drama or writing activities.

1. *Si ustedes fueran el erizo, ¿cómo se habrían sentido cuando los otros animales no querían estar con ustedes?* (If you were the hedgehog, how would you have felt when the other animals didn't want to be with you?)

2. *Si ustedes jugaran con alguien muy diferente de ustedes, ¿que dirían sus amigos? ¿Qué les dirían ustedes a ellos?* (If you were to play with someone very different from you, what do you think your friends would say? What would you say to them?)

3. *Si el erizo no hubiera conocido a la tortuga amigable, ¿cómo habría terminado el cuento?* (If the hedgehog had not met the friendly turtle, how would the story ending have been different?)

4. *¿De qué cosas no nos daríamos cuenta si estuvieramos tan tristes que no notaramos el mundo a nuestro alrededor?* (What would we be missing if we were too sad to notice the world around us?)

5. *Si pensaramos solamente en cosas tristes, ¿cómo sería cada día? ¿Estaríamos más contentos si pensáramos en cosas felices? ¿Quién quiere platicarnos de algo que les causó sentimientos felices?* (If we were to have only sad thoughts, what would each day be like? Would we be happier if we thought about happy things? Who would like to tell us about a happy experience?)

V. INTEGRATING OTHER DISCIPLINES: *Historia de un erizo*
(Class Session Three and Ongoing)

The following activities are designed to enhance children's response to literature and expand *beyond* the story and its theme. The variety of activities gives teachers and students an opportunity to choose those most appropriate.

CREATIVE DRAMATICS

1. *Different Ending:* Using paper bag puppets from activity #9 in Art and Writing, have students act out the story with the original ending. Then, let cooperative groups plan a different story ending. Allow them to practice and dramatize the new ending scene for the class.

2. *My Feelings:* Ask the students to show how they would express their feelings under the following circumstances:

   «*Todos reciben un cono de nieve menos ustedes.*» ("Everyone gets an ice cream cone except you.")

   «*Ustedes ganan un trofeo por escribir el poema mas hermoso.*» ("You win a trophy for writing the most beautiful poem.")

   «*Su amigo les dice que tiene un amigo nuevo.*» ("Your friend tells you that he/she has a new friend.")

   «*Alguien ha quebrado sus colores y ha escrito sobre sus libros.*» ("Someone has broken your crayons and has written all over your books.")

3. *Feelings Stick Puppets:* Have children sit in a circle. Use emotion stick puppets from activity #10 in Art and Writing for children to hold while expressing their feelings. Tell them that each must choose two feelings to talk about; e.g., When a child chooses the happy face, he might say, "I feel happy when I'm with my mom and dad." or "I feel excited when we have a party at my house."

4. *Feelings Through Music:* Provide children with crepe paper streamers. Have them express their feelings to a variety of musical pieces while exaggerating or emphasizing the movement of the streamer.

ART AND WRITING

1. *Caring:* Have students express how they feel about the hedgehog. Then discuss the illustrations in the book and the medium used. Using mixed media—watercolors for the setting and ink finger prints and crayons for the characters—have children illustrate the part that made them feel like being the hedgehog's friend. Have children write about their illustrations. Collect the illustrations and writings for a class book.

2. *Sculpture:* Using clay or playdough, have students create a hedgehog and a turtle. (Toothpicks may be used for the hedgehog's spikes.) Have students write about a fun place where the hedgehog and the turtle might play.

3. *Craft Characters:* Using a pinecone and clay, have students make a hedgehog. Then have students use a walnut shell and clay to make a turtle. Have them retell the story while manipulating the hedgehog and the turtle.

4. *Our Imagination:* Tell students that our imaginations can make us have many different feelings. Discuss how our imaginations may stir up our feelings. Have them close their eyes while you create a series of five peculiar noises; e.g., slam the door, knock loudly on a window, crumble paper, scream, and make a loud thump. Ask if they were imagining something strange happening. Instruct them to write a story using what they imagined.

5. *Happy Recollections:* Have students lie under a tree just to enjoy the peace and tranquility. Have them close their eyes and think about a happy occasion in their lives. Later, let them project their happy recollections in a watercolor painting. Allow them to write a description of this experience.

6. *Story Sequel:* Have students write a sequel to the hedgehog's story. Have them include a description of what the hedgehog and the turtle will do together; e.g., a vacation, a holiday, a birthday. Use Figure D (page 57) to make a shape-book cover for the sequel. Use toothpicks, spaghetti, or a traced child's hand to create hedgehog spikes.

7. *Mural:* Tack several long strips of butcher paper around the room. Have cooperative groups create murals depicting various feelings. Assign each group a feeling but instruct them not reveal it to the other groups; it can only be revealed through the drawings. One by one, have each student make a contribution to the group's mural. Have the class guess the emotion each mural depicts.

   Diamond Poem: Have each group create a diamond poem (see page 12 of Unit One) that describes the emotion depicted in their mural. Allow them to edit their poems and write them in their poetry logs. Have them share poems with the class.

8. *Moods with Music:* Explain that music can make us have many different moods; they will discover their own moods through music and painting. Expose them to classical, marching band, African, and rock'n roll music. Have them fingerpaint to the sound of various musical selections. Provide each student with four sheets of newsprint and fingerpaints; allow them to find a place on the floor where they can creatively express their "moods." Then, have them put their feelings into words by selecting a painting to write about. Let them share their work with the class.

9. *Character Bag Puppets:* Provide small paper bags and assorted media to have students create the story's characters. Allow them to write dialogues that the characters might say to each other and manipulate the puppets while performing the dialogues.

10. *Emotion Paper-Plate Puppets:* Provide small paper plates stapled to tongue depressors and have students draw emotions such as happiness, anger, amusement, sadness, excitement, and fear. Allow students to write short, humorous stories with themselves as the main characters and portraying varied emotions. Let them manipulate the puppets while reading their stories.

SCIENCE

1. *Fictional Versus Real Animals:* The animals in the story are fictional characters; so that young children can make a distinction between the behavior of real and story animals, have them compare and contrast Erizo with a real hedgehog. Record their ideas on a two-column chart. Show resources (film, illustrations, real animals) displaying the physical characteristics of hedgehogs and turtles. Discuss such characteristics as their seasonal behaviors, eating habits, and habitats. Have them record facts in their science logs.

SOCIAL STUDIES

1. *Feelings Discussion:* Engage students in a discussion about feelings. We do not see feelings, but we see the emotions caused by them—happiness, laughter, singing. When we are sad or afraid, we sometimes cry. When we are impatient, we sometimes do or say things that might hurt others. We all need to express our feelings; talking to someone about them makes us feel better about ourselves.

   Circle of Feelings: Provide a face with removable mouth expressions: a smile, a frown, a grin, a look of surprise. Have children sit in a circle. Talk about one of your own feelings first. Then ask for volunteers to complete the sentences you initiate. For example, place the frown on the face and model an example:

   «Me pongo triste cuando mis estudiantes están enfermos y faltan a la escuela.» ("I am sad when my students are ill and miss school.")

   «Estoy contenta/o cuando . . . .» ("I am happy when . . . .")

   «Me enojo cuando . . . .» ("I get mad when . . . .")

   «Cuando estoy cansada/o, yo . . . .» (When I am tired, I . . . .")

   «Cuando me asusto, yo . . . .» (When I am frightened, I . . . .")

   This exercise can be done rapidly and each sentence used more than once. Allow this experience to prompt students' personal journal writing.

2. *Accordion Book:* Using 6" x 18" sheets of construction paper, have students make accordion books. Have them illustrate and write about a different feeling on each face of the accordion; for example, *«Estoy contento/a cuando . . . .»* ("I am happy when . . . ."), *«Estoy triste cuando . . . .»* ("I am sad when . . . .")

3. *Memories:* Share some emotional memories that tell something about you (the teacher) as a seven-year old child. After sharing some of your memories, have students recollect and share some of their memories; then have them write about them in their personal journals. If needed, have students choose any of the following writing starters:

   «Mi recuerdo más feliz es cuando . . . .» ("My happiest memory is when . . . .")

   «Me sorprendió mucho cuando . . . .» ("It was surprising when . . . .")

   «Una cosa que realmente me hizo enojar es . . . .» ("The one thing that really made me angry is . . . .")

4. *Moods and Feelings:* Explain to students that pictures of different scenes or animals can create different feelings and moods in people. To demonstrate this point, provide several large pictures of animals, places (seascape, forest, city, spooky house), or covers of books from the Literature Input. Label signs with adjectives such as *emocionante, solitario, triste, feliz, calmado, furioso,* and *espantoso.* Post them around the room. As you show each picture to the students, have them position themselves in front of the label that best describes the feelings they get when they look at the picture. Allow volunteers to describe the feelings created by the pictures. Have students choose one of the pictures to describe the feelings evoked. Have them illustrate or write about this in their personal journals.

5. *My Fears:* With children, brainstorm and list fears that children commonly have. Convey the idea that we all have fears at one time or another. Have them describe the fears they think animals might have and allow them to compare the animal fears to their own. Have children write about their fears in a personal journal.

6. *Feelings about Places:* Explain to students that different places such as hospitals, churches, elevators, or amusement parks may create different feelings in us. Have them write about the feelings experienced as they have been in different places. If needed, choose one of the following writing starters:

   «*El lugar más triste que he visitado es . . . .*» ("The saddest place I've visited is . . . .")

   «*El lugar más espantoso que he visitado es . . . .*» ("The spookiest place I've visited is . . . .")

   «*Cuando me acosté y miré las estrellas, yo sentí . . . .*» ("When I lay under the stars, I felt . . . .")

   «*Me siento muy feliz cuando voy a . . . .*» ("I feel happiest when I go to . . . .")

POETRY

Los patitos

Patito, patito, color de café;
Si tú no me quieres, yo ya sé por que.
Perdí a mi patita color de café;
por eso estoy triste y triste estaré.
La pata voló y el pato también
y allá entre la milpa
contentos se ven.

Folklore

El burrito enfermo

A mi burro, a mi burro
le duele la garganta;
el médico le ha puesto
una corbata blanca.

A mi burro, a mi burro
le duelen las orejas;
el médico ha ordenado
que tome miel de abejas.

A mi burro, a mi burro
ya no le duele nada;
ahora esta contento
tomando limonada.

Folklore

El patio de mi casa

El patio de mi casa
es muy particular
que llueve y se moja
como los demás.
¡Agáchate!
y vuélvete a agachar!
que los agachaditos
sí saben cantar.
Chocolate, molinillo
ya no llores
buen amigo.
¡A cantar, a cantar!
y después a descansar.

Folklore

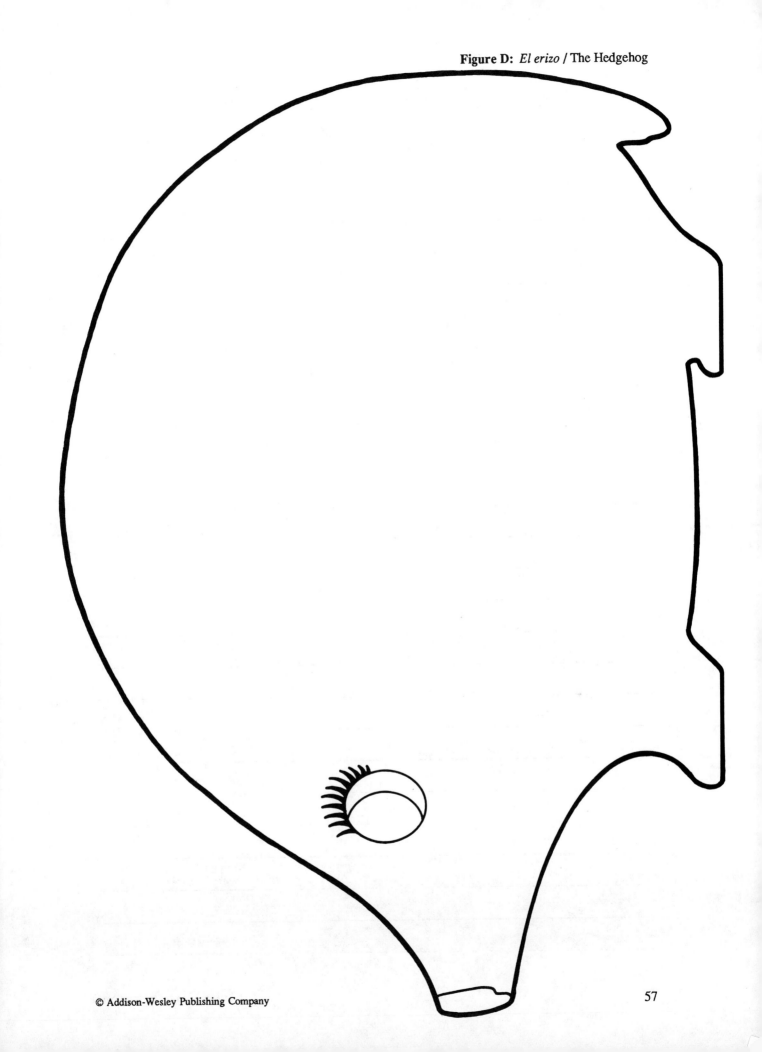

MY OWN CREATIVE TEACHING IDEAS FOR UNIT FOUR

Books: _____

_____

_____

_____

_____

Ideas: _____

_____

_____

_____

_____

_____

_____

_____

_____

_____

_____

_____

_____

_____

_____

UNIT FIVE

FELIZ DE SER COMO SOY

HAPPY TO BE ME

At an early age, children begin to develop a self-image and a concept of self-esteem. Coping with feelings about their individuality can be a challenge, especially since family, peers, and environment influence how they feel about themselves. They can attain a greater sense of self, of their own individuality, and of the value of self-esteem from stories such as *Oliver Button es un nena.*

As with the psychological aspects of self-esteem, children begin to ascribe physical attributes to the people, animals, and objects within their world. They begin to perceive differences and similarities as part of their natural learning. As part of growing up, they form attitudes about these differences and similarities and to form attitudes about distinctions such as "pretty," "unusual" and "ugly" in themselves and others. *El patito feo* and other stories from this unit help children understand how physical attributes influence self-esteem.

CONCEPTS AND VALUES

Psychological Self-Esteem

1. It can be valuable to be unique or different.
2. We have preferences in the things that we like to do.
3. We have a right to express our preferences.
4. We look for similarities and differences between ourselves and others.
5. People may judge others fairly or unfairly.
6. When we have a sense of worth, there are no limits to what we can do and be.

Physical Self-Esteem

1. People display differences in color, height, weight, physical maturity, and physical abilities.
2. We may like or dislike our own physical attributes.
3. We may like or dislike others' physical attributes.
4. Sometimes we judge others' physical differences as "limitations" when they really are not.
5. When we like ourselves, we, in turn, like others.

CHOOSE THE MAIN SELECTION

Before reading the Main Selection aloud, take your students through the Literature Input and Observation/Experience phases which follow.

de Paola, Tomie.

Andersen, Hans Christian. Adapted by Rossana Guarnieri.

Oliver Button es un nena.
Spain: Editorial Miñón, S.A., 1982.

El patito feo.
Mexico: Fernández Editores, S.A., 1984.

The author reveals Oliver Button's sense of individuality when Oliver suffers the scorn of his friends for being himself. Fortunately, his friends end up recognizing his talents and his broad interests.

This is the story about an "ugly duckling" who suffers rejection from family and neighbors because of his physical appearance. He finally discovers his true identity as a swan, and he is accepted as the beautiful creature that he always was.

If you choose *Oliver Button es un nena* as your selection, turn to page 64 to begin the Observation/Experience phase.

If you choose *El patito feo* as your selection, turn to page 68 to begin the Observation/Experience phase.

I. LITERATURE INPUT: *Both Selections*

Select five or more titles from the following list to read aloud. Read at least one selection per day to the students. Make available and incorporate the suggested titles for voluntary independent reading. Titles marked with * are Spanish translations of the original English story; titles marked with + are recommended for more proficient listeners.

1. Balzola, Asun. *Historia de un erizo.* Spain: Editorial Miñón, S.A., 1982. Erizo, the hedgehog, is saddened by those who shun him. No one will play with him because of his peculiar appearance.

*2. Bornstain, Ruth. *Gorilita.* New York: Scholastic, 1978. This is a delightful story about a gorilla who is loved by all, as a baby and as a fully grown gorilla.

3. Brennan, Gale, and Tom La Fleur. *Claudio el dinosaurio.* México: Editorial Trillas, S.A., 1984. In this delightful story, a sensitive dinosaur prefers to be brotherly.

4. —. *Dante el elefante.* México: Editorial Trillas, S.A., 1984. Dante feels self-conscious because his peers make fun of his peculiar ears and trunk, but his "differences" turn out to be valuable in a time of need.

5. —. *Donato el pato*. México: Editorial Trillas, S.A., 1984. Donato, the duck, is a very peculiar duck. He plays unusual games, hates to get wet, and is not afraid of the bad wolf.

6. —. *Tristán el hipopótamo*. México: Editorial Trillas, S.A., 1984. Tristán is a hippo who needs a boost in his self-image. By being in the right place at the right time, he saves a baby lion and is finally recognized and valued.

7. Busquets, Carlos. *El patito feo*. Spain: Editorial Susaeta, 1985. This is a colorful version of the classic *The Ugly Duckling*. This book may be used as an alternate for the Main Selection.

8. Díaz, Oralia A. *El sapito hablador*. Guatemala: Editorial Piedra Santa, 1984. A toad discovers that he can gain popularity by telling tall tales, but he later pays a stiff price for such behavior.

9. —. *El ave más linda*. Guatemala: Editorial Piedra Santa, 1986. All the birds in the jungle come to a competition to select the most beautiful bird, but instead they learn an important lesson.

10. García Sánchez, J. L. *La niña sin nombre*. Spain: Editorial Altea, 1979. A girl is found in the middle of the ocean and brought to a new land. She feels different because she does not speak the language, but she discovers that she is the same when she helps a prince recover from an illness.

11. Goldman, Judy. *Una rana en un árbol*. México: Editorial Trillas, S.A., 1986. A frog yearning to be different, exaggerates and lies, but his friends teach him a valuable lesson.

12. González de Tapia, Graciela. *La abeja coja*. México: Editorial Trillas, S.A., 1984. This is a story about a physically handicapped bee who had not recognized her potential because of her overprotective family and friends.

+13. Hemingway, Ernest. *El buen león*. Spain: Editorial Debate, 1984. An unusual lion travels to Africa where he is not welcomed by the other lions because he is "different." Unable to adapt to a new environment, he returns home to Venice.

+14. —. *El toro fiel*. Spain: Editorial Debate, 1985. An aggressive bull goes through life fighting. He finally stops when he meets a beautiful cow, but his romance ends when he re-enters the bullring.

15. Heuer, Margarita. *Antenita*. México: Editorial Trillas, S.A., 1983. In this interesting story, an ant's social behavior is unusual because she does not like to work.

16. —. *El conejo Carlitos*. México: Editorial Trillas, S.A., 1983. Charlie Rabbit decides he would rather be a lion. He tries to be very fierce, but he never manages to scare anyone.

17. Horacio, Helena. *Majo el rinoceronte*. Spain: Editorial Miñón, S.A., 1980. Majo, the rhino, is tricked into making himself look ridiculous. A child helps Majo discover that beneath his disguise, he is really a warm and beautiful rhino.

18. Janosch. *El cocodrilo feliz*. Spain: Ediciones S.M., 1985. A happy crocodile was content with himself, but his father felt ashamed of his son's gentle behavior. Feeling rather incompatible with his father, he leaves the kingdom to live in a peaceful zoo.

+19. Kipling, Rudyard. *El pequeño elefante*. Spain: Editorial Debate, 1985. This beautifully illustrated book tells the story of a curious elephant who wants to learn about crocodiles.

*20. Kraus, Robert. *Leo el capullo tardío*. New York: Windmill Books, 1977. Leo matures at a slower rate than his friends. Leo's father is concerned, but his wise mother knows that Leo will bloom one day, just as the flowers bloom when they are ready.

21. La Fontaine. *La ratoncita del campo y la de la ciudad*. Spain: Editorial La Galera, S.A., 1972. Two cousins, a country mouse and city mouse, have very different lifestyles and values.

*22. Leaf, Munro. *El cuento de Ferdinando*. New York: Scholastic, 1962. This is the story about Ferdinando, the bull, who chooses to be mild-mannered, contrary to others' expectations.

*23. Lionni, Leo. *Un pez es un pez*. Argentina: Editorial Kapelusz, 1980. This is a story about a fish who, wanting to imitate his best friend, the frog, leaves his home to travel upon the land. Recognizing his limitations, he finally returns to his natural niche, content to be a fish.

*24. —. *Frederick*. Spain: Editorial Lumen, 1982. While Frederick's four brothers busily gather food for the winter, he collects colors, images and words. His uniqueness proves to be valuable in coping with the long winter.

*25. —. *Nadarín*. Spain: Editorial Lumen, 1984. Nadarín uses his color as camouflage to escape the danger of the larger fish. A school of small fish forms a giant fish and Nadarín serves as the eye. His physical uniqueness and his intelligence help to save them all.

26. Mayne, William. *El ratón que voló*. Spain: Editorial Anaya, 1987. A mouse discovers that bats can fly, and he becomes obsessed with doing the same. He tries very hard and succeeds in his own way.

+27. Osorio, Marta. *El caballito que quería volar*. Spain: Editorial Miñón, S.A., 1982. A wooden carousel horse is not content traveling from fair to fair and yearns to fly. His dream is to be free and to fly like a bird.

28. Parramón, J.M., Jose Eduard, and María García. *Las mentiras de Koko*. Spain: Editorial Parramón, 1984. Koko tries to make himself appear more interesting by lying in order to attract more friends.

29. Perera, Hilda. *Rana, Ranita*. Spain: Editorial Everest, 1981. Toad wants to marry Rana Ranita, but she refuses because she would rather be someone else. When she finally accepts herself, she returns home to marry the toad.

30. Pierini, Fabio. *El niño que quería volar*. Spain: Editorial Miñón, S.A., 1982. A little boy, who wants to fly, learns that one must accept limitations when trying new pursuits.

31. Regals, Leo. *La pesada casa de Paso Lento*. México: Editorial Trillas, S.A., 1986. When Paso Lento, the turtle, experiences life without his heavy house, he learns to accept himself and never to complain again.

32. Rico de Alba, Lolo. *Angelita la ballena pequeñita*. Spain: Editorial Miñón, S.A., 1975. Angelita, the smallest whale, feels that she does not belong in the ocean and decides to try the land. She finally realizes that home, in the water, is the best place to be.

33. —. *El mausito*. Spain: Editorial Miñón, S.A., 1975. A strange-looking mouse tries to find out who he is. When he encounters several animals, he tries to imitate them but realizes he is not like any of them.

34. Spier, Peter. *Gente*. Venezuela: Ediciones Maria Di Mase, 1980. This book beautifully illustrates and describes similarities and differences among people throughout the world.

+35. Turin, Adela. *Rosa Caramelo*. Spain: Editorial Lumen, 1976. The young elephants had always met adult expectations until one of them, deciding to be different, influences a change in all the other females.

36. Turk, Hanne. *Jerónimo*. México: Editorial Trillas, S.A., 1985. Jerónimo, the chameleon, prefers to have a different color than his own and experiments with things to make him look different.

*37. Ungerer, Tomi. *Rufus*. Spain: Editorial Alfaguara, 1983. An adventurous bat tries to live his life by daylight. Unable to adapt, he decides to go back to his own nocturnal lifestyle.

RELATED TITLES IN ENGLISH FOR SECOND LANGUAGE ACQUISITION

Brandenberg, Franz. *Otto is Different*. New York: Greenwillow Books, 1985.

Brown, Marc. *Arthur's Nose*. New York: M. A. Little, 1986.

Duvoism, Roger. *Donkey, Donkey*. New York: Parent's Magazine Press, 1968.

Hazen, Barbara. *To Be Me*. Illinois: The Child's World Inc., 1975.

Howe, James. *I Wish I Were a Butterfly*. California: Harcourt, Brace Jovanovich, 1987.

Isadora, Rachel. *Max*. New York: Macmillan, 1976.

Rosenthal, Marya D. *Some Things Are Different, Some Things Are the Same*. Illinois: Albert Whitman and Company, 1986.

Sharmat, Marjorie W. *I'm Terrific*. New York: Holiday, 1977.

Simon, Norma J. *Why Am I Different?* Illinois: Albert Whitman and Company, 1976.

Stone, Elberta. *I'm Glad I'm Me*. New York: G. P. Putnam and Sons, 1971.

II. OBSERVATION/EXPERIENCE: *Oliver Button es un nena*
(Class Session One)

Guide students in the following observation/experience sequence to set the stage for reading the Main Selection.

Focus: Part of being ourselves includes being able to make our own choices.

1. Display toys or pictures of toys and have students categorize them according to their preferences. Graph the results on a chart labeled with the three categories: *«Niños solamente, Niñas solamente, Niños y niñas»* ("Boys Only, Girls Only, Boys and Girls"). Discuss the graph and have students justify their selections, telling why they think specific toys should be exclusively for boys or girls or for both.

2. Tell them that in a story titled *Oliver Button es un nena,* they will meet a boy who enjoyed doing things that both boys and girls can do. However, he ran into a problem when his classmates thought he should do only what all boys were expected to do.

3. Have students predict what Oliver's classmates will expect him to do and why. Following the story, have students discuss whether their predictions were correct.

III. READ AND DISCUSS THE MAIN SELECTION: *Oliver Button es un nena*
(Class Session One)

Read the Main Selection from page 60 to the students. Highlight the unit's theme by relating this story to other selections from the Literature Input list on pages 60 - 63. Then, guide students in discussing some of the following questions.

1. *¿En qué sentido era Oliver distinto a los otros niños?* (How was Oliver different from the other boys?)

2. *¿Qué pensaba la otra gente sobre las cosas que le gustaba a Oliver hacer? ¿Qué piensan ustedes?* (What did other people think about the things Oliver liked to do? What do you think?)

3. *¿Cuáles son algunas cosas que hacía Oliver y que a ustedes les gustaría hacer? ¿Qué otras cosas les gustan hacer a ustedes?* (What are some things that Oliver did that you would like to do? What are some other interests you have?)

4. *¿Qué les han dicho otras personas para hacerles sentir bien sobre las cosas que ustedes hacen? ¿Qué les dirían ustedes a otras personas para hacerlos sentir bien acerca de lo que ellos deciden hacer?* (What have people said to make you feel good about the things you do? What would you say to others to make them feel good about the things they choose to do?)

5. *¿Deberían forzar a Oliver a hacer cosas que solo hacen los niños? ¿Por qué? ¿Por qué no? Si esto les hicieran a ustedes, ¿cómo se sentirían? ¿Por qué?* (Should Oliver be forced to do things that only boys do? Why or why not? If this were done to you, how would you feel? Why?)

IV. "WHAT IF" STORY STRETCHER: *Oliver Button es un nena*
(Class Session Two)

Next, re-read the Main Selection and choose one or more of the following questions to develop students' critical thinking skills. Story stretchers may also prompt discussion, drama or writing activities.

1. *Si Oliver hubiera sido una niña, ¿cómo habría cambiado el cuento?* (If Oliver had been a girl, how would the story have been different?)

2. *Si Oliver hubiera dejado de hacer las cosas que a él le gustaban, solo para complacer a otros, ¿cómo se habría sentido? ¿Por qué?* (If Oliver had stopped doing all the things he liked, just to please others, how would he have felt? Why?)

3. *Si Oliver fuera su amigo, ¿qué cosas harían juntos?* (If Oliver were your friend, what things would you do together?)

4. *Si ustedes fueran Oliver, ¿cómo se sentirían y qué dirían y harían?* (If you were Oliver, how would you feel and what would you say and do?)

5. *Si ustedes hubieran estado con Oliver cuando los otros compañeros de clase escribieron «Oliver Button es un nena» ¿qué le habrían dicho ustedes a él?* (If you had been with Oliver when the other classmates wrote "Oliver is a sissy," what would you have said to him?)

V. INTEGRATING OTHER DISCIPLINES: *Oliver Button es un nena*
(Class Session Three and Ongoing)

The following activities are designed to enhance children's response to literature and expand *beyond* the story and its theme. The variety of activities gives teachers and students an opportunity to choose those most appropriate.

CREATIVE DRAMATICS

1. *Likes and Dislikes:* After the children have heard the story *Oliver Button es un nena,* have them pantomime the things Oliver liked and disliked doing.

2. *My Friend Oliver:* Have children pretend that Oliver is a friend and improvise things they would do together.

3. *I Would Like to . . . :* Have groups brainstorm games Oliver might play or things he might want to learn. Let them pantomime actions while observers guess. Next, allow students to brainstorm and list the different things each would like to play or learn if given the choice and opportunity. Have them pantomime these choices while observers identify them.

ART AND WRITING

1. *Interests Collage:* Have students make a group or an individual collage by cutting out magazine pictures that display interests common to boys and girls. Using their collages, have them select and write about the activities that both boys and girls can do, especially if an individual is willing to try new and different things (being a risk-taker). If needed, have the students use the following writing starters:

   «Los niños tienen el derecho de . . . (llorar, jugar con muñecas).»
   ("Boys have the right to . . . .")

   «Las niñas tienen el derecho de . . . (jugar beisbol, ser astronautas).»
   ("Girls have the right to . . . .")

   «Los niños y las niñas pueden . . . (hacer ballet, ser quienes dirigen).»
   ("Boys and girls can . . . .")

2. *Shoebox Character:* Have students make shoebox dolls representing Oliver. Have them decorate the boxes by drawing Oliver's clothes on them or by designing clothes using construction paper or wallpaper. Then have them tie on a ball made of pink crepe paper for the head, adding construction paper arms, legs, facial features and a hat.

   Oliver's Note: Have children pretend to be Oliver and write notes responding to those children who wrote, *«Oliver es un nena.»* ("Oliver is a sissy.") or *«Oliver es fenomenal.»* ("Oliver is a star.")

3. *Oliver and I:* Have students paint pictures of themselves with Oliver. Have them use the following writing starter to write in their personal journals:

   «Si Oliver y yo fueramos amigos, nosotros . . . .» ("If Oliver and I were friends, we . . . .")

4. *Self-Portrait:* Using 12" x 18" sheets of construction paper, have students make self-portraits on one half of the paper. (Provide colored yarn to use for hair.) On the other half, have students write using the following writing starter:

   «Estoy orgulloso/a de mi mismo/a porque . . . .» ("I am proud to be me because . . . .")

5. *Namegrams:* Using capital letters, have the students write their names vertically. Then, for each letter of the child's name, have her/him write a word that describes herself/himself, e.g.

Amigable	Adorable
Niña	Nice
Afectuosa	Affectionate

6. *Name Drawing:* Have students write their names in varying sizes and shapes inside illustrations that they have created with bold outlines.

7. *Sunshine Card:* Have the students trace and cut out two suns and then staple them together at the top. Have them border the outline of the sun with yarn and draw self-portraits on the covers. Inside the "sunshine" card, have them complete the following writing starter:

   «Yo brillo como el sol cuando . . . .» ("I shine like the sun when . . . .")

SOCIAL STUDIES

1. *Portrait Mirror:* Remind students that each of them is unique, with his/her very own name, birthdate, body, features, feelings, interests, and ideas. Using construction paper, have students trace and cut two oval mirror frames. Have them trace and cut out a smaller oval in the center of each. Then have them insert one lined paper and one plain, back to back between the two frames, stapling the frames together. Have them draw self-portraits on the plain side. On the lined side, have them write about what makes them one of a kind.

2. *Silhouette Autobiography:* Have students make silhouette booklets titled *«Feliz de ser como soy»* ("Happy to Be Me"). Pair students to take turns tracing each other's profile. In the classroom with the lighting dimmed, student "A" sits facing toward the left while student "B" uses a film projector to project light on the partner's profile in order to create a shadow. Student "B" traces the silhouette on dark construction paper. Repeat the activity, alternating students. Have students cut out their own silhouettes. Then have the students use the patterns to trace and cut out two sheets of lined paper and a second dark silhouette. Have them make individual booklets by placing the lined pages between the two dark silhouette covers and stapling on top.

   Brainstorm and record students' interests, likes and dislikes. Have them write brief autobiographies which include their interests, and likes and dislikes. Have them use white chalk to write titles on the covers. If necessary, younger writers may participate in this activity by having aides or volunteers trace the profiles and take dictations of the autobiographies.

3. *"Me" Mobile:* Using clothes hangers, index cards and string, have students make "me" mobiles. Have them use different colored cards to write about each of the following topics:

   > *Mi nombre, sexo, y edad.*
   > *Mi comida favorita es . . . .*
   > *En mi tiempo libre me gusta . . . .*
   > *En la escuela me gusta . . . .*
   > *Mi animalito (mascotita) favorito es . . . porque . . . .*
   > *Mi mejor amigo es . . . porque . . . .*

   > (My name, sex, and age.
   > My favorite food is . . . .
   > In my spare time I enjoy . . . .
   > In school I like . . . .
   > My favorite pet is . . . because . . . .
   > My best friend is . . . because . . . .)

   Have the children decorate the hangers with colorful yarn and attach the cards using varied lengths of yarn. Have the children include one of their photographs and a memento. Younger students may draw pictures and talk about their "me" mobiles.

4. *Driver's License:* Use large index cards to have students write vital information—birthday, name, address, weight, height, and eye and hair color—on a "driver's license." Have them draw self-portraits to user instead of photographs. (Weigh and measure students prior to writing.) Have them take turns pretending to be drivers that the police have stopped. Instruct them to show their driver's license and read their vital

information. Next, have a police officer collect several driver's licenses. The officer will read each license, describing the owner (but leaving out the name), while the children guess to whom it belongs.

5. *My Choice:* In **Oliver Button es un nena,** others made the choice to accept or reject Oliver. Discuss how children often choose their friends by the way they look or by their actions. Allow this to prompt personal journal writing.

I.   LITERATURE INPUT: *El patito feo*
See pages 60 - 63.

II.   OBSERVATION/EXPERIENCE: *El patito feo*
(Class Session One)

Guide students in the following observation/experience sequence to set the stage for reading the Main Selection.

Focus: Sometimes our physical differences are not appreciated by others.

1. Before class, prepare simple construction paper wings and bills for three different kinds of birds; e.g., duck, parrot, goose. Have three children wear the wings and bills and make bird noises.

2. Guide the class in discussing physical similarities and differences among these birds. Ask them which bird they think is the most beautiful, which the least, and why.

3. Show students the book cover and tell them that in the story *El patito feo,* they will meet a baby duckling who, because he looked different from the other ducklings, was not appreciated.

4. Have them predict what the baby duckling will think, say and do. Following the story, have students discuss whether their predictions were correct.

III.   READ AND DISCUSS THE MAIN SELECTION: *El patito feo*
(Class Session One)

Read the Main Selection from page 60 to the students. Highlight the unit's theme by relating this story to other selections from the Literature Input list on pages 60 - 63. Then, guide students in discussing some of the following questions.

1. *¿En qué forma era el Patito Feo distinto de los otros patitos? Explíquennos.* (How was the Ugly Duckling different from the other ducklings? Explain.)

2. *¿Qué pensaban los otros patos y los otros animales de la forma en que se veía el Patito Feo? ¿Creen ustedes que la gente hace esto a otras personas?* (What did the other ducks and other animals think of the way the Ugly Duckling looked? Do you think people do this to other people?)

3. *¿Cómo trataron al Patito Feo los otros animales? ¿Estuvo esto correcto o estuvo mal haberlo tratado así? Nos pueden decir.* (How did the other animals treat the Ugly Duckling? Was it right or wrong to treat him this way? Explain.)

4. *¿Cómo creen que se sentía el Patito Feo? ¿Creen ustedes que la gente se puede sentir así? Platíquennos.* (How do you think the Ugly Duckling felt? Do you think people can feel as he did? Tell about it.)

5. *¿Qué cosas puede uno decir o hacer para hacer que otra persona se sienta bien consigo mismo? ¿Nos pueden decir de alguna vez cuando alguien los hizo a ustedes sentirse bien de sí mismos?* (What are some things one could say or do to make another person feel good about him/herself? Can you tell us about a time when someone made you feel good about yourselves?)

IV. "WHAT IF" STORY STRETCHER: *El patito feo*
(Class Session Two)

Next, re-read the Main Selection and choose one or more of the following questions to develop students' critical thinking skills. Story stretchers may also prompt discussion, drama or writing activities.

1. *Si el huevo del Patito Feo hubiera sido el huevo de otro animal, imagínense un lagarto, un águila, o una tortuga, ¿cómo habría cambiado el cuento?* (If the Ugly Duckling's egg had been another animal's egg, suppose an alligator, an eagle, or a turtle, how would the story have been different?)

2. *Si el Patito Feo fuera el animalito (mascota) de ustedes, ¿cómo sería distinta la vida de él viviendo con ustedes?* (If the Ugly Duckling were your pet, how would his life be different living with you?)

3. *¿Cómo pudo haberse portado de otra manera el Patito Feo con los que se burlaron de él?* (How might the Ugly Duckling have behaved differently toward those who made fun of him?)

4. *Si ustedes fueran el Patito Feo y alguien se burlara de ustedes, ¿qué les dirían o que harían ustedes?* (If you were the Ugly Duckling and someone made fun of you, what would you say or do?)

5. *Si el Patito Feo hubiera sido aceptado y querido desde el principio, ¿cómo habría cambiado el cuento?* (If the Ugly Duckling had been accepted and liked from the beginning, how would the story have been different?)

V. INTEGRATING OTHER DISCIPLINES: *El patito feo*
(Class Session Three and Ongoing)

The following activities are designed to enhance children's response to literature and expand *beyond* the story and its theme. The variety of activities gives teachers and students an opportunity to choose those most appropriate.

CREATIVE DRAMATICS

1. *A New World:* Have children pantomime being the Ugly Duckling as he hatches and discovers a new world. Let them pantomime what the little bird might discover.

2. *Welcome:* Have children discuss and dramatize what it would be like if all the animals had welcomed the Ugly Duckling and treated him lovingly.

3. *Happy and Sad Times:* Review the sequence of events, select characters, and establish settings to have children dramatize the entire story from beginning to end. Allow several groups to dramatize the story, emphasizing the Ugly Duckling's saddest and happiest moments.

ART AND WRITING

1. *Friendly Letter:* Have the students pretend to be friendly animals and write letters to the swan inviting him to visit their "niche," a place where people and animals welcome and appreciate others, no matter how they look.

2. *Milk-Carton Swan:* Have the children cut off the top halves of small milk cartons to use as the bodies. The swans' heads and necks can be made by cutting and rolling one end of 5" x 1" strips of construction paper. Have the students cut construction paper wings and feathers. (Real feathers may be used.) Have them glue these parts on the milk cartons and add beaks and eyes.

   Notes of Praise: Have the students write short, kind notes to the Ugly Duckling—*Eres bello.* (You are beautiful.); *Te quiero.* (I love you.); *Nunca te sientas feo.* (Never feel ugly.)—on five to ten small eggs cut from paper. Have the students put them inside the milk-carton swans.

3. *Big Book:* In cooperative groups, have students make big books about the story. Have each group member select and draw a story event using mixed media (watercolors and crayons). Instruct them to write a description of each event. Have each group arrange the pictures in proper story sequence, bind their books, and read them to other groups.

4. *TV Story Scroll:* Using a shoebox, two pencils, and a narrow four-foot long strip of paper, have several cooperative groups illustrate four to six sequential events from the story. Have the groups write captions for their illustrations. Slip pencils through the top and bottom sides of a shoe box and tape one end of the scroll to each of the two pencils. Allow them to read their scrolls to other groups or classes.

5. *Secret-Pal Note:* Have students draw pictures of other characters from the Literature Input list who felt like the Ugly Duckling. As secret pals, allow them to write notes of praise to those characters. Have the children acknowledge the characters' good qualities so that the characters can feel good about themselves even when others try to make them feel bad.

6. *Favorite Character:* From the Literature Input list, have students select favorite story characters who, in some ways, remind them of how children can feel or be. Have them draw pictures of the characters and write about them in their literature logs.

SCIENCE

1. *Fictional Versus Real Birds:* The Ugly Duckling is a fictional character; to present him as a real bird, show resources (films, illustrations, real birds) displaying the physical characteristics of different birds. Make reference to the color of birds' feathers—among birds, males tend to be colorful and females are a camouflage brown—and

differences in beaks and feet. Guide the children in observing, discussing, and comparing the swan to other birds. With children, record facts on a two-column chart and then have the children read them. Allow them to record bird facts in their science logs.

2. *Egg Hatching:* In the story, the Ugly Duckling hatched from an egg. As an on-going project, have the students observe the hatching of an egg and record observations in their science logs. They may also illustrate the hatching process.

3. *Seasonal Behavior:* In the story, the swan's seasonal behavior is noted. Talk about the seasonal behavior among ducks, swans, and other birds. Have the students record facts in their science logs.

4. *"Birds of a Feather" Poem:* Talk about a bird's prominent feature, its feathers. Allow children to touch feathers and observe the qualities of color, texture, and weight. Use the tactile experience with feathers to create a class poem. Write it in a poetry log.

5. *Fingerprints:* Using magnifying glasses, have cooperative groups study their unique fingerprints. Have students use fingerprint painting to illustrate before and after pictures of the Ugly Duckling. (As a little swan, have them use the pinky print; and as a full grown one, a thumbprint). Have children discuss the setting of the story and illustrate it in their fingerprint pictures. Have them write descriptions of the Ugly Duckling first as a baby swan and finally as a full-grown swan.

SOCIAL STUDIES

1. *Our Similarities:* The Ugly Duckling was noticed because he looked different, but no one ever stopped to see that in some ways, he was just like the other birds. Discuss physical similarities among classmates and graph physical attributes—hair and eye color, hair length and texture, and height—to show that we are more alike than different. Talk about the fact that all of us share common human feelings and needs. Use this experience to prompt journal writing.

2. *Who's Who Display:* Pair children to trace each other from head to waist. Let students draw and color in their facial features and clothing. Provide tissue paper in assorted colors for hair, and let them shape and paste on the hair. Have students write five facts about themselves but not their names; e.g.,

   Tengo seis años.
   En mi familia somos cinco.
   Mi amigo es Alex.
   Me faltan dos dientes.
   ¿Quién soy?

   (I am six years old.
   There are five people in my family.
   My friend is Alex.
   Two of my teeth are missing.
   Who am I?)

   Attach the written facts under the pictures and display the students' artwork in a large area titled «*¿Quién es quien?*» ("Who's Who?") This activity is particularly interesting when parents visit since it really keeps them guessing.

3. *I Am:* Using Figure E (page 73), have children observe themselves in the mirror and write several unique attributes about themselves, using the title *«Así soy yo»* ("I Am"). Have them add features to the body pattern to create a boy or a girl and color the picture. Share project among classmates.

4. *Self-Esteem:* In their personal journals, have the children write about things that they like about themselves—talents, interests, personality—and one thing that they would like to develop or improve in themselves.

5. *Physical "Limitations":* Discuss physical limitations of the handicapped and how handicapped individuals compensate for limitations. Place the students in several role-playing situations which encourage them to focus on the use of alternate faculties (sight, touch, smell, hearing, taste) when faced with blindness, deafness, or another physical handicap. Allow this experience to prompt personal journal writing.

POETRY

El cisne

Al cisne lo confundieron
con un patito muy feo;
pero al crecer tan hermoso,
¡la sorpresa que se dieron!

Raquel C. Mireles

Los pájaros

En la cumbre de un cardón
cantaban tres animales,
uno parecía gorrión
y los otros cardenales.
¡Ay! que parecidos son,
pero nunca son iguales.

Folklore

La ardilla

La ardilla vuela.
La ardilla salta
como locuela.

—Mamá, ¿la ardilla
no va a la escuela?
Ven ardillita,
tengo una jaula
que es muy bonita.

—No, yo prefiero
mi tronco de árbol
y mi agujero.

Amado Nervo

Figure E: *Así soy yo* / This Is Me

MY OWN CREATIVE TEACHING IDEAS FOR UNIT FIVE

Books: _____

_____

_____

_____

_____

_____

Ideas: _____

_____

_____

_____

_____

_____

_____

_____

_____

_____

_____

_____

_____

_____

_____

_____

_____

UNIT SIX

PUEDO AYUDAR Y COMPARTIR

I CAN HELP AND SHARE

As young children begin to grow out of their egocentric selves, they begin to become more socially adapted—helping, sharing, and cooperating. They learn that these behaviors not only bring self-satisfaction, but are qualities valued by others. Encouraging children to work together helps them develop their sense of sharing, cooperation, decision-making, leadership, and camaraderie. They begin to find commonalities among themselves, to accept and value different ideas, and to communicate ideas and feelings for a real purpose. *Lucecita, La Gallina Paulina* and other stories from this unit allow children to recognize these qualities in the story characters so that they may value and take on these qualities for themselves as well.

CONCEPTS AND VALUES

1. Helping and sharing with others can be rewarding and self-fulfilling.
2. Being overly preoccupied with ourselves may cause us to overlook the needs of others.
3. Being sensitive and caring may generate the same behavior in others.
4. Being thoughtless and uncooperative can bring adverse consequences.
5. Cooperating and working together can help solve problems and produce results.
6. Teamwork can help us learn different ways to do things and to communicate our ideas.
7. By cooperating, we learn to accept and value what others are willing to share.
8. There are times when it is best to work alone, especially when we need time alone with our thoughts.

CHOOSE THE MAIN SELECTION

Before reading the Main Selection aloud, take your students through the Literature Input and Observation/Experience phases which follow.

Heuer, Margarita.	Alonso, Fernando.
Lucecita. México: Editorial Trillas, 1983.	*La Gallina Paulina.* Spain: Santillana Publishing Company, 1979.
Lucecita is a firefly who loses her shining light when she refuses to help others in need. A fairy plans several trials to test Lucecita's willingness to help others. When she learns the value of helpfulness, her light is restored.	This is the classic story of *The Little Red Hen.* When Paulina tries to recruit help from her friends, they are unwilling to lend a helping hand. Eventually, she finds a way to make them realize their selfish behavior.
If you choose *Lucecita* as your selection, turn to page 79 to begin the Observation/Experience phase.	If you choose *La Gallina Paulina* as your selection, turn to page 84 to begin the Observation/Experience phase.

I.   LITERATURE INPUT: *Both Selections*

Select five or more titles from the following list to read aloud. Read at least one selection per day to the students. Make available and incorporate the suggested titles for voluntary independent reading. Titles marked with * are Spanish translations of the original English story; titles marked with + are recommended for more proficient listeners.

*1. Ada, Alma Flor. *La gallinita roja.* Reading, MA: Addison-Wesley, 1989. An industrious hen teaches her friends about the benefits of cooperation in this beautifully illustrated big book version of the classic tale of *The Little Red Hen.*

+2. Alcántara, Ricardo S. *La bruja que quiso matar al sol.* Spain: Editorial Hymsa, 1981. Afkitan, the mean witch, hates the sun and the water, and is determined to destroy them. All the animals are frightened and cooperatively devise a plan, with a humble goose as their emissary, to get rid of her.

*3. Bishop, Dorothy Sword. *Leonardo el león y Ramón el ratón.* Illinois: National Textbook Company, 1973. This is a well-known fable about a great lion who refuses to play with Ramón because a small mouse is too "insignificant."

*4. Bright, Robert. *Jorgito y los ladrones.* New York: Scholastic, 1978. Jorgito is a friendly ghost who never scares anyone until, one night, he and his friends work together to scare some robbers.

5. Broger, Archim. *Historia de Dragolina.* Spain: Editorial Juventud, 1982. Dragolina, the last dragon on this planet, is the most adaptable and friendly creature in the land. She never gives up trying to find a home.

6. Clement, Elena. *Triste historia del sol.* México: Editorial Trillas, S.A., 1986. The sun is sad and all are concerned. The people cooperatively and compassionately bring things to make him happy.

7. Flores, Rosa. *Caracolitos: Me siento feliz al ayudar*. Oklahoma: Economy Co., 1979. A young boy becomes aware of the importance of helping others.

+8. Fuentes, Gloria. *El dragón tragón*. Spain: Editorial Escuela Española, S.A., 1982. A dragon becomes ill when he swallows a motorcycle and burns himself, but the whole town comes to his rescue to help him get better.

9. Gispert, M., and C. Peris. *Martín quiere leer*. Spain: Editorial Teide, S.A., 1984. Martín's love for books causes his imagination to run wild with story characters. One day his hometown is flooded and his favorite book is ruined. This misfortune is sad, but a new friendship emerges because of it.

10. Grimm, Brothers. Adapted by Rossana Guarnieri. *Los músicos de Brema*. México: Fernández Editores, S.A., 1983. This is an adaptation of the classic folktale about four animals who work together to solve a problem.

*11. Gross, Ruth Belos. *Los músicos de Brema*. New York: Scholastic, 1979. This amusing tale by the Brothers Grimm tells how four friends cooperate and work together to make the best of a situation.

12. Heuck, Sigrid. *El poni, el oso y el manzano*. Spain: Editorial Juventud, 1986. This is a beautifully illustrated story about a horse and a bear who search for some lost apples.

+13. Jucker, Rita. *Kivitán*. Spain: Ediciones S.M., 1985. Kivitán is a generous bird that helps find different objects in places no one else can.

+14. Kouzel, Daisy, and Earl Thollander. *El premio del cuco*. New York: Doubleday, 1977. This is a Mexican folktale about a courageous bird that loses his colorful feathers and his beautiful voice while helping his fellow birds.

*15. Kraus, Robert. *José el gran ayudante*. New York: Windmill Books, 1977. José loves to help. He helps his family, his friends, his entire community, and most importantly, he helps himself.

16. Kudlacek, Jan. *La gran aventura*. Colombia: Editorial Kapelusz Colombiana, S.A. Ediciones El Barco de Papel, 1984. Lola, the intelligent frog, devises a hilarious plan to protect herself and her friends from a dangerous serpent.

+17. Kurusa and Doppert, Morika. *La calle es libre*. Venezuela: Ediciones Ekaré-Banco del Libro, 1983. The children of San José need a place to play, and after a long struggle, all the people cooperate and build a park.

18. La Fleur, Tom, and Gale Brennan. *Lucho el aguilucho*. México: Editorial Trillas, S.A., 1984. This is a fable about a near-sighted eagle and a fly. They become good friends and together they make a perfect flying team.

19. La Fontaine. Adapted by Ma. Eulalia Valeri. *El asno y el perro*. Spain: Editorial La Galera, 1975. This is a beautiful fable about a faithful dog who helps a donkey in time of need in spite of previous problems between them.

20. Larreula, Eric. *La mona saltarina*. Spain: Editorial Teide, 1984. A little monkey is always active. When the little monkey bravely and skillfully rescues his friends, they learn that it pays to keep physically fit.

*21. Lionni, Leo. *Nadarín*. Spain: Editorial Lumen, 1982. Nadarín uses his color as camouflage to escape from the danger of the larger fish. He advises a school of fish to form a giant fish, and in this way, they protect each other from dangerous fish.

22. Lisson, Asunción. *El cuento de Ratapón*. Spain: Editorial La Galera, 1972. Mother rabbit is instinctively alerted to come to Ratapón's rescue when he has a dangerous encounter with a hungry snake.

*23. Minarik, Else Holmelund. *Un beso para Osito*. Spain: Editorial Alfaguara, 1986. Osito's grandmother sends him a kiss and all of his friends help deliver it.

24. McQueen, Lucinda. *La gallinita roja*. New York: Scholastic, 1988. This well-illustrated version of *The Little Red Hen* is also available in big book format. (This is another version of *Gallina Paulina,* one of the main selections for this unit.)

25. Moodie, Fiora. *El unicornio y el mar*. Spain: Ediciones S.M., 1987. A brave unicorn that saves a princess is rewarded with a new life in the sea.

26. Pecanins, Ana María. *La cometa*. México: Editorial Trillas, S.A., 1986. A girl and a flock of birds rescue a trapped kite and become the best of friends. They all fly together everyday and have a wonderful summer.

+27. Pettersson, Aline. *El papalote y el nopal*. México: CONAFE, CIDCLI, S.C., 1985. A kite flies freely until the rain gets it wet. When it lands on a cactus, it longs to be free again. But luckily, the humble cactus tries very hard to help free it, and succeeds.

28. Rius, María. *El principe feliz*. Spain: Editorial Bruguera, 1980. This heart-warming tale about a statue of a prince and a swallow shows how compassion can help diminish misery.

29. Ruille, Bertrand. *Historia de la nube que era amiga de una niña*. Spain: Editorial Miñón, S.A., 1973. A cloud comes down to earth to play with a friendly girl and notices that the plants need water. It waters every plant and animal until it begins to shrink. The girl and all the animals get together to save the generous cloud.

30. Ungerer, Tomi. *Los tres bandidos*. Spain: Editorial Lumen, 1980. An orphan girl, who is kidnapped by three bandits, is instrumental in helping a large number of orphans and in rehabilitating the bandits.

31. Valeri, Ma. Eulalia. *La gallinita roja*. Spain: Editorial La Galera, 1977. This is the traditional folk tale of *The Little Red Hen*. This is another version of *Gallina Paulina,* one of the main selections for this unit.

32. Vásquez, Zoraida. *Los músicos de Bremen*. México: Editorial Trillas, S.A., 1986. This humorous tale tells how several animals use team spirit to get rid of some adversaries.

+33. Velthuys, Max. *El gentil dragón rojo*. Spain: Editorial Miñón, S.A., 1975. A gentle red dragon is found and held captive. A wise person, recognizing the dragon's capabilities, uses him to help the town.

+34. Verley, Susan. *Gracias Tejón*. Spain: Editorial Altea, 1985. When Tejón, a wise elderly friend of the community, dies, he is remembered by his friends because of the time he shared with them and the things he taught them.

35. Watson, Jane Werner. *Colección de oro: La garra del león.* México: Editorial Trillas, S.A., 1987. This small book is a nice complement to the story of *The Little Red Hen.*

36. Wensell, Ulises. *La niña invisible.* Spain: Editorial Altea, 1979. María is a peacemaker. Her tears wash away her body, and though invisible, she becomes the unifying force between the green and blue children.

+37. Zavrel, Stepan. *El abuelo Tomás.* Spain: Ediciones, S.M., 1984. The city mayor decides to recruit all the elderly in town to send them to a rest home away from the young people. The grandchildren miss their grandparents so much that they devise a hilarious and successful plan to rescue them.

RELATED TITLES IN ENGLISH FOR SECOND LANGUAGE ACQUISITION

Addison-Wesley Big Book Program. *The Little Red Hen.* Reading, MA: Addison-Wesley, 1989.

—. *The Farmer and the Beet.* Reading, MA: Addison-Wesley, 1989.

—. *The Rabbit and the Turnip.* Reading, MA: Addison-Wesley, 1989.

Cauley, Lorinda Bryan. *The Cock, the Mouse and the Little Red Hen.* New York: G. P. Putnam's Sons, 1982.

+ Charlie, Remy. *Harlequin and the Gift of Many Colors.* New York: Parents Magazine Press, 1973.

Hines, Anna Grossnickle. *Maybe a Band-Aid Will Help.* New York: E.P. Dutton, 1984.

Hoban, Russell. *A Best Friend for Frances.* New York: Harper and Row, 1969.

Lionni, Leo. *It's Mine!* New York: Alfred A. Knopf, 1986.

Rockwell, Anne Harlow. *Can I Help?* New York: Macmillan, 1982.

Solasko, Fainna. *The Turnip.* New York: Malish, 1984.

II. OBSERVATION/EXPERIENCE: *Lucecita*
(Class Session One)

Guide students in the following observation/experience sequence to set the stage for reading the Main Selection.

Focus: Cooperation and helpfulness are valuable traits.

1. Instruct cooperative groups to create a large rainbow. Provide glue, tissue paper in assorted colors, scissors, and long strips of butcher paper. Under the rainbow, students may incorporate a spring scene such as a garden setting with colorful flowers and busy insects or children playing.

2. Guide the class in a discussion in which they describe the cooperation that went into creating the mural. Ask them what they would have done if one of the children had been too busy to help. How might they teach that person to be more helpful or cooperative?

3. Tell students that in a story titled **Lucecita,** they will meet a little firefly that has more important things to do than to help her friends. A fairy finds a way to help her understand the importance of being helpful and cooperative.

4. Have them predict what the fairy will do to teach Lucecita about being a more helpful and cooperative friend. Following the story, have students discuss whether their predictions were correct.

III. READ AND DISCUSS THE MAIN SELECTION: *Lucecita*
(Class Session One)

Read the Main Selection from page 76 to the students. Highlight the unit's theme by relating this story to other selections from the Literature Input list on pages 76 - 79. Then, guide students in discussing some of the following questions.

1. *¿Por qué no paró Lucecita para ayudar a la ardilla?* (Why didn't Lucecita stop to help the squirrel?)

2. *Cuando el hada dirigió a Lucecita a la montaña, ¿qué creen ustedes que ella quería que Lucecita hiciera? ¿Han ustedes necesitado a alguien quien les ayude? Platíquennos.* (When the fairy directed Lucecita to the mountain, what do you think she wanted Lucecita to do? Have you ever needed someone to help you? Tell us about it.)

3. *¿Cómo pudo Lucecita recobrar su luz? ¿Han ustedes ayudado a alguien? ¿Cómo?* (How was Lucecita able to get her light back? Have you ever helped someone? How?)

4. *¿Creen ustedes que Lucecita aprendió una lección de esta experiencia? Explíquennos.* (Do you think Lucecita learned a lesson from her experience? Explain.)

5. *¿Pueden acordarse de otros personajes que les recuerden a Lucecita?* (Can you think of other characters that remind you of Lucecita? Tell us about them.)

IV. "WHAT IF" STORY STRETCHER: *Lucecita*
(Class Session Two)

Next, re-read the Main Selection and choose one or more of the following questions to develop students' critical thinking skills. Story stretchers may also prompt discussion, drama or writing activities.

1. *Si Lucecita no hubiera encontrado al hada, ¿habría cambiado ella? Explíquennos.* (If Lucecita had not met the fairy, would she have changed? Explain.)

2. *Si Lucecita no hubiera ayudado a la mosca y al pájaro, ¿cómo habría sido su vida?* (If Lucecita had not helped the fly and the bird, how would her life have been different?)

3. *Si ustedes hubieran sido Lucecita, le habrían hecho caso al hada? ¿Por qué? ¿Por qué no?* (If you were Lucecita, would you have listened to the fairy? Why? Why not?)

4. *Piensen en alguien de su familia a quien ustedes ayudan. Si dejaran de ayudarle, ¿qué pasaría?* (Think of someone in your family that you usually help. If you stopped helping, what would happen?)

5. *Piensen en alguien en la escuela a quien ustedes ayudan. Si dejaran de ayudarle, ¿qué pasaría?* (Think of someone in school that you usually help. If you stopped helping, what would happen?)

V. INTEGRATING OTHER DISCIPLINES: *Lucecita*
(Class Session Three and Ongoing)

The following activities are designed to enhance children's response to literature and expand *beyond* the story and its theme. The variety of activities gives teachers and students an opportunity to choose those most appropriate.

CREATIVE DRAMATICS

1. *Dramatization with Props:* Using teacher-prepared story props (rabbit ears, wings for the firefly and a wand), have groups re-enact the story.

2. *Creative Movement:* Have the students recreate the movements of the story's characters: flying, crawling, hopping, running, floating. Have them move in unison to the beat of a drum as you call out the character and the character's action(s).

3. *Pantomime Scramblers:* Give several cooperative groups a set of sequence cards that have a simple written description of a group working together; these might include gardening, washing a car, painting a mural. Instruct the students to practice pantomiming the actions from the cards, but scramble the sequence so that they imitate the actions out of sequence. Each group shares its set of actions while the observers place the actions in order by positioning the participants in proper sequence.

ART AND WRITING

1. *Story Sequence:* Have cooperative groups illustrate all the major story scenes. Have each group display the illustrations out of sequence. Ask observers to position the students holding the pictures in the correct order.

   Big Book: Each group may make a big book using the illustrations. Have students write captions on separate sheets of paper, edit them, and then rewrite them on the illustrations. Have them tie the book together with yarn. Allow the students to read the books to other groups.

2. *Thank-You Note:* Have children write a thank-you note to someone who has been caring, helpful and thoughtful (friend, family member, school nurse, custodian). Have them design a cover and make the note into a card.

3. *Make a Firefly:* Using an egg carton for the body, tissue paper for the wings, and gold glitter for the light, have the students create fireflies. They can then staple their fireflies on large sheets of construction paper and draw a desired setting from the story. Have them write a descriptive caption for the illustration.

4. *Firefly Puppet:* Using Figure F (page 91), have the students make paper bag firefly puppets. They can use pipe cleaners for legs and tissue paper for wings. Have the children write a note to commend Lucecita or someone who reminds them of helpful Lucecita. Have them write on the lines of the fireflies:

   «*Lucecita, ha sido usted muy . . . . ; o* »
   «*Mamá, usted siempre . . . .*»

   ("Lucecita, you have been very . . . . "; or
   "Mom, you always . . . . ")

5. *Cooperation Mural:* Have cooperative groups create a class mural using mixed media to depict the theme. Provide assorted colors of tissue paper, construction paper, crayons, and paints as well as scissors and glue. While the children work together, photograph their cooperative behaviors—cutting, pasting, drawing, painting, hanging up murals, cleaning up. This activity may also be used as an alternative Observation/Experience.

   Class Album: When the photographs are developed, display them and discuss the cooperative teamwork. Relate the team experience to the theme of helping and sharing. Allow this to prompt personal journal writing. Use the photographs to make a class album (this may be a pop-up album). Students may write a descriptive caption for each photograph.

6. *"Cooperation Cupcake" Recipe:* With students, discuss and brainstorm qualities of being helpful and cooperative. Have the class dictate a recipe for "cooperation cupcakes" (or have cooperative groups write their own recipes). Record the class recipe on a chart and display it as a reminder to be cooperative. For example:

   Pastelillos de Cooperación

   > *5 tazas de ayuda*
   > *3-1/2 tazas de voluntad para compartir*
   > *2-1/2 cucharadas de humor*
   > *2-1/2 cucharadas de voluntad para esperar nuestro turno*
   > *4 cucharadas de amabilidad*

   Cooperation Cupcakes

   > 5 cups of helping
   > 3-1/2 cups of sharing
   > 3 cups of humor
   > 2-1/2 tablespoons of taking turns
   > 4 tablespoons of kindness

   As an added activity, students may make thumbprint children all around the recipe chart. They may add features such as balloons, flowers, books, umbrellas, animals, sports equipment.

7. *Print Mural:* Have cooperative groups select a theme that they would like to illustrate on a large mural. Provide a box of assorted materials such as small plastic bottles, bottle caps, sponges in assorted shapes, plastic cookie cutters, blocks, toy tires, large

paper clips, sliced potatoes or carrots, jar lids, tree bark, corks. Also set out several pie pans containing tempera paints and several long strips of butcher paper. Have each group draw the illustrations for its theme. Next, have them dip objects into the paints to print onto the illustrations, covering every inch of the mural. (It really involves planning and cooperation to get the job done!)

My Impressions: Have the students write about their impressions of this experience in their journals. You may wish to use the following writing starters:

«*Trabajando juntos . . . .*» ("Working together . . . .")

«*Cuando trabajo en el grupo . . . .*» ("When I work in the group . . . .")

«*Cuando todos trabajamos . . . .*» ("When we all help . . . . ")

SCIENCE

1. *Insect Study:* Lucecita is a fictional insect, but students can learn about real insects. Outdoors, have students observe some insects in their natural habitat. Let them capture some insects for later observation. Have them note the following characteristics in insects: insects have six legs, three body parts—head, thorax (middle area), abdomen—and two antennae (feelers). Some have one or two pairs of wings and some have no wings at all. Explain that there are four stages in an insect's life: egg, larva (wormlike), pupa, and finally the real insect.

Have the students brainstorm and list all the insects they normally see in their own backyards: ants, flies, mosquitos, moths, butterflies, grasshoppers, bees, crickets, beetles, fireflies, ladybugs, junebugs, dragonflies.

As a home project, have students explore their own backyards to find eggs on the underside of leaves, on tree trunks or on garden plants. Or have them collect caterpillars, fly and worm larvae and pupa, or insects. Have them record, in their science logs, what they collected and where, together with any additional observations that they have made. Have them share the information and the specimens with the class.

SOCIAL STUDIES

1. *Who Helps?:* Explain that our world is made up of people who help each other. Each of us helps out in our own special way. Help the children brainstorm, cluster, and record ideas about those who help us and how. Have the children trace both of their hands and, within each finger, write descriptive words (from the cluster) that tell how we help others.

2. *Class Ambassadors:* Class ambassadors can ease the new school experience for new students. Explain to students that we can be helpful by making new students feel comfortable and welcomed. Brainstorm and list all the possible things that a class ambassador could do to help a new student. Recruit class ambassadors to welcome and orient new students and visitors. (This is especially helpful when younger students come from other classes during team teaching.)

3. *Self-Help:* Guide students in a discussion about the value of helping ourselves. What are some things we can do to help ourselves? What are some things we expect our parents or others to do for us even though we can do them ourselves? If we always

depended on others to do everything for us, would we learn how to do things for ourselves? Why is it important to try doing things even if they are a little bit difficult to do? Should we always expect to do things right or perfectly the first time? What is the best thing we can do for ourselves?

Have students draw a self-portrait. Have them write about helping themselves. If needed, use the following writing starter:

«*Antes acostumbraba a . . . pero ahora haré . . . .*»
("I used to . . . but now I will . . . .")

I. LITERATURE INPUT: *La Gallina Paulina*
See pages 76 - 79.

II. OBSERVATION/EXPERIENCE: *La Gallina Paulina*
(Class Session One)

Guide students in the following observation/experience sequence to set the stage for reading the Main Selection.

Focus: It is important to be helpful and cooperative.

1. To prepare a setting for the story, have the class create a farm mural. Allow each group to have a turn painting anything (except animals, which will be added in a later phase) they decide to add to the farm. They must cooperate and help each other to accomplish the task. To obtain feedback regarding their cooperative experience, guide the students in a discussion.

2. Tell the students that in a story titled *La Gallina Paulina,* they will meet a hard-working hen that had a job to do and tried to involve her friends in helping.

3. Have them predict what her job will be and how she will get it done. Following the story, have students discuss whether their predictions were correct.

III. READ AND DISCUSS THE MAIN SELECTION: *La Gallina Paulina*
(Class Session One)

Read the Main Selection from page 76 to the students. Highlight the unit's theme by relating this story to other selections from the Literature Input list on pages 76 - 79. Then, guide students in discussing some of the following questions.

1. *¿Por qué creen que la Gallina Paulina pidió ayuda de sus vecinos? ¿Cuándo han pedido ustedes ayuda?* (Why do you think Gallina Paulina asked her neighbors for help? When have you asked for help?)

2. *¿Creen ustedes que la Gallina Paulina tenía razón en no compartir su pan? ¿Por qué? ¿Que habrían hecho ustedes?* (Do you think Gallina Paulina was right in not sharing her bread? Why? What would you have done?)

3. *A veces nos portamos como los amigos de la Gallina Paulina. Platíquennos de alguna vez que los niños se pueden portar así.* (Sometimes we behave as Gallina Paulina's friends did. Tell us about a time when children might behave like them.)

4. *¿A qué otros animales de la granja podía haber pedido ayuda la Gallina Paulina? ¿Qué excusas habrían dado esos animales?* (What other farm animals could Gallina Paulina have asked for help? What excuses would those animals have given?)

5. *¿Por qué es mejor trabajar juntos, en lugar de solos, en algunos trabajos?* (Why is it better to work together, rather than alone, on some tasks?)

IV. "WHAT IF" STORY STRETCHER: *La Gallina Paulina*
(Class Session Two)

Next, re-read the Main Selection and choose one or more of the following questions to develop students' critical thinking skills. Story stretchers may also prompt discussion, drama or writing activities.

1. *¿Qué habrían pensado si, cuando estaban pintando el mural, alguien no hubiera querido ayudar?* (What would you have thought if, when painting the farm mural, someone had been unwilling to help?)

2. *La Gallina Paulina estaba calmada aun cuando los otros no querían ayudar. Si ustedes estuvieran en esa situación, ¿qué habrían hecho? ¿Que habrían hecho o dicho a sus amigos?* (Gallina Paulina was calm even when the others were unwilling to help. If you were in that situation, what would you have done? What would you have said or done to your friends?)

3. *¿Qué habría pasado si todos los animales hubieran ayudado? Cuenten la historia con los animales cooperando con la Gallina Paulina.* (What would have happened if all the animals had helped? Tell the story with the animals cooperating with Gallina Paulina.)

4. *Si la Gallina Paulina les hubiera pedido ayuda, ¿qué le habrían contestado ustedes? ¿Por qué?* (If Gallina Paulina had asked you to help, what would you have answered? Why?)

5. *¿Cómo sería nuestro mundo si la gente no quisiera ayudar?* (What would our world be like if people were unwilling to help?)

V. INTEGRATING OTHER DISCIPLINES: *La Gallina Paulina*
(Class Session Three and Ongoing)

The following activities are designed to enhance children's response to literature and expand *beyond* the story and its theme. The variety of activities gives teachers and students an opportunity to choose those most appropriate.

CREATIVE DRAMATICS

1. *Seed Growth Pantomime:* Have children pretend to be seeds. Have them describe and dramatize their experience as they grow from the soil to being harvested and then finally being made into bread. Allow some children to be the seeds and others to take

the role of elements and demonstrate their role in the seeds' growth. Another group of students can be the bakers.

2. *Puppets:* Using animal puppets, have children present the story, depicting the uncooperative characters. Then, have the students present the story again, but this time substituting cooperative characters.

3. *Cooperation Pantomimes:* Discuss situations in which cooperation is necessary and have cooperative groups pantomime the following:

   - building a sand castle
   - painting a house
   - cleaning an entire house
   - decorating a Christmas tree
   - rescuing a person or animal

4. *Parachute Activity:* Gather children around a parachute and place a ball in the center. The group must work together to keep the ball from bouncing out. The parachute must be raised and lowered at the right time, demonstrating that cooperation is needed to accomplish the task.

5. *Comparison:* Read the supporting story, *La gallinita roja* by Ma. Eulalia Valeri. Discuss similarities and differences with regard to characters, setting and plot. In cooperative groups, have children choose and dramatize one of their favorite story variants while observers guess which one is being presented.

ART AND WRITING

1. *Story Characters:* Have the children, in cooperative groups, create large drawings of the story characters (Gallina Paulina and the other farm animals), cut them out and place them on the farm mural created during the Observation/Experience phase. Have them write letters to the different characters expressing their opinions regarding their uncooperative behavior.

2. *Seed Collage:* Provide dried beans, wheat, rice, other grains, and cardboard. Have students draw a picture or design of their choice on the cardboard and glue the seeds or grains onto the drawing. Have students write a description of their collage.

3. *Excuses, Excuses!:* Allow children to brainstorm excuses for not helping and for being uncooperative. Cluster excuses on the board. Have groups make up humorous excuses to write in a book titled *«Excusas para no trabajar»* ("Excuses for Not Wanting to Work"). Have them create humorous illustrations to accompany their excuses. Have the students share books and display them.

4. *Animal Masks:* Have cooperative groups create Gallina Paulina, the cat, the dog, the goose, the turkey, and two additional farm animals of their choice. Using several large 12 x 18 inch sheets of white construction paper, have them trace an oval as large as a child's face near the top of the 12-inch side. Have the students create the full animal figure around the oval (the oval is for the face). Have them color the animals and cut out the ovals.

   "What Am I?": Have a child from each group hold the face masks up to his/her face without looking at the front of the illustration. That student will ask the other group members, *«¿Qué soy?»* ("What am I?") The group members may give several clues

but must not reveal the name of the animal. The person giving the clue that enables the mask wearer to correctly identify the animal is next to wear the masks. As a variation, have students retell the story to another group while wearing the masks.

Riddles: Have students write a five-line riddle for any one of the animal masks. For example,

> *Trabajo mucho.*
> *Ayudo cuando me necesitan.*
> *Tengo plumas.*
> *Sembré una semilla.*
> *Mi pan era sabroso.*
> *¿Quién soy? (Gallina Paulina)*

> I am a hard worker.
> I help when I'm needed.
> I have feathers.
> I planted a seed.
> My bread was delicious.
> Who am I? (Gallina Paulina)

5. *Animal Sculptures:* Have the students create paper animal sculptures as another cooperative group project. Provide glue along with paper strips and scraps in assorted colors. Allow the students to decide which animals they would like to create and who will perform which tasks. As each group's animals will be unique, have the groups write the step-by-step instructions for making the animals so that other groups may make replicas of them.

6. *Mosaic Mural:* Provide large sheets of white construction paper, construction paper in assorted colors, scissors, and glue. Have cooperative groups draw large pictures (perhaps using ideas from the unit's Literature Input) on the white paper using simple outlines and designs. Have them cut the colored paper into small triangles, rectangles, squares, and circles and then arrange and glue the paper pieces within the shapes on the drawing. The students may use long, thin black paper strips to highlight the drawing so that it will appear as a bold illustration. Have each group write a poem for its mosaic mural.

7. *Three-Dimensional Art:* Provide construction paper in assorted colors, scissors and paste. Allow cooperative groups to cut strips in different lengths and widths; have them curl, pleat, tear, fringe, slit, wad, box, twist, braid, and layer the paper strips. Have them position the strips on a large sheet of black construction paper, weaving them over, under and through while adding paste to hold them in place. Have the cooperative groups explain, in writing, the process used in making their three-dimensional creations.

8. *Continued Story:* Seat cooperative groups in circles. Have one child begin to retell the Gallina Paulina story and stop after a few sentences. The person to the right must continue the story. Each person continues the story, adding to it until everyone has had a turn. For a variation of this activity, have students within the cooperative groups add on sentences about the story in writing. When completed, allow each group to share its story with the other groups.

MATH

1. *Seed Sorting:* Provide a variety of seeds for the students to sort by size, color and other characteristics. They may also create individual graphs or a large class graph with the information they obtained in the seed sorting.

SCIENCE

1. *Seeds:* Talk about the planting of seeds, the growth of seeds, and the making of flour. Present visuals representing these three stages. Engage children in group projects for recording information about the planting and growth of seeds.

2. *Making Bread Together:* Write a bread recipe together using illustrations where possible. Talk about the process of bread becoming a solid from a semi-liquid dough. As the bread is being mixed and baked, allow them to record their observations in their science logs. Read the recipe in unison. Make the bread by following directions.

Cranberry Bread

2 cups sifted flour
1 cup sugar
1 1/2 tsp. baking powder
1 tsp. salt
1/2 tsp. baking soda
1/4 cup butter or margarine
1 egg, beaten
1 tsp. grated orange peel
3/4 cup orange juice
1 1/2 cups light raisins
1 1/2 cups fresh or frozen cranberries, chopped

Sift flour, sugar, baking powder, salt, and baking soda into a large bowl. Cut in butter or margarine until mixture is crumbly. Add egg, orange peel, and orange juice all at once; stir just until mixture is evenly moist. Fold in raisins and cranberries.

Spoon into a greased 9x5x3-inch loaf pan. Bake at 350° for 1 hour and 10 minutes, or until a toothpick inserted into the center comes out clean. Remove from pan; cool on wire rack.

3. *Bread-Tasting Party:* Discuss different kinds of bread eaten by people in other countries. Have children share experiences they have had eating different breads. Have a bread-tasting party that includes as many varieties of bread as possible. To enhance the children's sense of smell and taste, have the students write descriptions of the bread-tasting experience.

4. *Bread Booklet:* Allow children to illustrate the steps needed to make bread from wheat. Have them title a bread recipe booklet «*Desde una semilla hasta el pan*» ("From a Seed to Bread"). Have them illustrate the steps on separate sheets with a descriptive sentence for each page.

SOCIAL STUDIES

1. *Caretakers' Responsibilities:* Have students consider the endless responsibilities that mothers and fathers and other caretakers have. Have them list all the jobs that parents and other caretakers have and the jobs that children might have. Have them determine those things that they could help with if they made an effort to do so. Guide them in a discussion in which they place themselves in their caretakers' shoes.

2. *Classroom Tasks:* Talk about what teachers do to organize a classroom. Have students pretend to be teachers and have them list those tasks where students could provide help.

3. *Thanksgiving:* Talk about how Pilgrims and Native Americans helped each other for the first Thanksgiving. Show pictures, books or a film about the holiday. If possible, have students bring food and prepare a Thanksgiving lunch. In a whole class setting, have students discuss the lunch preparation and compare their cooperative experience to that of the Pilgrims and the Native Americans. Have children think of a special person (family member, friend) who has been helpful to them. Have them write a thank-you note at this time of Thanksgiving.

4. *"How Would I Help?":* Seat several groups in circles and give each group a situation (problem) to brainstorm various ways that they could offer help. Cooperatively, have them write their answers to the problems and share them with the other groups.

POETRY

Solidaridad

Alondra, ¡vamos a cantar!
Cascada, ¡vamos a saltar!
Riachuelo, ¡vamos a correr!
Diamante, ¡vamos a brillar!
Aguila, ¡vamos a volar!
Aurora, ¡vamos a nacer!
   ¡A cantar!
   ¡A saltar!
   ¡A correr!
   ¡A brillar!
   ¡A volar!
   ¡A nacer!

Amado Nervo

La niñita hacendosa

Muy temprano yo me levanté
porque ayudo a mi mamá
me doy un bañito tibio
y me pongo a trabajar.

Pongo la mesa, hiervo la leche
voy corriendo por el pan
mamacita hizo el almuerzo
podemos desayunar.

Rosario Roldán de Alvarado

Vamos a jugar

Ven compañero,
¡vamos a jugar!
Si quieres a las canicas,
las podemos compartir.

O hacer un castillo de arena
sería mucho mejor,
porque los dos juntos
haríamos la labor.

Pero si prefieres
que leamos cuentos,
¿me ayudas a buscarlos?
y así estaremos mas
contentos.

Raquel C. Mireles

El trigo

Buen trigo sembramos en primavera
y lo regamos
con paciencia y alegría.

Difícil fue esperar a que creciera;
pero ahora,
ricas tortillas comemos cada día.

Raquel C. Mireles

MY OWN CREATIVE TEACHING IDEAS FOR UNIT SIX

Books: _____

_____

_____

_____

_____

Ideas: _____

_____

_____

_____

_____

_____

_____

_____

_____

_____

_____

_____

_____

_____

_____

_____

UNIT SEVEN

VOY CAMBIANDO MIENTRAS CREZCO

I AM CHANGING AS I GROW

A child's mind is naturally inquisitive about the world. This natural curiosity allows literature to broaden the child's perspective on the changes occurring in the child and in the world around her/him as both natural and positive. *Un diente se mueve* and other stories from the Literature Input phase present a child's physical growth as a natural part of development.

CONCEPTS AND VALUES

1. We experience change as we grow.
2. We are aware of our growth.
3. Changes sometimes cause anxiety.
4. At times we resist change.
5. Sometimes we are impatient for change.
6. Eventually, we adjust to change.

MAIN SELECTION

Before reading the Main Selection aloud, take your students through the Literature Input and Observation/Experience phases which follow.

Barbot, Daniel.

Un diente se mueve.
Venezuela: Ediciones Ekaré-Banco del Libro, 1981.

When Clarisse loses a tooth, this common experience prompts an imaginative dream about the land of mice where children's teeth are precious jewels.

I.   LITERATURE INPUT: *Un diente se mueve*

Select five or more titles from the following list to read aloud. Read at least one selection per day to the students. Make available and incorporate the suggested titles for voluntary independent reading. Titles marked with * are Spanish translations of the original English story; titles marked with + are recommended for more proficient listeners.

+1. Balzola, Asun. *Los zapatos de Munia.* Spain: Ediciones Destino, S.A., 1983. Munia discovers that her body is growing because her old shoes no longer fit.

*2. Berenstain, Jan and Stan. *El bebé de los osos Berenstain.* New York: Scholastic, 1982. The bear family prepares for the arrival of a new baby. When the baby arrives, big brother bear helps but worries about how the event will change his life.

*3. Bornstein, Ruth. *Gorilita.* New York: Scholastic, 1978. This is a delightful story about a gorilla who is loved as a baby and wonders whether he is going to be loved when he is fully grown.

4. Busquets, Carlos. *El patito feo.* Spain: Editorial Susaeta, 1985. In this classic story, an ugly duckling hatches in the wrong nest and is shunned by all the animals in the pond until he grows and develops into an elegant swan.

5. Claude, Levert, and Carme Solé Vendrell. *Pedro y su roble.* Spain: Editorial Miñón, S.A., 1981. Pedro watches the changes taking place in the oak tree he so dearly loves. As the seasons change, Pedro learns that the changes are a natural part of growth.

6. Cutts, David. *Como son las mariposas.* México: Sistémas Técnicas de Edición, S.A. de C.V., 1988. This attractively illustrated book depicts the life of a butterfly in all its stages.

7. D'Atri, Adriana. *Así es nuestro hermano pequeño.* Spain: Ediciones Altea, 1984. Child development, as told by siblings, is the topic of this nicely illustrated book.

*8. Flores, Rosa. *Caracolitos: El árbol de Rita.* Oklahoma: Economy Company, 1979. Señor García explains to Rita what a tree needs in order to grow from a small seed into a beautiful healthy tree.

*9. Kraus, Robert. *Leo el capullo tardío.* New York: Windmill Books and E. P. Patton, 1977. Leo, a late bloomer, wonders if he will ever mature, but in time he does, to everyone's delight.

*10. Krauss, Ruth. *La semilla de zanahoria*. New York: Scholastic, 1978. A boy plants a carrot seed. He cares for it and is rewarded when he harvests a huge carrot.

*11. Kwitz, Mary Deball. *La historia de la pollita*. New York: Scholastic, 1978. In this short story, a chicken lays five eggs and keeps one that develops into her dear little chick.

12. Moonen, Ries, and Martin Hongeweg. *¿Cómo vive una rana?* Spain: Ediciones Altea, 1980. This book documents the life of a frog in a pond through an entire year's development.

13. Noriega, Luisa de. *Yo soy el durazno*. México: Editorial Trillas, S.A., 1983. In this story, a peach grows from a blossom to a peach tree.

*14. Parramón, J. M. Illustrated by Carme Solé Vendrell. *Los jóvenes*. New York: Barron's, 1987. This is a nicely illustrated book about young people and how they function in daily life.

*15. —. Illustrated by María Rius. *Los niños*. New York: Barron's, 1987. This nicely illustrated book depicts children and how they function in daily life.

*16. de Podendorf, Illa. *La vida*. Illinois: National Textbook Company, 1979. This book provides a comprehensive account of the growth and changes in humans and other species.

*17. Selsam, Millicent E. *Teresita y las orugas*. New York: Harper & Row, 1969. In this interesting and true-to-life story, Teresa gives loving care to her silkworms as they go through the stages of metamorphosis.

18. Shapiro, Larry. *Animales pequeños*. Spain: Editorial Montena, 1983. A caterpillar is transformed into a butterfly, a tadpole into a frog, and a chick into a hen with the pull of a ribbon.

19. —. *Familias de animales*. Spain: Editorial Montena, 1983. Animals and their mothers are followed through a year of growth.

20. Soutter-Perrot, Andrienne. *El mosquito: El primer libro de la naturaleza*. Venezuela: Ediciones Maria D. Mase, 1985. In this beautifully illustrated book, the life of a mosquito is described.

21. —. *El sapo: El primer libro de la naturaleza*. Venezuela: Ediciones Maria D. Mase, 1985. This beautifully illustrated book describes the life of a frog.

22. Torres, Daniel C., and Angelina R. de Torres. *La papita*. California: Global Publications, 1986. This poem in book form describes the origins of the potato and its importance to us.

23. Vásquez, Zoraida, and Julieta Montelongo. *El naranjo que no daba naranjas*. México: Editorial Trillas, S.A., 1980. A boy wonders why his orange tree does not bear fruit and discovers that in order to grow, it needs water.

+24. Williams, Leslie. *El oso nuboso*. Spain: Ediciones Hymsa, 1979. A boy has an adventure with a cloud that changes shape and speaks in words that rhyme.

RELATED TITLES IN ENGLISH FOR SECOND LANGUAGE ACQUISITION

Bates, Lucy. *Little Rabbit's Loose Tooth*. New York: Crown Publishers, 1975.

Braithwaite, Althea. *Butterflies*. England: Longman House, 1984.

—. *Frogs*. England: Longman House, 1984.

Carle, Eric. *The Very Hungry Caterpillar*. New York: Philomel Books, 1970.

De Groat, Diane. *Alligator's Toothache*. New York: Crown Publishers, 1977.

Heller, Ruth. *The Reason for a Flower*. New York: Grosset E. Dunlap, 1983.

Kellogg, Steven. *Much Bigger Than Martin*. New York: The Dial Press, 1976.

II. OBSERVATION/EXPERIENCE: *Un diente se mueve*
(Class Session One)

Guide students in the following observation/experience sequence to set the stage for reading the Main Selection.

Focus: Children experience natural changes and become aware of themselves.

1. Have children bring in photos of themselves at different ages. Discuss physical changes that they have gone through including physical changes in stature, weight, hair, teeth, and abilities such as crawling, walking, running, grabbing, and holding. Have them describe the changes and compare their abilities with those of babies.

2. Tell students that in the story titled **Un diente se mueve,** a girl named Clarisse will go through a change that we are all familiar with.

3. Have children predict what that change will be. Following the story, have children discuss whether their predictions were correct.

III. READ AND DISCUSS THE MAIN SELECTION: *Un diente se mueve*
(Class Session One)

Read the Main Selection from page 94 to the students. Highlight the unit's theme by relating this story to other selections from the Literature Input list on pages 94 - 96. Then, guide students in discussing some of the following questions.

1. *¿A cuántos de ustedes se les ha caído un diente? ¿Cómo se sintieron? O si no se les han caído, ¿cómo se sentirían? Explíquennos.* (How many of you have lost a tooth? How did you feel? Or if you have not lost any, how would you feel? Explain.)

2. *¿Cómo se les cayó su primer diente? ¿Cuál podría ser la razón por haber perdido el primer diente?* (How did your first tooth fall out? What could be the reason for losing your first tooth?)

3. *Si pusieron su diente debajo de la almohada, ¿qué pasó la mañana siguiente? ¿Por qué creen que pasó o pasaría eso?* (If you put your tooth under your pillow, what happened the next morning? Why do you suppose that happened or would happen?)

4. *Clarisse soñó que a su diente se lo llevó el ratón. ¿Qué creen ustedes que pasó con sus dientes?* (Clarisse dreamed that her tooth had been taken by the mouse. What do you think happened to your teeth?)

5. *¿Qué otros cambios pueden suceder mientras Clarisse crece? ¿Qué cambios tendrán ustedes?* (What other changes may take place as Clarisse grows? What changes will you experience?)

IV. "WHAT IF" STORY STRETCHER: *Un diente se mueve*
(Class Session Two)

Next, re-read the Main Selection and choose one or more of the following questions to develop students' critical thinking skills. Story stretchers may also prompt discussion, drama or writing activities.

1. *Si la mamá de Clarisse no le hubiera sacado el diente, ¿cómo se le habría caído?* (If Clarisse's mother had not pulled the tooth, how would it have fallen out?)

2. *Si los gatos se hubieran comido a todos los ratones, ¿cómo habría cambiado el cuento?* (If the cats had eaten all the mice, how would the story have been different?)

3. *Si nadie hubiera venido por el diente, ¿por qué podría haber pasado eso?* (If no one had come for the tooth, why might that have happened?)

4. *Si Clarisse hubiera soñado con el mundo de las hadas, ¿cómo habría cambiado su aventura?* (If Clarisse had dreamed of the land of fairies, how would her adventure have been different?)

5. *Si ustedes pudieran crecer y cambiar ahora mismo, ¿cómo serían y que harían?* (If you could grow and change right now, how would you look and what you would do?)

V. INTEGRATING OTHER DISCIPLINES: *Un diente se mueve*
(Class Session Three and Ongoing)

The following activities are designed to enhance children's response to literature and expand *beyond* the story and its theme. The variety of activities gives teachers and students an opportunity to choose those most appropriate.

CREATIVE DRAMATICS

1. *Stages of Growth:* Provide a box with different objects and pictures of people at different ages. Have children pantomime a growth period using the object and matching the object to the picture as the class observes. The box may include rattles, a baby bottle, baby food, blocks, a tennis ball, a football, a baseball, car keys, books for different ages, and shoes of different sizes.

2. *Dramatize a Story:* In small groups, have the children dramatize one of the stories from the Literature Input. Later, encourage the audience to discuss and list the changes that the characters experienced.

3. *World of Fairies:* Have children dramatize fairies gathering children's teeth. Have small groups prepare questions to ask the fairies about their world, their duties, the purpose and dangers of tooth gathering, etc. For fun, have other groups respond as the imaginary fairies.

ART AND WRITING

1. *Why I Need Teeth:* Discuss teeth and their importance. Include the following points: Teeth are bones covered with enamel. The enamel makes them hard enough to chew our food. Our stomachs would not be able to digest big chunks of unchewed food. Teeth also make beautiful smiles when they are well cared for. Invite children to write about and/or illustrate themselves in a booklet titled *«Por que necesito mis dientes»* ("Why I Need My Teeth").

2. *Tooth Chart:* Keep a large tooth made of construction paper for every month, and use it on a chart titled *«Se me cayó un diente»* ("I Lost a Tooth"). Also, keep a large smiling mouth with teeth on which to place photographs of children who have not yet lost teeth. Allow children to dictate or write about what they believe happened to their lost teeth. Collect compositions to place in a tooth-shaped book.

3. *Tooth Collage:* Allow children, in groups, to construct "tooth" collages by cutting pictures from magazines. Collages may be titled with creative names chosen by children; e.g., *«Una sonrisa de perlas»* ("A Smile Full of Pearls"). Collages may also be used as interesting book covers for writing activities that follow.

4. *Do's and Don't's:* Have children write the "do's and don't's" of tooth care. Compile and make group books.

5. *Tooth Book:* Using construction paper, have students cut out two large teeth and use one as a healthy tooth and the other as an unhealthy tooth. Have the students cut a variety of food pictures from magazines, sort the pictures into healthy or unhealthy foods, and paste them on the appropriate tooth. On a separate lined tooth, have the children write about the consequences of eating either group of foods. Put the pages together to make a tooth book.

6. *Tooth Jewelry:* Children can use macaroni or popcorn to pretend that they are mice making jewelry out of a string of teeth. Have the students tell, in writing, where they got all the teeth to make the jewelry.

7. *Body Scroll:* Have children use three photocopies each of photographs of their faces and draw their bodies at three different stages in their lives. Have them place the bodies under the three faces. They may make booklets or scrolls. Have them dictate or write their own descriptions for each picture.

8. *Food on Me:* Have children provide samples of healthy snacks to share with the class and unhealthy snacks to show. Have children trace their bodies on butcher paper and cut out. Have them draw healthy foods on one side and unhealthy foods on the other side. Discuss the difference. Let them write on both halves of the tracings, on one half describing what their bodies need, and on the other half describing what they do not need.

9. *A New Me:* Have students draw pictures as they are now, and others showing any changes they will experience as they grow older. Let them describe, in writing, the changes that they will see in themselves; e.g., *«Cuando crezco ....»* ("When I grow ....") Have them tell, in writing, if they would like to stay the same forever. Why or why not?

10. *Growth Chart:* Using objects or animals, have children measure themselves and describe their height; e.g., "I am 20 caterpillars high." Height may be taken at the beginning and the end of the school year. Students may write in their personal journals why they want to grow up.

11. *Big Book:* Assign cooperative groups to use any of the stories from the Literature Input to illustrate the concepts of change and growth. Have them write descriptive captions for each illustration and then share books and place them in a library corner.

SCIENCE AND HEALTH

1. *Dental Casts and X-rays:* Ask your dentist for old dental casts (made from cement impressions of different patients' mouths) or old tooth x-rays. Have the students compare dental casts or, using a mirror, have students compare their own teeth. Hold up x-rays to the window and ask if children can find teeth of different shapes. Discuss their different functions—biting, chewing, and grinding. Have children take the role of different kinds of teeth and present information about themselves. Allow them to ask questions and record the information in their science logs.

2. *Talking Teeth:* With older children, discuss names and functions—incisors for biting, cuspids for tearing, molars for grinding. Children may write as talking teeth, expressing the importance of their functions; e.g., *«Soy importante porque ....»* ("I am important because ....")

3. *Brushing Contract:* Invite the school nurse to show children the proper way to brush and floss teeth. Using Figure G (page 101), have children get into the habit of daily brushing by using the weekly contract. Children will shade in a bristle every time they brush. The contract is to be signed by the child and the parent. Reward brushers with sugarless gum.

4. *Growing Our Own:* The following activities demonstrate growth and are easily managed in the classroom: (a) Silkworms are available through science catalogues and may be easily cared for by children. The complete metamorphosis takes place in a few weeks. (b) A sweet potato placed in a glass of water quickly sprouts roots and leaves. (c) Lima beans, corn, kidney beans, sweet peas, or radish seeds may be soaked in water for a few hours. Place a sponge inside a glass with a half-inch of water and six seeds placed between the sponge and the side of the glass. Place seeds two inches apart. Growth is rapidly evident. Allow the children to illustrate and record their observations.

Tres veces al día

Mis dientes los lavo
tres veces al día:
tenerlos muy sanos
me causa alegría.

No quiero que nunca
me vaya a pasar,
que algún dientecito
me llegue a faltar.

Anónimo

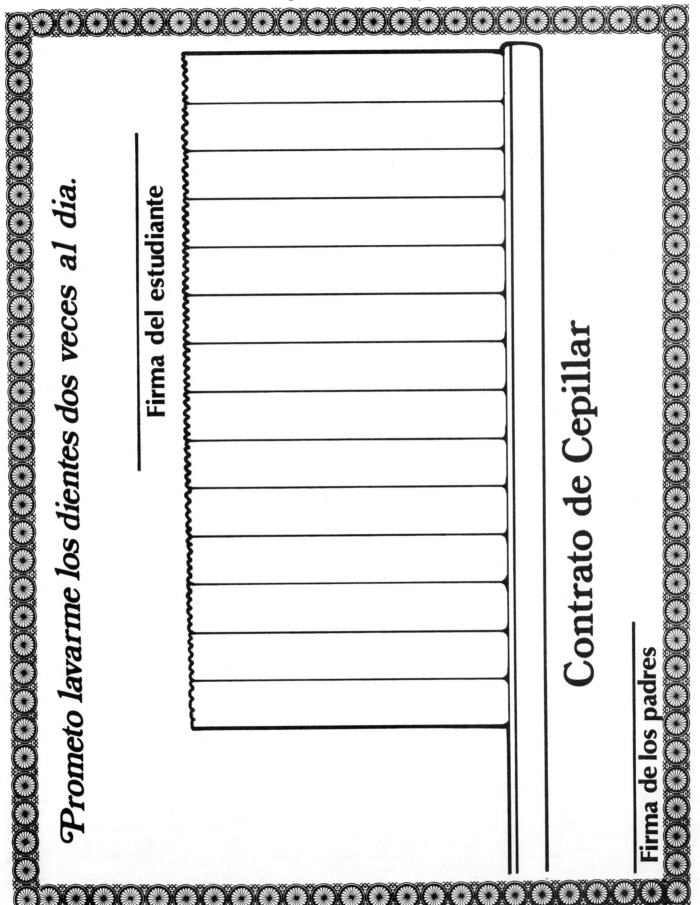

Prometo lavarme los dientes dos veces al día.

Firma del estudiante

Contrato de Cepillar

Firma de los padres

MY OWN CREATIVE TEACHING IDEAS FOR UNIT SEVEN

Books: _____

_____

_____

_____

_____

_____

Ideas: _____

_____

_____

_____

_____

_____

_____

_____

_____

_____

_____

_____

_____

_____

_____

_____

_____

UNIT EIGHT

VAMOS A EXPLORAR

LET'S EXPLORE

Being able to hear and see the adventures of others, whether real or imaginary, will allow a child's world to open up a little wider. Stories that allow children to explore new and unusual experiences encourage them to use their creativity and imagination to deal with adversity and challenges. Through the reading of **El lago de la luna** and other adventure stories, it is hoped that children will be encouraged to try the new and the unusual.

CONCEPTS AND VALUES

1. We learn about our world when we experience new places.
2. There are many ways to see and enjoy our world.
3. Our imagination can take us to new and unusual experiences.
4. We need not fear the new or unusual; they may be positive experiences in disguise.
5. We need to take "risks" in order to explore all possible opportunities.

MAIN SELECTION

Before reading the Main Selection aloud, take your students through the Literature Input and Observation/Experience phases which follow.

Gantschev, Ivan.

El lago de la luna.
México: Editorial Trillas, S.A., 1985.

In this beautifully told adventure, a boy named Pedro, while searching for a lost sheep, finds Moon Lake and precious jewels. A fox warns him that he must leave before sunrise. He obeys, but Moon Lake proves to be very dangerous for other greedy souls.

I. LITERATURE INPUT: *El lago de la luna*

Select five or more titles from the following list to read aloud. Read at least one selection per day to the students. Make available and incorporate the suggested titles for voluntary independent reading. Titles marked with * are Spanish translations of the original English story; titles marked with + are recommended for more proficient listeners.

+1. Alonso, Fernando. *El hombrecillo de papel.* Spain: Editorial Miñón, S.A., 1984. A little girl cuts a paper doll out of newspaper and it comes to life in this imaginative tale.

2. Altamirano, Francisca. *El viaje de Isaac.* México: Editorial Trillas, S.A., 1986. Isaac finds a beautiful, peaceful island where he discovers how enriching one's experience with nature can be.

+3. Baumann, Kurtz. *El tesoro de la isla.* Spain: Ediciones S.M., 1986. A brother and sister have an adventure looking for treasure and find an old tree that is more valuable than gold.

+4. Bolliger, Max. *La montaña de los osos.* Spain: Ediciones S.M., 1983. In this adventure, two bears overcome a wolf and a third bear runs away. The two brave bears find him and he too learns to overcome his fear.

*5. Burningham, John. *Trubloff.* Spain: Editorial Miñón, S.A., 1975. Trubloff, the Russian, has a yearning to play the *balalaica* (an instrument similar to a guitar). He eventually succeeds and is able to benefit his loved ones.

6. Capdevila, Juan. *Colección: Teo descubre el mundo.* Spain: Editorial Timún Más, S.A., 1983. This collection of books describing Teo's experiences includes: *Teo se disfraza, Teo en barco, Teo en tren, Teo en avión, Teo va de camping, Teo en la nieve, Teo en la feria,* and *Teo va de vacaciones.*

7. Cos, Rosa M. *Colección: Historias fantásticas de Ivo y Tina.* Spain: Editorial Timún Más, S.A., 1981. This collection is about the strange adventures of Ivo and Tina:
El bosque encantado. Ivo and Tina have an adventure in an enchanted forest.
El rey sol. While visiting an astronomer, Ivo and Tina dream they go through the universe with the sun as their guide.
La isla feliz. Ivo and Tina are shipwrecked on an imaginary island that looks more like another planet.
El país de la música. While listening to a concert, Ivo and Tina are transported magically to a world of music.

8. Delgado, Eduard. *Colección: Los Mecs*. Spain: Editorial Timún Más, S.A., 1982. *Los Mecs juegan en la playa*. The Mecs and their grandfather discover the animals that live in the ocean as they enjoy a wonderful day near the sea.
Los Mecs van en bicicleta. After watching a bicycle race, the Mecs are inspired to be cyclists. They learn to build and ride bicycles.

9. Delgado, Eduard, and Francesc Rovira. *Mientras Tim juega en el puerto*. Spain: Editorial Ariel, S.A., 1984. In this beautifully illustrated adventure, Tim and his friends bravely save zoo animals from a sinking ship.

+10. Denou, Violeta. *Los tres y Tío Pek*. Spain: Ediciones Hymsa, 1980. Tío Pek gives Tino, Cleta and Nicolas a ride in his hot air balloon as they explore different cities and towns.

11. Fuchshuber, Annegert. *Toribio y el sombrero mágico*. Spain: Editorial Juventud, 1978. A man named Toribio has hilarious adventures after he finds a magic hat.

12. Fujikawa, Gyo. *Lanudo y su sueño*. Argentina: Editorial Atlántida, 1981. Samuel's dog, Lanudo, dreams he is a tiny dog. The world is suddenly a very large and dangerous place. He learns to have compassion for smaller creatures.

13. Hernández Jiménez, Miguel. *Colección: Max quiere un mundo mejor*. Spain: Editorial Ponaire, S.A., 1980. Max has four wonderful adventures while trying to make the world a better place: *Max en la ciudad triste, Una escuela para Max, Max y los dragones,* and *Max en el planeta feliz.*

14. Heuer, Margarita. *X - cua - cua*. México: Editorial Trillas, S.A., 1984. Martín is a curious boy who meets an extraterrestrial friend and flies with him on a most unusual adventure.

*15. Loof, Jan. *Historia de una manzana roja*. Spain: Ediciones S.M., 1984. This is an interesting story of an apple that the reader follows through various adventures in the city.

16. Ortells, Estela. *Simón en el aire*. Spain: Editorial Alfredo Ortells, 1985. Simón joins Tadeo, the duck, on several adventures in a hot air balloon.

*17. Rey, H. A. *Jorge el curioso*. Boston: Houghton Mifflin, 1967. Jorge, a curious monkey brought from Africa, has many adventures.

18. Robles Boza, Eduardo (Tío Patota). *¿A dónde vas, Tomás?* México: Editorial Trillas, S.A., 1986. Tomás decides to create his own car and allows nature to help him.

19. —. *Cuatro letras se escaparon*. México: Editorial Trillas, S.A., 1986. Four letters escape from a book and have perilous adventures that end in the formation of the word *proeza,* which means *bravery.*

20. Sacre, María-José, and Guy Counhaye. *Victor, el hipopótamo volador*. Spain: Editorial Everest, S.A., 1982. We are taken along on the fantastic adventures of a hippo with wings.

*21. Stevenson, James. *No nos podemos dormir*. Spain: Ediciones Generales Anaya, 1983. Luisito and Ana María fall asleep after listening to the adventures of their grandfather.

+22. Zatón, Jesús. *Los sueños de Ana.* Spain: Ediciones Jucar, 1985. Ana has an adventure while trying to put color back into her dreams.

23. Zimnik, Reiner. *El viaje en globo de Guillermo.* Spain: Editorial Miñón, S.A., 1981. Guillermo has an adventurous flight while holding on to a bunch of balloons.

RELATED TITLES IN ENGLISH FOR SECOND LANGUAGE ACQUISITION

Charlip, Remy. *Fortunately.* New York: Parents Magazine Press, 1964.

Gackenback, Dick. *Little Bug.* New York: H. M. Clarion Books, 1981.

Keats, Ezra J. *Over in the Meadow.* New York: Four Winds Press, 1971.

Rey, H. A. *Curious George.* Boston: Houghton Mifflin, 1941.

—. *Curious George Flies a Kite.* Boston: Houghton Mifflin, 1941.

—. *Curious George Gets a Medal.* Boston: Houghton Mifflin, 1941.

Sawyer, Ruth. *Journey Cake, Ho!* New York: Viking Press, 1953.

II. OBSERVATION/EXPERIENCE: *El lago de la luna*
(Class Session One)

Guide students in the following observation/experience sequence to set the stage for reading the Main Selection.

Focus: Life may present a variety of unexpected surprises.

1. Have children observe you (the teacher) looking for something in the classroom. Unexpectedly find an object and show great pleasure in finding it. Provide a box filled with shredded paper or styrofoam peanuts and several small objects. Allow several children to dip their hands into the box looking for a surprise.

2. Lead the children in a discussion about whether they have ever tried looking for something but instead found something else unexpectedly.

3. Explain that many great things can come about accidently or unexpectedly because life can offer many wonderful surprises.

4. Tell students that in the story *El lago de la luna,* they will meet a boy named Pedro who will have an unexpected experience while looking for his lost sheep. Have them predict what Pedro will unexpectedly find. Following the story, have the children discuss whether their predictions were correct.

III. READ AND DISCUSS THE MAIN SELECTION: *El lago de la luna*
(Class Session One)

Read the Main Selection from page 104 to the students. Highlight the unit's theme by relating this story to other selections from the Literature Input list on pages 104 - 106. Then, guide students in discussing some of the following questions.

1. *¿Qué secreto murió con el viejecito?* (What secret died with the old man?)

2. *Si ustedes visitaran a Pedro, ¿qué cosas verían o harían?* (If you visited Pedro, what things would you see or do?)

3. *Pedro pensó en todas las cosas que podría comprar con las piedras preciosas. ¿Qué harían ustedes si encontraran piedras preciosas?* (Pedro thought of all the wonderful things he could buy with the precious stones. What would you do if you found valuable stones?)

4. *¿Qué clase de persona era Pedro? ¿Cómo lo saben?* (What kind of person was Pedro? How do you know?)

5. *Describan el jefe de policía. ¿Que piensan acerca de lo que le pasó?* (Describe the chief of police. What do you think about what happened to him?)

IV. "WHAT IF" STORY STRETCHER: *El lago de la luna*
(Class Session Two)

Next, re-read the Main Selection and choose one or more of the following questions to develop students' critical thinking skills. Story stretchers may also prompt discussion, drama or writing activities.

1. *Si Pedro no hubiera perdido a su oveja, ¿cómo podría haber encontrado al lago?* (If Pedro had not lost his sheep, how might he have found Moon Lake?)

2. *Si Pedro no hubiera escuchado a la zorra, ¿cómo habría salido la aventura?* (If Pedro had not listened to the fox, how would the adventure have turned out?)

3. *Si pudieran visitar al lago, ¿qué verían allí? ¿Qué harían allí?* (If you could visit Moon Lake, what would you see? What would you do there?)

4. *Si pudieran tener una aventura en cualquier sitio en el mundo, ¿a dónde irían y que harían?* (If you could go on an adventure anywhere in the world, where would you go and what would you do?)

5. *Si pudieran inventar sus propias aventuras imaginarias, ¿qué serían?* (If you could create your own imaginary adventures, what would they be?)

V. INTEGRATING OTHER DISCIPLINES: *El lago de la luna*
(Class Session Three and Ongoing)

The following activities are designed to enhance children's response to literature and expand *beyond* the story and its theme. The variety of activities gives teachers and students an opportunity to choose those most appropriate.

CREATIVE DRAMATICS

1. *Alien Creature:* Have the children imagine being from another planet and discovering our world for the first time. Have them dramatize the aliens' actions.

2. *Changing Creature:* Have the children dramatize being tiny creatures showing how enormous the world would be. Then have them become giants and show how tiny the world would be.

3. *Different Environments:* Circulate pictures representing different environments among small groups. Allow the children to describe the pictures, and then have the groups dramatize being in different environments for the first time; e.g., they are in a jungle trying to find their way out, at the North Pole, in the desert, on a tropical island. Using imagery, guide them in seeing, touching, hearing and smelling a given environment.

4. *Space Pantomime:* Have children imagine that they are astronauts on the moon. Let them move effortlessly in the weightlessness of space—gliding, jumping, floating. How would they eat, walk and run in space? Have them pantomime these activities.

5. *Imaginary Experiences:* On cards, write experiences that the children are familiar with but have probably not experienced—being in an airplane, being a passenger on a train or boat, being a firefighter or a police officer, playing in the snow, or seeing a play. You may also include imaginary experiences such as being an ant or a fish, visiting the moon, and so on. Have a group of children pick cards and pantomime the actions while observers guess what each child is doing. Then, guide the children in a discussion of the experience.

ART AND WRITING

1. *Precious Stones:* Provide pictures or books showing real precious stones to expand children's meaning. Then, have the children create precious stones, using crumpled paper dipped in glue and rolled in glitter, or using clay and glitter. Have children write stories about what they would do if they found precious stones while on a great adventure.

2. *Moon Lake:* Have the children illustrate Moon Lake as they believe it looked. Pedro accidently found the lake; allow cooperative groups to write about how they might discover Moon Lake. Have them share their stories.

3. *Cotton Sheep:* Have children illustrate Pedro and his sheep. The children may fill the illustrations of the sheep in with cotton to create the appearance of wool. Have small groups prepare questions to ask the lost sheep. Have children exchange questions and answer as sheep would.

4. *Adventure Walk:* Have children set up an adventure trail with props such as boxes, hoops, cones, blocks and stuffed animals to form an imaginary jungle, river, mountain forest, island or other exciting terrain. Have them imagine that the sheep go on the adventure walk. Allow them to write about their feelings if they accompanied the sheep.

5. *What If:* Have the children use their imaginations to think of incredible adventures they would like to experience if they could be anyone, do anything, or go anywhere. Allow them to illustrate their ideas and write about their incredible adventures.

6. *List of Supplies:* Have the children pretend that they will be traveling with a friend to Moon Lake. Have them make a list of supplies needed to make the long trip.

7. *Pop-Up Picture:* Have students create a pop-up Moon Lake picture. Have them fold a card stock sheet in half, color the bottom blue, and place cellophane on it. Then have them shape the mountains and moon, cut them out, and glue them on to the top half by attaching small accordion-folded papers to give the three-dimensional appearance.

Allow students to draw the characters to place within the pop-up picture. In their literature logs, have them complete the following writing starter:

«Si pudiera ir al lago de la luna, yo haría . . . .» ("If I could go to Moon Lake, I would . . . .")

8. *Reflections:* Discuss what a reflection is and any experiences children might have had with reflections. Mention stories that make reference to reflections. Have students pretend to look at the moon's reflection in the lake and relate what surprising things begin to happen; e.g., the moon falls into the lake, it shrinks and disappears, talks to the child, or grows enormously. Have students create a mural depicting their images of Moon Lake. Allow them to write an imaginary story about the moon's reflection.

9. *Rod Puppets:* Using Figures H1 and H2 (pages 111 - 112), have children make tagboard rod puppets of the lost lamb, the fox, Pedro, and his grandfather. Have them decorate figures using paint, material, yarn, construction paper, cotton, buttons, or any other scraps. Have them secure the shapes to sticks on rod handles. Allow children to use the characters to retell the story.

10. *Adventure Story:* Have the students select stories from the Literature Input and invite themselves into the stories to have an adventure with the main characters. Allow them to write descriptions of the adventures in their literature logs.

11. *I Want To:* Have children illustrate themselves doing some activity they would like to try, but have never experienced; e.g., playing a musical instrument, dancing, swimming, mountain climbing, skiing, canoeing, camping. Allow them to share their illustrations with the class. Have them write descriptions of what they imagine the experience would be like.

SOCIAL STUDIES

1. *Places of Interest:* The story's mountain and lake settings were interesting places to explore. With the children, brainstorm places they would like to explore—mountains, an island, a cave. Brainstorm and write a list of things they know about these places and those things that they would like to know.

2. *Explore New Places:* Have students explore new places through books, brochures, people that have been there, artifacts or souvenirs. Children may create postcards to send as if they were visiting the designated place.

3. *New Experiences:* Embarking on a new experience such as a trip to a new place, going to school for the first time, moving to a new home, trying swimming or horseback riding for the first time, can make us feel apprehensive; but taking a risk to try new experiences can prove to be worthwhile. Have children write in their personal journals about new experiences they have had or experiences they would like to try.

Nuestras aventuras

A todos los niños del mundo
nos gustan las aventuras,
explorar lugares nuevos
y hacer algunas travezuras.

Ya sea en un barco de velas,
en una nave espacial,
o en un ligero caballo,
cualquier cosa sería genial

Buzear debajo del mar,
o volar en las alturas;
explorar una densa selva
¡qué fantásticas aventuras!

Raquel C. Mireles

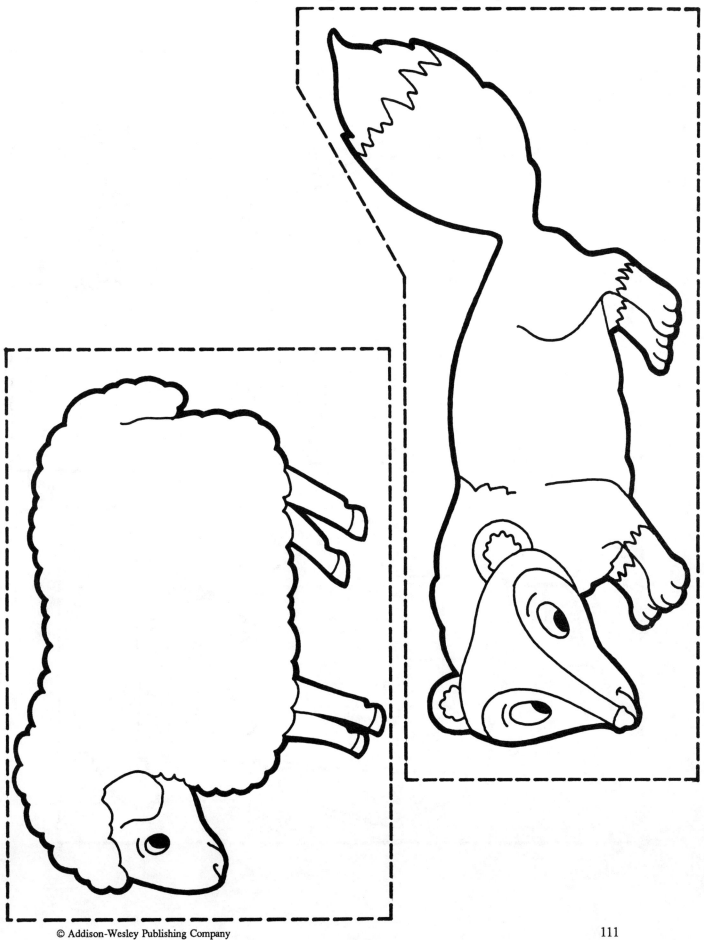

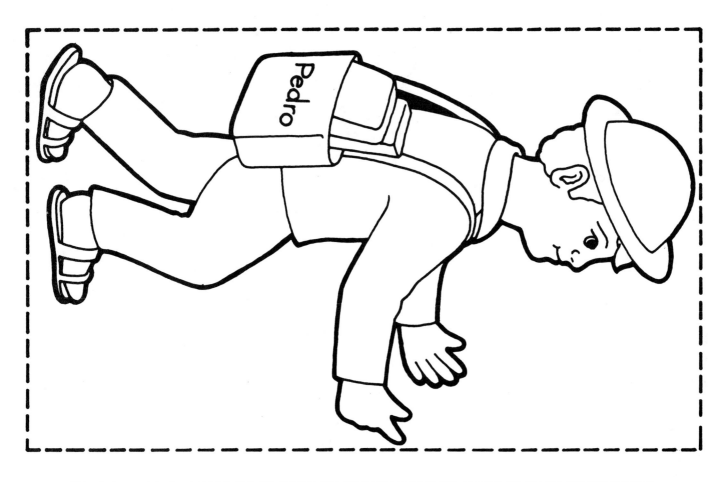

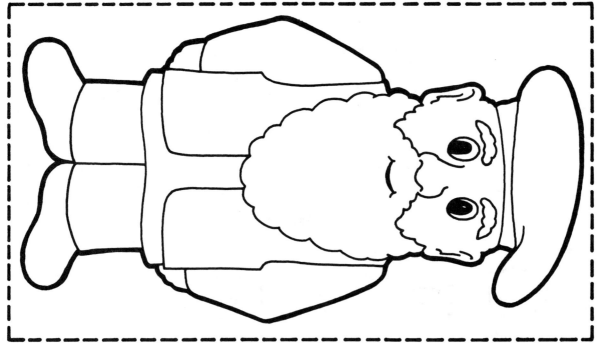

MY OWN CREATIVE TEACHING IDEAS FOR UNIT EIGHT

Books: _____

_____

_____

_____

_____

_____

Ideas: _____

_____

_____

_____

_____

_____

_____

_____

_____

_____

_____

_____

_____

_____

_____

_____

UNIT NINE

APRENDO POR MIS EXPERIENCIAS

I LEARN THROUGH MY EXPERIENCES

Children grow and change as they experience their world. Although their common experiences may cause negative feelings, they often serve as positive, valuable life-long lessons. Children may receive comfort in knowing that most of their everyday fears are shared by others at one time or another. Literature, through stories such as *El primer día de clase* and *Pedrín, el conejo travieso,* presents common childhood experiences through colorful, likeable characters. It is hoped that children will grow and learn from the mistakes made by endearing characters much like themselves.

CONCEPTS AND VALUES

1. Being afraid of a new experience is normal.
2. Many children have similar experiences.
3. There are many positive aspects of change.
4. We need time to adjust to new experiences.
5. We can learn from both negative and positive experiences.

CHOOSE THE MAIN SELECTION

Before reading the Main Selection aloud, take your students through the Literature Input and Observation/Experience phases which follow.

Carruth, Jane.	Potter, Beatrix.
El primer día de clase. Argentina: Editorial Sigmar, 1978.	*Pedrín, el conejo travieso.* London: Frederick Warne and Company,1985.
Nico is afraid to go to school because it is a new experience. He learns that new experiences can be wonderful and positive if given a chance.	This is the classic story of Peter Rabbit.
If you choose *El primer día de clase* as your selection, turn to page 119 to begin the Observation/Experience phase.	If you choose *Pedrín, el conejo travieso* as your selection, turn to page 122 to begin the Observation/Experience phase.

I. LITERATURE INPUT: *Both Selections*

Select five or more titles from the following list to read aloud. Read at least one selection per day to the students. Make available and incorporate the suggested titles for voluntary independent reading. Titles marked with * are Spanish translations of the original English story; titles marked with + are recommended for more proficient listeners.

*1. Ada, Alma Flor. *Ricitos de Oro y los tres osos*. Reading, MA: Addison-Wesley, 1989. This is a beautifully illustrated big book adaptation of the classic tale of Goldilocks and the Three Bears.

2. Armijo, Consuelo. *Moné*. Spain: Editorial Miñón, S.A., 1982. This is the story of a little girl and her love for Moné, her teddy bear. Together they have many interesting experiences.

3. Barbot, Daniel. *Un diente se mueve*. Venezuela: Ediciones Ekaré-Banco del Libro, 1981. When Clarisse loses a tooth, this common experience prompts an imaginative dream about the land of mice where children's teeth are precious jewels.

4. Blanco, Cruz, and Lolo Rico. *Colección Kalamito*. Spain: Ediciones Altea, 1983. This collection of books imaginatively depicts childhood experiences as a natural part of life: *Kalamito quiere otra familia, Kalamito se aburre, Kalamito se equivoca, Kalamito tiene miedo, Kalamito tiene una hermanita, Kalamito va a la escuela, Kalamito y sus dos amigos,* and *Kalamito y sus fantasías.*

*5. Blyton; Enid. *La niña que encontró una moneda*. Spain: Plaza & Janes, S.A. Editores, 1983. Jeanie learns a lesson about greed when the money she "finds" brings her nothing but misfortune.

*6. Carruth, Jane. *Colección Chiquilines*. Argentina: Editorial Sigmar, 1982. *Los anteojos de la suerte*. Tobi must wear glasses but he refuses to. When he goes to the fair with his friend, he discovers that there is a whole world he would miss if he did not wear his glasses.

El diente molesto. Nucho learns how important it is to brush his teeth and visit the dentist regularly.

Una nueva casa. Upi, very unhappy about having to move to a new home, tries to avoid the move. She finds her new home to be a wonderful place with new friends.

La nueva maestra. Porquispinita is afraid she will not like her new teacher and is reluctant to cooperate. She soon learns her new teacher is just as wonderful as her first.

La ola gigante. Carla visits her uncle who lives by the sea. Her first experience with a large wave frightens her, but she later learns that the ocean has much to offer.

*7. —. *Caperucita Roja.* London: Victoria House Publishing, 1982. This is the classic tale of Little Red Riding Hood.

*8. —. *Los tres osos.* London: Victoria House Publishing, 1982. This is the classic tale of the Three Bears.

*9. Chlad, Dorothy. *Los desconocidos.* Chicago: Children's Press, 1984. Excellent illustrations and information teach caution around strangers.

*10. —. *Cuando cruzo la calle.* Chicago: Children's Press, 1986. Safety in street crossing is presented in a manner that is easy to understand.

*11. —. *Es divertido andar en bicicleta.* Chicago: Children's Press, 1986. Rules for safe cycling are discussed in easy-to-understand language.

*12. —. *Los venenos te hacen daño.* Chicago: Children's Press, 1986. Poison safety is presented in language that is very easy to understand.

*13. Flores, Rosa. *Caracolitos: Para nuestra seguridad.* Oklahoma: Economy Company, 1979. This book cautions children to be aware of dangers and reminds them that careful behavior can prevent accidents.

14. Fujikawa, Gyo. *El cumpleaños de la osita.* Argentina: Editorial Atlántida, 1977. Osita is happy because it is her birthday, but she is saddened when none of her friends appears to remember. In the end, she finds that they did remember her after all.

15. Gerson, Sara. *El escondite.* México: Editorial Trillas, S.A., 1986. Grandmother plays hide and seek with her grandchildren and finds little Ana inside an old treasure chest.

16. Goldman, Judith. *Pepe, Sandra y la barda.* México: Editorial Trillas, S.A., 1987. Sandra and Pepe mischievously paint a fence with many colors. In the process, they accidently paint the barnyard animals the colors of the rainbow.

17. Gómez, Ermilio A. *Doña Estrella y sus luceros.* México: CIDCLI, 1987. This is a delightful, colorfully illustrated story about being disobedient and having mother as a firm disciplinary model.

18. López Remolina, María Teresa. *Un ciempiés descalzo.* México: Editorial Trillas, S.A., 1986. Mother caterpillar knits sixteen rainbow shoes for her son. Insistent upon wearing hard-soled shoes, he learns a valuable lesson about true gratitude.

19. Martínez, María I. Vendrell. *Colección: Hablamos de uno más.* Spain: Ediciones Destino S.A., 1986. This series explores such natural childhood fears as visiting the hospital, leaving home, darkness, and having a new baby in the family. Children will easily relate to these situations and the characters in *Como duele, Hola y adiós, La noche, Uno más,* and *Reir y llorar.*

*20. Mayer, Mercer. *Una pesadilla en mi armario*. Spain: Editorial Altea, 1982. The imaginary monster in the closet is really afraid of the boy holding the cork gun and ends up needing his care and comfort.

*21. Oxenbury, Helen. *Con el médico*. Spain: Editorial Juventud, S.A., 1983. This book may help to alleviate fear of hospitals and doctors.

*22. —. *En el auto*. Spain: Editorial Juventud, S.A., 1983. We can all relate to the experience of trying to maintain our sanity and arrive at our destination safely while in the car with the whole family.

*23. —. *En el restaurante*. Spain: Editorial Juventud, S.A., 1983. It is easy to relate to the incidents that occur as the family decides to go out for dinner.

*24. —. *El primer día de clase*. Spain: Editorial Juventud, S.A., 1983. This book describes the typical experiences of the first day of school.

25. Palombini, Ugo. *Voy al colegio*. Spain: Editorial Everest, S.A., 1980. This book presents experiences that commonly take place at school.

26. Puncel, María. *El premio*. Spain: Editorial Altea., 1980. Fernando enters an art contest and wins first place. His prize is twenty tickets to go to the zoo with all his friends.

*27. Scarry, Richard. *El conejito travieso*. México: Editorial Trillas, S.A., 1987. When a very mischievous bunny learns that his behavior makes his mother very unhappy, he changes so that he can see his mother happy again.

*28. Serrano, María Laura. *Colección Orejitas*. Argentina: Editorial Sigmar, 1985. These are durable, washable books with illustrations and concepts appealing to the K-1 child. Children will easily relate to Orejitas' experiences in this collection: *Orejitas en el supermercado, Orejitas está con su niñera, Orejitas hace una torta, Orejitas sale de viaje, Orejitas se va a bañar*, and *Orejitas se va a dormir*.

29. Válderrama Zaldívar, Rosario. *Cuando voy a la escuela*. México: Fernández Editores, 1987. We are taken through a typical school day from the sound of the alarm clock to the last activity of the day.

*30. Vincent, Gabrielle. *César y Ernestina han perdido a Gedeón*. Spain: Editorial Timún Más, 1981. When Ernestina loses Gedeón, César, her wonderful friend, does everything in his power to make up for the loss and finally succeeds.

*31. —. *César y Ernestina van de picnic*. Spain: Editorial Timún Más, 1981. This is one of several humorous stories about the adventures of a bear and a little rat. In this story, the friends go on a picnic and not even the rain spoils their fun together.

RELATED TITLES IN ENGLISH FOR SECOND LANGUAGE ACQUISITION

Addison-Wesley Big Book Program. *Goldilocks and the Three Bears*. Reading, MA: Addison-Wesley, 1989.

Brown, Marcia. *Runaway Bunny*. New York: Harper and Row, 1977.

Harper, Anita, and Susan Hellard. *It's Not Fair*. New York: G.P. Putnam's Sons, 1986.

Hoban, Russell. *Bedtime for Frances.* New York: Harper and Row, 1968.

Kraus, Robert. *Where Are You Going, Little Mouse?* New York: Greenwillow Books, 1986.

Mayer, Mercer. *Just for You.* New York: Western Publishing, 1975.

Turkel, Brinton. *Deep in the Forest.* New York: E. P. Dutton and Company, 1976.

II. OBSERVATION/EXPERIENCE: *El primer día de clase*
(Class Session One)

Guide students in the following observation/experience sequence to set the stage for reading the Main Selection.

Focus: Fear of new childhood experiences is natural.

1. Present a boy and a girl doll to the students. Tell them that the dolls would like to be real children for one day but would like to ask a few questions before trying the new experience. Using your voice to represent each doll, have the dolls interview the children, asking the following questions:

    ¿Hay algo de lo cual debemos tener miedo? (Is there anything we should be afraid of?)

    ¿Qué experiencias debemos tratar de hacer? (What experiences should we try?)

    ¿Cuáles nos gustarán? ¿Cuáles no nos gustarán? (Which will we like? Which will we not like?)

    ¿Qué podemos hacer para divertirnos con otros niños? (What can we do to have fun with other children?)

2. Tell students that after listening to their answers, the dolls need to decide whether they want to come into the world as real children to try the new experiences.

3. Tell them that maybe Nico, from *El primer día de clase,* will help them decide because Nico will be trying a new experience.

4. Show the children the book cover and have them predict what the experience will be and how Nico will change because of it. Following the story, have the children discuss whether their predictions were correct.

III. READ AND DISCUSS THE MAIN SELECTION: *El primer día de clase*
(Class Session One)

Read the Main Selection from page 116 to the students. Highlight the unit's theme by relating this story to other selections from the Literature Input list on pages 116 - 119. Then, guide students in discussing some of the following questions.

1. *¿Cómo se sentía Nico al tener que ir a la escuela por primera vez? ¿Cómo se sintieron ustedes al ir a la escuela por primera vez? ¿Por qué?* (How did Nico feel about going to school for the first time? How did you feel about going to school for the first time? Why?)

2. *¿Qué fue lo que hizo que a Nico le gustara la escuela? ¿Qué es lo que hace que a ustedes les guste la escuela?* (What was it that made Nico like school? What makes you like school?)

3. *¿En qué se parecen Nico y Cuque? ¿En qué forma son distintos?* (How are Nico and Cuque alike? How are they different?)

4. *Cuando llegaron a la escuela por primera vez, ¿qué fue lo que les hizo a ustedes sentirse mejor? ¿Por qué?* (When you came to school for the first time, what helped you feel better? Why?)

5. *¿Qué es lo que mas extrañaban cuando no estaban en sus casas? Cuando están en sus casas, ¿qué es lo que más extrañan de la escuela?* (What did you miss most about being away from home? When you are at home, what do you miss most about school?)

IV. "WHAT IF" STORY STRETCHER: *El primer día de clase*
(Class Session Two)

Next, re-read the Main Selection and choose one or more of the following questions to develop students' critical thinking skills. Story stretchers may also prompt discussion, drama or writing activities.

1. *Si la mamá de Nico hubiera dejado que se quedara en casa, ¿creen ustedes que habría sido una buena decisión? ¿Por qué o por qué no?* (If Nico's mother had allowed Nico to stay home, do you think it would have been a good decision? Why or why not?)

2. *Si ustedes fueran la mamá de Nico, ¿que cosas harían ustedes que la mamá de Nico no hizo?* (If you were Nico's mother, what things would you do that Nico's mother did not do?)

3. *Si ustedes fueran la maestra de Nico, ¿qué cosas harían ustedes que la maestra de Nico no hizo?* (If you were Nico's teacher, what would you do that Nico's teacher did not do?)

4. *Si tuvieran un hermanito quien tuviera miedo de venir a la escuela, ¿cómo le ayudarían para que no tuviera miedo?* (If you had a younger brother or sister who was afraid of coming to school, how would you help him/her not be afraid?)

5. *Si ustedes nunca quisieran probar experiencias nuevas, ¿se perderían de aprender algo nuevo? ¿Por qué? ¿Por qué no?* (If you never wanted to try new experiences, would you be missing out on learning something new? Why? Why not?

V. INTEGRATING OTHER DISCIPLINES: *El primer día de clase*
(Class Session Three and Ongoing)

The following activities are designed to enhance children's response to literature and expand *beyond* the story and its theme. The variety of activities gives teachers and students an opportunity to choose those most appropriate.

CREATIVE DRAMATICS

1. *What's in the Trunk?:* Nico's mother had a trunk with all the things Nico would need on the first day of school. Provide a box that represents a trunk. Allow children to pretend to place things in the trunk that are important for the first day of school. Have

each child look into the trunk, take out an imaginary object, and show how it is used. Have observers guess what the item is.

2. *Facial Expressions:* Have the children be Nico, and as you read different sentences in the story, have them express how Nico felt by changing their facial expressions.

3. *My First Day:* Have children re-enact the first day of school. Go over some of the same activities and try to bring out some of the students feelings on that first day.

ART AND WRITING

1. *Paper-Plate Mask:* Have students make paper-plate masks having happy faces on one side and sad faces on the other. Have the children make a list of experiences taken from the Literature Input and have them express their feelings by putting on the masks as the list is read. Discuss why they put on the happy or sad masks.

2. *Group Letter:* Have the children brainstorm and on the blackboard cluster fears they had on the first day of school. Then have the children write a group letter to the kindergarten class that will come next year. The letter should include things that they were afraid of and how their fears were overcome because of all the fun things they experienced.

3. *Paper Quilt:* Have the students make colorful drawings to illustrate all the things the newcomers should expect. Tie their drawings together with yarn to form a paper quilt. Tell them that you will keep it to share with the incoming kindergarten class.

4. *Welcome Cards:* Invite a kindergarten class to your classroom. Have children design and write welcome cards that they may read to the kindergarten class. Keep some of the cards to read to the incoming class.

5. *Experience Chart:* Using Figure I (page 128), allow children to color and cut figures to represent experiences that are often difficult for children. Provide a two-column chart with one column titled *«Difícil»* ("Difficult") and the other *«Fácil»* ("Easy"), or use a happy face and a sad face. Allow children to place completed figures in the appropriate column according to their feelings about the experiences.

6. *Advice Pamphlet:* Have children design and author a pamphlet for parents with advice on what to do when their child is afraid of trying something new, such as swimming or riding a bicycle.

7. *Doll Drawing:* Have students draw the two dolls from the Observation/Experience activity in new, real-life situations. Allow them to write descriptions of the new experiences chosen for the dolls.

8. *Favorite Experience:* Encourage children to share their favorite experiences. Children may illustrate and write about their favorite experiences and share them with the class.

9. *Story Starter:* Make a story starter book by having students bring photos of favorite experiences to be placed in a photo album. Have children use one of the photographs as a story prompt for writing a letter to a friend telling of the wonderful experience.

10. *First-Time Experiences:* Using Figure I (page 128), have students write about the feelings associated with common first-time experiences.

SOCIAL STUDIES

1. *Parent Interview:* As a homework assignment, have students interview parents questioning them about their childhood experiences. Prepare an interview sheet containing some of the following questions:

   ¿Cuáles fueron algunas cosas divertidas que hacía a mi edad? (What were some of the fun things you did at my age?)

   ¿Tenía miedo de algo? ¿Qué era? (Were you afraid of anything? What was it?)

   ¿Cuál es su recuerdo más feliz? (What is the happiest memory you have?)

   ¿En qué se parecía a mí? (How were you like me?)

   Allow children to share their written interviews with the class.

I. LITERATURE INPUT: *Pedrín, el conejo travieso*
See pages 116 - 119.

II. OBSERVATION/EXPERIENCE: *Pedrín, el conejo travieso*
(Class Session One)

Guide students in the following observation/experience sequence to set the stage for reading the Main Selection.

Focus: Our childhood experiences may lead to dangerous situations, especially when we go beyond set limits and choose to disobey.

1. Provide picture cards or word cards having potentially dangerous objects such as a stove, a swimming pool, medicine, a bicycle, matches. Guide students in the following discussion:

   ¿Les han explicado sus papas u otros adultos los peligros de algunos de estos objetos? Platíquennos. (Have your parents or other adults ever warned you about the dangers of some of these objects? Tell us about it.)

   ¿Creen ustedes que los niños pueden tener problemas por haber usado estos objetos de una forma peligrosa? (Do you suppose children ever get into trouble for using these objects in a dangerous way? Explain.)

   ¿Hay niños que desobedecen a sus papas cuando ellos les advierten sobre las cosas peligrosas? Platíquennos. (Do children ever disobey their parents' warning about these things? Explain.)

2. Tell students that in the story *Pedrín, el conejo travieso,* they will meet a little rabbit who will not listen to his mother's warning about a dangerous situation.

3. Have them predict what the dangerous situation will be and what will happen to Peter for disobeying his mother's warning. Following the story, have children discuss whether their predictions were correct.

III. READ AND DISCUSS THE MAIN SELECTION: *Pedrín, el conejo travieso*
(Class Session One)

Read the Main Selection from page 116 to the students. Highlight the unit's theme by relating this story to other selections from the Literature Input list on pages 116 - 119. Then, guide students in discussing some of the following questions.

1. *¿Qué fue lo que la mamá de Pedrín dijo que podían hacer y que no podían hacer?* (What did Peter's mother say they could and could not do?)

2. *Describan a Pedrín. ¿Qué les gusta de él? ¿Qué es lo que no les gusta? ¿Por qué?* (Describe Peter. What do you like about him? What don't you like? Why?)

3. *¿Cómo era el Señor McGregor? ¿Cómo podía haber protegido a su jardín sin hacerles daño a los conejos?* (What was Mr. McGregor like? How could he have protected his garden without hurting rabbits?)

4. *¿Qué aprendió Pedrín de su experiencia en la huerta?* (What did Peter learn from his experience in the garden?)

5. *¿Alguna vez han tenido ustedes tantos deseos de algo que hasta pensaron en desobedecer a sus padres para obtenerlo? ¿Cómo podrían obtener lo que quieren sin tener que ser desobedientes?* (Have you ever wanted something so much that you thought of disobeying your parents to get it? How might you get what you want without being disobedient?)

IV. "WHAT IF" STORY STRETCHER: *Pedrín, el conejo travieso*
(Class Session Two)

Next, re-read the Main Selection and choose one or more of the following questions to develop students' critical thinking skills. Story stretchers may also prompt discussion, drama or writing activities.

1. *¿Cómo habría cambiado el cuento si todos los conejos hubieran desobedecido a la mamá?* (How would the story be different if all the rabbits had disobeyed the mother?)

2. *Si Pedrín hubiera sido un conejito muy obediente, ¿cómo habría cambiado el cuento?* (If Peter had been an obedient rabbit, how might the story be different?)

3. *Si ustedes fueran la mamá de Pedrín, ¿qué le habrían dicho a él?* (If you were Peter's mother, what would you have said to him?)

4. *Si ustedes fueran el Señor McGregor, ¿cómo habría cambiado el cuento?* (If you were Mr. McGregor, how would the story be different?)

5. *Si ustedes fueran amigos de Pedrín, ¿habrían ido con él? Por qué? Por qué no?* (If you were Peter's friends, would you have gone with him? Why? Why not?)

V. INTEGRATING OTHER DISCIPLINES: *Pedrín, el conejo travieso*
(Class Session Three and Ongoing)

The following activities are designed to enhance children's response to literature and expand *beyond* the story and its theme. The variety of activities gives teachers and students an opportunity to choose those most appropriate.

CREATIVE DRAMATICS

1. *Dramatize Story:* Using paper-plate puppets from Art and Writing #1, have children dramatize the story.

2. *Eating Vegetables:* Have children pantomime Peter eating different vegetables. See if observers can guess which vegetables are being eaten.

3. *Another Ending:* Have the students retell the story with Peter being caught by Mr. McGregor. Have them plan and improvise what the ending with this twist might be.

4. *Mr. McGregor:* Have children be Mr. McGregor by pantomiming the steps in creating and caring for a garden.

5. *Mischievous Peter:* Have cooperative groups plan and improvise other possible mischief Peter might get into.

ART AND WRITING

1. *Paper-Plate Masks:* Using Figure J (page 129), have children make paper-plate masks by coloring and cutting Peter's ears and Mr. McGregor's hat and attaching them to paper plates. Children may create their own faces. Have them cut out holes for eyes. Both characters have good reason for needing to say "I'm sorry." Have students choose the character that they believe should apologize, and have them write a dialogue for that apology. Have the students use the masks while sharing their apologies in small groups.

2. *Animated Objects:* On large pieces of cardboard, have children make large drawings representing different animals and objects described in the story. Have them make holes large enough for their faces. While the children hold up the cardboard pictures, have a news reporter interview the animals or objects for their points of view of the story—«*Yo sabía que ese conejito causaría problemas cuando lo ví pasar por debajo de mí.*» ("I knew that little rabbit would cause trouble when I saw him go under me.") (fence) «*Cuando comió al primo zanahoria, pensé que me iba a comer a mí. ¡Qué gusto me dió ver al Sr. McGregor venir!*» ("When he ate cousin carrot, I thought he was going to eat me. I was sure glad to see Mr. McGregor coming.") (carrot)

   Another Viewpoint: Children may write their points of view as objects or animals in the story. Have them share their points of view with the class while listeners guess the identity of the object or animal.

3. *Garden Map:* Have students draw maps of the garden with Peter and Mr. McGregor in the picture. Have them write their plans for Peter's great escape.

4. *Easter Bunny Adventures:* Have students create a rabbit friend for whom Peter is to help deliver Easter eggs. (The friend may be naughty, silly, adventurous or a "goody two shoes.") Have them draw illustrations of Peter with his friend delivering Easter eggs and have them write about their adventures.

5. *What If:* Have the students select "what if" story twists to expand upon in writing. For example, what if all of Peter's brothers and sisters had disobeyed their mother? Have them draw illustrations to accompany their stories and share them with the class.

6. *Scenery Story:* Using shoebox lids, marking pens and glue, have students make finger puppet characters and design Mr. McGregor's garden inside the lids. Have them manipulate finger puppets while retelling the story. Allow them to write dialogues for the characters.

7. *Other Stories:* In their literature logs, have children write about characters from other stories, describing their experiences. If they could join one of these characters, who would it be and why?

SCIENCE

1. *Vegetable Graph:* Allow the children to color their favorite vegetables from teacher-provided patterns, or have them draw their own favorite vegetables. Create a graph using the different vegetables chosen by the children. Discuss the variety of choices and the number of each chosen.

   Vegetable Tasting Party: Provide children with an opportunity to taste some of the vegetables that they have chosen for the graph. Repeat the vegetable graph activity to see if there is a difference in preferences after the students have tasted the vegetables. You may decide to cook vegetable soup, and have children write the recipe as you make the soup.

2. *Pedrín Cookies:* Using rabbit cookie cutters, have children decorate their cookies with blue frosting for the jacket and M & M's for buttons. Have the students bring cookie recipes from home and swap them in small groups. Children may vote for a favorite recipe to make cookies.

3. *Types of Eaters:* Tell the students that Peter is a herbivore because he eats only plants. Brainstorm the names of other herbivores with the students. Discuss what other animals eat and what the three kinds of eaters are called—herbivores (plant eaters), carnivores (meat eaters), omnivores (both plants and meats). Have students create different types of animals and place them on a chart under one of these three classifications.

4. *All Kinds of Rabbits:* Provide children with information about rabbits—different kinds of rabbits, their habits, habitats. Allow children to illustrate and record facts about rabbits in their science logs.

SOCIAL STUDIES

1. *Disobedience:* Peter was disobedient but learned from his experience. Have students share similar experiences when they may have been disobedient but also learned a lesson. Children may write about experiences that helped them learn a valuable lesson.

2. *Dangerous Experiences:* Peter's experience in the garden with Mr. McGregor was dangerous. Have students relate similar experiences that may have happened to someone they know or that they heard about on the news. Have them draw pictures to illustrate the experiences. Then, let them write about the experiences and place them in a class book titled *«Experiencias con el peligro»* ("Experiences With Danger").

3. *Danger Now:* Have students explore ideas about things that are dangerous to them now but which may not be so dangerous later in their lives; e.g., crossing streets, cutting food, using stoves or irons, going long distances, or driving cars. Record their ideas on a chart: Have them write about one thing they cannot wait to do.

4. *Best/Worst Experiences:* Discuss and brainstorm best and worst experiences that children commonly have. Allow them to describe their best experiences and to create accompanying illustrations.

HEALTH

1. *Tea Party:* Peter's mother comforted him by giving him tea. Have a tea party. Ask children what their moms or dads do when they have stomach aches. Make different teas and allow children to taste them. To enhance their sense of smell and taste, have children describe the tea-tasting experience.

POETRY

Doña Semanita

Doña Semanita
tiene siete hijos:
unos son flacos
y otros gorditos

Son lunes y martes,
miércoles y jueves,
viernes y sábado,
y el domingo en fín.

Doña Semanita
siempre recomienda
a sus siete hijitos
que se porten bien.

Todos muy felices
van a trabajar,
menos el domingo
que prefiere jugar.

Folklore

Mi escuelita

(sing to the tune of "La Cucaracha")

Mi escuelita, mi escuelita.
Yo la quiero con amor,
porque en ella, porque en ella
yo aprendo mi lección.

Cuando vengo en la mañana,
lo primero que yo hago
es saludar a mi maestra
y después a mi trabajo.

Anónimo

En el agua clara

En el agua clara
que brota en la fuente
un lindo pescado
sale de repente.

Lindo pescadito,
¿no quieres venir
a jugar con mi arco?
Vamos al jardín.

Mi mamá me ha dicho:
no salgas de aquí
porque si te sales
te puedes morir.

Folklore

Figure I: *Gráfica de experiencias* / Experience Chart

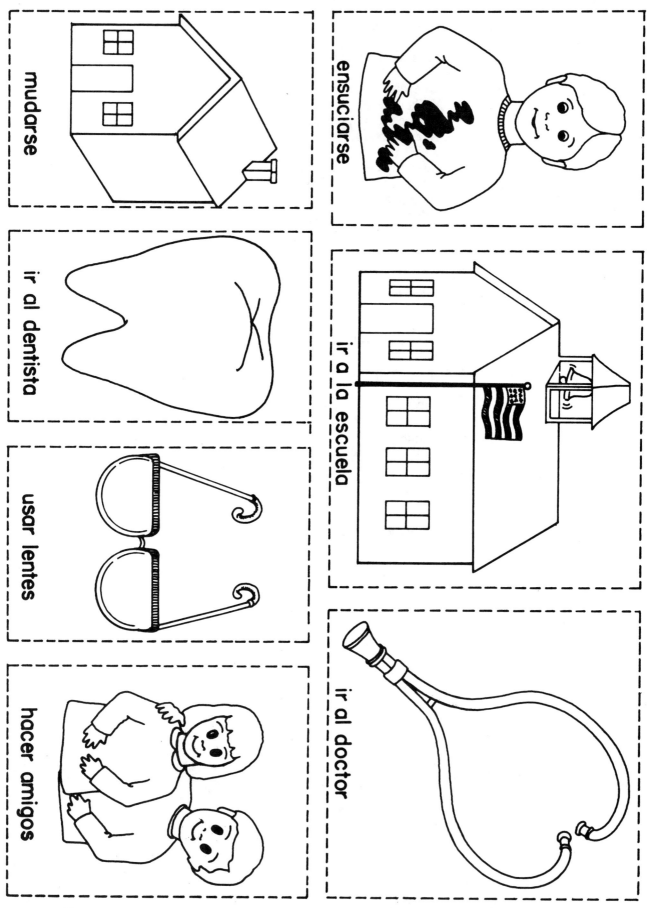

mudarse

ensuciarse

ir al dentista

ir a la escuela

usar lentes

hacer amigos

ir al doctor

128

Figure J: *Máscaras del Pedrín y el Señor McGregor* / Peter Rabbit and Mr. McGregor Masks

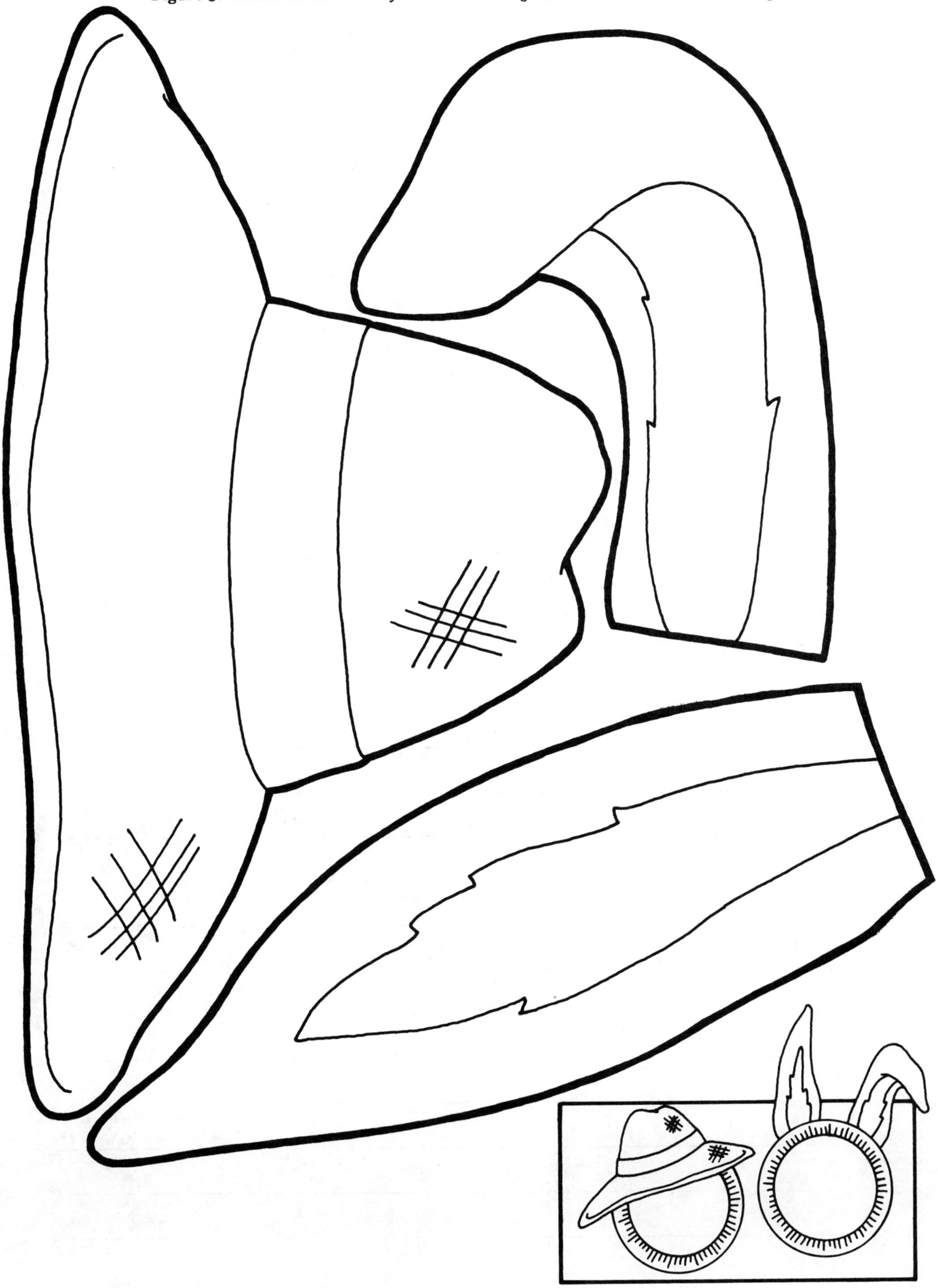

MY OWN CREATIVE TEACHING IDEAS FOR UNIT NINE

Books: _____

_____

_____

_____

_____

_____

Ideas: _____

_____

_____

_____

_____

_____

_____

_____

_____

_____

_____

_____

_____

_____

_____

_____

UNIT TEN

LO QUE PUEDO LLEGAR A SER

WHAT I CAN BECOME

It is very important for children to put no limits on what they can aspire to become. Throughout life, many opportunities, as well as obstacles, will present themselves. However, when children are exposed to positive male and female role models, they are instilled with a spark of inspiration. *¿Qué seré... cuando sea mayor?* and other stories present professions and occupations as attainable goals that may allow children's dreams to become reality in the future.

CONCEPTS AND VALUES

1. Effort and hard work bring rewards.
2. There are many occupations and professions.
3. It is important to believe that we can reach our goals.
4. We can make choices as to what we want to be.

MAIN SELECTION

Before reading the Main Selection aloud, take your students through the Literature Input and Observation/Experience phases which follow.

Aleu Ferrer, J.

¿Qué seré . . . cuando sea mayor?
Spain: Plaza & Janes, 1981.

We are introduced to a variety of occupations and professions as the question is asked, "What will I be . . . ?" The narration describes the responsibilities and pleasures of various jobs.

I.   LITERATURE INPUT: *¿Qué seré . . . cuando sea mayor?*

Select five or more titles from the following list to read aloud. Read at least one selection per day to the students. Make available and incorporate the suggested titles for voluntary independent reading. Titles marked with * are Spanish translations of the original English story; titles marked with + are recommended for more proficient listeners.

* 1.   Behrens, June. *Puedo ser conductor de camión.* Chicago: Children's Press, 1984. The daily experiences of a truck driver are depicted in an appealing manner.

* 2.   ——. *Puedo ser un astronauta.* Chicago: Children's Press, 1984. This appealing book presents the life of an astronaut.

  3.   Belloz, Jesús. *Colección Ibai: Aventuras de la imaginación.* Spain: Editorial Timún Más, 1982. The following books are contained in this collection:
Ibai: Astronauta. Ibai dreams he is an astronaut and explores the red planet. His mission is to bring back the red stone.
Ibai: Detective. Ibai dreams of searching for a missing sword. He and his friends search in a castle where they have many adventures.
Ibai: Granjero. Ibai dreams that his uncle and aunt invite him to spend his vacation on their farm.
Ibai: Piloto. Ibai dreams of being a cross-country race car driver. He encounters obstacles and dangers and overcomes them.
Ibai: Reportero. Ibai dreams he is a reporter and goes after a story at the cold North and South Poles. His films help people see the need for conservation.
Ibai: Socorrista. Ibai helps rescue a hurt colt in the mountains.
Ibai: Submarista. Ibai explores undersea life and finds sunken treasure.

 *4.   Broekel, Ray. *La policía.* Chicago: Children's Press, 1984. Photographs of real situations are used to present the varied duties of a police officer.

  5.   Capdevila, Juan. *Colección Nico y Ana quieren ser.* Spain: Editorial Timún Más, 1981.
Nico y Ana hacen fotos. Nico and Ana want to know how photographs are made, so they find out by spending time with a photographer.
Nico y Ana pescadores. Nico and Ana spend several days with a cousin who lives in a small fishing village. They learn all about the life of a fisherman.
Nico y Ana quieren ser bomberos. The fire chief invites Nico and Ana to visit the fire station. They go to several fires and learn about the dangerous life of the firefighter.

6. Delgado, Eduard. *Colección Los Mecs*. Spain: Editorial Timún Más, 1982.
—. *Los Mecs cocineros*. The cook asks the Mecs to help in the restaurant because he has no help.
—. *Los Mecs juegan a carteros*. The Mecs find a mail carrier's bag full of packages and letters. They spend the day delivering the mail to different homes.
—. *Los Mecs juegan a ser actores*. The Mecs put on a show. The show involves music, costumes, and making scenery.

+7. Dupasquier, Philippe. *Colección aquí se trabaja*. Spain: Ediciones Generales Anaya, 1985. This series allows children to explore some of the very different environments in which people work. The series includes: *El aeropuerto, La estación de ferrocarril, La fábrica, El garaje, La obra,* and *El puerto.*

*8. Flores, Rosa. *Caracolitos: Abraham Lincoln*. Oklahoma: Economy Company, 1979. This is one of Flores' biographies of famous Americans. Others in the series include: *George Washington; Martin Luther King; El sueño de Amelia* about Amelia Earhart; *Gwen Brooks, una poeta;* and *La doctora Susana,* the inspiring true-life story of a poor Indian girl who becomes a doctor and a leader among her people.

* 9. —. *El agricultor as un amigo*. Oklahoma: Economy Company, 1979. This book describes different types of farms and the importance of farmers as well as the difficulties they face.

*10. —. *Un día de trabajo en la ciudad*. Children are exposed to various occupations and professions as people go about their business.

*11. —. *Lo que hacen las madres*. Ten mothers have a variety of jobs besides being loving mothers.

*12. —. *Mis amigos policías*. A girl describes the daily experiences of the on-duty policemen as she rides with them.

13. Gergely, Tibor. *Ocupaciones de gente ocupada*. Argentina: Editorial Sigmar, 1978. We explore the city and countryside to see the many occupations that play such important roles in our daily lives.

*14. Greene, Carol. *Puedo ser jugador de béisbol*. Chicago: Children's Press, 1984. This book presents the daily experiences of a baseball player.

15. Huacuja, Verónica. *Colección mis personajes favoritos*. Editorial Trillas, 1987. These biographies of important personalities include large illustrations that may be colored. The collection includes: *Agustín Lara, Jorge Washington, Josefa Ortiz de Domínguez, Simón Bolivar,* and *Sor Juana Inez de la Cruz.*

*16. Lepscky, Ibi. *Amadeus*. Spain: Ediciones Destino, 1985. A biography of Mozart is written and illustrated at an interest level that appeals to children. Others in this series of biographies written at a level appealing to children include: *Pablito,* a biography of Picasso; *Albert,* about Albert Einstein; and *Leonardo,* a biography about Leonardo da Vinci.

+17. Maury, Inez. *Mi mamá la cartera*. New York: The Feminist Press, 1976. Lupita, an appealing four-year-old, tells the story of her mother, the mail carrier. Her point of view makes for a colorful story all children will enjoy.

18. Palombini, Ugo. *Los hombres que trabajan.* Spain: Editorial Everest, S.A., 1980. This book gives brief descriptions of twelve different professions and occupations.

19. Puncel, María. *Colección cuando sea mayor seré.* Spain: Ediciones Destino, 1979. This series of splendidly illustrated and narrated stories for different occupations includes: *Comerciante, Construir casas, Enfermera, Haré cine, Marino, Mecánico, Periodista,* and *Trabajar en una granja.*

20. Solano Flores, Guillermo. *El periódico.* México: Editorial Trillas, S.A., 1987. This book describes the process involved in getting a news item into the newspaper.

21. Válderrama Zaldívar, Rosario. *El cartero.* México: Fernández Editores, 1987. We are invited to spend the day with the mail carrier.

RELATED TITLES IN ENGLISH FOR SECOND LANGUAGE ACQUISITION

Burnett, Carol. *What I Want To Be When I Grow Up.* Simon and Schuster, 1975.

Lasker, Joe. *Mothers Can Do Anything.* Chicago: Albert Whitman and Company, 1972.

Powell, M., and G. Yokubinas. *What To Be?* Regensteiner Publishing Enterprises, 1972.

Roche, A.K. *I Can Be.* New Jersey: Prentice-Hall, 1967.

Rockwell, Harlow. *My Doctor.* New York: Macmillan, 1973.

Rothman, Joel. *I Can Be Anything You Can Be!* New York: Scroll Press, 1973.

II. OBSERVATION/EXPERIENCE: *¿Qué seré . . . cuando sea mayor?*
(Class Session One)

Guide students in the following observation/experience sequence to set the stage for reading the Main Selection.

Focus: When we learn about people from different occupations and professions, it helps us explore what we may become in the future.

1. Have two or three guests describe their occupations or professions to the children. Perhaps a carpenter can bring his/her tools, a librarian may share books, a police officer or a firefighter may come as a representative of the community. Use resource people from the school, such as the principal, secretary, another teacher, the psychologist, speech therapist, cafeteria worker, and maintenance workers.

2. Encourage dialogue between guests and children to focus on the following:

   * what guests did to prepare for their jobs
   * what they need to perform their duties
   * why their jobs are important
   * what they like or dislike about their work
   * what made them want to become (job titles).

3. Tell students they will meet other people who will have important jobs in *¿Qué seré . . . cuando sea mayor?*

4. Have students predict the professions and occupations they will learn about and the duties performed by these people. Following the reading presentation, have the children discuss whether their predictions were correct.

III. READ AND DISCUSS THE MAIN SELECTION: *¿Qué seré . . . cuando sea mayor?*
(Class Session One)

Read the Main Selection from page 132 to the students. Highlight the unit's theme by relating this story to other selections from the Literature Input list on pages 132 - 134. Then, guide students in discussing some of the following questions.

1. *¿Qué les gustaría ser cuando sean grandes?* (What would you like to be when you grow up?)

2. *¿Cuáles de los trabajos mencionados creen que les gustaría? ¿Por qué?* (Which of the jobs mentioned do you think you would enjoy? Why?)

3. *¿Va toda la gente a trabajar en la misma forma? Mencionen algunas formas como la gente llega al trabajo.* (Do all people get to work in the same way? Name some ways people get to work.)

4. *¿Qué creen ustedes que tendrán que hacer para prepararse para hacer este trabajo?* (What do you think you will have to do to prepare yourself for this job?)

5. *Llegar a ser lo que quieren ser será su decisión. ¿Qué les podrá ayudar a ser lo que ustedes desean? ¿Qué les podría impedir?* (Becoming what you want to be is your choice. What can help you become what you want to be? What could stop you?)

IV. "WHAT IF" STORY STRETCHER: *¿Qué seré . . . cuando sea mayor?*
(Class Session Two)

Next, re-read the Main Selection and choose one or more of the following questions to develop students' critical thinking skills. Story stretchers may also prompt discussion, drama or writing activities.

1. *¿Qué tal si fueran un/una . . . ? ¿Por qué serían importante?* (What if you were a . . . ? Why would you be important?)

2. *Si pudieran conocer a un/una . . . , ¿qué preguntas le harían?* (If you could meet a . . . , what questions would you ask?)

3. *Si pudieran ser lo que quisieran, ¿qué les gustaría ser? ¿Por qué?* (If you could be anything you wanted, what would you be? Why?)

4. *Si pudieran entrevistar a quien quisieran, ¿quién sería esa persona? ¿Por qué?* (If you could interview anyone you wanted, who would that person be? Why?)

5. *Si no hubieran trabajadores para prestar servicios a la comunidad, ¿cómo sería nuestra comunidad?* (If there were no workers to provide services to the community, what would our community be like?)

V. INTEGRATING OTHER DISCIPLINES: *¿Qué seré . . . cuando sea mayor?*
(Class Session Three and Ongoing)

The following activities are designed to enhance children's response to literature and expand *beyond* the story and its theme. The variety of activities gives teachers and students an opportunity to choose those most appropriate.

CREATIVE DRAMATICS

1. *Act in a Hat:* Provide a selection of hats representing a variety of occupations. As the children wear the hats, allow them to role play situations such as building a house, being sick, having a toothache, and being lost.

2. *Pantomime Occupations:* Pair children to pantomime different occupations or professions—doctor/patient, teacher/student, carpenter/house. Have the class guess what the occupations or professions are and what is happening.

3. *What Am I?:* Provide a large box with a square cut out so that children can look out of the box and speak. Also provide hats associated with different occupations/professions. Have different children go in and give three hints about the duties of a given job. Allow the class time to ask questions and guess what the occupation is. The child in the box responds to the correct answer by putting on the hat that reflects that occupation or has the name of the occupation written on it.

4. *What with Whom?:* Put items in a box, and as children take different items out, they decide what professions or occupations might use them. (There may be several answers for each item.) Allow children to describe how the items will be used. Have children illustrate an item and play the same game using their illustrations.

5. *Workers in Many Places:* In a creative dramatics corner, set up several places of business such as a market, hospital, restaurant, dental office, or library, and allow children to role play being workers in one of these places.

ART AND WRITING

1. *A . . . for a Day:* Have the students begin with sheets of newspaper; have them fold the paper in half, then fold the top corners into the center and fold the bottom edges up for hats. Have children write the titles of professions or occupations on their hats. Have small groups brainstorm and cluster the duties or responsibilities corresponding to the hat titles. Allow them to write group stories describing themselves in their chosen occupations during a typical day.

2. *Join My Profession:* In cooperative groups, have children select professions for which they will create the uniforms and necessary equipment. Have them trace a group member's body, then create, color, label and cut out the uniform and equipment to fit the life-size body. Allow children to write about themselves in their chosen occupations, describing the positive aspects of the job and inviting others to join the profession.

3. *What Will I Be?:* Guide the children in a clustering activity with occupations and professions. Pair children and have each child tell the partner what she/he would like to be when grown up and why. The listening partner must repeat what she/he heard to the class. Ring a bell for the children to switch roles. Have children illustrate what they would like to be. To accompany their illustrations, allow them to use titles of clustered occupations and write about what they would like to be and why.

4. *Worker Puppets:* Using Figure K (page 139), have children color and cut out hats and glue them on the cut-out figures. Have the children use the finger puppets to create impromptu dialogues which focus on situations related to the occupation/profession. Allow the puppets to be shared among small groups. Alternatively, cut off the finger holes and have the children glue the figures on tongue depressors to make stick puppets. Have the class brainstorm and write questions to be used for interviewing the stick puppets. Pair children to allow each an opportunity to interview the partner's puppet.

5. *What Will I Be?:* From the discussion of a "What If" story stretcher, have children write and illustrate what they would like to be in the future.

6. *I Am a . . . .:* Have children paint pictures of themselves in desired professions. Allow them to list all the things they would do during their busy work day.

7. *Create a Collage:* Brainstorm and discuss different community workers and service employees and some of their tasks. Using magazines, scissors, and paste, have students fold sheets of construction paper in half. Have them label one half «*Ayudantes de la comunidad*» ("Community Workers") and the other half «*Servicios de producción*» ("Service Employees"). Allow them to cut and paste on pictures that correspond with the titles. Have them write captions to describe each type of service.

8. *Paper-Bag Puppets:* Using paper bags and colorful construction paper, have children create their favorite community workers on one side of the bags. Have them make charts describing the job and duties of the workers and paste them on the back of the bags. Allow them to read their charts among the groups.

SOCIAL STUDIES

1. *Workers in the City:* With children, discuss and brainstorm the many workers that are needed to help run a city smoothly. Then, on large pieces of butcher paper, have cooperative groups draw city murals. Instruct them to include work places for occupations that have been previously mentioned, homes, stop signs, and whatever children may want to include. The children can then drive little cars or walk with their finger puppets through the city to visit busy workers. Have each group write descriptions of workers in the city during a typical day.

2. *The Making of . . . :* Provide several common objects—cartons of milk, food, cotton, wool, pieces of clothing—and discuss all the different jobs that were necessary in the production of the items. Have children make books in the shape of the items with each page representing a step in the process of producing the item. Children may write descriptive captions for each step.

3. *Praising Helpers:* Allow children to brainstorm all the people representing a variety of occupations that helped them or that had an effect on them the previous day—bus driver, mother, father, grocer, delivery person, teacher, principal, crossing guard, clergy, T.V. or movie star. Have the children choose one of these people, and write notes of commendation to them.

4. *City into Action:* Provide children with background information and field trip experiences to places in your city where children can see people in real situations and functioning for real purposes. Guest speakers such as city council members, the mayor, bankers, merchants, and club and organization leaders may be invited to make presentations and to be interviewed by the students. Later, have cooperative groups select, brainstorm, and plan which city officials or workers they would like to represent. (Make certain that all sectors of the community are represented.) Guide the students in putting their plans into action; e.g., city officials deciding policies, merchants running businesses, organizations helping the community, bankers functioning to serve their patrons, consumers frequenting businesses, and other workers performing their duties. Much problem solving and evaluation should follow each active experience. You will need to determine an appropriate time span for carrying out this challenging and fruitful endeavor.

POETRY

El ayudante

(May also be sung to the music of "Did You Ever See a Lassie?")

Yo deseo ser bombero,
bombero, bombero.
Yo deseo ser bombero
para ayudar.

Ayudante quiero ser,
quiero ser, quiero ser.
Ayudante quiero ser
para servir.

Anónimo

Quiero ser

Quiero ser una flor
para darla a mi amor.
Quiero ser caracol
para dormir en el sol.

Quiero ser la media luna
y cantarle una runa.
Quiero ser un mal pirata
en buen barco de lata.

Anónimo

NASA

cut out

59

221

MY OWN CREATIVE TEACHING IDEAS FOR UNIT TEN

Books: _____

_____

_____

_____

_____

_____

Ideas: _____

_____

_____

_____

_____

_____

_____

_____

_____

_____

_____

_____

_____

_____

_____

_____

_____

UNIT ELEVEN

MI MUNDO CAMBIA

MY WORLD CHANGES

The seasons are, for children, a natural introduction to the changing world. The changes in temperature, colors, weather, activities, and animal behavior stimulate children's curiosity to discover the world around them. ***Pedro y su roble*** presents the concept of seasonal change through an imaginary story that children can understand.

CONCEPTS AND VALUES

1. Our environment changes with the seasons.
2. Our activities change as the seasons change.
3. We eat different foods at different times of the year.
4. We dress differently as the seasons change.
5. There are places without apparent seasonal changes.

MAIN SELECTION

Before reading the Main Selection aloud, take your students through the Literature Input and Observation/Experience phases which follow.

Levert, Claude and Carme Solé Vendrell.

Pedro y su roble.
Spain: Editorial Miñón, S.A., 1979.

This is a warm story about Pedro's love and concern for his beautiful oak tree. Pedro does not understand the seasonal changes his tree goes through but finally realizes it is natural and wonderful.

I. LITERATURE INPUT: *Pedro y su roble*

Select five or more titles from the following list to read aloud. Read at least one selection per day to the students. Make available and incorporate the suggested titles for voluntary independent reading. Titles marked with * are Spanish translations of the original English story; titles marked with + are recommended for more proficient listeners.

Las cuatro estaciones / The Four Seasons

*1. Blocksma, Mary. *Manzano! manzano!* Chicago: Children's Press, 1983. A caterpillar finds a home in an apple tree that changes as the seasons pass. This book is written in the form of a poem.

+*2. Buscaglia, Leo. *El otoño de Freddy la hoja.* Spain: Emece Editores, 1982. This beautifully told story of the life of a leaf depicts all the changes that take place as the year progresses.

*3. Charles, Donald. *El año de Gato Galano.* Chicago: Children's Press, 1984. Gato Galano enjoys activities during the four seasons.

4. Dalmais, Anne-Marie. *El señor Erizo.* Spain: Editorial La Galera, S.A., 1970. Mr. Hedgehog experiences life with different creatures through the four seasons.

*5. Flores, Rosa. *Caracolitos: Doce meses de felicidad.* Oklahoma: Economy Company, 1979. Photographs show twelve months of activities.

+6. Heathen, Anne. *Cuatro perritos.* México: Editorial Trillas, S.A., 1987. Four puppies experience the fun and beauty that the seasons bring.

+*7. Lionni, Leo. *¡Prohibido a los gatos!* Spain: Editorial Lumen, 1984. Mice give us a month by month account of their experiences with the changes in weather.

8. Llimona, Mercedes. *Colección Bibi.* Spain: Editorial Hymsa, 1983. Bibi, her friends, and family are active through each season of the year. The series includes: *Bibi y el otoño, Bibi y el invierno, Bibi y la primavera,* and *Bibi y el verano.*

9. Palombini, Ugo. *Colección Carlos y Sandra: Las estaciones.* Spain: Editorial Everest, S.A., 1982. The four seasons are explored through Sandra's experiences: *Sandra y el otoño, Sandra y el invierno, Sandra y la primavera,* and *Sandra y el verano.*

10. Pecanins, Ana María. *Manzanita*. México: Editorial Trillas, S.A., 1986. This is the adventure of a talking apple.

11. Satomi, Ichikawa. *Susana y Nicolás: El reloj de las cuatro estaciones*. Spain: Plaza and Jones, S.A., 1979. We travel through the seasons with Susana and Nicolas in this beautifully illustrated book.

El otoño / Autumn

12. Alonso, Fernando. *El árbol que no tenía hojas*. Spain: Santillana, S.A., 1975. A leafless tree learns he is ugly and asks the elements for help. The elements are not able to help, but through the kindness of thoughtful children, he becomes a beautiful tree.

*13. Flores, Rosa. *Caracolitos: El otoño para todo*. Oklahoma: Economy Company, 1979. Fall is described and explored through narration and photographs.

14. Heuck, Sigrid. *El poni, el oso y el manzano*. Spain: Editorial Juventud, 1977. In this beautifully illustrated story, a horse and a bear search for lost apples.

*15. Parramón, J.M. Illustrated by Ulises Wensel. . *El otoño*. Spain: Barrons Educational Series, 1984. Autumn is described and illustrated by all the changes and activities of fall.

16. *Soy el otoño*. Spain: Publicaciones Fher, 1980. This is a description of fall, written in the first person.

El invierno / Winter

17. Alberti/Wolfsgruber. *Simón y los animales*. Spain: Ediciones S.M., 1987. In this beautifully illustrated story, Simón finds that the noses on his snowmen are missing. He discovers they were taken by hungry animals and compassionately begins to feed them.

*18. Flores, Rosa. *Caracolitos: Así es el invierno*. Oklahoma: Economy Company, 1979. Winter is described as it occurs in different parts of the United States.

19. Garberi, Francesca, and María Dolores La Torre. *La hormiguita que iba a Jerusalem*. Spain: Editorial La Galera, S.A., 1970. This poem describes an ant's hazardous journey to Jerusalem.

*20. Nagasaki, Genosuke. *Mamá y el muñeco de nieve*. Spain: Editorial Planeta, 1982. Mother pig becomes impatient when all the family ignore her requests because of the unusual snowfall. She falls, and they show their affection by making a snowman that looks like mother.

*21. Parramón, J.M. Illustrated by Carme Solé Vendrell. *El invierno*. Spain: Barron's Educational Series, 1986. Winter is described and illustrated through all the changes and activities of winter.

22. Serrano, María Laura. *Tipi el gorrión*. Spain: Editorial Everest-Leon. 1980. Tipi, the sparrow makes friends with a snowman. Tipi replaces his friend's carrot nose, but as spring comes, his friend leaves.

23. *Soy el invierno*. Spain: Publicaciones Fher, 1983. Written in the first person, Winter describes the changes and events that occur during the coldest time of the year.

La primavera / Spring

24. Alsonso, Fernando. *La visita de la primavera*. Spain: Santillana, 1975. A town had never known spring. "Spring," through the concern of her husband, finds the town and her boredom disappears when she shares her beauty with everyone.

*25. Brown, Margaret Wise. *El conejito y el huevo*. México: Editorial Trillas, S.A., 1987. A bunny finds an egg and wonders what could be inside. He tries unsuccessfully to open the egg until, finally, what comes out of it becomes a good friend.

*26. Clifton, Lucille. *El niño que no creía en la primavera*. New York: E. P. Dutton and Company, 1976. Toni cannot find any signs of spring in the city and doubts there is a spring, but he finally finds it in the most unexpected place.

*27. Flores, Rosa. *Caracolitos: La linda primavera*. Oklahoma: Economy Company, 1979. This book describes all the changes unique to spring.

*28. —. *Caracolitos: El árbol de Rita*. Oklahoma: Economy Company, 1979. El Señor García explains to Rita what a tree needs in order to grow from a small seed into a beautiful tree.

29. Gerson, Sara. *Luisa y el arco iris*. México: Editorial Trillas, S.A., 1986. Luisa lives in a black and white town and longs for color. After a storm, a rainbow becomes attached to the wheel of her bike, and with every pedal she brings color into her town.

30. Larreula, Eric. *Las dos nubes amigas*. Spain: Editorial Susaeta, 1985. This story of two clouds during spring illustrates what occurs when the weather changes.

31. Marcus, Elizabeth. *La vida de las plantas*. México: Sistemas Técnicas de Edición, S.A. de C.V., 1987. This book with appealing illustrations explores plants and their importance in our world.

*32. Parramón, J.M. Illustrated by Asun Balzola. *La primavera*. New York: Barron's Educational Series, 1986. Spring is described and illustrated through all the special things that happen in the springtime.

33. *Soy la primavera*. Spain: Publicaciones Fher, 1980. This is a description of spring written in the first person.

El verano / Summer

34. Barklen, Jill. *Cuento de verano*. London: Editorial Bruguera, 1981. This story captures life during the summer as imaginary mice marry and work in hot weather.

*35. Carruth, Jane. *La ola gigante*. Argentina: Editorial Sigmar, 1982. Carla and her family go to visit her uncle. He lives by the sea and Carla has her first experience with a large wave.

*36. Flores, Rosa. *Caracolitos: El verano es para divertirse*. Oklahoma: Economy Company, 1979. Summer is described through all the different activities that only take place in the summertime.

37. Gerson, Sara. *Castillos de arena*. México: Editorial Trillas, S.A., 1986. The wonderful experience of building a sand castle stimulates Diana's imagination.

38. —. *Pedro aprende a nadar*. México: Editorial Trillas, S.A., 1986. Pedro nearly drowns because of his concern for his dog's safety. Instead, Pedro learns to swim the dog paddle.

*39. Parramón, J.M. Illustrated by Carme Solé Vendrell. *El verano*. New York: Barron's Educational Series, 1985. Summer is explored through simple descriptive phrases and beautiful illustrations.

40. Pecanins, Ana María. *La cometa*. México: Editorial Trillas, S.A., 1986. A girl and a flock of birds rescue a trapped kite. They become friends and have a wonderful summer together.

41. *Soy el verano*. Spain: Publicaciones Fher, 1980. This description of summer is written in the first person.

*42. Wylie, Joanne and David. *Un cuento de un pez grande*. Chicago: Children's Press, 1984. This is a nicely illustrated story of an imaginary fish.

*43. —. Chicago: Children's Press, 1984. *Un cuento curioso de colores*. This is a story of a fish of many colors.

RELATED TITLES IN ENGLISH FOR SECOND LANGUAGE ACQUISITION

Alington, Richard, L. *Summer*. Wisconsin: Raintree Publishers, 1981. (Additional seasons are available.)

Coleridge, Sara. *January Brings the Snow*. New York: Dial Books for Young Children, 1986.

Foster, Doris Van Liew. *A Pocketful of Seasons*. New York: Lothrop, 1964.

Gibbons, Gail. *The Seasons of Arnold's Apple Tree*. San Diego: Harcourt, Brace and Jovanovich, 1984.

Keats, Ezra Jack. *The Snowy Day*. New York: Viking, 1962.

Ryder, Joanne. *The Snail's Spell*. New York: Viking Penguin, 1982.

II. OBSERVATION/EXPERIENCE: *Pedro y su roble*
(Class Session One)

Guide students in the following observation/experience sequence to set the stage for reading the Main Selection.

Focus: Seasons change our environment.

1. Plan a nature walk. At the beginning of each season, take an early morning walk along the same route. Take a box or bag for the children to pick up treasures on the way. Take along magnifying glasses so the children may view small creatures. Help children look for signs of the season—clothing people wear, ice, smoke from chimneys, steam from the mouth, wet or dry windows, trees, flowers, insects, clothes hanging on the line.

2. Discuss the following questions as the walk continues:

¿Cómo estamos vestidos y cómo nos sentimos? (How are we dressed, and how do we feel?)

Fíjense como está vestida la gente. (Notice how people are dressed.)

Describan los árboles y las plantas. (Describe the trees and plants.)

¿Qué está haciendo la gente? (What are people doing?)

3. Remind students that they have seen some signs of (name of season). Tell them that in ***Pedro y su roble,*** they will read about a boy who did not understand the seasonal changes in his tree.

4. Have the students predict the changes Pedro will see in his tree during fall, winter, spring, and summer. Following the story, have children discuss whether their predictions about a particular season were correct.

III. READ AND DISCUSS THE MAIN SELECTION: *Pedro y su roble*
(Class Session One)

Read the Main Selection from page 142 to the students. Highlight the unit's theme by relating this story to other selections from the Literature Input list on pages 142 - 145. Then, guide students in discussing some of the following questions.

1. *¿Por qué pensaba Pedro que su árbol estaba enfermo?* (What made Pedro think his tree was sick?)

2. *¿Qué hizo Pedro para tratar de curar a su árbol?* (What did Pedro do to try to cure his tree?)

3. *Describan el ambiente alrededor del árbol de Pedro durante las cuatro estaciones.* (Describe the environment around Pedro's tree during the four seasons.)

4. *Describan el árbol de Pedro durante las cuatro estaciones.* (Describe Pedro's tree during the four seasons.)

5. Ask some of the following questions for each season:

   • *¿Qué ropa se usa en . . . ?* (What kinds of clothes are worn during . . . ?)

   • *Describan ustedes como es el/la . . . en otras partes del mundo.* (Describe what . . . looks like in different parts of the world.)

   • *¿Qué es lo que hacen algunos animales en el/la . . . ? ¿Por qué?* (What do some animals do in . . . ? Why?)

   • *¿Qué actividades hacen ustedes en el/la . . . que no pueden hacer en ningún otro tiempo?* (What are some activities you do in . . . that you cannot do any other time?)

   • *Nómbrenme los días de fiesta de el/la . . . .* (Name the holidays in . . . .)

- *¿Qué es lo que les gusta del/de la. . .?* (What do you like about . . . ?)

- *¿Qué alimentos encuentran en el/la . . . que no pueden encontrar en otras estaciones?* (What foods do you find in . . . that are not available in other seasons?)

IV. "WHAT IF" STORY STRETCHER: *Pedro y su roble*
(Class Session Two)

Next, re-read the Main Selection and choose one or more of the following questions to develop students' critical thinking skills. Story stretchers may also prompt discussion, drama or writing activities.

1. *Si Pedro hubiera sabido de los cambios naturales de un árbol, ¿qué cosas no habría hecho?* (If Pedro had known about the natural changes of a tree, what would he not have done?)

2. *Si no hubiera (nombre de estación), ¿qué es lo que más extrañarían?* (If there were no (name of season), what would you miss the most?)

3. *Si el año tuviera una sola estación, ¿cuál quisieran que fuera? ¿Por qué?* (If the year had only one season, what would you like it to be? Why?)

4. *Si tuvieran que pensar en otro nombre para (nombre de estación), ¿cómo la llamarían? ¿Por qué?* (If you had to think of another name for (name of season), what would you call it? Why?)

V. INTEGRATING OTHER DISCIPLINES: *Pedro y su roble*
(Class Session Three and Ongoing)

The following activities are designed to enhance children's response to literature and expand *beyond* the story and its theme. The variety of activities gives teachers and students an opportunity to choose those most appropriate.

Las cuatro estaciones / The Four Seasons

ART AND WRITING

1. *Thermometers:* Have the students trace thermometer patterns on white construction paper. Have them mark either degrees or "colder, cold, warm, hot." Have them cut patterns with slits one-half inch from the top and bottom. Then, have them cut pieces of red and white ribbon, glue them together, and insert them into the slots. Have them glue the other ends together on back. Have the children set temperatures on their thermometers and write weather reports for the selected temperatures.

2. *Seasonal Tree:* Using Figure L (page 157), have children illustrate the four seasons. Each child will need four copies of the tree. For fall, they may add orange, red, and yellow leaves with paint or torn pieces of construction paper. For winter, they may show snow by adding white paint, cotton or soap flakes. For spring, they may add blossoms of tissue paper or colored popcorn. They may add green leaves and/or fruit

for summer. When completed, the four illustrations may be put together in a booklet. Children may write as the trees, describing themselves in that particular season, «*Todas mis hojas se me han caído . . . .*» (My leaves have all fallen . . . .)

3. *Favorite Season:* Discuss activities of a certain season. Have children illustrate and write about their favorite time of year.

4. *Vegetable People:* Have the children make vegetable people, using the vegetables available during that particular season. Have children write recipes for making their vegetable people.

5. *Shopping List:* Have children make up a shopping list of items to be purchased for a particular season. Children may illustrate a seasonal catalogue of clothing with descriptions and prices.

6. *Fruits and Vegetables:* Using fruits and vegetables unique to a particular season, engage the children in the following activities:

   • Have them estimate the number of seeds found in the fruit or vegetable.
   • Have them estimate how many blocks, unifix cubes, or other items will equal the weight of a particular fruit or vegetable.
   • Provide recipes using fruits and vegetables to permit children to measure. Allow children to copy recipes they want to use at home.

SCIENCE

1. *Seasonal Animal Behavior:* Talk about animals and the behavior they display during a particular season—they hibernate, gather food, have babies, hunt, migrate. Have the children write as if they were animals, telling of life during a particular season. Allow them to draw and attach accompanying illustrations.

El otoño / Fall

Trees shed their leaves in fall to protect themselves from the cold of winter. When a tree loses its leaves, the living interior is sealed off and protected inside the bark. The leaves change color because the tree draws back foods such as sugars and proteins. Everything needed to survive the winter is drawn back into the sap of the tree. The tree is now ready to face the hard winter.

CREATIVE DRAMATICS

1. *Be a Tree:* Have the children pretend that they are trees, and it is September, then October, and finally November. Have them describe what is happening to them—they feel colder; they are feeling dry; they are losing their leaves. Ask them what kinds of insects are on them. Ask them to show what the wind does to them.

2. *Be a Leaf:* Have the children pretend that they are leaves falling off a tree. Have them imagine the sensation of falling. Ask them what happens once they reach the ground: Are they raked, stepped on, crumbled, whisked away, carried away by insects? Do they dance in the wind? Have students pantomime the different consequences.

3. *Pantomime:* Have children pantomime the following actions common to the fall season:

- walking on dry leaves, raking leaves, piling leaves, jumping on the leaves, tossing them in the air
- running through a pumpkin patch and holding the different size and shaped pumpkins
- picking apples and pears from trees
- celebrating fall holidays

ART AND WRITING

1. *Leaf Graph:* Allow children to sort and graph leaves by color, shape and size. Have them draw and label different leaves in leaf books. Have the students compare the number of leaves in each group.

2. *Sponge Painting:* Have the children pin leaves to pieces of paper. Have them use small pieces of sponge dipped in paint to dab all around the leaves. Have them remove the leaves to display the outline. Talk about the different shapes of leaves. Use as a book cover for the leaf book in Activity 1 above.

3. *I Wish I Had:* Use the following as a writing starter: *«Ojalá tuviera un árbol....»* ("I wish I had a ... tree.") Encourage children to be as imaginative and descriptive as possible and to incorporate some of the information from the discussion of leaves.

4. *Leaf Rubbing:* Have the students make leaf rubbings by covering leaves with pieces of paper (make sure the vein side is up) and rubbing crayons over the leaves. To add a little more beauty, the children may paint them with watercolors. Use the leaf rubbings to make a bulletin board. Have the children brainstorm and cluster adjectives that describe the bulletin board.

5. *Thumbprint-Tree Invitations:* Children may invite another class to a party by making invitations that illustrate the season. Have children draw and cut out a tree trunk using textured wallpaper. Have them paste it on construction paper and have them dip their thumbs in yellow, orange and red paint to make thumbprint leaves. Have the children write who, what, where, when and why inside the invitations.

6. *Tissue Tree:* Have children draw outlines of tree trunks and branches, then glue on leaves made from torn colored tissue paper. (This activity is especially good after reading *El árbol que no tenía hojas* from the Literature Input.) Children may write as leaves, telling about changing colors and falling from the tree.

7. *Group Composition:* Allow children, in cooperative groups, to develop a composition centered around the questions for all seasons. Have them paint a group mural depicting a specific question relating to fall.

SCIENCE

1. *Kinds of Trees:* Talk about different kinds of trees. Discuss trees that do not lose their leaves and why. The leaves of some plants and trees can stand the cold winter because their leaf pores close off to protect the inside of the plant and their glossy exteriors prevent them from being damaged by frost—holly, laurel and ivy are good examples.

Pines, spruce and firs also remain green all winter. These conifers have tiny leaves, like needles, that are not affected by the cold. Have students record facts in their science logs.

2. *Edible and Non-Edible Leaves:* Discuss the dangers of eating poisonous leaves from plants such as holly, poinsettia or potato. Have students list the non-edible leaves in their science logs. Talk about and allow the children to eat edible leaves such as lettuce, spinach and cabbage. Follow with an edible-leaf-tasting party.

El invierno / Winter

Winter is the coldest time of the year. It is cold in winter because of the way the earth is tilted. If where you live is tilted toward the sun, it is summer; if it is tilted away from the sun, it is winter. In the tropics, the tilt makes little difference. At the poles, it is always cold, but much colder in the winter months. If the earth did not tilt, the temperature would stay the same all year long.

CREATIVE DRAMATICS

1. *Snowman:* Instruct children to build an imaginary snowman. Have children get down on their knees and roll a snowball together. Have them put one snowball on top of the other and mime adding some embellishments such as carrots for a nose or a buttons for the eyes.

2. *Cold Morning:* Tell students to imagine waking up to a very cold morning. Ask them what they think about. Then have them pantomime what they would do—wanting to stay under the covers, wishing the heater were on, deciding what to wear and what to eat. Serve hot chocolate to heighten the mood.

3. *Ice Skating:* Show children pictures of ice skaters. Explain the freezing of water. Relate this to what they are familiar with such as ice cubes and popsicles. Tell them that when water turns to ice, people can get on it and skate, wearing special shoes called ice skates. Have waltz music available. Instruct them to get down on the floor and put on their imaginary ice skates. Then have them imagine that they are getting out onto the ice (uncarpeted, bare floors are best). Once they get this skating motion under way, you can introduce other moves, spins and turns. Allow the children to create their own skating dance.

ART AND WRITING

1. *Winter Home:* Have partners make pairs of cards to match the animal with its animal winter home: butterfly-cocoon, bear-cave, rabbit-hole in the ground, beaver-lodge. Have them write as one of the animals, describing their winter homes.

2. *Pasta Snowflakes:* Using pasta of different shapes, such as wagon wheels corkscrews, and bow ties, have students place them on pieces of waxed paper and glue the pasta together. The finished flakes can be sprayed gold or silver and hung. Have students write group charts or poems about snowflakes.

3. *Button Snowman:* Using three large white buttons glued onto paper, have students make snowmen. They may add yarn for scarves and draw on hats. Have the children name their snowmen and write stories about how they survived to see the following winter.

4. *Cotton Snowman:* Have students glue cotton balls onto colored paper to make snowmen. Have them create additional scenery. Children may interview the snowman to find out what he likes about being a snowman.

5. *Creative Writing:* Have children, in cooperative groups, write about «*Lo que me gusta de un día de invierno*» ("What I Like about a Winter Day").

6. *Weather Report:* Read weather reports from the newspaper to the children or allow them to listen on the radio or television. Have them make up weather reports for a winter day. The weather report should include what should be worn or any precautions that should be taken.

SCIENCE

1. *Winter Survival:* Talk about how animals survive in winter. Animals need more food in winter to give them energy to maintain their body temperature. Despite all the problems of snow and ice covering the feeding grounds, and plants stopping growth, animals have found ways to survive through migration, hibernation, and thicker, longer, and often different colored coats. Allow the children to make a three-column chart of animals, showing how the animals cope with winter.

2. *Crystal Christmas Tree:* Discuss how trees are affected by extreme cold. Have students trace a tree and cut it out. Allow them to design the colorful "ornaments." Mix a quart of water and 1/2 - 3/4 cup of epsom salts. Stir with a brush and have students brush "crystals" on the trees. Let students record, in their science logs, what happened to the epsom salts and describe how snow-capped trees have a similar appearance.

3. *Edible Snowman:* Have the children make snowman treats by attaching large marshmallow balls together with toothpicks and adding raisin features with corn syrup. Have children write directions for making marshmallow snowmen.

La primavera / Spring

We hear more birds singing in the spring because males are setting up their territories and trying to attract the female birds. Flowers with bright petals and sweet scents attract insects that are busy gathering food and fulfilling their roles as pollinators.

CREATIVE DRAMATICS

1. *Pantomime:* Have children pantomime the following activities often seen in the springtime:

   - sowing seeds
   - mowing the lawn
   - using garden tools
   - smelling flowers
   - picking strawberries
   - celebrating spring holidays

2. *Be a Gardener:* Using a set of plastic garden tools or other objects that can serve as make-believe tools—pail, watering can, hose for imaginary water, empty seed packets, fake flowers—have children make believe that they are gardeners. In the imaginary garden, the rug can be grass; the children can pretend to plant seeds, water them, watch them grow, pick them, and smell or eat them.

3. *Spring Things:* Children may pantomime spring insects, flowers, birds in a garden, bees looking for pollen, birds hatching from their eggs, butterflies going through metamorphosis.

ART AND WRITING

1. *Seed Plaque:* Provide seeds of various types, glue, and posterboard. Have students draw designs on the posterboard and then place seeds within the drawings and glue them in place. Students may display their plaques with descriptions of their plaques and the kinds of seeds used.

2. *Magic Seed:* Have the students write about a magic seed. Use the following as a title: «Si yo tuviera una semilla mágica . . . .» ("If I Had a Magic Seed . . . .")

3. *Popcorn Blossoms:* Have the students make flower blossoms with tinted popcorn. Have them shake the popped popcorn with powdered tempera paints in brown paper bags. Let the children glue tinted popcorn on small twigs glued onto construction paper. They may create group poems about their blooming trees.

4. *Newspaper Dip:* Have children dip crumpled newspaper into paint and dab it onto construction paper. After they let the construction paper dry, they can cut out kites, butterflies or other spring objects. These can be used as book covers with creative spring titles.

5. *Sensory Booklet:* Have the students go outside to take a good look and to feel spring. Later, have them write sensory descriptions of spring to place in sensory booklets.

6. *Marble Painting:* Have the students place a cut-out paper shape of a butterfly, a flower, or any other spring object in a shallow cardboard box. Then have them put several paint-covered marbles in each box. Let the children roll the marbles back and forth. The marbles leave a trail of color on the paper. Use as the cover for a book of creative writing and illustrations titled «Los signos de la primavera» ("The Signs of Spring"). Display on a bulletin board with the same title.

SCIENCE

1. *Paper Towel Planting:* Let the students place several bean seeds between sheets of paper toweling. Have them cover the towels with plastic wrap to keep the moisture in and place seeds in areas that vary from dark to very sunny. Children may keep a record of the seed growth in their science logs.

2. *Seed Collection:* Have children bring in seeds for a collection of different seeds. The seeds may be placed on a bulletin board or chart along with a picture of the fruit it produces. Children may also place seeds in envelopes with pictures of fruit on the outside along with pertinent information on planting.

3. *Fruit Salad:* Prepare a fruit salad with one of the activities being to locate all of the different types of seeds found in the fruit. Allow children to sort and graph seeds by color, texture, size, and shape. Children may write the recipe as the salad is prepared.

El verano / **Summer**

In summer, the part of the earth where you live is tilted towards the sun. It is a time of plentiful fruits, vegetables, cold drinks and outdoor fun.

CREATIVE DRAMATICS

1. *Pantomime Situations:* Have children pantomime the following activities often seen during the summer:

   - wading in the shallow water in a swimming pool
   - running through sprinklers
   - picking apricots, peaches, or other summer fruit
   - watering the lawn
   - resting under a shady tree with the breeze cooling their skin
   - sunbathing
   - building sandcastles

2. *Summer Discussion:* Brainstorm with the children about the summer. Have the children take an imaginary trip to the beach to cool off. Have them take off their shoes and stroll along, pretending to be on the sand. Have them wiggle their toes in the "sand." Encourage creative descriptions of their experiences on the sandy beach.

3. *I'm a Wave:* Have students pretend to be waves and roll onto the shore. Show them make the motion of a wave by curling and uncurling the spine. Have them ride the waves and move with the force of a wave hitting their bodies.

4. *Hot Summer Day:* Have students make believe they are playing on a hot summer day. Have the children show how we wipe off our perspiration, how slowly we walk, how tired and thirsty we become. Allow children to describe what they are wearing and what they feel like eating or drinking. Allow children to pantomime what they do to keep cool:

   - walking barefoot in the cool sand
   - standing near a fan
   - sitting near the ocean
   - sitting near an open window
   - drinking something cold
   - washing their faces with cold water
   - having a water-balloon fight

ART AND WRITING

1. *Summer Chart:* Create a chart titled «*¿Les gusta el verano?*» ("Do You Like Summer?") Allow children to write their names under the happy face for yes or under the sad face for no. Allow children to express their feelings as to why the answer is yes or no. Allow them to illustrate and write a few sentences telling of the good and bad things of summer. Share and collect their creations for a class book. Allow the class to decide on a title.

2. *Magnetic Fishing:* Let the children go "fishing." Cut out fish shapes from cardboard. Have the children color them and attach magnetic strips. Have them tie paper clips onto pieces of string and attach them to sticks. Allow more mature children to research different kinds of fish and attach their names to the cut-out fish. When a fish is caught, the children may share the information about that particular catch.

3. *Mosaic Fish:* Have the students cut a large fish pattern out of heavy cardboard. Working in small groups, have the children apply white glue to cardboard, a small area at a time, and then add corn, split peas, navy beans, and rice to make designs. Have children write about a talking or imaginary fish that they caught.

4. *Paper-Plate Fish:* Have the students create paper-plate fish or shellfish. Children may glue small paper plates together, concave sides in, and add features with any odds and ends available. These may be used on a class bulletin board with blue fingerpainting as the background for the sea creatures. Share sea poems and have children create their own poems about sea creatures.

MATH

1. *Watermelon Math:* Allow children to estimate the width of a watermelon with all of the children cutting strings the length of their estimates. They can also estimate how many seeds their slices contain and confirm their estimates by counting the seeds.

   Have children create watermelons by cutting large green half-circles and slightly smaller red half-circles from construction paper. Tell them to place the smaller red half-circles on the green half circles and glue on real watermelon seeds to produce slices of construction-paper watermelon. Children may write the directions for making the construction-paper watermelons, using the correct measurements for each item.

SCIENCE

1. *Hula-Hoop Bubble:* In a child's plastic pool, pour liquid dishwashing soap into the water to make suds. Have one child at a time, wearing a bathing suit, get into the pool, and stand in the center of a hula-hoop. Have them lift the hula-hoop and it will form a bubble with the child inside. Give the children a number of objects of different shapes—plastic strawberry baskets, bottomless styrofoam cups, geometric stencils cut from styrofoam. Have them compare the sizes and shapes of the bubbles. Have students observe the colors of the prism and the effect that a breeze has on the bubbles. Have them record their observations in their science logs.

2. *Insect Book:* Summer being such a busy time for insects allows for a plentiful supply. Provide pictures and information about insects. Have each child make up a list of questions to be answered and choose an insect to illustrate. The answers and illustrations may become a class book.

Las estaciones

¿Cómo te llamas, hermosa niña?
Me llamo Primavera.
Yo traigo los pájaros y las flores.
Cuando llego los árboles se cubren de hojas nuevas y
el labrador echa la semilla en el surco.

¿Quién eres tú?
Soy el Verano.
Conmigo viene el calor.
Cuando llego los pájaros cantan en sus nidos
y las abejas hacen su panal.

¿Cómo te llamas, niño?
Mi nombre es Otoño.
A mi me acompañan siempre las nubes y la lluvia.
Yo pinto los árboles y los campos de color de oro.

¿Quién eres tu, niño?
Soy el Invierno.
Cuando llego los pajaritos se van.
Los niños se ponen sus abrigos y no salen a jugar.
Yo quito las hojas secas de los árboles para que cubran
las pequeñas plantas.

Amado Nervo

Hojitas de otoño

Las hojas de otoño,
de lindos colores
se caen con el viento,
en leve rumor.

Se ven tan hermosas
vestidas de gala,
como mariposas
bañadas de sol.

Anónimo

Cuadro de primavera

(sung to the tune of "Vuelo de
pájaros")

Ha despertado la tierra
de su sueño invernal
los pajaritos alegres
cantan sin cesar.

Y en sus cantos ellos dicen
primavera, primavera
ha llegado ya.

Anónimo

Frío

Hoy en la mañana
no ha salido el sol
hace tanto frío
que entumido estoy.

Para calentarme
yo quiero jugar
a manos calientes
también a brincar.

Anónimo

Invierno

Suéter, abrigo
guantes y gorra,
botas de cuero
yo me pondré,
y con la nieve
haré un muñeco
y en un trineo
me subiré;
pues quiero darle
la bienvenida
al blanco invierno
que siempre trae
dulces, regalos,
dicha, alegría,
amor, ternura,
unión y paz.

Anónimo

MY OWN CREATIVE TEACHING IDEAS FOR UNIT ELEVEN

Books: _____

_____

_____

_____

_____

_____

Ideas: _____

_____

_____

_____

_____

_____

_____

_____

_____

_____

_____

_____

_____

_____

_____

_____

UNIT TWELVE

OBSERVANDO MI MUNDO

OBSERVING MY WORLD

Providing enriching experiences for children should be the foundation upon which our instruction is based. Science can help teachers integrate all learning into experiences children can see, hear, touch, understand and remember. The earth's elements—earth, air, water, and fire—as presented in J.M. Parramón's books, are a means of using what children know so that familiar experiences are integrated with new interactions in their world.

ELEMENTO: LA TIERRA
ELEMENT: EARTH

CONCEPTS AND VALUES

1. The earth is larger than what children may imagine.
2. The earth is made up of many environments.
3. People live differently in different environments.
4. Earth as a planet is part of a larger universe.
5. We must keep our earth clean.

MAIN SELECTION

Before reading the Main Selection aloud, take your students through the Literature Input and Observation/Experience phases which follow.

J.M. Parramón. Illustrated by Carme Solé Vendrell.

La tierra.
New York: Barron's Educational Series, 1985.

A simple text and beautiful watercolor illustrations allow children to achieve a greater understanding of their world.

I. LITERATURE INPUT: *La tierra*

Select five or more titles from the following list to read aloud. Read at least one selection per day to the students. Make available and incorporate the suggested titles for voluntary independent reading. Titles marked with * are Spanish translations of the original English story; titles marked with + are recommended for more proficient listeners.

1. Catchpole, Clive. *Colección mundo vivo.* Spain: Ediciones Generales Anaya, 1985. The books in this collection explore the natural habitats of animals, plants, and insects: *Desiertos, Junglas, Montañas,* and *Praderas.*

2. *Colección el hombre y la naturaleza: El campo y sus productos.* Spain: Editorial Hymsa, 1984. This beautifully illustrated selection shows country life and all that is produced there to serve our needs.

3. *Colección los elementos: La tierra.* Spain: Ediciones Generales Anaya, 1985. This beautifully illustrated book explores the element "*la tierra.*"

4. *Colección Piñata: El campo y la ciudad.* México: Piñata, 1985. The country and city are beautifully compared with illustrations that are appealing and highly appropriate.

+ 5. Denou, Violeta. *Colección el hombre y la naturaleza: La tierra y sus riquezas.* Editorial Hymsa, 1984. This well-illustrated book about the earth is a good selection for more mature learners.

*6. Flores, Rosa. *Caracolitos: El agricultor es un amigo.* Oklahoma: Economy Company, 1979. The importance of what a farmer does and how it affects our lives is simply and beautifully shown.

*7. —. *Caracolitos: Una ciudad limpia.* We have a responsibility to keep our world a clean place to live.

*8. —. *Caracolitos: Contaminación y solución.* This book shows ways that we pollute our world and suggests things that we can do to prevent and solve our pollution problems.

*9. —. *Caracolitos: Nuestras tierras.* This book describes and illustrates different environments found in the United States.

+10. Herrera, Miguel Angel, and Julieta Fierro. *Colección nuestro mundo: La tierra.* México: Sistemas Técnicas de Edición, S.A. de C.V., 1987. This book poses and then answers some interesting questions about the earth.

11. Ortells, Fernando. *Colección Simón*. Spain: Editorial Alfredo Ortells, 1985. In *Simón en Japón,* Simón visits Japan and the volcano, Mt. Fujiyama. In *Simón en Africa,* Simón is given a tour by a monkey who introduces him to typical African animals.

12. Palombini, Ugo. *El campo*. Spain: Editorial Everest, S.A., 1980. This book describes life in rural areas, including people as well as plant and animal life.

13. —. *El mar*. Spain: Editorial Everest, S.A., 1980. This book describes life for people as well as plants and animals in and around the sea.

14. —. *Carlos montañero*. Spain: Editorial Everest, S.A., 1982. Carlos looks at the changing earth as he explores mountain environments.

*15. Parramón, J. M.. Illustrated by María Rius. *El campo*. New York: Barron's Educational Series, 1987. This description of the country has beautiful illustrations.

*16. —. *La ciudad*. New York: Barron's Educational Series, 1987. This book describes the abundant activity commonly found in the city through interesting, lively illustrations.

*17. —. *La montaña*. New York: Barron's Educational Series, 1987. This description of a mountain and its scenery has wonderful illustrations.

*18. —. *La vida bajo la tierra*. New York: Barron's Educational Series, 1987. This book illustrates and describes animal life under the earth.

*19. —. *La vida sobre la tierra*. New York: Barron's Educational Series, 1987. This book depicts life on the surface of the earth for animals as well as humans.

20. *¿Qué es . . . la madera?* Spain: Interediciones J.M., 1981. Trees in our world and their usefulness as sources of wood are well-illustrated and explained to the reader.

+*21. Rydell, Wendy. *Colección quiero conocer: Las islas*. México: Sistemas Técnicas de Edición, S.A. de C.V., 1988. The history, formation, and inhabitants of islands are explored. Information and illustrations are very appealing to children.

22. Solano Flores, Guillermo. *El campo*. México: Editorial Trillas, S.A., 1985. This book depicts life in the country with animals and plants shown in their natural habitats.

*23. Spier, Peter. *Gente*. Venezuela: Ediciones Maria Di Mase, 1980. This book beautifully illustrates and describes similarities and differences among people throughout the world.

RELATED TITLES IN ENGLISH FOR SECOND LANGUAGE ACQUISITION

Branley, Franklin M. *What Makes Day and Night*. New York: Harper and Row, 1986.

Branley, Franklin M. *Volcanos*. New York: Harper and Row, 1986.

Cole, Joanna. *The Magic School Bus inside the Earth*. New York: Scholastic, 1987.

Lewis, Thomas P. *Hill of Fire*. New York: Harper and Row, 1971.

II. OBSERVATION/EXPERIENCE: *La tierra*
(Class Session One)

Guide students in the following observation/experience sequence to set the stage for reading the Main Selection.

Focus: What is the earth?

1. Provide a white sheet of construction paper and have students draw a map of what they think our earth looks like.

2. Following the drawing activity, show them a globe and ask them what the blue, brown and green colors represent. Ask if they have the blue oceans, brown mountains, and green lands in their drawings. Have them compare their illustrations with the globe.

3. Tell them that in the text, *La tierra*, they will learn that the earth is full of wonderful things and places to see, hear, touch and explore.

4. On two separate charts, record a list of facts (assumptions) they know about the earth, and those questions they would like to have answered. Following the text, have the children discuss whether their predictions were correct. (Record answers to their questions as provided through children's discovery).

III. READ AND DISCUSS THE MAIN SELECTION: *La tierra*
(Class Session One)

Read the Main Selection from page 160 to the students. Highlight the unit's theme by relating this story to other selections from the Literature Input list on pages 160 - 161. Then, guide students in discussing some of the following questions.

1. *¿Creen que toda la tierra se ve igual?* (Expand on different environments.) (Do you think all the earth looks the same?)

2. *¿Han ido ustedes alguna vez al mar o a un río? Describan lo que vieron.* (Have you ever been to the ocean or a river? Describe what you saw.)

3. *¿Han vivido en el campo? ¿Cómo es distinto el campo a la ciudad?* (Have you ever lived in the country? How is the country different from the city?)

4. *¿Por qué es importante permitirle a los animales que vivan en sus ambientes naturales?* (Why is it important to allow animals to live in their natural environments?)

5. *¿En qué son diferentes los niños de todo el mundo? ¿En que se parecen?* (Teacher may record ideas.) (How are children different all over the earth? How are children alike?)

IV. "WHAT IF" STORY STRETCHER: *La tierra*
(Class Session Two)

Next, re-read the Main Selection and choose one or more of the following questions to develop students' critical thinking skills. Story stretchers may also prompt discussion, drama or writing activities.

1. *Si pudieran escoger un lugar en donde vivir, ¿cuál sería? ¿Por qué?* (If you could choose one type of environment to live in, which one would it be? Why?)

2. *Si no cuidamos el ambiente donde vivimos, ¿qué pasaría?* (If we don't take care of our environment, what would happen to it?)

3. *Si pudieran cambiar una cosa en nuestra tierra, ¿cuál sería?* (If you could change one thing about our earth, what would it be?)

4. *Si la tierra ya no nos diera ni agua, ni comida, ni materia prima para elaborar nuestras necesidades, ¿cómo podríamos vivir?* (If the earth no longer gave us water, food, or raw materials to make our goods, how would we be able to live?)

5. *¿Qué pasaría si no hubiera ni sol, ni luna, ni viento en la tierra?* (What would happen if there were no sun, moon, or wind on the earth?)

V. INTEGRATING OTHER DISCIPLINES: *La tierra*
(Class Session Three and Ongoing)

The following activities are designed to enhance children's response to literature and expand *beyond* the story and its theme. The variety of activities gives teachers and students an opportunity to choose those most appropriate.

CREATIVE DRAMATICS

1. *Pantomime Animals:* Have children pantomime different land and sea animals while observers guess in which environment they would be found.

2. *Earth's Rotation:* Have children demonstrate their understanding of the earth's rotation by having them become the earth, sun and moon.

3. *Environments:* Assign different environments to small groups—desert, beach, mountains, forest, plains. Have them plan and then pantomime what they might do in these settings, while observers guess the environment. Have some students pantomime the trees and animals indigenous to the environment.

4. *Exploring an Object:* Have students pretend that they have never been on earth and that everything on earth—insects, animals, water, people, grass—is totally unfamiliar. Have them pantomime one thing they would like to see, touch, hear, smell, taste, and learn about. Let the observers guess the object being explored.

5. *Flying High:* Allow children to be birds, planes, kites, or balloons. They are to describe the earth as they see it from above—grass with cows grazing, trees in a forest, oceans and fishing boats, a polluted river.

ART AND WRITING

1. *Rock Craft:* Using rocks, have children paint features and add other craft items. Then instruct children to write about a "day in the life of a rock," what a rock might say to the seasons of the year, or a dialogue between two rocks in a rock collection.

2. *Rock Painting:* Have children paint objects, designs, or characters on large rocks. Tell them to imagine that the rocks have magical qualities and to write about all the fantastic things they can do.

3. *Sand-Painting Postcards:* Have the students create sand-painting postcards. First, have them draw postcards. Then, have them brush on glue and sprinkle the postcard with sand. After they shake off any loose sand, have them spray the card with clear varnish so that the sand will not rub off. Have students write a greeting to a friend from a sandy beach of their choosing.

4. *Conservation "Plea":* Have children write a "plea" for the earth, expressing the importance of conservation. Let them illustrate what needs to be conserved.

5. *Earth Speaks Out:* Have students think of the earth as if it were personified; e.g., «*Miren como me trata la gente.*» ("Look how people treat me.") «*No me contaminen.*» ("Do not contaminate me.") Have them write what the earth would say to them and what they would reply. Have them illustrate how this idea would appear in a picture book.

6. *Earth Book:* Have students fold an 18" x 11" piece of yellow construction paper in half. Duplicate Figures M1-5 (pages 185 - 189). Use M1 as a front cover and have children cut out the oval window. Duplicate M2 on brown (earth), M3 on green (plants), M4 on blue (water), and M5 on white (sun and wind) construction paper. Have children cut along the dotted lines and place M2, M3, M4, and M5 in sequence. Staple the booklet together. Children may color M5 to highlight the sun and wind, or they may cut out the sun so that the yellow back cover of the booklet shows through. Have students write about the earth and its features on M5.

SCIENCE

1. *Dirt Exploration:* Have the students explore dirt of different textures and describe what they find in dirt—insects, dead leaves, pebbles, bones. Bury a surprise object and see if children can guess if it was artificially placed or not. Children may record "findings" in their science logs.

2. *Earth and Water:* Use sand and water to show how water affects the earth, from forming rivers to oceans. With the children, discuss the observation and and have them record or illustrate facts in their science logs.

3. *Earth's Rotation:* With a globe and a light, show how the earth rotates as it revolves around the sun. Discuss the observation, allowing children to touch the globe. Ask students if they have ever wondered how night and day come. Explain that night comes when the earth turns away from the sun. Ask students if they think that night and day come at the same time for people living in other parts of the world. Explain that when we are sleeping, people in other parts of the world are busy, and when they are sleeping, we are busy. Have them record facts in their science logs.

4. *Earth's Size:* To develop the children's concept of the earth's size in relation to the moon and sun, have students draw the earth, moon and sun. Tell them to draw them showing their relative sizes.

   Then, show them three balloons—yellow for the sun, white for the moon, and green for the earth. Have them estimate how much each balloon should be inflated. Tie a knot when they say "Stop!" Show them the correct size relationship by inflating another set of balloons. Let them compare their drawings to the balloons and have them draw the accurate size. Let them record facts in their science logs.

5. *Rock Collections:* Have students bring rocks to class and discuss their appearance, size, weight, texture, and color. Have them sort and graph the rocks.

SOCIAL STUDIES

1. *Adapting:* This theme lends itself nicely to the study of different cultures. Talk about how people have had to adapt to given environments all over the world. (National Geographic journals and films are an excellent source of material for this topic.) Have students record facts in their science logs. Discuss how we adapt to the seasons in our environment.

2. *Globe:* Using the globe, allow children to locate oceans, land features, the United States, Mexico, Canada, other continents, and the poles. Let them view the same features on a flat map. Have them draw these features on a round balloon. Let them explain to a partner where such features and countries are located and where they live on the balloon.

3. *Earth's Environments:* Provide large pieces of butcher paper to have students create different environments on earth such as forests, jungles, deserts, and plains. A variety of projects can be carried out using these created environments:

   Students may draw houses and place them in the environments of their choice with an explanation about why living in a given environment would be different or interesting.

   Children may illustrate people living in these environments and the clothing they would use. Children may create a catalogue of clothing for a given environment.

   Children may discuss, compare, and, if possible, taste the foods grown and eaten in the different environments.

   Children may place animal pictures in the different environments. Pictures may be children's drawings or photographs cut from magazines. Allow children to discuss how the inhabitant is suited to the environment.

   Children may research and obtain factual information about particular environments to compare them to others.

4. *Map:* Provide a large black and white map of the earth showing only outlines of continents and oceans. Have students paint or color the oceans blue and the continents brown. Allow for some conceptualization of the earth's physical features such as mountains, valleys, rivers, lakes and sandy beaches. These may be identified and discussed using a large map which shows some of these features. Allow them to label the continents, oceans and other important features.

ELEMENTO: EL AGUA
ELEMENT: WATER

CONCEPTS AND VALUES

1. There are many uses for water.
2. All living things need water.
3. Water has different forms.
4. Water affects things.
5. Water must be conserved.

MAIN SELECTION

Before reading the Main Selection aloud, take your students through the Literature Input and Observation/Experience phases which follow.

J.M. Parramón. Illustrated by Carme Solé Vendrell.

El agua.
New York: Barron's Educational Series Inc., 1985.

Through a simple text and beautiful watercolor illustrations, water is discussed, including all the different places it is found and its uses.

I. LITERATURE INPUT: *El agua*

Select five or more titles from the following list to read aloud. Read at least one selection per day to the students. Make available and incorporate the suggested titles for voluntary independent reading. Titles marked with * are Spanish translations of the original English story; titles marked with + are recommended for more proficient listeners.

+*1. Adler, David. *El mar y sus maravillas.* México: Sistemas Técnicas de Edición, S.A. de C.V., 1987. This wonderful exploration of the ocean is written at a child's interest level.

+2. *Colección los elementos: Agua.* Spain: Ediciones Generales Anaya, 1985. This is a beautifully illustrated exploration of the element *el agua.*

+3. Denou, Violeta. *Colección el hombre y la naturaleza: El río.* Spain: Ediciones Hymsa, 1984. A river and all the ways it touches our lives are beautifully illustrated.

+*4. Dickinson, Jane. *El agua.* México: Sistemas Técnicas de Edición, S.A. de C.V., 1987. This exploration of water has information at a level highly appropriate for children.

*5. Flores, Rosa. *Caracolitos: Agua para todos.* Oklahoma: Economy Company, 1979. The uses and conservation of water are discussed in this book.

*6. —. *Caracolitos: El árbol de Rita.* Oklahoma: Economy Company, 1979. El señor García explains to Rita what a tree needs to grow from a small seed into a beautiful tree.

7. García Sánchez, J. L. *Soy una gota.* Spain: Ediciones Altea, 1974. This book traces the life cycle of a drop of water and explores our uses of water.

8. Giron, Nicole. *El agua.* México: Editorial Patria, S.A., 1981. This book shows the different uses of water.

*9. Kraus, Robert. *José, el gran ayudante.* New York: Windmill Books, 1977. José, an octopus, loves to help everyone in his sea community.

10. Larreula, Eric. *Colección Grao: El arca de Noe.* Spain: Editorial Teide, S.A., 1984. If children have ever wondered how the world's animals fit into Noah's ark and what they did during their forty-day journey, this charming story will spark their imagination.

*11. Manley, Deborah. *La playa.* Spain: Editorial Molino, 1980. Activities that can take place in a day at the beach are described.

*12. Negrete, A. L. *El agua.* México: Editorial Trillas, S.A., 1986. This book tells us, in a simple manner, about the need for water, its uses, and its forms.

+13. Palombini, Ugo. *Carlos marino.* Spain: Editorial Everest, S.A., 1982. The ocean's secrets are revealed as Carlos takes us on a trip.

*14. Parramón, J. M. Illustrated by María Rius. *El mar.* New York: Barron's Educational Series, 1986. The vivid and thought-provoking illustrations depict life near the sea.

*15. —. *La vida en el mar.* New York: Barron's Educational Series, 1987. This book explores life in the sea.

16. *¿Qué es . . . el agua?* Spain: Interediciones, J.M., 1981. The many uses of water in our daily lives is discussed.

17. Solano Flores, Guillermo. *La lluvia.* México: Editorial Trillas, S.A., 1985. This beautifully illustrated book recounts the many things that rain touches.

18. Vásquez, Zoraida, and Julieta Montelongo. *El naranjo que no daba naranjas.* México: Editorial Trillas, S.A., 1984. An Indian boy wants his orange tree to bear fruit, but he does not give it water. When the orange tree is finally watered, it produces fruit.

+19. Wade, Harlan. *El agua.* Wisconsin: Raintree Children's Books, 1979. Water is explored through interesting illustrations.

RELATED TITLES IN ENGLISH FOR SECOND LANGUAGE ACQUISITION

Bartlett, May. *Water, Rain and Hail.* New York: Thomas Y. Crowell Company, 1983.

+ Cole, Joanna. *The Magic School Bus at the Waterworks.* New York: Scholastic, 1986.

Gans, Roma. *Water for Dinosaurs and You.* New York: Thomas Y. Crowell Company, 1972.

Garelick, May. *Where Does the Butterfly Go When It Rains?* Massachusetts: Addison-Wesley, 1961.

II. OBSERVATION/EXPERIENCE: *El agua*
(Class Session One)

Guide students in the following observations/experience sequence to set the stage for reading the Main Selection.

Focus: What is water?

1. Stimulate children's thinking by asking if water always looks, feels, and smells the same. Provide ice and, as the discussion takes place, allow it to melt. If possible, and with caution, boil water and allow the children the opportunity to see water as vapor. Use a mirror or paper over the steam to demonstrate that steam is only water in another form.

2. Elicit from children those facts they know about water and those they would like to know. Record ideas on two separate charts.

3. Tell them that in a book titled *El agua,* they will learn about the many uses of water and the places where it is found.

4. Following the reading and the extended experiences relating to water, have children discuss whether their previously recorded known assumptions were correct. In answer to information children wanted to learn, record the newly learned facts on charts as answers are provided through children's discovery.

III. READ AND DISCUSS THE MAIN SELECTION: *El agua*
(Class Session One)

Read the Main Selection from page 166 to the students. Highlight the unit's theme by relating this story to other selections from the Literature Input list on pages 166 - 167. Then, guide students in discussing some of the following questions.

1. *¿Por qué es importante tomar agua?* (Why is it important to drink water?)

2. *¿Cómo llega el agua a nuestras casas?* (How does water get to our homes?)

3. *¿Qué cosas necesitan agua en nuestro mundo?* (What things need water in our world?)

4. *¿De dónde viene el agua de un río y a dónde va?* (Where does the water in a river come from and where does it go?)

5. *¿En qué forma hace el agua que nuestro mundo sea más bello?* (How does water make our world more beautiful?)

IV. "WHAT IF" STORY STRETCHER: *El agua*
(Class Session Two)

Next, re-read the Main Selection and choose one or more of the following questions to develop students' critical thinking skills. Story stretchers may also prompt discussion, drama or writing activities.

1. *¿Qué pasaría si no hubiera agua en nuestro mundo? Describan nuestro mundo sin agua.* (What would happen if there were no water in our world? Describe our world without water.)

2. *Cuenten que pasaría si lloviera durante dos semanas. ¿Qué harían con su tiempo?* (Tell what would happen if it rained for two weeks. What would you do with your time?)

3. *¿Qué tal si solamente pudieran usar una taza de agua al día? ¿Cómo utilizarían sus porciones?* (What if you were told that you could only use one cup of water each day? How would you use it?)

4. *¿Qué harían si toda el agua se congelara? ¿Qué podrían hacer para convertirla de sólida a líquida?* (What would you do if all our water froze? What could you do to change it from a solid to a liquid?)

5. *Si pudieran vivir como peces en el mar, ¿qué verían y qué harían?* (If you could live as fish in the sea, what would you see and do?)

V. INTEGRATING OTHER DISCIPLINES: *El agua*
(Class Session Three and Ongoing)

The following activities are designed to enhance children's response to literature and expand *beyond* the story and its theme. The variety of activities gives teachers and students an opportunity to choose those most appropriate.

CREATIVE DRAMATICS

1. *Pour Me:* In pairs, have children pantomime being water poured into a glass. The glass is held by one child while the other child is the water being poured into the glass. Have them show how they would handle a glass of water filled to the brim.

2. *Acting Out Situations:* Have the children imagine that they are sticks lying on the ground. It begins to rain. It rains hard. What happens to them?

   They are raindrops falling from the clouds. They fall in many different places. What happens to them?

3. *Brainstorm and Pantomime:* Have students pantomime the things we do with water:

   • drinking water
   • swimming
   • brushing teeth
   • putting out a fire
   • scrubbing the floor
   • washing ourselves
   • washing things
   • running in the sprinklers
   • watering plants

ART AND WRITING

1. *Raindrop Biography:* In a raindrop-shaped book, have children write as raindrops and tell of their adventures.

2. *Water Mural:* Using diluted tempera paints, have groups make a large mural showing different bodies of water. Have them write about real or imaginary experiences that they have had in one of the bodies of water.

3. *Water-Use Chart:* Provide magazines for students to find pictures of water being used. Have the students divide the pictures into three groups: water used for work, water used for food, and water used for play. Have them put the pictures on the charts. Have cooperative groups make lists of different ways that they used water the day before. Have them write a prioritized list of how they would use water if they had a very limited supply. Graph the children's responses.

4. *Magic Goggles:* Put goggles on children and have them look at different objects placed in a small tub of water. Have them write descriptions of changes in objects under water for a long time.

5. *Bubble Trouble:* Have students write an imaginary adventure about getting into trouble while traveling around in a giant bubble.

6. *Deserts and Jungles:* Using pictures or films, show and discuss the differences between deserts and jungles. Emphasize the importance of water in each of these environments. Have the students illustrate and write conversations that would fit the following situations:

    • a raindrop and a frog living in a pond
    • a leaf and the morning dew in the jungle
    • a bird and a cactus living in the desert
    • a waterhole and a traveler on foot in the desert

7. *Magic Swimming Pool:* Have students imagine that the water in a swimming pool has magical properties—an ability to shrink, expand, disappear, and transform. Using one of these magical properties, let them create and illustrate their own stories.

8. *Paper Boat:* Have students make paper boats by folding newspapers. Tell them to imagine they are the boats and that they are floating in a stream, river, or ocean. Have them write about their adventures.

9. *Ice Pictures:* Allow children to make large outlines of objects of their choice. Have them place tempera (either dry or liquid) within the outline of the object and use ice cubes as the paint brushes. Allow this to prompt sensory descriptive writing.

SCIENCE

1. *Evaporation:* Provide children with large paint brushes and buckets of water. Have them paint outdoor furniture, the side of the building, and sidewalk. Have them make their own puddles and then draw chalk rings around the puddles. Periodically, let them observe what happens to the puddles. With students, discuss why they think their water paintings and puddles evaporated. They may record observations in their science logs.

2. *Water Volume:* Use an uncovered glass of water marked with a rubber band (or permanent marker) at the water line. Have students observe the water line every day and discuss where the water has gone.

Have students observe an increase in volume as water turns into a solid when frozen. Draw a line on the container or place a rubber band around the container along the water line. Have them record their observations in their science logs.

3. *Sink or Float:* Place ice cubes in a glass and pour water over them. The ice rises because the ice cubes are less dense than water. Collect items brought in by children and have them predict what they think will sink and what will float. Provide a tub of water to have them check if their predictions were correct. Allow them to record facts in their science logs.

4. *Dirty Water:* Provide a microscope, an eyedropper, and slides for children to have a microscopic view of dirty water. Furnish a bowl so that the entire class can wash their hands. Have them suction water with the dropper and place droplets on a slide. Let them observe their germs swimming like little creatures. Have them describe and illustrate the shapes they observe and record their observations in their science logs. Have them paint imaginary germs, give them creative names, and write stories.

5. *Liquid Floats:* To show students that liquid can float, provide empty juice bottles, and the following liquids: colored water, salad oil, petroleum, liquid wax, and paint. With supervision, have them pour three ounces of water and one tablespoon of each of the remaining liquids into bottles. After they have closed the lids tightly, have them turn the bottles upside down and observe the stratified liquids. Discuss why the layers exist. They may write observations in their science logs.

6. *Absorption:* To focus on the principle that some materials absorb water, provide different materials—rubber, waxed paper, sponges, paper towels, construction paper, tissues, cotton, cardboard. Allow children to test absorbency with eyedroppers and water. Encourage children, in groups, to describe the results and record in their science logs.

7. *Dissolving:* To emphasize the principle that some materials dissolve in water, provide children with a chart with columns for materials that dissolve and materials that do not dissolve. Allow children to test provided materials—salt, baking soda, beans, flour, sugar cubes, flour, butter. Ask questions to help children focus on the results, and allow them to test other materials of their choosing. Have the children write the name of the material in the proper column of the chart or place the testing cup in the proper column. Children may record their results in their science logs.

ELEMENTO: EL AIRE
ELEMENT: AIR

CONCEPTS AND VALUES

1. We and all living things need air to survive.
2. We use air in many ways.
3. Air takes up space.
4. Air moves things.
5. It is important to keep our air clean.

MAIN SELECTION

Before reading the Main Selection aloud, take your students through the Literature Input and Observation/Experience phases which follow.

Parramón, J.M. Illustrated by María Rius.

El aire.
New York: Barron's Educational Series, 1985.

Beautiful illustrations and simple phrases paint a vivid picture of the importance of air in our lives and its many uses.

I.   LITERATURE INPUT: *El aire*

Select five or more titles from the following list to read aloud. Read at least one selection per day to the students. Make available and incorporate the suggested titles for voluntary independent reading. Titles marked with * are Spanish translations of the original English story; titles marked with + are recommended for more proficient listeners.

+1. *Colección los elementos: Aire.* Spain: Ediciones Anaya, 1985. This is a beautifully illustrated exploration of the element *el aire.*

2. Díaz, Oralia A. *El jardinero.* Guatemala: Editorial Piedra Santa, 1987. A gardener dreams about being a hummingbird. In his dream, he fails to praise the wind, so it destroys all the beautiful flowers. Awakened by the strong wind, the gardener gives due praise to the wind.

*3. Ets, Marie Hall. *Gilberto y el viento.* New York: The Viking Press, 1963. A beautifully illustrated story relates Gilberto's experiences with the wind.

4. Fujikawa, Gyo. *El vuelo del barrilete.* Argentina: Editorial Atlántida, 1981. This beautifully illustrated story tells how Nicolas lost his friend's kite. When asked what happened to the kite, he uses his imagination to create exciting events that never took place.

5. García Sánchez, J. L. *Soy el aire.* Spain: Ediciones Altea, 1974. The air describes himself and all that he causes and changes.

+6. Posadas, Carmen de. *El Señor Viento Norte.* Spain: Ediciones S.M., 1984. María and Arturo decide to try to convince Señor Viento Norte to change to a breeze because it is spring and winter is over.

*7. Mayne, William. *El ratón que voló.* Spain: Editorial Anaya, 1987. Orejitas, a mouse, is inspired by the flight of a bat and wants to fly. As the result of a very dangerous situation, he experiences his fantasy of flight.

8. Negre, María I. *El cuento del flautín.* Spain: Editorial La Galera S.A., 1975. The wind makes it possible for a boy to get a flute from a dog in exchange for some bread.

9. Parramón, J. M. Illustrated by María Rius. *La vida en el aire.* New York: Barron's Educational Series, 1987. This book beautifully illustrates life found in the air.

10. Pierini, Fabio, and Carme Solé Vendrell. *El niño que quería volar.* Spain: Editorial Miñón, S.A., 1982. The beautiful flight of a bird inspires a child to want to fly. He searches for an answer from books, people, and animals, but to no avail. He finally finds contentment in being himself.

+11. *¿Qué es . . . el aire?* Spain: Interediciones, J.M., 1981. This book illustrates and describes the different qualities of air.

*12. Scarry, Richard. *Mi primer gran libro del aire.* Spain: Editorial Bruguera, S.A., 1975. The characters explore all the various ways air affects our lives.

13. Solano Flores, Guillermo. *El viento.* México: Editorial Trillas, S.A., 1985. The wind is a force that causes many things to move as demonstrated through illustrations.

14. Zimnik, Reiner. *El viaje en globo de Guillermo.* Spain: Editorial Miñón, S.A., 1981. Guillermo has an incredible adventure in the air with his bunch of balloons.

RELATED TITLES IN ENGLISH FOR SECOND LANGUAGE ACQUISITION

Addison-Wesley Big Book Program. *How the Moon Got in the Sky.* Reading, MA: Addison-Wesley, 1989.

Branley, Franklin M. *Air Is All Around You.* New York: Thomas Y. Crowell, 1979.

Hatch, Shirley. *Wind Is to Feel.* New York: Coward, McCann & Geoghegan, 1973.

Lloyd, David. *Air.* New York: Dial Press, 1982.

II. OBSERVATION/EXPERIENCE: *El aire*
(Class Session One)

Guide students in the following observations/experience sequence to set the stage for reading the Main Selection.

Focus: What is air?

1. Provide the children with straws, glasses of water, and balloons. Say to the children:

> *Extiendan sus brazos y den vueltas. ¿Sienten el aire pasar? Noten la sensación en sus cabellos.»* (Put your arms out and whirl around. Do you feel the air as it rushes past you? Notice the sensation in your hair.)

Soplen por los popotes contra sus manos. ¿Qué sienten? (Blow through straws onto your hands. What do you feel?)

Soplen por los popotes en los vasos de agua. ¿Sienten el aire? ¿Pueden ver el aire? (Blow through the straws into the glasses of water. Can you feel the air? Can you see the air?)

Inflen los globos y suéltenlos. ¿Qué hizo que los globos se volaran? (Blow up the balloons and let them go. What made the balloons fly?)

2. Tell students that in a book titled *El aire,* they will learn more about the importance of air and its many uses.

3. Have the students contribute facts that they know about air, and have them ask questions indicating what they would like to know about air. Record them on two separate charts: *«Lo que sé del aire»* ("What I Know About Air") and *«Lo que me gustaría saber del aire»* ("What I Would Like to Know About Air"). As answers are provided through children's discovery, record newly learned facts on charts .

4. Following the reading of the text, have them discuss whether their previously recorded assumptions were correct.

III. READ AND DISCUSS THE MAIN SELECTION: *El aire*
(Class Session One)

Read the Main Selection from page 172 to the students. Highlight the unit's theme by relating this story to other selections from the Literature Input list on pages 172 - 173. Then, guide students in discussing some of the following questions.

1. *¿Quién o qué necesita aire?* (Who or what needs air?)

2. *¿Pueden decirme cuál es la diferencia entre una brisa y el viento? ¿Qué experiencias han tenido con el viento?* (Can you tell me what the difference is between a breeze and the wind? What experiences have you had with the wind?)

3. *¿Han volado alguna vez cometas? Describan sus experiencias.* (Have you ever flown kites? Describe your experiences.)

4. *¿Qué hace que un bote de vela se mueva? ¿Qué lo hace mover más rápido? ¿Qué lo hace mover más despacio?* (What makes a sailboat move? What makes it move faster? What makes it move more slowly?)

5. *¿Qué puede parar la respiración de una persona?* (What can stop a person from breathing?)

IV. "WHAT IF" STORY STRETCHER: *El aire*
(Class Session Two)

Next, re-read the Main Selection and choose one or more of the following questions to develop students' critical thinking skills. Story stretchers may also prompt discussion, drama or writing activities.

1. *Si no hubiera aire, ¿cómo sería diferente nuestro mundo?* (If there were no air, how would our world be different?)

2. *¿Qué tal si el viento les levantara y les llevara consigo? ¿Cómo creen que se sentirían.* (What if the wind were to lift you and carry you away? How do you think you would feel?)

3. *¿Cómo sería si ustedes fueran pájaros?* (What would it be like if you were birds?)

4. *Si tuvieran un ratoncito en una caja encerrada, ¿qué sería necesario para que el ratón se mantuviera vivo?* (If you had a pet mouse in a box with a lid, what would be needed to make sure the mouse would live?)

5. *¿Qué creen ustedes que verían o que se sentirían si estuvieran en un avión?* (What do you think you would see or feel if you were on an airplane?)

V. INTEGRATING OTHER DISCIPLINES: *El aire*
(Class Session Three and Ongoing)

The following activities are designed to enhance children's response to literature and expand *beyond* the story and its theme. The variety of activities gives teachers and students an opportunity to choose those most appropriate.

CREATIVE DRAMATICS

1. *Move with the Wind:* Have children pretend they are one of these: a paper, a leaf, a tree, a bird, or a blade of grass. Ask them to show how they think they would be moved by the wind in each of the following situations as you call out the items.

   • It is calm and then the sun comes out from behind the clouds.
   • March winds blow.
   • The ocean breeze is nearby.

2. *Be a Kite or a Balloon:* Have students improvise being kites or balloons. Have them show and tell what they would do and where they might land.

3. *Pantomime:* Have students imagine themselves in the following situations as you call them out:

   • They are in a hurricane.
   • They try to walk against the wind.
   • They are riding in a car without a top such as a jeep or sportscar.
   • They are sitting under a large fan.
   • They are near an airplane with spinning propellers.
   • They chased their friends all the way home from school.

4. *Moving Like the Wind:* Have students look outside and see if they can find evidence of the wind—smoke, trees, clouds, or leaves moving. Have them move like the objects they observe.

5. *Balloon Pantomime:* Pair students and have one student pretend to be a balloon while the other pretends to blow it up. Let them use their imagination to decide what would happen next.

ART AND WRITING

1. *Paper Airplanes:* Have students make paper airplanes, decorate them, and have a contest for the best long-distance aircraft. Allow them to create adventure stories about the paper airplanes and themselves.

2. *Kite Fun:* In cooperative groups, have the children make and decorate kites or allow them to bring kites from home. Go out and fly them together. Have children name their kites and write of the kites' failures and successes.

3. *What Flies?:* Have children illustrate things that fly—airplanes, birds, insects, balloons, bubbles, kites. With the children, discuss how all these things use air to move. Have them create adventure stories centered around one of the above.

4. *Straw Painting:* Create modern art by allowing children to blow tempera paint onto paper through straws. They may write about what they see in their art to share with the class.

5. *Pinwheels:* Instruct students to take square pieces of paper and draw big "X's" on them. Tell them to place nickels in the middle of the "X's." They should trace around the coin. Have them decorate the pinwheels by coloring triangles different colors. Then tell them to cut the lines that make the "X," but not to cut into the circle that they traced. Have them bend every other corner into the center of the circle. Tell them to put a straight pin carefully through all four corners at the center of the circle and press the pin into the eraser on the end of the pencil.

   Working in pairs have one partner explain to another partner how the pinwheel was made. Then, from memory, have them write the pinwheel instructions for another friend.

6. *Swirl Painting:* Spin art machines are available at most art or toy departments. Have children create their own unique whirl paintings. Have them create a chant about the colors in their paintings.

7. *Parachute:* To make parachutes, have students use 5" x 5" plastic sheets which can be made by cutting plastic garbage bags. Have them tie strings to each corner and then tie the other end of the strings around a small plastic figure such as an army man. Have them throw it up into the air and watch it float down. Tell students to imagine themselves in the parachutes, and to describe, in writing, the view from the sky.

8. *Balloon Launch:* Organize a helium balloon launch commemorating some special occasion; e.g., "poems for all reasons," "let's make our world a better one," "launching a new school year." Let students decorate the balloons with permanent marking pens. Have them write goals, poems, or special thoughts to place inside their balloons before they are blown up. Have them include self-addressed envelopes so that "receivers" can return them.

9. *Kite-Shaped Book:* Instruct students to pretend they are kites flying high in the sky. Have them imagine what they look like, what they see, and how the world looks. Allow them to write their ideas in a kite-shaped book, using crayon resistant media to create an illustration on the cover of the kite book.

10. *Wind Sock:* Have students draw pictures of windy days on 4" x 11-1/2" strips of card stock. Have them glue on five or six colorful crepe paper streamers at the bottom edge and then staple the sides together to form tubes. Have them make three holes and tie

on thin yarn or string. Have them join the strings together and tie knots. Take the wind socks outside to see the wind run through the streamers. Allow them to write poems about the wind and the wind socks.

SCIENCE

1. *What We Breathe:* To focus on the principle that the air we breath is important, guide students in the following activities:

   - Have students jog in place for one minute and ask what they feel coming out of their bodies (air made up of carbon dioxide).
   - Have them hold their breath while you count to fifteen. Ask children how they feel. Discuss the importance of air (oxygen) to our bodies and how our bodies use oxygen.
   - Discuss the use of oxygen tanks by deep sea divers and astronauts. Dramatize using oxygen tanks in these situations. Encourage them to record facts in their science logs.

2. *Air Moves Things:* To focus on the principle that air can move things, play "raising the ball." Provide bendable plastic straws and ping pong balls. Have the students position the straws so that the short ends stick straight up when the children blow. Have them blow very hard into the long ends to raise the balls and trap them in the stream of air. Children may time and graph how long they can keep the balls up.

3. *Air and Fire Experiment:* Engage students in the following experiment involving air: Show students a lit candle and explain that fire needs oxygen. Have them predict what will happen when a jar is placed over the candle. Turn the jar upside down and place it over the candle. Afterward, ask them to explain what happened when the oxygen supply was cut off (the flame was extinguished).

4. *Air Pressure:* Provide a small glass tank, a large glass jar and a flexible plastic tube. Place the jar open end down into a water-filled tank. Have students notice how the water looks inside the jar. Then, tilt the jar just enough to slip the tube under the jar and hold it in place. Blow hard through the other end of the tube. Have students notice what happens inside the water-filled jar. Ask them why they think the water level went down and later came back (air pressure).

   Demonstrating the same principle, provide a bowl of water, a clear plastic cup, and a note with a secret message. Show students the note, but do not read the message. Crumple it up and put it at the bottom of the cup. Turn the cup upside down and put it into the bowl of water. Have students predict what will happen to the note. Pull up the cup and read them the dry note. Repeat the procedure but this time tilt the cup. Have students notice what happens to the note. Ask them why they think the note got wet (air escaped and water entered). Allow them to record air experiment facts in their science logs.

5. *What Needs Air?:* Create an illustration or a chart labeled «*Cosas que necesitan aire/ Cosas que no necesitan aire*» ("Things That Need Air/Things That Do Not Need Air"). Have students bring in objects that need air and others that do not need air. Discuss their characteristics. Graph the children's responses. Have them record the lists in their science logs.

6. *Air and Space:* To emphasize the concept that air takes up space, provide several plastic bags and balloons. Give children the experience of catching air in a plastic bag and inflating balloons. Demonstrate that there is air in the bags and balloons by

allowing the children to fly the balloons or to move paper with the air released from the balloons. They can blow a horn by placing a plastic bag around it and squeezing the bag. Children may record the experiences in their science logs.

SAFETY

1. *Little or No Air:* Discuss safety relating to such hazards as refrigerators, plastic bags and use of barbecues indoors. Have the students write safety bulletins based on the discussion.

ELEMENTO: EL FUEGO
ELEMENT: FIRE

CONCEPTS AND VALUES

1. Fire is necessary in our daily lives.
2. Fire may be destructive.
3. We must learn fire safety.
4. Fire is part of nature.

MAIN SELECTION

Before reading the Main Selection aloud, take your students through the Literature Input and Observation/Experience phases which follow.

Parramón, J. M. Illustrated by María Rius.

El fuego.
New York: Barron's Educational Series, 1985.

Simple phrases and beautiful illustrations of children and the many colors, uses, and dangers of fire make fire a vivid reality.

I.   LITERATURE INPUT: *El fuego*

Select five or more titles from the following list to read aloud. Read at least one selection per day to the students. Make available and incorporate the suggested titles for voluntary independent reading. Titles marked with * are Spanish translations of the original English story; titles marked with + are recommended for more proficient listeners.

1. Alonso, Fernando. *Baira y el fuego.* New Jersey: Santillana, 1982. This book recounts the legend of how people came to possess fire.

2. de Armellada, Fray Cesareo. *El cocuyo y la mora.* Venezuela: Ediciones Ekaré-Banco del Libro, 1978. An Indian legend explains how the firefly came to be black with a light on its tail.

3. Bofill, Francesc. *El dragón del lago.* Spain: Editorial La Galera, S.A., 1979. A fire-breathing dragon eats children and is unconquerable until, magically, a change occurs.

4. Capdevila, Juan. *Nico y Ana quieren ser bomberos.* Spain: Editorial Timún Más, 1984. Nico and Ana are invited by the fire chief to visit the fire station. They also witness several fires and learn about the dangerous life of a firefighter.

*5. Chlad, Dorothy. *Cuando hay un incendio sal para afuera.* Chicago: Children's Press, 1984. This book stresses how dangerous fire can be if proper precautions are not taken.

6. Climent, Elena. *Triste historia del sol.* México: Editorial Trillas, S.A., 1986. The sun is sad and all are concerned. The people cooperatively and compassionately bring things to make him happy.

7. *Colección biblioteca educación infantil: Allí vienen los bomberos*. Spain: Editorial Molino, 1981. Firefighters and their duties are described.

+8. *Colección los elementos: Fuego*. Spain: Ediciones Generales Anaya, 1985. This is a beautifully illustrated exploration of the element *el fuego*.

9. Díaz, Oralia A. *El rayito de sol*. Guatemala: Editorial Piedra Santa, 1984. This is a story of the warm relationship between a little ray of sun and two children.

+10. Gantschev, Ivan. *El volcán*. México: Editorial Trillas, S.A., 1985. This is a well-told tale of an unhappy giant crab and how he convinced the river to try to quiet the volcano, thus causing the volcano to burst.

11. García Sánchez, J. L. *Soy el fuego*. Spain: Ediciones Altea, 1974. This book describes how people perceive fire and the effect that the other elements have on fire.

12. MacDonald, John. *Luz y calor*. Spain: Editorial Molino, 1974. Heat and light are explored in an interesting manner.

+*13. Marcus, Elizabeth. *Colección quiero conocer: Montañas y volcanes*. México: Sistemas Técnicas de Edición, S.A. de C.V., 1987. This book explores the formation of mountains and volcanos.

+14. *¿Qué es . . . el fuego?* Spain. Interediciones J. M., 1981. This book illustrates and describes the characteristics of fire.

15. Roa, Jorge Anaya. *Los bomberos*. México: Editorial Novaro, S.A., 1975. This book relates what firefighters do to put out a fire from beginning to end.

RELATED TITLES IN ENGLISH FOR SECOND LANGUAGE ACQUISITION

Chlad, Dorothy. *Matches, Lighters, and Firecrackers Are Not Toys*. Chicago: Children's Press, 1982.

Chlad, Dorothy. *When There Is a Fire . . . Go Outside*. Chicago: Children's Press, 1982.

Gibbons, Gail. *Fire! Fire!* New York: Thomas Y. Crowell, 1984.

II. OBSERVATION/EXPERIENCE: *El fuego*
(Class Session One)

Guide students in the following observations/experiences to set the stage for reading the Main Selection.

Focus: What is fire?

1. Turn the lights off, seat children in a circle and cautiously place a lit candle in the center of the circle. Let children observe the flame, and have them volunteer what the flame makes them think about.

2. Ask students what they know about fire and what they want to know about fire. Record their ideas with chalk on black sheets of paper.

3. Tell students that in a book titled *El fuego,* they will learn about the many uses and dangers of fire.

4. Following the reading of the text and the extended experiences, have them check whether their previously recorded "facts" were correct. Allow them to form questions about what they want to learn about fire and record. As answers are provided through children's discovery, record newly learned facts on charts.

III. READ AND DISCUSS THE MAIN SELECTION: *El fuego*
(Class Session One)

Read the Main Selection from page 179 to the students. Highlight the unit's theme by relating this story to other selections from the Literature Input list on pages 179 - 180. Then, guide students in discussing some of the following questions.

1. *Nombren los colores que encuentran en el fuego.* (Name the colors found in fire.)

2. *¿Qué puede causar un incendio?* (What can start a fire?)

3. *¿Qué puede destruir un fuego cuando se extiende?* (What can a fire destroy when it spreads?)

4 *¿Han necesitado un fuego alguna vez? ¿Cuándo?* (Have you ever needed a fire? When?)

5. *¿Cómo usamos el fuego para ayudarnos?* (How do we use fire to help us?)

IV. "WHAT IF" STORY STRETCHER: *El fuego*
(Class Session Two)

Next, re-read the Main Selection and choose one or more of the following questions to develop students' critical thinking skills. Story stretchers may also prompt discussion, drama or writing activities.

1. *¿Qué tal si no tuviéramos fuego? ¿Cómo serían las cosas diferentes?* (What if we had no fire? How would things be different?)

2. *Si no somos cuidadosos con el fuego, ¿qué puede pasar?* (If we are not careful with fire, what can happen?)

3. *Si vieran un incendio empezando en la cocina, ¿qué harían?* (If you saw a fire starting in the kitchen, what would you do?)

4. *Si estuvieran cuidando a un hermanito/a, ¿qué precauciones tomarían para evitar que se queme?* (If you were babysitting a younger brother or sister, what precautions would you take to prevent him/her from getting burned?)

5. *Si sus amigos estuvieran jugando con fósforos, ¿qué dirían y qué harían?* (If your friends were playing with matches, what would you say and do?)

V. INTEGRATING OTHER DISCIPLINES: *El fuego*
(Class Session Three and Ongoing)

The following activities are designed to enhance children's response to literature and expand *beyond* the story and its theme. The variety of activities gives teachers and students an opportunity to choose those most appropriate.

CREATIVE DRAMATICS

1. *Fire! Fire!:* Have the children role play waking up to a fire. What are the right things to do; the wrong things to do?

2. *Forest Fire:* Have children improvise being different animals escaping from a forest fire. Use tissue paper as flames and allow some children to be the spreading fire. Other children may be the water that saves the animals.

3. *Where Is Fire?:* Provide object cards and have groups pantomime where fire can be— a stove, fireplace, cigarette, lighter, candle, barbecue, bonfire, lantern, welding torch, hot water heater, something on fire. Allow observers to identify the source.

4. *Musical Flames:* Engage children in creative movement using music that lends itself to the children acting as flames.

5. *Stop, Drop, Roll Chant:* Have students make up a chant for "stop, drop and roll." Have them perform actions during the chant.

ART AND WRITING

1. *Flames:* Provide the children with red, yellow, and orange paint, large brushes, and large sheets of paper. Let them paint their interpretation of a fire burning. Have them write a cluster around the word «*Fuego*» (Fire).

2. *Fire Prevention:* Discuss real experiences children have had with fire, such as being burned, witnessing someone getting burned or hearing of someone's experience. With students, brainstorm and list ten things that can be done to prevent accidents with fire. Allow them to design a fire prevention flyer listing their ten tips for fire prevention.

3. *Dialogue:* Have students write dialogues using the following writing starters:

   • *Un cohete y un fósforo ven a un niño que se los lleva. ¿Qué se dicen uno al otro?* (A firecracker and a match see a small child carrying them. What do they say to each other?)
   • *Una olla de agua hirviendo y una silla ven a un niño subirse a la silla para ver la olla. ¿Qué se dicen uno al otro?* (A boiling pot of water and a chair see a child climbing the chair to look into the pot. What do they say to each other?)
   • *Una lata de gasolina y un fósforo están en una mesa. ¿Qué se dicen uno al otro?* (A can of gasoline and a match are on the table. What do they say to each other?)
   • *La llave de agua caliente y la tina de baño ven a un niño de dos años tratando de abrir la llave. ¿Qué se dicen uno al otro?* (The hot water faucet and the bathtub see a two-year old child trying to turn on the water. What do they say to each other?)

4. *Kettle-Shape Book:* Provide two pot or kettle patterns for students to cut out. Let them write about what's cooking in the kettle, including its temperature, aroma, taste, consistency, and appearance.

5. *Fire Chief Puppet:* Have the children use paper bags and construction paper to create talking puppets. Pair students and have them use puppets to explain the "stop, drop and roll" procedure. Allow them to write a stop, drop and roll skit on a fire chief brochure.

SCIENCE

1. *Evaporation:* Have children wash out doll clothes and hang them out to dry. Place the wet clothes in different places. Later, discuss why some clothes dried faster than others. Have children estimate how long the same object will take to dry in different places. Allow them to record facts in their science logs.

2. *Barbecue Lunch:* Children may prepare hamburgers and/or hotdogs. Allow them to observe and discuss the use of fire in the preparation of their food. Have them list the ways fire can be used to cook food—broiling, frying, boiling, steaming.

3. *Food Collage:* Have children construct a collage using magazine pictures of foods that require cooking. Brainstorm a list of hot foods and have students write a school menu featuring hot foods for a one-week period.

4. *Combustible Items:* To stimulate a discussion on combustible items found in the home, provide empty containers from gasoline, lighter fluid, charcoal lighter, and matches. Discuss how these items are used in the home and the "do's" and "don't's" with respect to the items. Have the children role play the "do's" and "don't's." Have children illustrate and write about «*Lo que se hace y lo que no se hace al usar. . . .*» ("The "Do's" and "Don't's" of Using. . . .")

5. *Fire and Oxygen:* Provide a half-pint, a quart and a half-gallon jar. Carefully set up three lit candles on a table. Have three students, each with one of the containers, stand in front of a candle. At a given signal, have them place their jars over their candles. The flames will go out relative to the amount of oxygen within each container. Have children write an explanation of what took place in their science logs. **Note:** This activity is for older students and requires careful supervision.

SOCIAL STUDIES

1. *Fire Prevention:* Make up a bulletin board of news items in which fire was involved. Children may bring in and share articles. Allow children to write about a precaution that could have been taken to prevent a fire that occurred in a news item.

2. *Interview:* Invite a firefighter as a guest speaker and have an interview session. Invite children to "step into the boots of a firefighter," and write a letter to warn families of the dangers of kitchen and garage fire hazards.

El campo

Si yo pudiera escoger,
viviría siempre en el campo;
sembraría mi buena tierra
y trabajaría contento.

Gozaría las mañanas frescas
y también los días de sol;
bebería agua del río
y el aire puro sería mejor.

Raquel C. Mireles

La lluvia

Que linda la lluvia
que todo refresca,
que baña los campos,
que corre en la cuesta;
que forma charquitos
que limpia las casas,
y da por las noches,
gentil serenata.

Anónimo

Ya llueve

Ya llueve, ya llueve
comienza a llover
menudas gotitas
yo miro caer.

Ya llueve, ya llueve
¿por qué lloverá?
las flores del campo
muy secas están.

Las nubes dijeron
no es justo que mueran
que rieguen los campos
preciso es que llueva.

Ya llueve, ya llueve
comienza a llover
y un fuerte aguacero
pronto he de ver.

Letra y música de V. Lozano

El viento

El amigo viento
viene hoy a jugar
nos trae las cometas
que saben volar.

Juega con las hojas
que en el árbol hay
y mece a los nidos
como una mamá.

El amigo viento
se pone a jugar
y silba que silba
¿no lo oyes silbar?
uh uh uh uh.

Anónimo

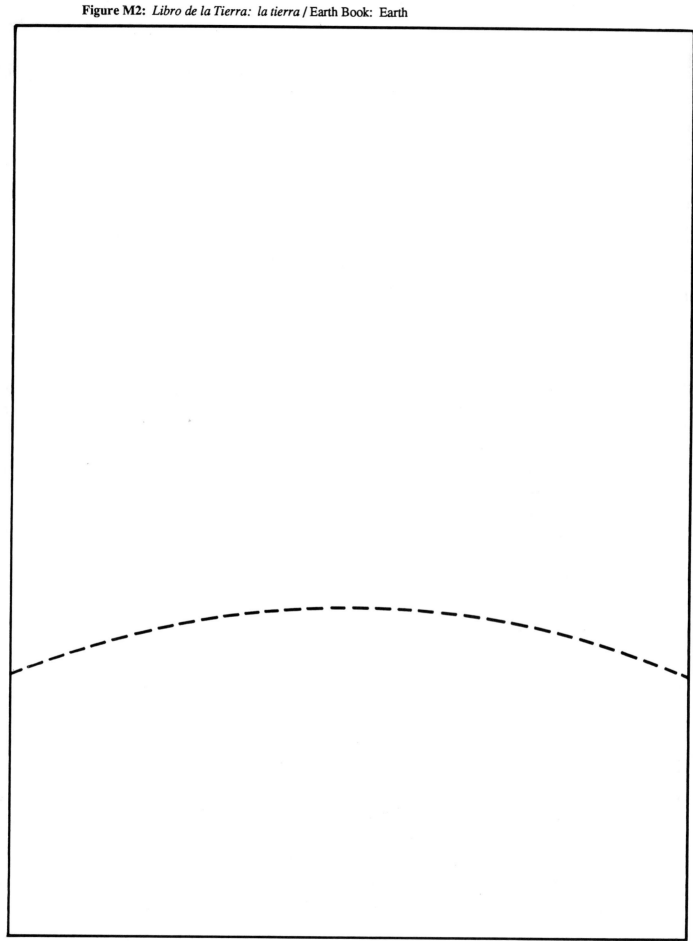

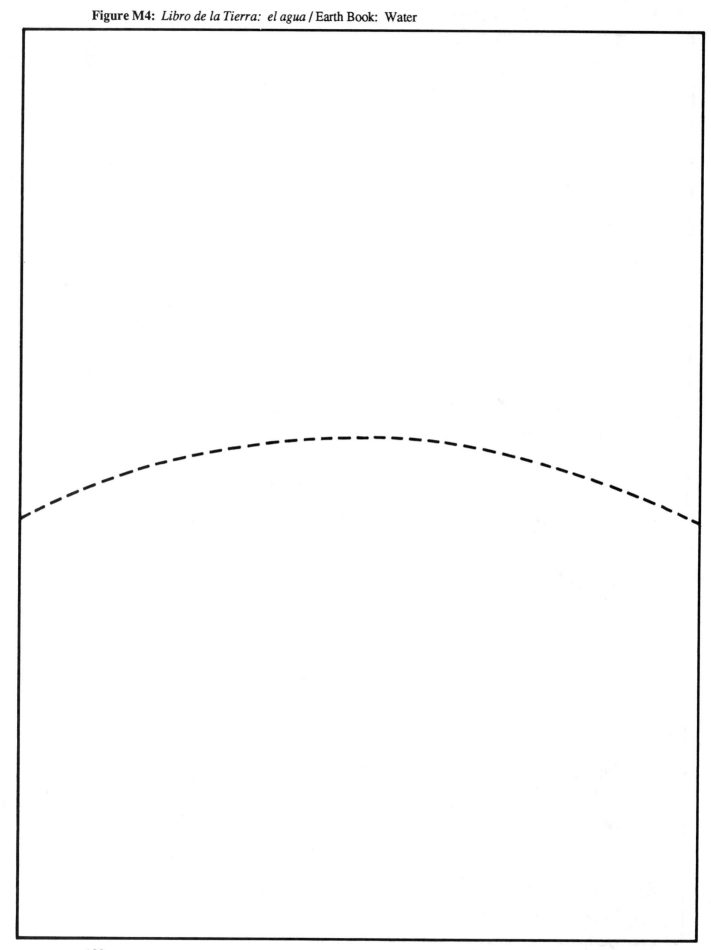

MY OWN CREATIVE TEACHING IDEAS FOR UNIT TWELVE

Books: _____

_____

_____

_____

_____

_____

Ideas: _____

_____

_____

_____

_____

_____

_____

_____

_____

_____

_____

_____

_____

_____

_____

_____

_____

UNIT THIRTEEN

APRENDO CON MIS SENTIDOS

I LEARN THROUGH MY SENSES

It is through our sensory system that all learning takes place. Our senses of sight, hearing, touch, taste and smell feed our minds, including all creative thoughts. We all require continuous stimulation to keep in touch with ourselves and our world. Exposing children to literature about the five senses allows them to become aware of the many possibilities for exploring their world. It can also allow them to appreciate their sensory systems, the learning tools so often taken for granted.

CONCEPTS AND VALUES

1. We are able to learn with our senses.
2. We use our senses to enjoy our environment.
3. We use our senses to survive.
4. There are people who do not have all of their senses.
5. We use some of our senses more than others.

I. LITERATURE INPUT: *All Selections*

Select five or more titles from the following list to read aloud. Read at least one selection per day to the students. Make available and incorporate the suggested titles for voluntary independent reading. Titles marked with * are Spanish translations of the original English story; titles marked with + are recommended for more proficient listeners.

Los cinco sentidos / The Five Senses

*1. Brenner, Barbara. *Caras*. New York: E. P. Dutton, 1977. Photographs show the reaction of the senses to both pleasant and unpleasant stimuli.

2. Broekel, Ray. *Tus cinco sentidos*. Chicago: Children's Press, 1988. The book explores the five senses through photographs and answers questions posed by the author.

3. Larreula, Eric. *El país de los cinco sentidos*. Spain: Editorial Teide, S.A., 1984. In this fantasy world all senses are separate and only one sensation can be experienced at a time. The senses unite and become what we are today.

+4. Murphy, Chuck. *Tus sentidos*. Colombia: Editorial Norma S.A., 1986. This pop-up book of the senses describes the location of each of the senses and how each helps us know our world.

El gusto / Taste

5. *Colección Piñata: El azúcar*. México: Editorial Piñata, 1985. Everything about sugar is explored through beautiful illustrations depicting Mexican society.

6. *Colección Piñata: El chocolate*. México: Editorial Piñata, 1985. Interesting facts are presented about the origin and the characteristics of chocolate with illustrations depicting Mexican society.

*7. Flores, Rosa. *Caracolitos: Lo sabroso sabrosito*. Oklahoma: Economy Company, 1979. All of the different tastes that our tongues can distinguish are depicted with illustrations of children and food.

8. Lasa, Maite. *Voy a cocinar*. México: Sistemas Técnicas de Edición, S.A. de C.V., 1988. This recipe book for children has recipes that are culturally appealing.

*9. Parramón, J. M., and J. J. Puig. Illustrated by María Rius. *El gusto*. New York: Barron's Educational Series, 1985. This book beautifully illustrates all the different tastes.

+10. Rodríguez, Ana, and Jorge Blanco. *Cocinar es un juego muy sabroso*. Venezuela: Ediciones María Di Mase, 1982. This beautifully illustrated cookbook has recipes that are very appealing to children.

11. Smith, Kathie Billingslea, and Victoria Crenson. *Colección mil preguntas: Gustando*. Argentina: Editorial Sigmar, 1988. The sense of taste is explored through questions and answers with interesting explanations and illustrations.

El olfato / Smell

*12. Flores, Rosa. *Caracolitos: La nariz de Pepito*. Oklahoma: Economy Company, 1979. Mother rabbit tells Pepito that his nose is for smelling and he learns to enjoy the smells found in his environment.

*13. Parramón, J. M., and J. J. Puig. Illustrated by María Rius. *El olfato*. New York: Barron's Educational Series, 1985. This book vividly illustrates the most memorable smells in life.

14. Smith, Kathie Billingslea, and Victoria Crenson. *Colección mil preguntas: Oliendo*. Argentina: Editorial Sigmar, 1988. The sense of smell is explored through questions and answers with interesting explanations and illustrations.

El oído / Hearing

15. *Colección Piñata: Ritmos y sonidos*. México: Editorial Piñata, 1985. This book explores the wonders of sound.

*16. Flores, Rosa. *Caracolitos: Escucha*. Oklahoma: Economy Company, 1979. Nora and Gabriel meet Escuchi, a small animal that helps them become aware of sounds they had never stopped to listen to.

17. Gerson, Sara. *La orquesta*. México: Editorial Trillas, S.A., 1987. While listening to the instruments play, a cat and mice become music lovers, not enemies.

+*18. Knight, David. *Colección quiero conocer: El mundo del sonido*. México: Sistemas Técnicas de Edición, S.A. de C.V., 1988. Experiments and colorful illustrations are used to explore sound.

*19. Parramón, J. M., and J. J. Puig. Illustrated by María Rius. *El oído*. New York: Barron's Educational Series, 1985. this book illustrates the most enjoyable sounds in the world.

20. de Podendorf, Illa. *Sonidos*. Illinois: National Textbook, 1979. This is an interesting presentation of sounds and how they are a part of our daily lives.

21. Smith, Kathie Billingslea, and Victoria Crenson. *Colección mil preguntas: Oyendo*. Buenos Aires: Editorial Sigmar, 1988. The sense of hearing is explored through questions and answers with interesting explanations and illustrations.

22. Wolf, Bernard. *Ana y su mundo de silencio*. New York: J. B. Lippincott, 1979. This is a true story of Ana's daily life experiences as a deaf child.

La vista / Sight

*23. Flores, Rosa. *Caracolitos: Ojitos*. Oklahoma: Economy Company, 1979. Carlota meets an octopus with eight eyes that tells how he sees different things with each eye.

24. García Sánchez, J. L. *El niño que tenía dos ojos*. Spain: Ediciones Altea, 1978. This is the beautiful story of a boy born with two eyes on a planet where all inhabitants have one eye. He learns to overcome his "defect" and lives a full life.

*25. Parramón, J. M., and J. J. Puig. Illustrated by María Rius. *La vista*. New York: Barron's Educational Series, 1985. This book explores, through beautiful illustrations, the wonders of our sense of sight.

26. Smith, Kathie Billingslea, and Victoria Crenson. *Colección mil preguntas: Viendo*. Argentina: Editorial Sigmar, 1988. The sense of sight is explored through questions and answers with interesting explanations and illustrations.

27. Williams, Leslie, and Carme Solé Vendrell. *¿Qué hay detrás del árbol?* Spain: Ediciones Hymsa, 1985. Before discovering the truth, two children allow their imagination to run freely as they try to guess what could possibly be behind a tree.

El tacto / Touch

28. *El Rey Midas*. Spain: Editors S.A., 1980. This is the classical story of King Midas.

*29. Flores, Rosa. *Caracolitos: El libro de Toco el tucán*. Oklahoma: Economy Company, 1979. Toco the toucan introduces us to the world of touch.

*30. Parramón, J. M., and J. J. Puig. Illustrated by María Rius. *El tacto*. New York: Barron's Educational Series, 1985. This book illustrates and describes the different textures we find in the world.

31. Smith, Kathie Billingslea, and Victoria Crenson. *Colección mil preguntas: Tocando*. Argentina: Editorial Sigmar, 1988. The sense of touch is explored through questions and answers with interesting explanations and illustrations.

RELATED TITLES IN ENGLISH FOR SECOND LANGUAGE ACQUISITION

Alexander, Martha. *Pigs Say Oink: The First Book of Sounds*. New York: Random House, 1978.

Aliki. *My Five Senses*. New York: Harper and Row Junior Books, 1962.

Allington, Richard. *Smelling*. Wisconsin: Raintree Publishers, 1980. (Additional titles are available for the other senses.)

Brighton, Catherine. *My Hands, My World*. New York: Macmillan Publishing, 1984.

Gardner, Beau. *Guess What?* New York: Lothrop, Lee and Shephard, 1985.

Kline, Suzy. *Don't Touch*. Illinois: Albert Whitman and Company, 1985.

Martin, Bill Jr. *Brown Bear, Brown Bear, What Do You See?* New York: Holt, Rinehart and Winston, 1970.

Pluckrose, Henry. *Smelling*. New York: Franklin Watts Inc., 1986. (Additional titles are available for the other senses.)

Tymme, Jean. *I Like to See: A Book of the Five Senses*. Wisconsin: Western Publishing Company, 1978.

YO PUEDO SABOREAR
I CAN TASTE

Our tongue helps us tell one food from another. The tongue must be coated with saliva in order to distinguish tastes. The taste buds are bumps on the tongue. The tip and front of the tongue taste sweet foods, while salty and sour are on the sides of the tongue, and bitter is in the back. Most foods are a combination of tastes and, sometimes, what one may think is taste, is really smell. *La zorra y la cigüeña* is a humorous, yet meaningful, way to introduce the concept of how important our sense of taste can be.

MAIN SELECTION

Before reading the Main Selection aloud, take your students through the Literature Input and Observation/Experience phases which follow.

Valeri, Eulalia Ma.

La zorra y la cigüeña.
Spain: Editorial La Galera, S.A., 1973.

The fox and the stork each prepare food without considering the other's needs.

I. **LITERATURE INPUT:** *La zorra y la cigüeña*
See pages 192 - 194.

II. **OBSERVATION/EXPERIENCE:** *La zorra y la cigüeña*
(Class Session One)

Guide students in the following observations/experience sequence to set the stage for reading the Main Selection.

Focus: Exploring our sense of taste.

1. Provide a variety of foods for children to sample. Put a blindfold on each child and place a dab of each food on the tongue. Here are some suggested items—ketchup, mustard, peanut butter, salt, canned fruit, toothpaste, honey, lemon. Encourage children to describe the taste and compare it to other tastes.

2. During tasting, ask the following questions:

   • *¿Reconocen el sabor?* (Do you recognize the taste?)

   • *¿Es un sabor que les disgusta o les gusta?* (Is it a taste you dislike or like?)

   • *¿Qué clase de sabor es—dulce, salado, amargo, o agrio?* (What kind of taste is it— sweet, salty, bitter, or sour?)

3. Tell the students that in the story *La zorra y la cigüeña,* they will see how a fox and a stork are placed in a situation in which they intentionally plan to prevent each other from being able to taste.

4. Show the book cover and have the children predict what will keep the fox and stork from tasting. Following the story, have children discuss whether their predictions were correct.

III. READ AND DISCUSS THE MAIN SELECTION: *La zorra y la cigüeña*
(Class Session One)

Read the Main Selection from page 195 to the students. Highlight the unit's theme by relating this story to other selections from the Literature Input list on pages 192 - 194. Then, guide students in discussing some of the following questions.

1. *¿Alguna vez han querido saborear lo que otra persona estaba comiendo? ¿Por qué querían probarlo?* (Have you ever wanted to taste something someone else was eating? Why did you want to taste it?)

2. *La zorra y la cigüeña usaron uno de los sentidos en una manera cruel. ¿Qué sentido usaron y por qué creen que fue cruel?* (The fox and the stork used one of the senses in a cruel way. Which sense did they use, and why do you think it was cruel?)

3. *¿Qué podemos hacer con el sentido de sabor?* (What are we able to do with the sense of taste?)

4. *¿Qué extrañarían si no tuvieran el sentido de sabor?* (What would you miss if you did not have the sense of taste?)

5. *¿Cuáles son algunos peligros que debemos evitar cuando usamos el sentido del gusto?* (What are some dangers we must be aware of when we use the sense of taste?)

IV. "WHAT IF" STORY STRETCHER: *La zorra y la cigüeña*
(Class Session Two)

Next, re-read the Main Selection and choose one or more of the following questions to develop students' critical thinking skills. Story stretchers may also prompt discussion, drama or writing activities.

1. *Si ustedes fueran la cigüeña, ¿qué le habrían hecho a la zorra?* (If you were the stork, what would you have done to the fox?)

2. *Si no pudieran saborear, ¿cómo sería la comida?* (If you could not taste, how would mealtime be?)

3. *Si pudieran sentir un solo sabor de comida—salado, dulce, amargo, agrio, desabrido, ¿cúal escogerían? ¿Por qué?* (If you could only taste one type of food—salty, sweet, bitter, sour, bland—which would you choose? Why?)

4. *Si vieran a un hermano/a menor probar algo que no debiera, ¿qué dirían o qué harían ustedes?* (If you saw a younger brother or sister tasting something he/she shouldn't, what would you say or do?)

5. *Si ustedes pudieran invitar a sus amigos a una cena muy especial, ¿qué comidas deliciosas les servirían?* (If you could invite your friends to a very special dinner, what delicious foods would you serve?)

V. INTEGRATING OTHER DISCIPLINES: *La zorra y la cigüeña*
(Class Session Three and Ongoing)

The following activities are designed to enhance children's response to literature and expand *beyond* the story and its theme. The variety of activities gives teachers and students an opportunity to choose those most appropriate.

CREATIVE DRAMATICS

1. *Invisible Foods:* As a group, have the students prepare and eat invisible foods—mashed potatoes, carrots, ice cream cones, steak, spaghetti. Then have them try it once again with partners and have them ask questions such as: *¿Se come con los dedos? ¿Necesitan un tenedor o un cuchillo? ¿Cómo sabe?* (Do you eat it with your fingers? Do you need a fork or knife? What does it taste like?)

2. *Imaginary Dinner:* Have groups plan menus for imaginary dinner parties. Combining silent actions with conversation, let them react to the food served from the menus. Encourage them to try to create varied menus with foods of many different tastes.

3. *Potluck Supper:* Invite the children to an imaginary potluck supper. Have each child bring a food to the party. Let the child pantomime tasting the contribution while observers pose questions about the food until they can guess what the food is. (The person eating the food may not speak.)

4. *Pantomime Situations:* Have students imagine themselves in some of the following situations:

   • They are trying a food for the first time. They examine it first, and by their expressions, show their reactions.
   • They come home from school and the smell of food is in the air. They investigate.
   • They are touching, peeling, and eating lemons.
   • They are eating messy, but delicious food—pizza, ribs, tacos, chili dogs.
   • They must take their medicine.

5. *Story Twist:* Have student re-enact ***La zorra y la cigüeña*** and add a twist portraying the characters as considerate, cooperative hosts.

ART AND WRITING

1. *Menus:* Have children make menus which include illustrations, prices, and descriptions. Cooperative groups may make different menus or different parts of the same menu such as sandwiches, salads, drinks, dinner, lunch, or breakfast. For variety, the students may create multicultural menus—Italian, Mexican, Cuban, Chinese. Allow the children to prepare and share one of the selections on the menus and have a multicultural potluck.

2. *Grocery Lists:* Have children make illustrated or written grocery lists. Children may think of meals they can make using the foods on the grocery lists.

3. *Food Labels:* Remove labels from cans and have children match the labels to the cans by tasting what is in the cans. As an alternative, instead of using labels, have them create labels for the foods. Then have them match labels with foods and compare their labels with the real labels.

4. *Invitations:* Have students create invitations for a food-tasting party, specifying the type of party and illustrating the food to be tasted at the party.

5. *No-Cook Menu:* Brainstorm foods prepared without cooking. Instruct children to make up a menu for "Joe's No-Cook Restaurant." All items on the menu must require no cooking.

6. *No Taste:* Have students imagine life without a sense of taste. Have them write descriptions of how it feels to eat soup, ice cream cones, spaghetti, or oranges for a person that cannot taste.

7. *Food Rating:* Have students write descriptions of either their breakfast, lunch or dinner. They may illustrate the foods they had, or they may cut pictures from magazines. For fun, let them give their meals one- to four-star ratings (* * * *) for poor to excellent.

8. *Food Activities:* Have students create artwork from the list below and then write and attach descriptions to the artwork for a "senses" art show.

   • Show the students a pear. Have them each draw eight pear shapes and create animals and/or people from the pear shapes.
   • Show the students a pretzel. Have them think of ways to incorporate it into a drawing. Provide pretzels and let them create the drawings.
   • Provide popcorn and have students incorporate it into illustrations.

9. *Gingerbread House:* Provide graham crackers, candy and frosting so that students, in groups or individually, can design a gingerbread house on a small milk carton. Have students imagine that they have come upon a gingerbread house like Hansel and Gretel did. Let them imagine tasting parts of the house. Then have them write descriptions of what they ate and how it tasted.

SCIENCE

1. *Our Taste Buds:* To demonstrate that our tongues have sensitive taste buds, provide large dittos of a tongue with our taste areas mapped but unlabeled. Provide four liquids such as grapefruit juice, salted water, lime or lemon juice, or jello. Have children drop different liquids on different parts of the tongue with toothpicks or cotton swabs. Allow children to label the different areas—sour, sweet, salty, and bitter—in the following manner: bitterness on the sides, sourness near the base, saltiness and sweetness at the tip.

2. *Our Sensitive Tongue:* To demonstrate that our tongues are sensitive to texture and temperature, allow children to taste foods that are mushy, crunchy, sticky, cold, or hot. Have the students brainstorm and list other foods that are in these categories.

3. *Tasting Parties:* Have food-tasting parties. These may include a flower-tasting party with cauliflower and broccoli buds; a leaf-tasting party to sample cabbage, spinach, mint, parsley, and cilantro (coriander); a seed-tasting party with sesame seeds, sunflower seeds, rice, green beans, lima beans, roasted pumpkin seeds, popcorn, and one giant seed—the coconut; a root-tasting party with parsnips, beets, radishes, carrots, and potatoes. You may also wish to hold dairy-, fruit-, meat- or protein-tasting parties. (Review the class allergy list.)

4. *Spice Cookies:* Have students bake spice cookies and let them sample the ingredients as they use them. Have the children taste the dough before the cookies are baked, when they are still warm from the oven, and after they have cooled. After sampling all three, let the students write about their preferences in their science logs.

5. *Applesauce:* Let students taste apples before they are cooked and afterward. Then add cinnamon and call their attention to the change in taste. Allow children to drink apple juice. Create a four-column chart labeled *«Así me gustan mis manzanas»* ("How I Like My Apples"). Give the children the four choices and have them place their names or pictures of apples under their preferences.

6. *Vegetable Soup:* Have the students taste, touch, smell, and identify the colors of each vegetable before and after the soup is made. Have the students describe each vegetable in terms of these four senses in their science logs.

7. *Edible Playdough:* With students, mix equal amounts of peanut butter and non-fat dry milk together to the consistency of playdough. Add more peanut butter or dry milk as needed. Make sure that hands and utensils are clean because the children will eat as they create. Allow students to experiment with consistency by adding milk or peanut butter. Have them record their observations in their science logs.

8. *Animal Tongues:* Display pictures of different animals. Discuss how different animals such as snakes, cats, and anteaters use their tongues for different purposes. Have the students record facts in their science logs.

YO PUEDO OLER
I CAN SMELL

The nose has nerves that tell the brain what we are smelling. The sense of smell is not as highly developed in humans as in other animals, but most people can identify approximately 4000 different smells. We can smell objects some distance away, but the nose must come in contact with the odor. *Ferdinando* illustrates how the sense of smell can enhance our lives.

MAIN SELECTION

Before reading the Main Selection aloud, take your students through the Literature Input and Observation/Experience phases which follow.

> Leaf, Munro.
>
> *Ferdinando.*
> New Jersey: Rae Publishing Company, 1982.
>
> This is a wonderful story about a bull that loves to smell flowers and hates behaving as a bull.

I. LITERATURE INPUT: *Ferdinando*
See pages 192 - 194.

II. OBSERVATION/EXPERIENCE: *Ferdinando*
(Class Session One)

Guide students in the following observations/experience sequence to set the stage for reading the Main Selection.

Focus: Exploring our sense of smell.

1. Provide a variety of fragrances for the group to identify. Small, empty jars will be needed so each item can be in its own container. Some suggested items are vinegar, coffee, flowers, spices, mouthwash, cocoa, mustard.

2. Encourage children to discuss their reactions.

   - *¿Es un olor agradable o desagradable?* (Is it a pleasant or unpleasant smell?)
   - *¿Reconocen el olor?* (Do you recognize the smell?)
   - *¿En qué les hace pensar el olor?* (What does the smell make you think of?)

3. Tell students that in the story *Ferdinando* they will meet a bull, unlike other bulls, that enjoys his sense of smell.

4. Have them predict what Ferdinando will enjoy smelling and what the other bulls will think of him. Following the story, have students discuss whether their predictions were correct.

III. READ AND DISCUSS THE MAIN SELECTION: *Ferdinando*
(Class Session One)

Read the Main Selection from page 200 to the students. Highlight the unit's theme by relating this story to other selections from the Literature Input list on pages 192 - 194. Then, guide students in discussing some of the following questions.

1. *¿Qué piensan de Ferdinando y de su comportamiento?* (What do you think of Ferdinando and his behavior?)

2. *Si quisieran darle un regalo a Ferdinando, ¿qué le darían?* (If you wanted to give Ferdinando a gift, what would you give him?)

3. *¿Por qué es importante el sentido de olor para nosotros?* (Why is the sense of smell important to us?)

4. *¿Hay algunas veces cuando ustedes no quieren usar el sentido de olor? Explíquennos.* (Are there times when you do not want to use the sense of smell? Explain.)

5. *¿Cómo sería diferente la vida sin el sentido de olor?* (How would life be different without the sense of smell?)

IV. "WHAT IF" STORY STRETCHER: *Ferdinando*
(Class Session Two)

Next, re-read the Main Selection and choose one or more of the following questions to develop students' critical thinking skills. Story stretchers may also prompt discussion, drama or writing activities.

1. *Si Ferdinando no se hubiera sentado en la abeja, ¿cómo habría cambiado el cuento?* (If Ferdinando had not sat on the bee, how would the story have been different?)

2. *Si ustedes fueran Ferdinando, ¿qué les dirían a los otros toros acerca de darse tiempo para oler?* (If you were Ferdinando, what would you say to the other bulls about taking time to smell?)

3. *Si no pudieramos oler, ¿en qué forma serían diferentes nuestras vidas?* (If we could not smell, how would our lives be different?)

4. *Si ustedes pudieran hacer un perfume, ¿qué usarían para hacerlo y cómo lo nombrarían?* (If you could create a perfume, what would you use to make it and what would you name it?)

5. *Si hubiera un incendio cerca, ¿cuál sentido les alertaría? ¿Por qué tiene valor su sentido del olfato?* (If there were a fire nearby, which sense would alert you to it? Why is your sense of smell valuable?)

V. INTEGRATING OTHER DISCIPLINES: *Ferdinando*
(Class Session Three and Ongoing)

The following activities are designed to enhance children's response to literature and expand *beyond* the story and its theme. The variety of activities gives teachers and students an opportunity to choose those most appropriate.

CREATIVE DRAMATICS

1. *Flowers and Insects:* Have some children pretend they are flowers opening their petals from a bud to full bloom. Have them move with the wind. Allow other children to take the role of insects that come by to gather pollen, drink nectar, hide or sleep in a flower. Another group of children may pretend to smell the flowers and tell what they would like to do with the beautiful-smelling flower—give it to someone they love, decorate something, wear someplace special.

2. *Pantomime Smelling:* Pose situations that stimulate the sense of smell—baking a cake, putting gasoline in the car, picking flowers, putting on perfume, passing by a dairy farm, being around trash or garbage. Have children pantomime actions. You or the students may write other ideas on cards to select for pantomime activities.

3. *Dramatize the Story:* Have students dramatize the Ferdinando story and add a twist to the story by having Ferdinando teach his bull friends about the joy of smelling.

4. *Baking a Pie:* Have students pantomime smelling a pie just out of the oven. Give cards that illustrate sequence of activities in producing a pie. One by one, let the students join in the group, pantomiming the steps.

ART AND WRITING

1. *Nose Collage:* Have cooperative groups make collages of different noses found in magazines. Encourage them to give a creative name to their collages.

2. *Cinnamon Necklace:* Cut sandpaper into three-inch squares. Let children rub a piece of sandpaper with a cinnamon stick. Tell them to punch a hole in the top of the squares, put a piece of yarn through them, and tie the necklaces around their necks. Children can then enjoy the spicy-smelling necklaces.

3. *Food Verse:* Have them write short verses incorporating foods and someone/ something that smelled it and ate it; e.g., "Lupe wore a popcorn necklace and guess what happened?" "A little bird smelled it and pecked it off her neck."

4. *Chart of Smells:* Have cooperative groups create an illustrated or written list of pleasant and unpleasant odors on a large piece of butcher paper folded in half. Title one side *«Olores que me gustan»* ("Smells I Like") and include a happy face. Title the other side *«Olores que no me gustan»* ("Smells I Don't Like") with a sad face. Cooperative groups can draw, paste and place pictures under each heading. A discussion and creative writing may follow; e.g., *«Mi fragancia favorita es . . . . Mi olor favorito me hace pensar en . . . .»* ("My favorite fragrance is . . . . My favorite smell makes me think of . . . .)

4. *Flower Show:* Have children make flowers and add fragrances of their choice. They may also bring flowers found in their gardens. Provide information about the flowers. Have the children put the information on cards to display with the real and child-created flowers.

5. *Picture Smells:* Put aromatic oils or extracts such as vanilla, peppermint, strawberry, and lemon in tempera paints. Allow children to create paintings and/or scratch and sniff pictures and write accompanying captions or stories for a senses art show.

SCIENCE

1. *Animal Noses:* Provide pictures or picture books of animal noses and have children name the animal that goes with the nose. (The stranger the nose, the better.) Discuss the many uses of noses. Let them select an imaginary nose to wear and pantomime the animal that belongs with the nose.

2. *Sniff the Cup:* Provide ten numbered containers in which contents can be smelled but not seen. Containers may include such things as vinegar, garlic, cinnamon, soap, toothpaste, mint, coffee, or celery. Have students number their papers from one to ten and write down what they smell as the containers are passed. Allow them to graph and compare the results.

3. *Match Smells:* Using small jars containing four different scents, allow children to find two jars containing the same smell. On a sheet of paper folded into four squares, have the children write the name of a scent within the square and place the jars in the proper squares.

4. *Senses Booklet:* Plan to take the children on a nature walk. Before going out, duplicate and cut out Figure N1, "*Las ideas* / Ideas" (page 219). Have the children write their predictions of what they think they will experience with their senses. After the nature walk, duplicate and cut out the remaining Figures N1 - N2 (pages 219 - 220). For the senses of hearing, smell, and sight, have students write their experiences. Have children assemble the booklets with brads. Have them use the booklets to compare their predictions and experiences.

YO PUEDO OIR
I CAN HEAR

The world is full of sounds that we often ignore. Bringing some of these sounds to a conscious level may help children become more aware of the world around them. *El flautista de Hamelín* dramatically shows that what children listen and respond to can greatly influence their lives.

MAIN SELECTION

Before reading the Main Selection aloud, take your students through the Literature Input and Observation/Experience phases which follow.

Hutchinson, Hanna.

El flautista de Hamelín.
New York: Kenworthy Educational Service, Inc., 1962.

A town finds a way of getting rid of its rats, but the town's people find their children gone also.

I. **LITERATURE INPUT:** *El flautista de Hamelín*
See pages 192 - 194.

II. **OBSERVATION/EXPERIENCE:** *El flautista de Hamelín*
(Class Session One)

Guide students in the following observations/experience sequence to set the stage for reading the Main Selection.

Focus: Exploring our sense of hearing.

1. To emphasize that each person interprets sounds in her/his own way, play the "telephone game." Have children seated in a circle. Instruct one to whisper a message into the ear of the next child. That child, in turn, whispers it into the ear of the next child, and so on. The last child tells the group what message was received and the message is compared to the original.

2. Discuss the importance of listening, and how what is heard is not always what was said.

   * *¿Alguna vez alguien les ha mal entendido lo que dijeron? Dígannos acerca de ello.* (Has someone ever misunderstood what you said? Tell us about it?)
   * *¿Alguna vez han mal entendido a alguien? Dígannos acerca de ello.* (Have you ever misunderstood someone? Tell us about it.)
   * *¿Cómo saben que alguien está realmente escuchando?* (How do you know that someone is really listening?)
   * *¿Por qué es difícil a veces hacer que otros escuchen?* (Why is it sometimes difficult to get others to listen?)

3. Tell students that in a story titled *El flautista de Hamelín,* a flautist will get others to listen to him in a most unusual way.

4. Tell students to predict what he will do to get others to listen to him. Following the story, have the children discuss whether their predictions were correct.

III. READ AND DISCUSS THE MAIN SELECTION: *El flautista de Hamelín*
(Class Session One)

Read the Main Selection from page 204 to the students. Highlight the unit's theme by relating this story to other selections from the Literature Input list on pages 192 - 194. Then, guide students in discussing some of the following questions.

1. *¿Por qué creen que los niños siguieron al flautista?* (Why do you think the children followed the flautist?)

2. *¿Por qué es importante el sentido de oír para ustedes?* (Why is the sense of hearing important to you?)

3. *¿Qué extrañarían si no tuvieran el sentido de oír?* (What would you miss if you did not have the sense of hearing?)

4. *¿Hay algunas veces cuando ustedes no quieren usar el sentido de oír? Explíquennos.* (Are there times when you do not want to use the sense of hearing? Explain.)

5. *¿Cuáles son algunos peligros que debemos evitar para cuidar el oído?* (What are some dangers we must avoid in order to take care of our hearing?)

IV. "WHAT IF" STORY STRETCHER: *El flautista de Hamelín*
(Class Session Two)

Next, re-read the Main Selection and choose one or more of the following questions to develop students' critical thinking skills. Story stretchers may also prompt discussion, drama or writing activities.

1. *Si el flautista hubiera usado otro sentido para atraer a las ratas ¿cuál habría usado? ¿Cómo habría cambiado el cuento?* (If the flautist had used another sense to attract the rats, which one would he have used? How would the story have changed?)

2. *Si no pudieran oír, ¿cómo cambiarían sus vidas?* (If you could not hear, how would your lives change?)

3. *¿Qué tal si el mundo no tuviera sonido? Describan el mundo a sus alrededores.* (What if the world had no sound? Describe the world around you.)

4. *Si estuvieran en un lugar oscuro, ¿qué sentido usarían más? ¿Por qué?* (If you were in a dark place, which sense would you use the most? Why?)

5. *Si tuvieran un amigo/a quien no pudiera oír, ¿qué harían para ayudarlo/a a entenderles?* (If you had a friend who could not hear, what would you do to help him/ her understand you?)

V. INTEGRATING OTHER DISCIPLINES: *El flautista de Hamelín*
(Class Session Three and Ongoing)

The following activities are designed to enhance children's response to literature and expand *beyond* the story and its theme. The variety of activities gives teachers and students an opportunity to choose those most appropriate.

CREATIVE DRAMATICS

1. *Story Twist:* Allow groups to add several different story twists by having the flautist become a drummer, violinist or guitarist. To lure different animals and children to different places, have groups plan, practice and improvise their story twists.

2. *Listening:* Invite the children to close their eyes, remain very still, and listen to several sounds in the classroom. Have the children quietly raise their hands when they have heard a sound. When most or all children have heard a sound or two, encourage them to identify the source. Challenge them to discover sounds they had not previously noticed.

3. *Pantomime Situations:* Have groups pantomime the following situations:

   • They are trying to sleep but a mosquito keeps buzzing in their ears.
   • The horn on the car gets stuck; it will not stop.
   • They are in a restaurant and someone is slurping soup.
   • They are trying to tell someone something, but the other person is far away and cannot hear.
   • They are trying to listen to someone in a very noisy place.

4. *School-Yard Sounds:* Have children close their eyes and listen to sounds in the school yard. Let them form a circle and tell them to show, through improvisation, some of the the sounds heard in the environment of the school yard—the sound of the wind, birds, rustling leaves, a ball bouncing, an airplane, a car, children walking, running. Allow the audience to guess the source.

5. *Making Sounds:* Model happy, angry, loud, soft, jerky, explosive, and nasal sounds. Have the children create a sequence of sounds imitating animals or objects.

6. *Do Your Thing:* Allow children to react to different styles of music—march, waltz, rock, and Mexican music. Play a march and move in the expected manner—knees high and arms swinging. Wait for the children to respond in their own creative way. Use the same technique with a waltz. Next, let students move spontaneously to rock or any festive music.

7. *Make-It-Yourself Band:* Allow children to make up their own instruments with things found in the classroom, or use things brought in from home—egg-beaters, old pots and wooden spoons, washboards, cardboard tubes from paper towels. Using their instruments, have groups participate in "jam" sessions for real "band lovers" (other students).

8. *Records:* Listen to records and have students pantomime or creatively move to music that they describe as being happy or sad, fast or slow, loud or soft. This activity may also be done using the radio.

9. *Guessing Game:* Have the children close their eyes. Select one child to touch another child's shoulder. The child who has been selected says, «*Quién Soy?*» ("Who am I?") The other child tries to guess who it is by the sound of the voice. The children may disguise their voices. Discuss our ability to vary our voices and how our voices are distinguishing features.

10. *With Expression:* Read a story twice, once without any expression and a second time with creative expression. Allow children to discuss the difference and determine which was the more interesting reading. Allow cooperative groups to select a popular tale to read with maximum expression in a readers' theater.

11. *What Dropped?:* Hang a sheet across a table, hiding it from the class, and provide eight to twelve unbreakable things such as aluminum pie tins, boxes, balls, cans, pencils, and other items that makes distinctive sounds when dropped. Behind the sheet, let a student drop one item at a time, pause, then drop the next item. See if the listeners can guess what was dropped.

12. *Sound in a Box:* Furnish objects to place in a tightly closed box. One at a time, place objects in the box and have children list characteristics they can distinguish from the sound the object makes when the box is shaken. See if they can guess what the object is.

    Another variation of the same game is to have ten or twelve different boxes containing things. Each box has an item that matches an object found in another box. The object is to find all the pairs by listening to the sounds made when the boxes are shaken.

ART AND WRITING

1. *Maracas:* Using paper towel rolls and beans or popcorn, have students make maracas. Have them attach tongue depressors for the handles and decorate the maracas. Allow them to write chants and incorporate the maracas as they chant.

2. *Telephone:* Have students make telephones using two cans or two yogurt containers and string. Have students write a short dial-a-story for a friend to listen to when using their phones.

3. *Listen and Draw:* Have students sit in groups of four. Provide each group with crayons and four pieces of paper divided into four rectangles each. Have each student write a two- to three-step direction for a drawing to be placed in one of the rectangles. One student reads his directions while the other three listen to directions for drawing on one of the rectangles; e.g., on rectangle #1, draw a square, a cat on the left side of the block, etc. The three listeners are not allowed to see the others' drawings. Each of the four has a turn giving directions. Students may compare drawings and discuss how several people may hear the same thing but visualize it much differently.

4. *Write and Seek:* In cooperative groups, have children hide object inside or outside the classroom. They are to write directions specifying the locations of the objects. Someone must look for each object by listening to the directions as they are read aloud.

5. *Sounds in Stories:* Invite children to create stories centered around sounds such as animal sounds or sounds that are common, unusual, or frightening. To stimulate creativity, provide many sounds from which the students can select. Allow them to create accompanying illustrations.

6. *"What If"* : Have students use a "what if" story stretcher as a topic for creative writing.

7. *Sound Effects:* Have a sound-effects day and tape interesting sounds created by students. Brainstorm sounds that would make interesting sound effects. Have the students use them as story starters. Allow students to paint or draw pictures to accompany their stories.

8. *Stories with Sounds:* Use recorded or live sound effects with familiar stories. Allow cooperative groups to come up with the ideas. Have them write the stories and incorporate the sound effects. Each group may present the sound-effects story to the class.

9. *Sounds and Other Senses:* Have children think about sounds and use the other four senses to describe how particular sounds taste, look, feel, and smell—thunder is black, feels rough, smells humid, and tastes like ice. Children may write their ideas and share them with the class.

10. *Outdoor Sounds:* Have the children go outside and listen to the wind, a bird, a tree moving, a ball bouncing, an airplane, a car, dry leaves being stepped on. While outside, children may make lists of what they hear. Upon returning, they may share and compare lists.

11. *Animal Sounds:* Have students imitate animal sounds and use them with well-known stories having animal characters. In cooperative groups, have children create stories with animal sounds.

SOCIAL STUDIES

1. *Taking Turns:* To demonstrate that listening involves active listening and taking turns talking, pair children to tell each other stories at the same time. The children will be telling their stories while listening to their partners' stories. How accurately can they recount their friends' stories? Is it necessary to take turns? Why? Have children brainstorm and list instances when listening is especially important.

SCIENCE

1. *Wind Instruments:* To demonstrate that the vibration of air in a container determines the pitch, use bottles of different sizes or bottles of the same size with differing amounts of water. Place your bottom lip on the edge of the opening and blow to get different pitches. The distance the sound must travel from the opening of the bottle to the bottom determines the sound. (The shorter the distance, the higher the pitch; the longer the distance, the lower the pitch.) Give children the opportunity to play with the sounds and bottles to create interesting sequences of sound. Children may record learned facts in their science logs.

2. *Senses Booklet:* Plan to take the children on a nature walk. Before going out, duplicate and cut out Figure N1, *"Las ideas / Ideas"* (page 219). Have the children write their predictions of what they think they will experience with their senses. After the nature walk, duplicate and cut out the remaining Figures N1 - N2 (pages 219 - 220). For the senses of hearing, smell, and sight, have students write their experiences. Have children assemble the booklets with brads. Have them use the booklets to compare their predictions and experiences.

YO PUEDO VER
I CAN SEE

Sight is the most developed of the senses, but some people "see" better than others. Often, we use our sight more than any other sense, sometimes to the point of overusing it. When we use our imagination to enhance this sense, as in *Las gafas maravillosas,* we see beyond the surface.

MAIN SELECTION

Before reading the Main Selection aloud, take your students through the Literature Input and Observation/Experience phases which follow.

> Munter, Anke.
>
> *Las gafas maravillosas.*
> Spain: Editorial Miñón, S.A., 1984.
>
> Life changes for Carlos as he begins to see interesting places through his "magic" glasses. He shares his adventures with his friends.

I. **LITERATURE INPUT:** *Las gafas maravillosas*
    See pages 192 - 194.

II. **OBSERVATION/EXPERIENCE:** *Las gafas maravillosas*
(Class Session One)

Guide students in the following observations/experience sequence to set the stage for reading the Main Selection.

Focus: Exploring our sense of sight.

1. To emphasize that we can see with our eyes and with our imaginations, provide a picture file and allow children to look at the pictures. Let them describe what they see. Then have them look at the pictures a second time as they search for things seen in their imagination—what is under the rock, inside the house or building, inside the pocket or purse?

2. Tell students that in the story *Las gafas maravillosas,* a boy uses his sense of sight and sees more by using his imagination.

3. Show them the book cover and have them predict what Carlos will see and how he will use his imagination.

4. Following the story, have the children discuss whether their predictions were correct.

III. READ AND DISCUSS THE MAIN SELECTION: *Las gafas maravillosas*
(Class Session One)

Read the Main Selection from page 209 to the students. Highlight the unit's theme by relating this story to other selections from the Literature Input list on pages 192 - 194. Then, guide students in discussing some of the following questions.

1. *¿Alguna vez alguien les ha descrito algo tan bien que pudieron imaginarlo? Platíquennos.* (Has someone ever described something so well you could see it in your mind? Tell us about it?)

2. *Carlos utilizó uno de sus sentidos al máximo. ¿Cuál sentido era? ¿Cómo han utilizado ustedes este sentido?* (Carlos made the most of one of his senses. Which sense was it? How have you used this sense?)

3. *¿Por qué es importante este sentido para nosotros?* (Why is this sense important to us?)

4. *¿Qué extrañarían si no tuvieran el sentido de vista?* (What would you miss most if you did not have the sense of sight?)

5. *¿Cuáles son algunos peligros que debemos evitar para cuidar el sentido de vista?* (What are some dangers we must be aware of in order to take care of the sense of sight?)

IV. "WHAT IF" STORY STRETCHER: *Las gafas maravillosas*
(Class Session Two)

Next, re-read the Main Selection and choose one or more of the following questions to develop students' critical thinking skills. Story stretchers may also prompt discussion, drama or writing activities.

1. *Si fueran Carlos, ¿qué verían con los lentes mágicos? Descríbanlo.* (If you were Carlos, what would you see with the magic glasses? Describe it.)

2. *Si ustedes no pudieran ver ¿cómo sería la vida diferente?* (If you could not see, how would life be different?)

3. *Si pudieran ver cualquier cosa en el mundo, ¿qué sería? ¿Por qué?* (If you could see anything in the world, what would it be? Why?)

4. *Si sus ojos pudieran ver el mundo de un solo color, ¿qué color sería? ¿Por qué?* (If your eyes could see the world in only one color, what color would it be? Why?)

5. *¿Cómo sería diferente la vida si nunca usáramos nuestra imaginación?* (How would life be if we never used our imagination?)

V. INTEGRATING OTHER DISCIPLINES: *Las gafas maravillosas*
(Class Session Three and Ongoing)

The following activities are designed to enhance children's response to literature and expand *beyond* the story and its theme. The variety of activities gives teachers and students an opportunity to choose those most appropriate.

CREATIVE DRAMATICS

1. *Pantomime Situations:* Have students pantomime the following situations:

    - They are looking for a word in the dictionary.
    - They are late for school and can't find their shoes; they find them and put them on quickly.
    - Their kitten is lost and they look for it up a tree; they coax it down.
    - They are looking for the exact amount of change in their purses or pockets
    - They are in a car looking for an address while following a map.
    - They are hungry and are looking for something delicious to eat.

2. *Blindfolded:* Have children wear blindfolds and experience, through improvisation, such activities as going to the store, eating in a restaurant, getting ready for school. Discuss how the blindfold made a difference.

3. *Leading the Blind:* Pair children and have one blindfolded while the other acts as a "seeing" guide. Allow the "blind" to explore their world outside with the guides directing them to interesting things to touch. They should focus on the textures of the objects rather than on the names.

4. *Re-Enact the Story:* Have students re-enact **Las gafas maravillosas**. Have cooperative groups incorporate a story twist putting themselves in the story using the magic glasses. Let them plan, practice improvisation, and share improvisations with the class.

5. *Find and Touch:* Ask children to locate and touch the objects the teacher calls for (include some silly items also):

    - Find a blue crayon.
    - Find a red book.
    - Find a brown box.
    - Find a yellow pencil.
    - Find a black eraser.
    - Find your own ankle.

    Have the students think of other things that can be found and touched.

6. *Perspective:* In the following two activities, assign recorders and participants and then have them switch roles. Inside the classroom, have children lie flat on their backs, heads on the floor, looking up. Have them describe, without naming the objects, all the things they see above. Have the partners record and report to the class.

    Looking Tall: Without putting the participants in any danger, allow them to climb outdoor playground equipment and describe what they see and how things look from above. Have the partners record and report to the class.

7. *Memory Game:* Place a number of objects on a tray. Pass the tray around. Let each person look at it for 30 seconds. Cover the tray. How many objects on the tray can the child remember? (They may say or write the names of the objects.)

8. *"It" Game:* Two or three students are chosen "it." The class looks them over very carefully. They are sent out and something about their appearance is changed. When they return, the class must guess what is different.

9. *Mind Sight:* Have children create, in their minds, actual, familiar scenes such as their own room, backyard, favorite place to play. Have them visualize the scene as a still picture. Guide children in noticing the placement of things, their colors, size, movement, and so forth. Pair students to orally share their descriptions.

10. *"Hole" Thing:* Pair students and give each one a small sheet of paper with a small hole pierced through it. While one student is looking at a single object seen through the hole, have the other ask questions inquiring about the object so that it can be identified; e.g., "Is it big or small?" "Is it made out of wood, plastic or glass?"

11. *Tight-Rope Race:* Lay two twelve-foot-long ropes on the ground about eight feet apart. Have students take off their shoes and form two even teams. Have two children put on blindfolds, turn around twice and receive a signal for them to walk on the rope feeling their way to the end. The first one to reach the end is the winner. This can also be a competitive race having students rush back to blindfold the next person in line. Allow students to describe this sensory experience.

ART AND WRITING

1. *Appearance Change:* Have a big mirror in the classroom so that children can look at themselves. Have them imagine that a change in appearance is taking place. Allow them to write descriptions of what they would imagine themselves turning into .

2. *Face Cup:* Have children glue pictures of eyes, ears, nose, eyeglasses, and mouth on a white styrofoam cup. Provide soil, spoons, water and bean sprout seeds so they may plant the cup's hair. Allow partners to give creative names and a character description to each others' face cup and share with the class.

3. *Make Binoculars:* Tape together two tissue paper rolls. Have children take turns focusing on one thing and giving clues as to what it is while other children write down the clues and their answers. Compare and discuss answers.

4. *See Beyond:* Use a picture file to prompt imaginative thinking and creative writing. Allow children to look beyond what is actually seen; e.g., «*¿Qué creen que hay en este bolsillo?*» ("What do you think might be in this pocket?") or «*¿Qué creen que hay detrás del árbol?*» ("What do you think might be behind the tree?") Have them select pictures and write about what they "see."

5. *Half a Picture:* Provide action pictures that are cut in half. Have children visualize what the other half of the picture might look like. Let them choose a picture that they would like to illustrate and complete. Have them write a description of their drawing.

6. *Big Book:* Patterned after the Literature Input selection, *Brown Bear, Brown Bear, What Do You See?* have cooperative groups create their own big books. Groups may read their books and share them with the class.

7. *Guess What Book:* Patterned after the Literature Input selection, *Guess What?,* have students create their own books. Have them draw part of an animal on one page and, on the reverse side, draw the complete animal. Allow them to illustrate several animals. On the page having part of an animal, have them write, «*Adivinen lo que es.*» ("Guess what this is.") On the reverse side, have them write the answer; e.g., «*Soy un caballo.*» ("I am a horse.")

8. *Look and Remember:* Have students look out of the window for two minutes. Instruct them to look carefully and to remember the things they see. Let them draw what they captured in their minds. Have them write descriptions of what they saw including such characteristics as size, color, number, position, and motion. Allow students to exchange their window-view descriptions and save them for the senses art show.

9. *Dark Drawing:* Have students draw while blindfolded. Provide a blindfold, pencil, and paper for each student within a group. Except for one "guide," have all group members sit down and put on the blindfold. The guide will call directions for others to follow; e.g., "Draw a bird's head. Now draw the beak. Give the bird two wings." (Each guide may select different animals or objects to draw.) When the guide is finished giving directions, have students take off the blindfolds. Let them share the drawings that were drawn without sight. Allow them to write descriptions of their unusual drawings.

10. *Where Was It?:* Change the location of a few familiar objects in the classroom and see if children can find the changes. Have them play the game at home and write about their family's response.

11. *Blindfolded:* Use Activity Number Two from Creative Dramatics to prompt writing about «*Vi con mis manos*» ("I Saw with My Hands"). Allow children to describe in writing what they felt and to share their descriptions with the class to find out if others can "see" through the description.

SCIENCE

1. *Camouflaged Animals:* Locate pictures of animals that blend into their environments such as a lion, fish, or praying mantis for hunting or a moth, bird, or chameleon for protection. Explain that we need to use our eyes when things are camouflaged. Have them trace a chameleon on wallpaper, cut it out and glue it on a background of the same wallpaper. They may attach the chameleon on an accordion paper to appear three-dimensional. Allow them to write about other instances of camouflage in our environment.

2. *Magnifying Glass:* Place objects under a magnifying glass and let the children see how large and detailed an object becomes. Children may record their observations in their science logs.

3. *Binoculars:* Go outdoors and let the children use binoculars, alternating between the close-up and distant lenses. In small groups, have children make lists of occasions when binoculars are used. Have them share the lists with the class. A microscope or telescope can also be used with this activity.

4. *Senses Booklet:* Plan to take the children on a nature walk. Before going out, duplicate and cut out Figure N1, "*Las ideas* / Ideas" (page 219). Have the children write their predictions of what they think they will experience with their senses. After the nature walk, duplicate and cut out the remaining Figures N1 - N2 (pages 219 - 220). For the senses of hearing, smell, and sight, have students write their experiences. Have children assemble the booklets with brads. Have them use the booklets to compare their predictions and experiences.

YO PUEDO TOCAR
I CAN TOUCH

Most people relate touch to hands, as in *El Rey Midas,* but we use our entire bodies to touch. The sense of touch includes five sensations—touch, pain, pressure, heat, and cold. Not all parts of the body are equally sensitive; it is highly developed on the tip of the tongue and is poorest on the back of the shoulders. Hair and fingernails have no receptors, while our fingers have hundreds of receptors that give us information about the world around us.

MAIN SELECTION

Before reading the Main Selection aloud, take your students through the Literature Input and Observation/Experience phases which follow.

El Rey Midas.
Spain: Susaeta Ediciones, 1981.

In his quest for gold, foolish King Midas makes a wish to have the touch of gold.

I. **LITERATURE INPUT:** *El Rey Midas*
See pages 192 - 194.

II. **OBSERVATION/EXPERIENCE:** *El Rey Midas*
(Class Session One)

Guide students in the following observations/experiences to set the stage for reading the Main Selection.

Focus: Exploring our sense of touch.

1. Put various objects into a bag and let the children feel the objects, naming and describing each. Use some of the following objects—cotton ball, paper clip, seashell, cardboard or plastic shapes, marble, penny, toy car, and sandpaper.

2. Ask the following questions:

   • *¿Cómo se siente el objeto—áspero, liso, suave, o duro?* (How does the object feel—rough, smooth, soft, or hard?)
   • *¿Qué objeto creen que es?* (What do you think the object is?)
   • *¿Qué piensan cuando tocan este objecto?* (What comes to your mind when you touch this object?)

3. Tell students that they will meet a king from the story *El Rey Midas,* who uses the sense of touch for greed and later regrets it.

4. Have them predict what will happen when King Midas touches things and why he will regret it later. Following the story, have children discuss whether their predictions were correct.

III. READ AND DISCUSS THE MAIN SELECTION: *El Rey Midas*
(Class Session One)

Read the Main Selection from page 214 to the students. Highlight the unit's theme by relating this story to other selections from the Literature Input list on pages 192 - 194. Then, guide students in discussing some of the following questions.

1. *El Rey Midas no tomó en cuenta que no solamente tocamos con las manos. ¿Cómo podemos tocar sin usar los manos?* (King Midas did not realize that we do not only touch with our hands. How can we touch without using our hands?)

2. *¿Por qué es importante este sentido para nosotros?* (Why is this sense important to us?)

3. *¿Qué extrañarían si no tuvieran este sentido?* (What would you miss if you did not have this sense?)

4. *¿Hay algunas veces cuando ustedes no quieren usar el sentido del tacto?* (Are there some times when you do not want to use the sense of touch?)

5. *¿Cuáles son algunos peligros que debemos evitar para cuidar este sentido?* (What are some dangers we must avoid in order to take care of this sense?)

IV. "WHAT IF" STORY STRETCHER: *El Rey Midas*
(Class Session Two)

Next, re-read the Main Selection and choose one or more of the following questions to develop students' critical thinking skills. Story stretchers may also prompt discussion, drama or writing activities.

1. *Si tuvieran "magia al tocar," ¿qué harían?* (If you had the magic touch, what would you do?)

2. *¿Qué pasaría si no pudieran ustedes tocar? ¿Cómo sería la vida?* (What would happen if you could not touch? How would life be?)

3. *Si todo lo que tocaran se volviera _____, ¿cómo serían sus vidas diferentes?* (If everything you touched turned to _____, how would your lives be different?)

4. *Si no pudieran sentir ni calor, ni frío, ni dolor, ¿cómo serían sus vidas?* (If you could feel neither heat, nor cold, nor pain, how would your lives be?

5. *Si fueran ciegos y sordos, ¿qué sentido necesitarían usar? ¿Por qué?* (If you were blind and deaf, which sense would you need to use? Why?)

V. INTEGRATING OTHER DISCIPLINES: *El Rey Midas*
(Class Session Three and Ongoing)

The following activities are designed to enhance children's response to literature and expand *beyond* the story and its theme. The variety of activities gives teachers and students an opportunity to choose those most appropriate.

CREATIVE DRAMATICS

1. *Pantomime Situations:* Have students pantomime the following situations:

   - They are selecting fruit at a fruitstand.
   - They are checking pockets before washing clothes.
   - They are trying to find the light switch in the dark.
   - They are looking for the right key to open the door and there is no light.
   - They are trying to connect a lamp in a socket behind the bed that they cannot see.

2. *"Be an Object":* While seated in a circle, show students pictures of objects such as trees, fire, steel, ice, clouds, sandpaper. Have them pretend to be holding the object in their hands; e.g., show an ice cube and have the observers pretend to toss it from hand to hand, lick it, feel it drip, and comment that it is cold.

3. *Basket Game:* Provide a basket with imaginary objects inside. Have students pantomime imaginary objects they pick up while observers guess what they are by the way they are handled.

4. *Touch Game:* In small groups, have a child touch an object in the room and name the object. That child then selects another child to touch the same object, name what was touched, and then add one more. The game continues until all the children in the group have successfully touched and named all of the objects. When the order and naming becomes too difficult, begin the game again. As an alternative, play the game by telling children to touch one part of their bodies to another part of their bodies—touch their knees to their ankles, touch their toes to their toes.

5. *Body Chain:* Make a body chain by seating children in a line on the floor. Tell them they are going to build a chain with their bodies. Tell the child seated at one end of the line to touch her/his elbow to the next child's knee. Tell them they are stuck with glue. Now tell each child, in turn, to touch her/his elbow to the knee of the next child until the chain is complete.

6. *What's in the Bag?:* Have each child bring a bag with an object from home. Allow the children to take turns reaching into the bags, describing the object they are touching. As an added activity on the following day, see if children can remember and describe what objects were in the bags without saying the object's name. Listeners must identify the objects.

7. *Who Am I?:* In groups, blindfold half the children and have them touch another partner's face and hair. Tell the children without the blindfolds to move to other locations. The blindfolded children must take off their blindfolds, draw their partners and tell who they were. Repeat with other groups.

ART AND WRITING

1. *Opposites:* Have students make charts that describe opposite qualities such as smooth/rough, soft/hard, hot/cold. Have children bring in objects from home that fit these descriptions. Using two undetailed animal shapes, have children create two animal shapes that have opposite textures. Provide materials of varying textures for the students to paste onto their animal shapes. Allow them to write sensory descriptions of the animal shapes.

2. *Mixed-Up Animal:* Have students create a mixed-up animal having combined animal textures. Provide mixed media to give the drawings a mixed-texture appearance. Have students write stories focusing on the textures of the mixed-up animal—scaly skin, furry neck, spiky back, bushy tail.

3. *Do Not Touch:* Make a list of things children are not allowed to touch. The ideas should come from the children. See if children can come up with reasons for not being allowed to touch certain things—health, safety, expensive, breakable, sacred. Have students create a story for the title *«No toque»* ("Do Not Touch").

4. *Once Upon a Time:* Read the big book, *Ricitos de Oro y los tres osos* (Addison-Wesley, 1989) with students. Have students imagine that Goldilocks is an intruder in their homes. Have the students describe all the things she should not have touched but did anyway. Have them incorporate it into *«Había una vez Ricitos de Oro....»* ("Once upon a time Goldilocks....") Have them illustrate the stories accordingly.

5. *Textures:* Provide paper of assorted textures—tin foil, waxed paper, corrugated paper, sandpaper, shelving paper, gift wrap, magazine pictures, paper towels, tissue paper—for students to create textured pictures. Have them glue their pictures on cardboard sheets. They may wish to create picture designs or sculptures of layered paper. Have them close their eyes and touch the textured pictures. Ask if they can "see" with their hands. In journal entries, have students describe the experience of being able to "see" with their hands.

6. *Touch Picture:* Provide a large sheet of paper with the word *«Tocar»* ("Touch") written across it in large block letters covering the whole sheet. Provide items of assorted textures such as egg shells, macaroni, seeds, marshmallows, or leaves for students to paste inside the letters. Have students write poems about the sense of touch.

7. *Clay-Figure Story:* Have students make two clay figures, one to keep and one to contribute for a writing exercise. Let them create an object of their choice and paint it when dried. To prompt story writing, place finished figures on a tray from which each child may select a figure to be the main character in the story. Have them share stories with class.

8. *Touching List:* As a homework assignment, have children make up a list of things they enjoy touching and why. Children may also make up a list of things they would rather not touch. Compare and share lists for a very "touchy" discussion.

9. *Textured Fingerpainting:* Have children mix coarse sand or salt in paint to fingerpaint. Allow them to write descriptions of their textured pictures.

10. *Facepainting:* Provide homemade make-up and allow children to do facepainting.

Non-toxic make-up

1 Tbsp. solid shortening
2 Tbsp. cornstarch
Food coloring

Mix together and store in small jars.

Allow cooperative groups to select several interesting faces to incorporate into a story about the peculiar-looking "characters." Encourage story sharing.

SCIENCE

1. *Feeling Fabric:* Collect samples of fabric and attach them to a board. Let the group feel the differences in texture and describe them—velvet, silk, vinyl, leather, suede, corduroy, lace, plastic, satin, wool, polyester. For each fabric that they touch, allow them to illustrate and write the name of an object or an animal that may feel like it, e.g., wool/sheep, suede/boots, corduroy/pants. With the students, discuss where the fabrics came from and/or how they were made (the process).

2. *Feeling Animals:* Before doing this activity, make sure there are no pet allergies among your students. Bring in a kitten, snake or turtle and allow children to carefully feel and describe. Have students incorporate the sensory experience into a group poem.

3. *Nature Walk:* Take the children on a nature walk. Have them predict and write about what they think they will experience with their senses. After the nature walk, have the children compare what they predicted with what they experienced on the walk.

POETRY

Los sentidos

Niño, vamos a cantar una bonita canción;
yo te voy a preguntar; tú me vas a responder:
Los ojos, ¿para qué son? Los ojos son para ver.
¿Y el tacto? Para tocar. ¿Y el oido? Para oir.
¿Y el olfato? Para oler. ¿Y el gusto? Para gustar.
¿El alma? Para sentir, para querer y pensar.

Amado Nervo

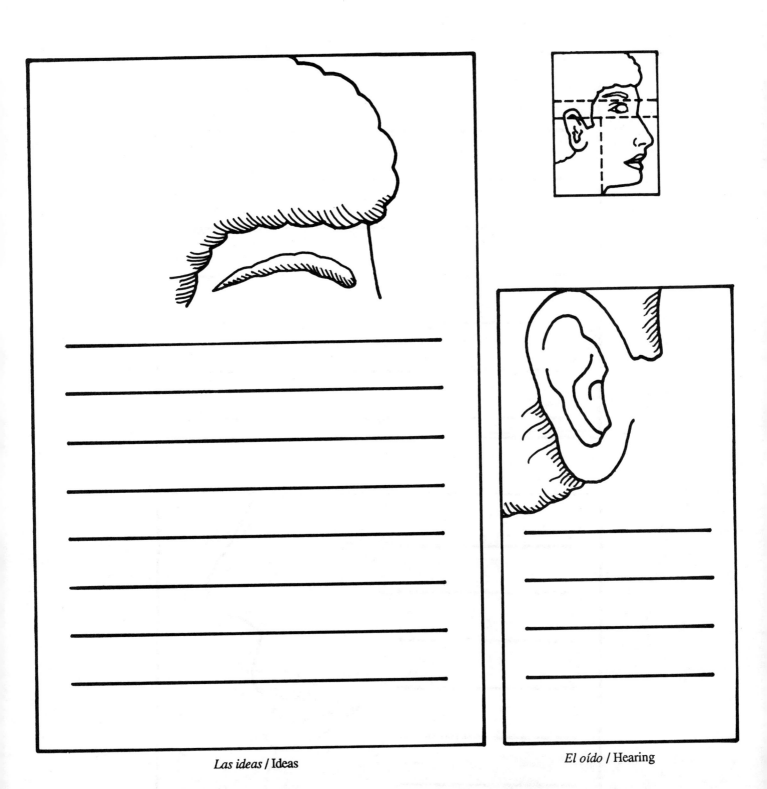

Las ideas / Ideas

El oído / Hearing

Figure N2: *Librito de los sentidos* / Senses Booklet

La vista / Sight

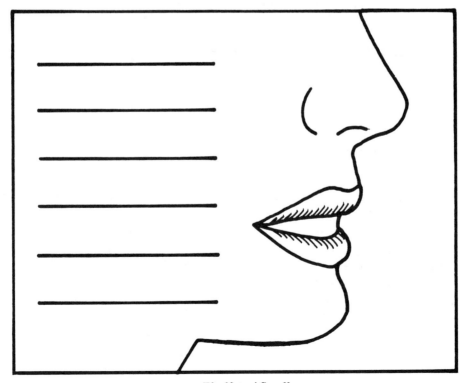

El olfato / Smell

MY OWN CREATIVE TEACHING IDEAS FOR UNIT THIRTEEN

Books: _____

_____

_____

_____

_____

_____

Ideas: _____

_____

_____

_____

_____

_____

_____

_____

_____

_____

_____

_____

_____

_____

_____

_____

UNIT FOURTEEN

EL MUNDO DE LA MAGIA Y LOS DESEOS

THE WORLD OF MAGIC AND WISHES

Stories of enchantment are found among all folktales. Frequently the enchantment is used as a curse or punishment; sometimes it serves goodness and happiness. Other forms of enchantment include enchantment of children, enchantment during a long sleep, and giving magical powers such as invisibility and strength. Magical objects are essential aspects of many tales. Dolls, rings, cloaks, tablecloths, lamps, musical instruments, and the like, add an imaginative dimension to the tales. Wishes, frequently granted in threes, are usually associated with character traits such as courage, greed, benevolence, and honesty. Another feature of this theme is transformation, such as the changing of inanimate objects to live characters. All of these elements make interesting and fanciful contributions to the folktale *El payaso y la princesa*, in which inanimate objects come to life in the most imaginative way.

MAIN SELECTION

Before reading the Main Selection aloud, take your students through the Literature Input and Observation/Experience phases which follow.

Gabán, Jesús.

El payaso y la princesa.
Spain: Editorial Destino, S.A., 1983.

In this imaginative, romantic tale about two marionettes—a princess and a clown—a magic raindrop touches them in movement, love, and spirit, bringing them to life and floating them away to a refuge of harmony and happiness. An award-winning *Appel les Mestres* book, this story kindles the imagination for creative literary response.

I. LITERATURE INPUT: *El payaso y la princesa*

Select five or more titles from the following list to read aloud. Read at least one selection per day to the students. Make available and incorporate the suggested titles for voluntary independent reading. Titles marked with * are Spanish translations of the original English story; titles marked with + are recommended for more proficient listeners.

1. *Aladino y la lámpara maravillosa.* Spain: Editors S. A., 1986. A magician helps Aladino find his fortune with a magic lamp. It breeds greed in those who seek power, but for Aladino, it represents a humble symbol of wealth and strength.

+2. Alonso, Fernando. *El hombrecillo de papel.* Spain: Editorial Miñón, S.A., 1981. A modern tale about a little girl's "life-like" paper doll. Made from newspaper, it comes to life and creates a wonderful experience for her and her friends.

3. *La Bella Durmiente.* Spain: Editors S. A., 1986. In this version of *Sleeping Beauty,* an interesting story twist occurs—the villainous witch causes her own accidental death when she battles with the prince who breaks the evil spell the princess is under.

4. Boada, Francesc. *El molinillo mágico.* Spain: Editorial La Galera, S.A., 1977. A humble man is given a magic grinder. It repays people according to their personalities, including the captain who is responsible for causing the ocean's water to be salty.

5. Bofill, Francesc. *Los guisantes maravillosos.* Spain: Editorial La Galera, S.A., 1980. In this Spanish version of *Jack and the Beanstalk,* Pedro is aided by a good fairy who helps him get rid of the villainous giant.

6. Busquets, Carlos. *El zapatero y los duendes.* Spain: Editorial Susaeta, 1980. This adaptation of *The Shoemaker and the Elves* tells about a shoemaker who constructs wooden elf dolls as gifts for three little orphans. When a fairy brings the elves to life, they reward the shoemaker for his good deed.

7. *La Cenicienta.* Editors S. A., 1986. In this simplified hardcover version of *Cinderella,* she is aided by birds that help with her chores to free her for the gala event.

+8. *Cuéntame un cuento: Las semillas mágicas y otros cuentos.* Spain: Editorial Altea, 1985. This is a wonderfully illustrated version of the classical story *Jack and the Beanstalk.*

9. Duplaix, Lily. *El conejo blanco.* México: Editorial Trillas, S.A., 1987. A little rabbit's magic works against him for using it in a naughty way.

10. Farris, Stella. *La manta mágica*. Spain: Editorial Montena, 1982. Curro and his teddy fly on a magic carpet to get a close-up view of pop-up insects and birds. The pop-up collection includes: *Teddy, el osito mágico; La pompa mágica* and *El castillo mágico*.

+11. Gantschev, Ivan. *El lago de la luna*. México: Editorial Trillas, S.A., 1985. This book tells of a child's adventure with the magical power of the moon.

+12. Guerrero García, J.J. *La pequeña cerillera*. Spain: Editorial Molina, 1984. In this heart-moving story, a little orphan match girl struggles for survival on a snowy Christmas Eve. As she holds on to the last thread of life, her matches bring imaginative, almost magical images that take her to a better world.

13. *Las habichuelas mágicas*. Spain: Editors S.A., 1986. This delightful adaptation of *Jack and the Beanstalk* tells how an ogre was reformed by a small child, Zock, and promised never to harass children again. This is one of twenty simplified and colorful hardcover versions of classic fairytales.

14. Heuer, Margarita. *La niña y el delfín*. México: Editorial Trillas, S.A., 1983. On the ocean floor where Griselda and her dolphin live, a luminous, human-like shadow with magical powers grants them their wish in return for a humble request—its freedom.

+15. Janosch. *El violín mágico de Yosa*. Spain: Ediciones S.A., 1986. A generous bird gives young Yosa a magic violin. The violin allows him to help everyone who comes his way.

16. Mathieu, Renada. *Los tres deseos*. Spain: Editorial La Galera, 1980. In this humorous tale, San Pedro grants a woodcutter three wishes. They are foolishly wasted, especially his last one, for how would his wife face life with a sausage on her nose?

+17. Moodie, Fiona. *El pescador*. Spain: Ediciones S.M., 1985. Emma is magically transformed into a mermaid when she accidentally falls into the sea. She is freed from this enchantment when her husband recognizes her and devises a plan to rescue her.

18. *Nariz de salchicha*. Spain: Editors S.A., 1986. This humorous tale recounts how a woodcutter and his wife foolishly waste three wishes.

19. *El pájaro azul*. Spain: Editorial Bruguera, 1982. A prince is transformed into a bluebird by a fairy when he refuses to marry the king's stepdaughter. His heart belongs to Florinda, the king's daughter, whose love bears the key to his freedom.

20. *Rosa Blanca, Roja Flor*. Spain: Editors S.A., 1986. Two kind-hearted sisters, Rosa Blanca and Roja Flor, an enchanted prince, and several ill-tempered dwarves introduce young readers to the world of enchantment when the prince is transformed into a bear.

+
*21. Sendak, Maurice. *El gran libro verde*. Spain: Editorial Lumen, 1983. When Jack finds a green book, he discovers the most amazing magical tricks.

+22. Steig, William. *Silvestre y la piedrita mágica*. Windmill Books, 1977. Silvestre, a donkey, finds a magic pebble that grants all wishes. Frightened by a lion on his way to school, Silvestre wishes that he were a rock. He becomes a rock and remains one through four seasons until his parents discover him during a picnic.

*23. Suigne, M.C. *La Bella Durmiente del bosque*. Belgium: Ediciones HEMMA, 1981. This classical fairy tale retains much of the original story line and includes beautiful illustrations and enriching language.

*24. —. *Cenicienta*. Belgium: Ediciones HEMMA, 1981. This is a marvelously illustrated and well translated book of the classic tale, *Cinderella*.

+25. Turín, Adela and Nadia Pazzaglia. *Las hierbas mágicas*. Spain: Editorial Lumen, 1985. This is an interesting tale about Hortense, who saves the queen's life by finding magical herbs to cure her.

26. Valeri, Ma. Eulalia. *El pez de oro*. Spain: Editorial La Galera, S.A., 1982. A golden fish grants a fisherman all that can be desired until it can no longer tolerate the fisherman's weakness and his wife's greed.

RELATED TITLES IN ENGLISH FOR SECOND LANGUAGE ACQUISITION

+   de Paola, Tomie. *Strega Nona*. New Jersey: Prentice-Hall, 1975.

Galdone, Paul. *The Gingerbread Boy*. New York: Houghton Mifflin, 1975.

Graig, Jean M. *The Three Wishes*. New York: Scholastic, 1986.

William, Jay. *One Big Wish*. New York: Macmillan, 1980.

II. OBSERVATION/EXPERIENCE: *El payaso y la princesa*
(Class Session One)

Guide students in the following observation/experience sequence to set the stage for reading the Main Selection.

Focus: Our imaginations allow us to create imaginary, magical transformations as in the motifs found in folktales.

1. Display marionettes, move them, and have students imitate the movements. Instruct half the class to pretend that they are lifeless marionettes inside a rickety old-time theater wagon.

2. While the other half observes, sprinkle "magic" dust or water droplets, or blow bubbles on the group. Instruct them to come to life as they experience a transformation from lifelessness. Discuss observations and repeat the activities with the other half of the class.

3. Tell students that they will listen to a story, *El payaso y la princesa,* in which marionettes come to life in much the same way.

4. Have them predict the adventures that the clown and the princess will have as free-roaming marionettes. Following the story, have students discuss whether their predictions were correct.

III. READ AND DISCUSS THE MAIN SELECTION: *El payaso y la princesa*
(Class Session One)

Read the Main Selection from page 224 to the students. Highlight the unit's theme by relating this story to other selections from the Literature Input list on pages 224 - 226. Then, guide students in discussing some of the following questions.

1. *De todos los títeres del Tío Tano, ¿cuáles eran más especiales? ¿Por qué?* (Of all Tío Tano's puppets, which ones were most special? Why?)

2. *¿Qué deseaban el payaso y la princesa? ¿Por qué?* (What did the clown and the princess desire? Why?)

3. *¿Qué hizo el payaso para darle vida a la princesa? Si fueran ustedes el payaso y no hubieran gotas mágicas, ¿en qué otra forma podrían darle vida a la princesa?* (What did the clown do to bring life to the princess? If you were the clown and there were no magic raindrops, how might you bring the princess to life?)

4. *Si ustedes pudieran ser títeres, ¿cuáles les gustarían ser? ¿Por qué?* (If you could be marionettes, which would you like to be? Why?)

5. *¿Qué pasó con el Tío Tano y los títeres románticos? ¿Qué otro fin podría tener este cuento?* (What became of Tío Tano and the romantic puppets? What other ending might the story have?)

IV. "WHAT IF" STORY STRETCHER: *El payaso y la princesa*
(Class Session Two)

Next, re-read the Main Selection and choose one or more of the following questions to develop students' critical thinking skills. Story stretchers may also prompt discussion, drama or writing activities.

1. *Si al Tío Tano le hubieran gustado los títeres vivientes, ¿cómo habría cambiado el cuento?* (If Tío Tano had liked the living puppets, how would the story have changed?)

2. *Si Parsimonia no hubiera causado el accidente durante la tormenta, ¿en qué otra forma podrían haber tocado las gotas mágicas al payaso y la princesa?* (If Parsimonia had not caused the accident during the storm, in what other way might the magic raindrops have touched the puppets?)

3. *Si todos los títeres hubieran recobrado vida durante una función, ¿qué habrían hecho y qué habrían dicho los títeres? ¿Y el público?* (If all the puppets had come to life during a performance, what would they have done and said? And the audience?)

4. *Si algo mágico les pasara a ustedes, ¿qué podría ser? Describan que pasaría.* (If something magical were to happen to you, what might it be? Describe what would happen.)

5. *Si ustedes pudieran compartir un deseo, tal como el payaso y la princesa, ¿qué sería? ¿Cómo lo compartirían?* (If you had one wish to share, just as the clown and princess did, what would it be? How would you share it?)

V. INTEGRATING OTHER DISCIPLINES: *El payaso y la princesa*
(Class Session Three and Ongoing)

The following activities are designed to enhance children's response to literature and expand *beyond* the story and its theme. The variety of activities gives teachers and students an opportunity to choose those most appropriate.

CREATIVE DRAMATICS

1. *Story Dramatization:* Have groups re-enact the following story scenes: (1) the clown and the princess marionettes coming to life; (2) the mule and the marionettes inside the cart during the storm; (3) Tío Tano's encounter with the living marionettes; (4) all the marionettes coming to life and running away. Allow them to dramatize the entire story. Use sound to enhance the dramatization—patting, brushing and snapping fingers for rain; and imaginative music for the magical scene when the puppets come to life.

2. *Living Mural:* Have the students sketch life-sized story characters and scenery on a strip of butcher paper. Plan a spot in the picture where arms and a face can become part of the picture. Have the students paint the mural and, when dry, cut out holes. Have students take turns being the characters and answering questions posed by curious observers.

3. *Magically Coming to Life:* For total class participation, form several groups and assign marionette characters to each group (clown, princess, prince, witch, and so on). Have groups think of alternate ways to bring the characters to life—blowing kisses, touching elbows, rubbing backs. Have them improvise their ideas while coming to life.

4. *Magic Box:* Present a box that has "magical" qualities. Tell students that its contents can become many things. Have them pantomime its contents; e.g. a kitten, banana, or camera.

5. *Magic Cloth:* Present a "magic" cloth that has the quality of transforming individuals into a desired character, object or animal. To model this, drape a cloth over yourself and then appear as a newly transformed character, object or animal; e.g., a ballerina, motorcycle, monster, or toy. Have students contribute their imaginative ideas.

ART AND WRITING

1. *String Puppets:* Using construction paper, cardboard rolls, string, straws, paper fasteners (brads), and crayons or markers, have the students create simple clown and princess marionettes. The students may use them to imitate character movements. Have students write dialogues that the puppets might say during given situations; e.g., when touched by the magic raindrop; scolded by Tío Tano; off to start new lives.

2. *Magic Raindrop:* Shape hangers in the form of raindrops. Glue two clear cellophane sheets to each of the shaped hangers and cut away the excess. On construction paper, have the students draw the clown and the princess. Have them color, cut out, and glue the figures on the raindrops. Then have them use permanent marking pens to draw pictures of a place where they live "happily ever after." (Have the students draw the scenery on the cellophane raindrop around the characters). Tell the students to write new story endings describing how the magic raindrop happily changed the puppets' lives.

3. *Magic Hats:* Have the children construct assorted hats from construction paper. The magic hats will "transform" the students into the marionettes of their choice. Within cooperative groups, allow students to improvise an adventure they might have and write a group story about the adventure.

4. *Autobiography:* Allow the students to pretend that they are marionettes—princesses, sailors, pirates—and ask them to think of all the magical things they might do. Have them describe what life is like as free-roaming, live marionettes. Have them write autobiographies of their adventures.

5. *Finger Puppets:* Using Figure O (page 232), have students color and cut out the clown and princess. Instruct them to cut out holes for index and middle fingers. Have the students cut out the four rectangles, and color, roll and glue them to use on their fingers as stockings and boots. Then have students glue the figures onto firm cardstock. Make a stage platform out of an inverted shoebox. Decorate and have finger puppets perform on the platform. Using the puppets, allow the children to improvise the story, or they may write skits for the puppets.

6. *Magic Pictures:* Have students draw colorful pictures of magical objects. Tell them to color, pressing firmly with crayons. Have them lightly brush thinned-out tempera paint over the pictures. Ask them to notice how the crayon area almost magically resists the paint. For variation, have them experiment with crayons and paper that match and see how the magic picture reappears. On another paper, have them write a description of the function of the magical object.

7. *I Can Make Magic:* Have students imagine themselves finding something that is magical. Where did it come from? Where did they find it? Was it placed there intentionally or was it lost? Instruct them to write stories and edit them for publication. Once the stories have been typed, duplicated and bound, have them illustrate their stories.

8. *Book Awards:* Have the students select favorite books from the Literature Input to honor with awards. Ask them to list the standards by which the book was chosen. Have them illustrate the book cover and write the standards on pre-designed award certificates. Display the illustrated book covers on a bulletin board titled *«Mi ventana mágica»* ("My Magic Window"). Present the awards at a class book-awards ceremony.

9. *Wishing Star:* Have students imagine what three wishes they would make on a magic wishing star. Have them tell how the wishes would come true. Have them write the stories in star-shaped books. Allow them to draw accompanying illustrations. If needed, use the following writing starters:

   «Si tuviera tres deseos . . . .» ("If I had three wishes . . . .")
   «Mi mayor deseo es . . . .» ("My biggest wish is . . . .")

10. *Magic Potion Recipe:* Have children write recipes for magic potions to sprinkle on favorite objects to make them magical. Ask them to draw the objects and write stories about their "magical" power.

11. *Stencil Magic:* Provide four-inch-high tagboard patterns, such as gingerbread girls and boys and animals, for the children to trace on construction paper with colored pastels. Without removing the patterns, have the students retrace the outline of the figures, using the pastels in a back and forth motion. Next, have the students use tissues

to sweep the pastel away from the outline on the construction paper. When they lift the tagboard shape, the figure will have the appearance of a magical transformation. Have the students write stories about interesting characters who have been transformed. Compile the illustrations and stories for a class book.

SCIENCE

1. *Magic Raindrops:* The raindrop in the story had a magical quality, but real raindrops can give the appearance of being magical, as when water droplets are observed on a variety of surfaces such as a flower, leaf, paper, or waxed paper. With the children, discuss how water is absorbed by some materials and repelled by others, how it flows and evaporates. Allow the children to record some of these observations in their science logs.

2. *Liquid Magic:* Allow the students to perform liquid magic with water by using food coloring and carnations. When the stems of white carnations are placed in colored water, color appears in the petals as the water travels upward. Have the students record the observation in their science logs.

3. *Liquid Emulsion:* Prepare liquid emulsions in baby jars, using dishwashing soap and water. Have the students shake the jars, observe what happens, and discuss. Allow them to record the observations in their science logs.

   Using the liquid emulsion and shaped pipe cleaners as wands, have the children blow bubbles and play a transformation game in which they are transformed into characters or objects. Form a circle and have several students pantomime actions inside the circle while others observe. Observers may record the activity of the floating and bursting air-filled bubbles and the actions of the "transformed" students.

SOCIAL STUDIES

1. *Restriction Versus Freedom:* A concept that can be drawn from this story is that we value our freedom, but restrictions are placed on our freedom for various reasons. Have students participate in an activity that is very restrictive (not allowing for freedom of movement), e.g., have them stand in a line for 30 seconds without moving, while lively music plays. As a contrasting activity, have them dance in a parade, expressing their individual creative movement to a variety of musical selections. Following these activities, allow them to compare their feelings, describing how each activity made them feel and why. Discuss how these experiences relate to the puppets' experiences. Use this experience to prompt personal journal writing.

2. *Good and Bad Aspects of Freedom:* In cooperative groups, have children brainstorm situations in which animals have lost their freedom. Allow them to write about the good and bad side of each situation; e.g., the zoo is a sad place for many animals, but good because we can see them. Next, instruct them to brainstorm situations which require restrictions for the children now but which will not pose a concern to them as adults. With the children, discuss the good and bad of each situation.

3. *Wish for a Friend:* We all experience moments when we wish that we could do something nice for others. With students, brainstorm a list of people who would be happy to have a wish come true. Have them write about one of those people having the wish come true.

POETRY

Muñequita

Esta muñequita bailará
con su vestidito muy ampón
dos pasitos para acá
y otros tantos para allá.

Llevará muy bien este compás
y las manos así moverá;
una vuelta para atrás
y así se quedará
para poder decir «mamá.»

Folklore

El payasito

El domingo fui al circo
y entre otras cosas vi
a un lindo payasito
que me hizo reir.

Yo soy ese payasito
que tanto te gustó;
a enseñarte mis gracias
he venido yo.

Anónimo

Los títeres encantados

Una princesita muy aburrida
con un payasito deseaba bailar.
¡Qué buena suerte tuvieron
cuando una gotita los vino a
encantar!

El dueño del teatro
muy disgustado los quiso castigar;
¡pero los títeres tan felices
se pudieron escapar!

Raquel C. Mireles

Figure O: *Títeres de la princesa y el payaso* / Princess and Clown Puppets

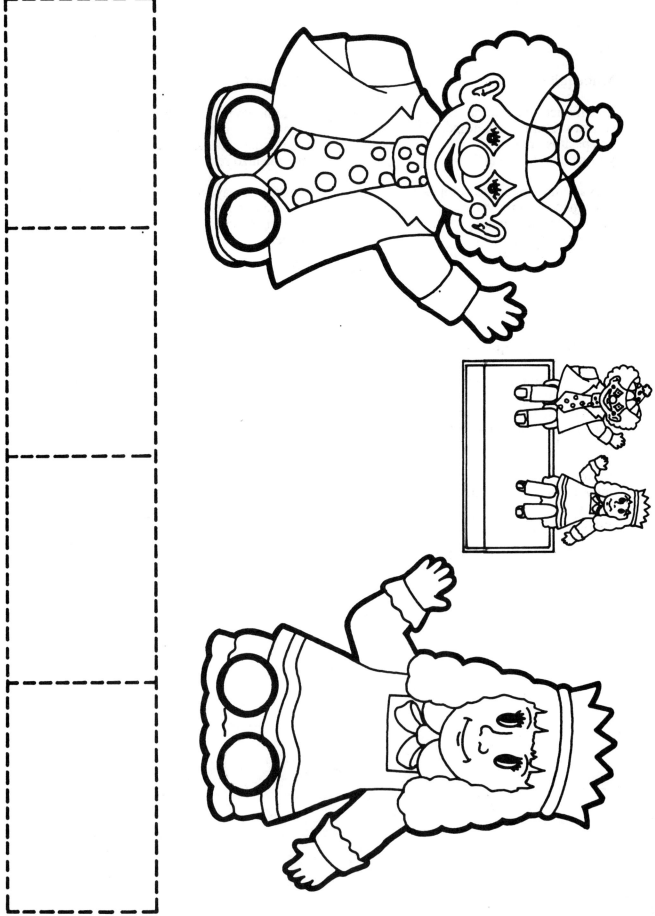

MY OWN CREATIVE TEACHING IDEAS FOR UNIT FOURTEEN

Books: _____

_____

_____

_____

_____

_____

Ideas: _____

_____

_____

_____

_____

_____

_____

_____

_____

_____

_____

_____

_____

_____

_____

_____

_____

_____

_____

UNIT FIFTEEN

ASTUCIA Y ENGAÑO

QUICK WITS AND TRICKS

In folktales, wit frequently prevails in children, little people, the youngest sibling, or in the humblest but noblest character. A character may use quick wit to solve problems, as in overcoming giants. Motifs about quick wits and trickery usually portray both animals and humans outsmarting their friends, caretakers, masters, or enemies. Gain in status, riches, recognition, marriage, or freedom are often the reward for extraordinary bravery or for jobs well done. *Caperucita Roja* illustrates these themes with a twist of adventure.

MAIN SELECTION

Before reading the Main Selection aloud, take your students through the Literature Input and Observation/Experience phases which follow.

Suigne, M.C.

Caperucita Roja.
Belgium: Ediciones HEMMA, 1981.

In this beautifully illustrated story, a shepherd, suspecting the wolf's evil intentions, rescues poor grandmother and grandchild from the wolf's stomach. Tricked by the shepherd, the wolf drowns. However, in this story, guess who is both the trickster and the "tricked"?

I.   LITERATURE INPUT: *Caperucita Roja*

Select five or more titles from the following list to read aloud. Read at least one selection per day to the students. Make available and incorporate the suggested titles for voluntary independent reading. Titles marked with * are Spanish translations of the original English story; titles marked with + are recommended for more proficient listeners.

*1. Ada, Alma Flor. *Los tres cerditos*. Reading, MA: Addison-Wesley, 1989. This story classic, adapted by Alma Flor Ada, is a beautifully illustrated big book for shared reading experiences.

2. Almendros, Herminio. *Había una vez. . . .* Cuba: Editorial Gente Nueva, 1982. This book contains an anthology of many of the classics and poems by Cuban poets. The selections represent the current theme and a variety of other themes from this handbook.

3. Almodóvar, A.R. *Los animales miedosos*. Spain: Editorial Algaida, 1985. This Spanish version of the *Musicians of Bremen* is humorous and the illustrations are delightful.

+4. —. *El medio pollito y el medio real*. Spain: Editorial Algaida, 1985. On his way to reclaim half a silver coin from an insincere king, a persistent chick calls upon the aid of his companions who face the king's wrath. Surrendering to the chick's invincibility, the king finally returns the silver coin.

+5. —. *El mono caprichoso*. Spain: Editorial Algaida, 1985. A conniving monkey trades several possessions, from bread to a child, until he gets what he wants.

+6. —. *La niña del zurrón*. Spain: Editorial Algaida, 1985. A beggar tricks a naive little girl; he kidnaps her but mistakenly returns her to her mother's village to experience the surprise of his life!

+7. —. *Los tres cochinitos*. Spain: Algaida Editores, S.A., 1985. The wittiest pig hires a bricklayer to build a sturdy brick house. When the wolf finally meets up with him, the wolf learns that he is no match for the clever pig.

8. Amades, Joan. *El pleito del gato*. Spain: Editorial La Galera, S.A., 1983. Four farmers, who are equal owners of a cat, must decide who owns the part of the cat that caused a fire. A judge cleverly resolves the dispute.

*9. Aruego, José. *El cuento de un cocodrilo*. New York: Scholastic Book Services, 1972. A witty monkey helps rescue a small boy from a starving crocodile. The monkey's only request for compensation is to be allowed to eat bananas from the boy's plantation.

*10. Burningham, John. *Harquín, el zorro que bajó al valle*. Spain: Editorial Miñón, S.A., 1982. Harquín's adventurous spirit places him at odds with a hunter, whom he manages to outwit to help save his family.

11. Carreño, Mada. *Clásicos Trillas: Pulgarcito*. México: Editorial Trillas, S.A., 1987. When witty Pulgarcito uses the magic boots to help the king, he receives a handsome reward. This story is one among a collection of fifteen colorfully illustrated classics and ethnic tales.

+12. Company, M., and R. Capdevila. *Las Tres Mellizas y el flautista de Hamelín*. Spain: Editorial Ariel, 1985. There is never a dull moment with those crazy triplets. When they get tangled in the story, humor is the end result.

13. —. *Las Tres Mellizas y Pulgarcito*. Spain: Editorial Ariel, 1985. Once again, when the unruly triplets meet up with Pulgarcito and his brothers, they are too much for the ogre and much too smart for the "stir-crazy" witch.

+14. —. *Las Tres Mellizas, Ali Baba y los cuarenta ladrones*. Spain: Editorial Ariel, S.A., 1986. The Mellizas devise a scheme to recover all the valuables that the forty thieves have taken from the town's people. Those poor thieves have a surprise in store for them with the Mellizas in the picture.

+15. *Cuéntame un cuento: Gato con botas y otros cuentos*. Spain: Editorial Altea, 1986. This classic tale, which is one of a series, is beautifully illustrated and contains an enriching text.

16. *El flautista de Hamelín*. Spain: Editors S.A., 1986. This is a classic tale about a king's ingratitude, miserliness, and insincerity. The flautist uses his wit to force the king into "singing a different tune."

17. *El gato con botas*. Spain: Editors S.A., 1986. The witty cat from *Puss in Boots* bribes the town's people to accomplish good.

+18. Grimm, Brothers. Adapted by Rossana Guarnieri. *Los músicos de Brema*. México: Fernández Editores, S.A., 1983. This Grimms' tale recounts how four animals—a donkey, a rooster, a dog, and a cat—use their wits to find their fortunes. It is a colorful paperback with easily comprehensible text.

+*19. Grimm, Brothers. *Hansel y Gretel*. Spain: Alianza Editorial, 1985. This hardbound version of Grimms' tale is beautifully illustrated with a richly appealing text.

20. Gwen, M.L. *Los tres pequeños cerditos*. Spain: Editorial Susaeta, S.A., 1971. This paperback version of *The Three Little Pigs* closely follows the original story, highlighting the serious, hardworking little pig that solves the problem as the wittiest character.

21. Jordi, Jane. *Juanote y las tres bolsas de oro*. Spain: Editorial La Galera, S.A, 1984. Juanote sets out to gain wisdom from people in other lands, but much to his surprise, he finds many foolish people. Instead, he uses his own wisdom to earn three bags of gold.

*22. Lionni, Leo. *Pulgada a pulgada*. New York: Col. Aston-Ivan Obolensky, 1960. A witty inchworm escapes an inevitable fate by inching his way out of sight when a naive bird requests that his song be measured.

*23. Lobel, Arnold. *Sopa de ratón*. Spain: Ediciones Alfaguara, S.A., 1984. A clever mouse tells four stories to cunningly trick a weasel into sparing his life.

24. Rius, María. *La casita de chocolate*. Spain: Editorial Bruguera, S.A., 1980. In this adaptation of *Hansel and Gretel*, the gingerbread house is made of chocolate and the main characters are Juan and Margarita. The parents abandon their children, but feeling remorse for their actions, they later rejoice upon the safe return of their children. Margarita's quick wit makes the reunion possible.

25. —. *Pulgarcito*. Spain: Editorial Bruguera, 1980. Pulgarcito in the fairytale collection by Rius is beautifully illustrated and told with simplicity and enriching language.

26. —. *El sastrecillo valiente*. Spain: Editorial Bruguera, S.A., 1980. A brave little tailor instigates a fight between two giants so that he capture them for the king and collect his royal reward.

27. Valeri, Ma. Eulalia. *La gallinita roja*. Spain: Editorial La Galera, 1977. This Spanish version of the *Little Red Hen* tells how the fox is tricked by the hen. An unexpected hot shower cures him of his bad habits forever.

28. —. *El lobo, el cerdito, el pato y la oca*. Spain: Editorial La Galera, 1977. This modified version of *The Three Little Pigs* includes a pig, a duck and a goose against a villainous wolf.

29. —. *Pluma dorada*. Spain: Editorial La Galera, S.A., 1977. A delightful story of a witty hen that finds a diamond and uses it to outsmart a selfish king.

30. —. *Los siete chivitos y el lobo*. Spain: Editorial La Galera, 1977. Seven little goats outwit a villainous wolf in this selection with delightful illustrations and bold print.

31. —. *El pajarillo*. Spain: Editorial La Galera, S.A.1982. A child, through a misfortune, is transformed into a little bird but finds a way to return to his normal state.

32. Vásquez, Zoraida. *Grandes cuentos para los pequeñitos*. México: Editorial Trillas, S.A., 1986. This collection has colorfully illustrated, bold-print texts with simplified, yet enriching narratives. Selections include: *El gato con botas, Los músicos de Bremen, El sastrecillo valiente,* and *Los tres cerditos*.

33. Vásquez, Zoraida, and Julieta Montelongo. *Chiquito pero listo*. México: Editorial Trillas, S.A., 1984. A miserable rabbit gets nothing but disrespect from a hippopotamus and an elephant until he cooks up a scheme to outwit them.

34. —. *Amigos con suerte*. Mexico: Editorial Trillas, S.A., 1985. The sly rabbit and gopher, who were supposed to be the dinner for Sr. Léon's family, trick baby lion into thinking they are invited guests.

*35. Wilson, Gage. *Kali-Kali y el oso*. Spain: Editorial Generales Anaya, 1983. Kali-Kali, the hunter, goes hunting for a bear; but the bear, without even trying, outsmarts the hunter.

+36. Zatón, Jesús. *El gato con botas*. Spain: Editorial Jucar Infantil, 1984. A witty cat, through masterful trickery, acquires wealth, a kingdom, and even a princess for his master.

The following selections should be read after the main selection has been presented. These supporting stories can be used for story comparisons, dramatizing variants, or for writing about story variants; such activities are described in Experiences with Literature.

+37. Bernadette. *Caperucita Roja*. Spain: Editorial Lumen, 1980. This beautiful version of Little Red Riding Hood tells of the grandmother's and granddaughter's rescue by a hunter. When Little Red Riding Hood and grandmother fill the wolf's stomach with rocks, he falls to his death.

38. Boada, Francesc. *Caperucita Roja*. Spain: Editorial La Galera, S.A., 1981. In this version of Little Red Riding Hood, a hunter frees grandmother and grandchild by snipping the wolf's stomach. The humorous illustrations prompt a great deal of discussion.

39. Capdevila, Juan. *Las Tres Mellizas y Caperucita Roja*. Spain: Editorial Ariel, 1985. Brace yourselves for some fun and excitement with these hilarious triplets and the trouble-seeking witch as they venture into Little Red Riding Hood's world.

+40. *Cuéntame un cuento: Caperucita Roja y otros cuentos*. Spain: Editorial Altea, 1986. This classic tale is one of eleven beautifully illustrated and well-translated books in the series.

+41. Tapia, Graciela. *Las dos Caperucitas*. México: Editorial Trillas, S.A., 1984. Little Red Riding Hood and Little Blue Riding Hood plan a brilliant scheme to outsmart the wolf and to get rid of him forever.

RELATED TITLES IN ENGLISH FOR SECOND LANGUAGE ACQUISITION

Addison-Wesley Big Book Program. *The Gingerbread Man*. Reading, MA: Addison-Wesley, 1989.

—. *The Three Little Pigs*. Reading, MA: Addison-Wesley, 1989.

Galdone, Paul. *Henny Penny*. New York: Clarion Books, 1968.

+ —. *The Monkey and the Crocodile*. New York: Clarion Books, 1969.

—. *The Gingerbread Boy*. Boston: Houghton Mifflin, 1975.

—. *What's in Fox's Sack?* New York: Clarion Books, 1982.

Hoban, Russell. *A Bargain for Frances*. New York: Harper and Row, 1970.

+ Hyman, Trina S. *Little Red Riding Hood*. New York: Holiday House, 1983.

Kincaid, Lucy. *Now You Can Read: Little Red Riding Hood*. Cambridge, England: Brimax Books, 1980. Other books in the collection include: *The Gingerbread Man, Puss in Boots, Three Little Pigs, and Chicken Little*.

Marshall, James. *Red Riding Hood*. New York: Dial Books for Young Readers, 1987.

Schmidt, Karen. *The Gingerbread Man*. New York: Scholastic, 1985.

II.   OBSERVATION/EXPERIENCE: *Caperucita Roja*
(Class Session One)

Guide students in the following observation/experience sequence to set the stage for reading the Main Selection.

Focus: Games may utilize quick wits and tricks, the same traits often portrayed in folktales.

1. Have children form a circle. Have a blindfolded student sit in a chair in the middle of the circle. A child knocks on the chair. The blindfolded student asks, *«Quién es?»* ("Who is it?") The child disguises his voice to trick the blindfolded child.

2. Playing another game, have one child leave the room while an object is hidden under a child seated in the circle. The object of the game is for the seeker to find out who has the object. Each student must try to trick the seeker into thinking that she/he has the object.

3. Discuss what both games have in common. Tell them that they will hear a famous folktale, titled *Caperucita Roja,* which has more than one character acting as a trickster.

4. Have children predict who will do the tricking and how. Following the story, have them discuss whether their predictions were correct.

III.   READ AND DISCUSS THE MAIN SELECTION: *Caperucita Roja*
(Class Session One)

Read the Main Selection from page 236 to the students. Highlight the unit's theme by relating this story to other selections from the Literature Input list on pages 236 - 240. Then, guide students in discussing some of the following questions.

1. *¿Para qué iba Caperucita Roja a la casa de su abuelita? ¿Por qué visitan ustedes a sus abuelitas?* (Why was Little Red Riding Hood going to her grandmother's house? Why do you visit your grandmother?)

2. *¿Cómo describirían ustedes al lobo? ¿Creen ustedes que hay alguna gente que actúa como el lobo? Explíquennos.* (How would you describe the wolf? Do you suppose some people might behave like the wolf? Explain.)

3. *¿Cómo describirían ustedes al pastor?   ¿Conocen alguna persona como él? Explíquennos.* (How would you describe the shepherd? Do you know some people like him? Explain.)

4. *¿Por qué creen ustedes que Caperucita Roja siempre recordará esta experiencia? ¿Qué lección aprendió?* (Why do you think Little Red Riding Hood will always remember this experience? What was the lesson she learned?)

5. *¿Les gustó el final? Díganme ¿por qué o por qué no?* (Did you like the ending? Why or why not?)

IV. "WHAT IF" STORY STRETCHER: *Caperucita Roja*
(Class Session Two)

Next, re-read the Main Selection and choose one or more of the following questions to develop students' critical thinking skills. Story stretchers may also prompt discussion, drama. or writing activities.

1. *Si el pastor no hubiera venido a ayudar a Caperucita Roja y a su abuelita, ¿como habrían podido escapar?* (If the shepherd had not come to Little Red Riding Hood's and her grandmother's aid, how might they have been able to escape?)

2. *Si Caperucita hubiera llegado a la casa de la abuelita antes que el lobo, ¿qué habría pasado?* (If Little Red Riding Hood had arrived at her grandmother's house before the wolf had, what would have happened?)

3. *Si la abuelita se hubiera dado cuenta del plan del lobo, ¿cómo lo habría podido engañar?* (If Grandmother had realized that the wolf was trying to trick her, how might she have tricked him instead?)

4. *Si ustedes fueran la mamá de Caperucita Roja, ¿qué truco podrían hacerle al lobo para rescatar a la abuelita y a Caperucita Roja?* (If you were the mother of Little Red Riding Hood, what trick might you play on the wolf to rescue grandmother and Little Red Riding Hood?)

5. *Describan la escena favorita de ustedes del cuento. Si ustedes fueran más listos que Caperucita Roja, ¿qué dirían y qué harían en esta escena?* (Describe your favorite scene in the story. If you were wittier than Little Red Riding Hood, what would you say and do during this scene?)

V. INTEGRATING OTHER DISCIPLINES: *Caperucita Roja*
(Class Session Three and Ongoing)

The following activities are designed to enhance children's response to literature and expand *beyond* the story and its theme. The variety of activities gives teachers and students an opportunity to choose those most appropriate.

CREATIVE DRAMATICS

1. *Story Dramatization:* Have groups re-enact the following scenes: (1) the forest scene where Little Red Riding Hood encounters the wolf; (2) the cottage scene when the wolf disguises himself as Grandmother; (3) the rescue scene when the shepherd tricks the wolf, causing the wolf's demise. Have each group practice a scene, then take part in the story by dramatizing the entire story from beginning to end.

2. *A Changed Personality:* Have groups plan and improvise the story, incorporating a personality change in Little Red Riding Hood; e.g., silly, wild, brave, mischievous.

3. *Different Story Ending:* Have groups re-enact scenes from other variants of Little Red Riding Hood in which the climaxes or endings differ; e.g., Grandmother escapes; Grandmother hides in a closet; Little Red Riding Hood escapes, seeking aid from a nearby woodcutter; rescuers chase the wolf away, and so on. Discuss other possible endings; plan and have groups improvise their ideas.

4. *Story Variant:* Have students re-enact a humorous scene from *Las Tres Mellizas y Caperucita.* Have them devise plans for the Mellizas to outwit the witch. Have cooperative groups create and improvise witty ways for the Mellizas to escape from the fairytale.

5. *Story Variant:* After reading *Las dos Caperucitas,* have groups re-enact the scene when Little Red Riding Hood and Little Blue Riding Hood devise a plan to outwit the wolf and the cottage scene when the town's people await the wolf's capture. Allow groups to discuss, plan, and improvise possible subsequent story episodes.

ART AND WRITING

1. *Cereal-Box Wolf Puppet:* Half-way down cereal boxes, have the students draw a line around the boxes, cutting only around the front and sides. To make the wolves' faces, have the children fold the boxes in half so that, using their fingers and thumbs, they can open and close the mouths. To decorate, tell them to place the boxes flat on construction paper, trace the outline of the boxes, cut along the outlines, and glue paper to the boxes. Have them draw and cut out features, and paste them on the boxes. Have the students write favorite repetitive dialogues or chants that the wolves might say.

2. *Paper-Bag Wolf Hat:* Have the students create hats from large, brown paper bags. Half-way along the bottom sides and bag bottoms, have them draw horizontal zigzags for teeth, and cut along the lines. Tell them to cut a hole for the head at the other end. Draw and cut two large eyes and ears and glue them to the top of the wolf's face. Slip the bag over head and tape ends closed. Now we have a talking wolf that the students can interview.

   Interview: In pairs, have students think of questions to ask the wolf and prepare short interview sheets. Use sock puppets for interviewers (this lessens inhibitions). Have the interviewers ask questions, solicit answers, record them. Then have the pairs switch roles. Share the interviews with other groups.

3. *Character Stick Puppets:* Using the wolf and Little Red Riding Hood patterns from Figure P (page 245), have students color, cut out, and glue the clothing on the story characters. Then have the children mount these characters on popsicle sticks. Students may include hand-drawn characters from story variants such as *Las dos Caperucitas* and *Las Tres Mellizas y Caperucita Roja.* Have them retell the story or their favorite story variants while manipulating the stick puppets.

   Bag Theater: On brown paper bags, have them draw and cut out a square to form a bag stage with a large window. Have them create scenery and designs around the window. While holding the bag in one hand, have them manipulate the stick puppets inside the windows.

   Skit: Have the students write brief skits demonstrating quick wits and tricks for the stick puppets. Allow them to perform the skit for friends.

4. *Story Booklet:* Have cooperative groups create fairytale sequence books. Have them illustrate, sequence, and staple the pages together. Have them write captions to describe favorite story scenes. Allow them to read and share their booklets with the class. If needed, students may dictate captions.

5. *Finger Puppets:* Using Figure P (page 245), have the students color and cut out the characters and cape and granny cap from tagboard or stiff paper. Allow them to glue red fabric on the cape for Little Red Riding Hood and fur or velour fabric on the wolf. Have the children dress the characters using the tabbed clothing. Staple a rubber band across the lower back of each puppet to slip two fingers through to "walk" across the scenery box or table top. (For story variants, duplicate two or three figure sheets per student and have students modify the illustrations.)

   Table-Top Theater: Finger puppets can be used for table-top theaters. Dimensional props such as forest trees, flowers, a stream, a bridge, and a cottage can make up the setting on the table. Have the students use the puppets to re-enact the story.

   Lap Story Box: Have the students decorate shoeboxes by drawing houses and trees, cutting them out, and glueing them onto the boxes. Allow them to use finger puppets to retell the story. Have them write about favorite story variants.

6. *Painting:* Have students paint pictures of Little Red Riding Hood or the wolf. Allow them to write captions describing their favorite tricksters.

7. *Secret Pal:* Have students imagine that they are witty, trickster-type characters. Instruct them to write letters to secret pals telling all about their wittiest, trickiest secrets. Allow them to design large folders having secret lift-up doors and windows with secrets written inside.

8. *April Fool's Day Scheme:* Tell the students to imagine that it is April Fool's Day and it is their chance to fool or trick a friend, a member of the family, or even the teacher. Have them think about their schemes and write out all the details. Let them illustrate what they think the outcome of their schemes will be. Put the stories into a class book for the library corner.

9. *Witty-Character Face Book:* Using two paper plates and construction paper strips for facial features and hair, have students make their favorite witty character's face. (Characters are from the Literature Input.) Staple the face of both plates together at the top. Inside the plates, have them write "brag" notes, telling why the characters are so witty and sly.

10. *Quick Wits Club:* To become honorary members of a "quick wits" club, have students tell how they would outsmart characters from one of the stories in the Literature Input. Then, welcome to the club! Allow them to be the authors and illustrators of their witty stories and share them with the other "clubs."

SCIENCE

1. *Forest Nature Walk:* As Little Red Riding Hood did, take students on a nature walk, and ask them to use as many sensory faculties as possible to explore an imaginary forest. Try using mental imagery to capture the forest's density, animals, plants, sounds, and mood. Following the experience, with students, brainstorm all of their descriptions. Have them write the descriptions that their imaginations created. Have

groups recapture ideas on paper by having them paint sensory and imaginary impressions on a mural using watercolors and crayons. Have them write a group poem inspired by the "real" and imaginary sensory experience.

HEALTH AND SAFETY

1. *Healthy/Unhealthy Foods:* Little Red Riding Hood had some healthy foods inside her basket to deliver to Grandmother. Have students brainstorm some healthy foods and some "not so healthy" foods to give Grandma. Have them draw two large baskets on construction paper and draw all the foods that they would like to give to Grandma or to the wolf. Have them label the foods, and then use the foods as examples to write ten tips for healthy eating.

2. *Do's and Don't's:* Engage students in a discussion about Little Red Riding Hood's experience with the wolf. List all the "do's and don't's." Have students role play the ideas and evaluate them.

3. *Danger Zones:* Little Red Riding Hood walked into a danger zone. Relate her experience to real-life situations in which potential dangers with strangers might arise. Discuss and role play. With the children, brainstorm and write ideas for a class safety bulletin listing ten tips to help children avoid dangerous strangers.

POETRY

La caperucita

La caperucita le tiene que llevar
a su dulce abuela mantequilla y pan.
«Linda caperuza»—le dice su mamá—
«por el bosque espeso tienes que
cruzar.»

«Anda con cuidado no vayas a tardar
porque la abuelita esperando está.»
Pero caperuza se puso a jugar
y al mirarla el lobo la quiso abrazar.

Anónimo

El lobo

Jugaremos en el bosque
mientras el lobo no está
porque si el lobo aparece,
enteros nos comerá.

«Lobo, ¿estás allí?»
«Me estoy vistiendo.»

Jugaremos en el bosque
mientras el lobo no está
porque si el lobo aparece,
enteros nos comerá.

«Lobo, ¿estás allí?»
«Me estoy afilando los dientes.»

Jugaremos en el bosque
mientras el lobo no está
porque si el lobo aparece,
enteros nos comerá.

«Lobo, ¿estás allí?»
«Voy corriendo hasta encontrarlos.»

Juego popular

Figure P: *Títeres de la Caperucita Roja y el lobo* / Little Red Riding Hood and Wolf Puppets

cut
out

245

MY OWN CREATIVE TEACHING IDEAS FOR UNIT FIFTEEN

Books: _____

_____

_____

_____

_____

Ideas: _____

_____

_____

_____

_____

_____

_____

_____

_____

_____

_____

_____

_____

_____

_____

UNIT SIXTEEN

CONOCIENDO LA GENTE DEL CASTILLO

MEETING PEOPLE FROM CASTLES

In many fairytales, royalty subject commoners to tasks and trials. In other tales, royalty are the subjects of such tribulations. Unworthy traits such as vanity, dishonesty, greed, or over-zealousness are often portrayed in royalty; but sometimes royalty display honorable virtues. Such is the love and compassion of a prince in *El Príncipe Feliz.*

Commoners form the central characters in some plots in which royal status or power is gained. Sometimes both royalty and commoners must prove their worthiness or noble virtues by performing challenging tasks. These tasks, often carried out in series, seem almost impossible for the character to accomplish unless aided by an assistant with magical power or extraordinary wit. Such is the case when a young maiden rises from rags to riches in *Cenicienta.*

CHOOSE THE MAIN SELECTION

Before reading the Main Selection aloud, take your students through the Literature Input and Observation/Experience phases which follow.

Vásquez, Zoraida.	Suigne, M.C.
Grandes cuentos para los pequeñitos: El Príncipe Feliz. México: Editorial Trillas, S.A., 1986.	***Cenicienta.*** Belgium: Ediciones HEMMA., 1981.
This is a heart-warming tale about a compassionate prince and a swallow that sacrifice themselves to ease the misery among the town's people. These two souls reach out to others and, in the end, are rewarded for their kind deeds. Children can learn how caring about others and how giving of one's self can bring immense inner-satisfaction.	This beautifully picturesque tale retains much of the traditional elements of Perrault's classical Cinderella. If you choose ***Cenicienta*** as your selection, turn to page 256 to begin the Observation/ Experience phase.
If you choose ***El Príncipe Feliz*** as your selection, turn to page 252 to begin the Observation/Experience phase.	

I.   LITERATURE INPUT: *Both Selections*

Select five or more titles from the following list to read aloud. Read at least one selection per day to the students. Make available and incorporate the suggested titles for voluntary independent reading. Titles marked with * are Spanish translations of the original English story; titles marked with + are recommended for more proficient listeners.

+1.   —. *Las tres preguntas del rey*. Spain: Editorial Algaida, 1985. A boastful general, who claims that he has no worries at all, is given plenty to worry about by the king— he has three days to answer three impossible questions or else face demotion.

2.   Amades, Joan. *Juana, la princesa de la sal*. Spain: Editorial La Galera, S.A., 1977. In this charming tale, a king throws out his youngest daughter for telling him that she loves him "as much as salt." The use of rhyme enhances this delightful tale.

3.   Andersen, Hans Christian. *La princesa del guisante*. Spain: Editorial Lumen, 1986. This is a beautiful version of *The Princess and the Pea*. Pastel illustrations and enriching text make this a wonderful reading experience.

+4.   —. Adapted by Rosanna Guarnieri. *El traje nuevo del emperador*. México: Fernández Editores, 1983. A child's innocence reveals the deceptiveness of the adult world. A colorful paperback series.

+5.   —. *El ruiseñor del emperador*. México: Fernández Editores S.A., 1983. This well done translation of *The Nightingale* is one of twenty-four tales from *Los más famosos cuentos*.

+6. Arredondo, Inés. *Historia verdadera de una princesa*. México: SEP CIDCLI, S.A., 1984. Children will appreciate México's rich cultural heritage in this wonderfully illustrated story which recounts the Mexican legend of La Malinche's childhood and romantic encounter with Hernán Cortés.

+7. Beaumont, L.P. Translated by Carmen Bravo Villasante. *La bella y la bestia*. Spain: Editorial Miñón, S.A., 1984. This version of the classic *Beauty and the Beast* retains the traditional story line and has handsome illustrations.

8. *La Bella Durmiente*. Spain: Editors, S.A., 1986. This is one of twenty simplified and colorful fairytales in hardback binding.

9. *Blancanieves*. Spain: Editors, S.A., 1986. In this version of *Snow White,* the villainous queen causes her own death, and the poisoned princess is aided by a prince who later marries her.

10. Boada, Francesc. *Las tres naranjas de la vida*. Spain: Editorial La Galera, S.A., 1979. In his dangerous quest to find the three oranges of life, a prince breaks an evil spell placed on a princess.

11. —. *La princesa y el guisante*. Spain: Editorial La Galera, S.A., 1982. A real princess proves her nobility when she feels a pea under a heaping stack of mattresses and blankets! The pea is later displayed in the museum.

+12. Bollinger, Max. *La canción más bonita*. Spain: Ediciones S.M., 1985. The king orders a flautist to find the bird with the magnificent song. Unable to meet the king's request, the flautist plays for the last time. His flute is the magnificent song! When the king discovers this, he sets all the birds and the flautist free.

+13. Capdevila, Juan. *Las Tres Mellizas, Blancanieves y los siete enanitos*. Spain: Editorial Ariel, S.A., 1984. There is never a dull moment with the terrible triplets and the crazy witch. Elena, one of the triplets, takes Snow White's role and is revived by Snow White's son, a little prince, who is also a triplet!

+14. —. *Las Tres Mellizas y el traje nuevo del emperador*. Spain: Editorial Ariel, S. A., 1986. This is a humorous creation. Children cannot resist an invitation to listen to this tale and his entire *Mellizas* series.

+15. Capek, Karel, and Josef Palecek. *La princesa de Solimania*. Spain: Ediciones S.M., 1985. A woodcutter uses his common sense to cure a Solimanian princess—healthy food, fresh air, and sunshine are his remedy.

16. Carreño, Mada. *Clásicos Trillas: El pájaro de oro*. México: Editorial Trillas, S.A., 1985. This is a beautifully illustrated version of Grimm's classic about an enchanted prince from a golden palace.

17. —. *Clásicos Trillas: Sirenita*. México: Editorial Trillas, 1986. This is a colorful paperback version of *The Little Mermaid*.

18. —. *Blancanieves*. México: Editorial Trillas, 1986. This is a well translated and charmingly illustrated picture book to read out loud.

19. —. *La Bella Durmiente*. México: Editorial Trillas, 1986. This is a beautifully illustrated paperback version of the classic tale *Sleeping Beauty*.

+20. *Cuéntame un cuento: La bella y la bestia y otros cuentos.* Spain: Editorial Altea, 1986. This is a marvelous colorful and well translated hardbound version of the classic *Beauty and the Beast.*

+21. *Cuéntame un cuento: La Bella Durmiente y otros cuentos.* Spain: Ediciones Altea, 1986. From a collection of several tales, this classic is told with richness and simplicity.

+22. Darío, Rubén. *Margarita.* Venezuela: Editorial Arte, 1983. *Margarita* is a beautiful story, told in verse, about a brave, imaginative little princess who reaches for the brightest star as the final touch for her poem.

23. *El enano saltarín.* Spain: Editors, S.A., 1986. This colorful version of Rumplestiltskin contains an added twist—the dwarf later returns as the baby's guardian.

+24. García Sánchez, J.L. *Los niños de los cuentos.* Spain: Ediciones Altea, 1978. All the popular fairy tale characters who experience problems in their stories teach us that children have the very same problems.

+25. González de León, Ulalume. *Las tres manzanas de naranja.* México: SEP CIDCLI, S.A., 1985. This is an interesting story of a princess who falls ill and can be cured only by a true love.

26. Grimm, Brothers. Adapted by Rosanna Guarnieri. *Los más famosos cuentos: Blancanieves y Rosaflor.* México: Fernández Editors S.A., 1987. This is one of twenty-four classics in colorful paperback format.

*27. Grimm, Brothers. *La Bella Durmiente.* Spain: Alianza Editorial, 1985. The illustrations are splendid and the text is enriching for young readers.

+*28. —. *Blancanieves y los siete enanos.* México: Promociones Editoriales Mexicanas, S.A, 1982. This beautifully illustrated Grimm's tale contains the traditional story elements such as the wicked queen who is punished for her vain, spiteful ways.

29. Paz Castillo, Fernando. *El príncipe moro.* Venezuela: Ediciones Ekaré-Banco del Libro, 1978. This is the story about a Moorish prince who finds a treasure on the ocean floor and later loses it.

+30. Perrault, Charles. Adapted by Rossana Guarnieri. *La gata blanca.* México: Fernández Editores, S.A., 1983. The youngest of three brothers helps free a beautiful princess. His loyalty and devotion to a white cat helps him win the princess and her six kingdoms!

+31. —. Adapted by Rossana Guarnieri. *Riquete, él del copete.* México: Fernández Editores, S.A., 1983. An ugly, charming prince and a beautiful, dull princess exchange their unattractive traits to become the most handsome, compatible couple in the kingdom.

+32. —. Adapted by Rosanna Guarnieri. *Cenicienta.* México: Editorial Fernández, 1983. This adapted version of Perrault's *Cinderella* is a colorfully illustrated paperback with an easily comprehensible text.

+33. *El Rey Midas.* Spain: Editors, S.A., 1986. King Midas' obsession is to build his wealth; everything that he touches turns to gold. One day he loses his daughter and is forced to re-examine his values.

34. Rius, María. *Blanca Nieves*. Spain: Editorial Bruguera, 1980. This beautifully illustrated version of the classical tale is told with simplicity.

+35. Santos, J.F. *El reino de los niños*. Spain: Editorial Debate, 1986. A bored little prince discovers the world outside his palace. Tired of the rigid, dull adult world, he creates a world of gaiety and liveliness.

*36. Suigne, M.C. *La Bella Durmiente del bosque*. Belgium: Ediciones HEMMA, 1981. This Sleeping Beauty tale closely follows the original story. The illustrations are charming and the narrative is easily comprehensible and very enriching.

*37. Vanhalewijn, Mariette. *Los 365 vestidos de la princesa Penélope*. Spain: Editorial Everest, 1981. A little princess trades places with a maid's daughter and learns from the little girl that being grateful is more valuable than being overly indulged in material possessions.

+38. Vásquez, Zoraida. *Grandes cuentos para los pequeñitos: El ruiseñor y el emperador*. México: Editorial Trillas, S.A., 1986. This is a well illustrated, well translated paperback book with bold print.

+39. —. *Grandes cuentos para los pequeñitos: El traje nuevo del emperador*. México: Editorial Trillas, 1986. The text is simplified for young children, containing bold print and delightful colorful illustrations.

The following selections should be read after the Main Selection has been presented. These supporting stories can be used for story comparisons, dramatization, or for writing about story variants—such activities are described in Experiences with Literature.

40. Rius, María. *El Príncipe Feliz*. Spain: Editorial Bruguera, S.A., 1980. This is a heart-warming story about a compassionate prince. This paperback has enriching text and colorful illustrations.

+*41. Wilde, Oscar. *El Príncipe Feliz*. Spain: Editorial Altea, 1985. Oscar Wilde's books are good selections for any literature program. This sensitive story shows the compassion of a prince for his fellow man.

+42. Company, M., and R. Capdevila. *Las Tres Mellizas y Cenicienta*. Spain: Editorial Ariel, S.A., 1985. The mischievous triplets stir up humor as they are flung into the Cinderella story by the crazy witch.

+43. *Cuéntame un cuento: Cenicienta y otros cuentos*. Spain: Editorial Altea, 1986. This is a well translated and beautifully illustrated classic in hardback binding.

+44. Llimona, Mercedes. *La Cenicienta*. Spain: Ediciones Hymsa, 1984. This adaptation of Perrault's Cinderella is enriching reading for students who have previously heard a simplified version.

45. Mistral, Silvia. *La Cenicienta china*. México: Editorial Trillas, S.A., 1986. Cinderella is a classic known the world over. This Chinese version is beautifully illustrated and contains an enriching text in paperback form.

RELATED TITLES IN ENGLISH FOR SECOND LANGUAGE ACQUISITION

DePaola, Tomie. *The Knight and the Dragon.* New York: G. P. Putnam's Sons, 1980.

Kincaid, Lucy. *Now You Can Read: Cinderella.* Cambridge, England: Brimax Books, 1980. (Additional titles include *Rapunzel, Rumplestiltskin,* and *Frog Prince.*)

Lobel, Arnold. *Prince Bertram the Bad.* New York: Harper and Row, 1963.

Shulevitz, Uri. *One Monday Morning.* New York: Charles Scribner's Sons, 1967.

II. OBSERVATION/EXPERIENCE: *El Príncipe Feliz*
(Class Session One)

Guide students in the following observations/experience sequence to set the stage for reading the Main Selection.

Focus: We can care about other people.

1. Display pictures of people lacking basic needs such as clothing, food, shelter, care. Discuss how others can help homeless and impoverished people.

2. From the book cover, show a picture of the prince. Tell them that the prince lives in the same town where homeless people live. Elicit the students' impression of the prince. Ask, for example, *¿Qué clase de príncipe piensan que es él?* (What type of prince do you think he is?)

3. Tell them that they will meet this prince from *El Príncipe Feliz,* who, unlike the usual prince who shares his riches with a princess, devotes himself to helping the needy such as those in the pictures.

4. Have them predict what he will do to help these people and why he will be known as "el Príncipe Feliz." Following the story, have students discuss whether their predictions were correct.

III. READ AND DISCUSS THE MAIN SELECTION: *El Príncipe Feliz*
(Class Session One)

Read the Main Selection from page 248 to the students. Highlight the unit's theme by relating this story to other selections from the Literature Input list on pages 248 - 252. Then, guide students in discussing some of the following questions.

1. *¿Cómo creen que el Príncipe Feliz obtuvo ese nombre?* (How do you think the Happy Prince got his name?)

2. *¿Por qué estaba llorando el príncipe? Si ustedes lo hubieran visto llorando, ¿qué le habrían dicho?* (Why was the prince crying? If you had seen him crying, what would you have said to him?)

3. *¿Cómo le ayudaba la golondrina al príncipe? ¿Cómo habrían ayudado ustedes?* (How did the swallow help the prince? How would you have helped?)

4. *¿Han querido ustedes ayudar a alguien así como lo hizo el príncipe? ¿En qué forma han ayudado a otros?* (Have you ever wanted to help someone as the prince did? In what ways have you helped others?)

5. *¿Por qué era el príncipe especial? ¿Por qué era la golondrina especial? ¿Por qué son ustedes especiales?* (Why was the prince special? Why was the swallow special? Why are you special?)

IV. "WHAT IF" STORY STRETCHER: *El Príncipe Feliz*
(Class Session Two)

Next, re-read the Main Selection and choose one or more of the following questions to develop students' critical thinking skills. Story stretchers may also prompt discussion, drama or writing activities.

1. *Si la estatua hubiera tenido mas joyas para regalar, ¿a quién más habría ayudado?* (If the statue had had more jewels to give, who else would he have helped?)

2. *Si la golondrina no se hubiera muerto y el príncipe no hubiera tenido mas joyas para regalar, ¿en qué otra forma habrían podido ayudar a la gente?* (If the swallow had not died, and the prince had had no more jewels to give, in what other ways could they have helped the people?)

3. *Si ustedes hubieran sido los ayudantes del príncipe, ¿cómo habrían ayudado al príncipe?* (If you had been the prince's helper, how might you have helped him?)

4. *Si ustedes se encontraran con la golondrina o con el príncipe, ¿qué les dirían ustedes?* (If you were to meet the swallow or the prince, what would you say to them?)

5. *¿Qué le dirían ustedes al alcalde del pueblo si ustedes estuvieran tratando de salvar a la estatua?* (What would you say to the mayor if you were trying to save the statue?)

V. INTEGRATING OTHER DISCIPLINES: *El Príncipe Feliz*
(Class Session Three and Ongoing)

The following activities are designed to enhance children's response to literature and expand *beyond* the story and its theme. The variety of activities gives teachers and students an opportunity to choose those most appropriate.

CREATIVE DRAMATICS

1. *Story Dramatization:* Have groups dramatize the story in three short parts: (1) the scene when the prince cries and tells the bird about the misery and despair among the town's people; (2) the scene when the swallow delivers the jewels to each of the needy people; and (3) the scene when the swallow dies on the statue and both the prince and the swallow are removed by an angel who carries them away. Allow each group to practice a scene and then dramatize the entire story from beginning to end.

2. *Swallow Pantomime:* Have students move as the swallow did in the story—flying as a healthy, helpful, and energetic friend; then as a weak, fragile, cold and dying friend. Present a given situation, during various seasons, while students pantomime actions. Have students improvise the swallow's flight and behavior during spring, fall, summer, and winter.

3. *Improvisation:* In groups, have students pretend to be in a situation which makes them unhappy. Have them improvise and discuss the situation. Next, have them relate, through spontaneous improvisation, how they might improve their situations.

4. *Emotion "Wall":* Using an "emotion wall," with a hole for a face and two small holes below for hands, have students express the intensity of their emotions when parts of the story are read out loud by the teacher. Observers may identify the emotion expressed.

ART AND WRITING

1. *Portrait:* Have students use broken jewelry and colored sequins to paste on a portrait of the Happy Prince and colored feathers to paste on a picture of the swallow. (Students may create these portraits or teacher may furnish them.) Students may write tributes on the bottom of the portraits.

2. *Thank-You Letter:* Have students pretend to be the children from the story and write thank-you letters to the prince and the swallow. If needed, use the following fill-in letter:

> *Querido Príncipe Feliz y Golondrina,*
>
> *Gracias por ser _____ . Ustedes tienen corazones _____ .*
> *Usé _____ (el oro o las joyas) para _____ .*
>
> > *Con cariño, _____*

> Dear Happy Prince and Swallow,
>
> Thank you for being _____ . You have a _____ heart. I used the _____ (gold or jewels) to _____ .
>
> > Love, _____

3. *Happy-Prince Statue:* Have students sculpt the prince out of clay. After it hardens, they may spray it with gold paint and then paint on jewels with tempera or colored markers.

4. *Balloon Swallow:* Have the students blow up round balloons and tie them. Draw wings, a tail, and a head on paper, and cut them out. Glue the body parts onto the balloon with rubber cement and tie on a string. Use the swallow or the prince statue in activity #3 to help inspire the creation of group poems about these characters.

5. *A Kind Deed:* Tell students that the Happy Prince and the swallow continue to help many people. Have them think of a kind deed that could help someone they know. How would the Happy Prince and swallow help this person? Allow them to rewrite the story using this person as one of the characters.

6. *Egg-Carton Swallow:* Have students paint egg cartons and after they dry, attach long strings. Have them draw, color, cut out, and glue on a head, wings, and a tail. Then let them pretend to make the swallow fly. Supposing the swallow had not died, have the students write dialogues about what the swallow would have said to his fellow birds about his experience with the Happy Prince.

7. *Prince's Heart:* Tell the students to fold large sheets of newsprint in half, trace or draw large hearts, and cut them out so that each has two hearts. On each heart, have students write their heartfelt thoughts about the Prince's kind nature. Then have them glue the edges of the hearts, leaving openings to fill with paper, and glue them closed.

8. *Castle Folder:* Using Figure Q (page 262), have students color the castle, cut it out, and make a lift-up door by cutting along the dotted lines. Have the students glue the castle on the inside top half of an open 8-1/2" x 11" manila folder. Have them draw members of a royal family inside the windows, with a surprise character under the lift-up door. On the inside bottom half of the folder, have them write a riddle about the characters in the castle. On the front cover of the folder, have students draw and title their favorite story about royalty.

9. *Royalty Plate Book:* Have students draw the faces of princes or princesses on the plate bottoms. Have them place the plate faces together and staple them at the top. Then have them design crowns and staple or glue them on the heads. They may use tissue paper or yarn for the hair. Have students use the poem *"El postre real"* (page 261), for a reader's theater. Tell them to paste copies of the poem inside, and have them read the stanzas.

10. *Fairy-Tale Mix:* Have students illustrate fairytales that combine parts of two to four other fairytales such as those on the Literature Input list. Have them write adapted fairytales that go along with their illustrations.

11. *Fairy-Tale Add-Ons:* Have several small groups sit in circles. Furnish one piece of paper and one pencil. Allow one child to write a sentence to begin a story. Have them pass the story around so that each child may add one sentence. If the story finishes before each child has had a chance to contribute, have the last child write an add-on sentence for a different story ending. Allow them to read the story aloud to other groups. Based on the group creations, have students become the artists and illustrate how their stories might appear in murals.

12. *News Fairy Tales:* Select a fairy tale to turn into a news story of the day. Title it with an "eye-catching" headline—"THE HAPPY PRINCE SAVES THE TOWN'S PEOPLE." Have the students create the accompanying illustrations (photos) and place the news clippings and "photos" in a class paper.

SCIENCE

1. *Bird Migration:* Relating the swallow's experience, talk about the migration of birds. (Books, films, and science magazines will enhance this topic). Have the students record facts in their science logs.

2. *Egg Hatching:* Allow the students to observe a real egg hatching. Have them sketch and label the hatching process in their science logs.

3. *Swallow Family:* Have children become members of a swallow family as they hatch from eggs, explore the new world, and fly together in a flock. Let them relate this to human families, discussing how human families explore and grow together. With children, brainstorm the similarities.

4. *Conservation:* The mayor made an effort to recycle the statue of the prince; with the children, brainstorm and record the types of material that are recyclable. Collect some recyclable items and recycle them for cash to use for a class project.

SOCIAL STUDIES

1. *Values:* While the class observes, pose several hypothetical situations in which helping and giving of one's self is evident. Have four students wear labels indicating the following situations: "I cut my finger;" "I have a broken leg;" "I forgot my lunch;" "I dropped my books." Orally, pose several situations requiring value judgments from the observers and spontaneous improvisations from the participants; e.g., *«Mientras ustedes iban caminando, encontraron a un niño quien no podía cruzar la calle él solo. ¿Qué harían ustedes?»* (As you were walking, you met a child who couldn't cross the street alone. What would you do?) Allow the observers to respond to each situation.

   Tie the concepts together by having children volunteer the one important thing that they learned from each situation (for example, that they can be helpful). Have them share their personal experiences helping others and the special feeling it gave them. Allow this experience to prompt personal journal writing.

2. *Something Special:* Assign students to say or do something special for an honored family member or someone other than family. Allow them to write about and share their experiences with the class.

3. *Giving:* As a class project, have students contribute canned food items to donate to needy people or families. Discuss the feelings associated with giving and relate this concept to the story. (This project is customarily done during Thanksgiving and Christmas but can be initiated at any time.)

4. *Compassion:* The Happy Prince and the swallow showed compassion for all people. Have children think of someone that they know can use some cheering up. Allow them to brainstorm and list actions that can bring cheer to others. Using mixed media, have them create "thinking about you" cards. Have them write cheerful messages to someone in need of a little cheer.

I. LITERATURE INPUT: *Cenicienta*
See pages 248 - 252.

II. OBSERVATION/EXPERIENCE: *Cenicienta*
(Class Session One)

Guide students in the following observations/experience sequence to set the stage for reading the Main Selection.

Focus: The rags to riches element is commonly characterized in fairytales.

1. Place one dressy, high-heeled shoe, a small pile of ashes, and a crown on the floor. Arouse children's curiosity by asking, *¿A quién pueden pertenecer estas cosas?* (Who might these things belong to?)

2. Have two students try on two sets of clothes: rags, and a crown and cape. Allow observers to describe the difference between the two students (one is in rags and one is royalty; or one is rich and the other is poor).

3. Tell students that in a story titled *Cenicienta,* a young maiden rises from rags to riches as displayed by the two children.

4. Have them predict how Cenicienta will rise from rags to riches (from being poor to rich). Following the story, have students discuss whether their predictions were correct.

III. READ AND DISCUSS THE MAIN SELECTION: *Cenicienta*
(Class Session One)

Read the Main Selection from page 248 to the students. Highlight the unit's theme by relating this story to other selections from the Literature Input list on pages 248 - 252. Then, guide students in discussing some of the following questions.

1. *¿Cómo era la vida de Cenicienta con su madrastra y sus hermanastras? ¿Cuál es la diferencia entre la familia de Cenicienta y las de ustedes?* (How was Cinderella's life with her stepmother and stepsisters? What is the difference between Cinderella's family and yours?)

2. *¿Cuáles eran las esperanzas de Cenicienta? ¿Han ustedes tenido esperanzas de algo? ¿Pueden contarnos sus ideas?* (What were Cinderella's hopes? Have you ever hoped for anything? Can you share your ideas?)

3. *Describan que fue lo que hizo el hada para ayudar a Cenicienta. ¿Cuál fue la promesa que tuvo que cumplir Cenicienta? ¿Han ustedes tenido que cumplir alguna promesa? Platíquennos de eso.* (Describe what the fairy godmother did to help Cinderella. What was the promise Cinderella had to keep? Have you ever had to keep a promise? Tell us about it.)

4. *¿Cuál fue la parte más feliz del cuento? ¿Cuál fue la más triste? ¿Cuál fue la más emocionante? ¿Y cuál fue la que les causó más sorpresa?* (Which was the happiest part of the story? Which part was the saddest? Which part was the most exciting? And which part was the surprising?)

5. *¿Cómo cambió la vida de Cenicienta? ¿Creen ustedes que esto podría pasarles a ustedes o a alguien que ustedes conocen? ¿Cómo?* (How did Cinderella's life change? Do you think that this could happen to you or to someone you know? If so, how?)

IV. "WHAT IF" STORY STRETCHER: *Cenicienta*
(Class Session Two)

Next, re-read the Main Selection and choose one or more of the following questions to develop students' critical thinking skills. Story stretchers may also prompt discussion, drama or writing activities.

1. *Si Cenicienta no hubiera tenido un hada, ¿cómo habría podido ella ir al baile?* (If Cinderella had not had a fairy godmother, how might she have been able to go to the ball?)

2. *Si la madrastra y las hermanastras de Cenicienta la hubieran reconocido en el baile, ¿cómo habría cambiado la experiencia de ella en el baile?* (If Cinderella's stepmother and stepsisters had recognized her at the ball, how would her experience at the ball have changed?)

3. *Si Cenicienta no hubiera hecho caso de regresar a las doce de la noche, ¿cómo habría cambiado el cuento?* (If Cinderella had ignored the twelve o'clock curfew, how might the story have been different?)

4. *Si la zapatilla les hubiera quedado a más muchachas—supongamos que le hubiera quedado a una de las hermanastras—¿cómo habría terminado el cuento?* (If Cinderella's slipper had fit more than one girl's foot—suppose it had fit one of the stepsisters—how would the story have ended?)

5. *Si Cenicienta hubiera tenido hermanastros en vez de hermanastras, ¿cómo habría cambiado el cuento?* (If Cinderella had had stepbrothers instead of stepsisters, how would the story have been different?)

V. INTEGRATING OTHER DISCIPLINES: *Cenicienta*
(Class Session Three and Ongoing)

The following activities are designed to enhance children's response to literature and expand *beyond* the story and its theme. The variety of activities gives teachers and students an opportunity to choose those most appropriate.

CREATIVE DRAMATICS

1. *Re-enact the Story:* In groups, have students re-enact the story in four parts: (1) the scene when Cinderella is made to work very hard by her stepmother and stepsisters; (2) the scene when the fairy godmother appears; (3) the scene at the palace when the prince falls instantly in love with Cinderella, and she flees leaving the glass slipper behind; and (4) the scene when the sisters try on the slipper, but, surprisingly, Cinderella tries it on and shows her other slipper. Have each group practice a scene, then like a jigsaw puzzle, dramatize the entire story from beginning to end.

2. *Characterization:* In groups, have children mimic the stepsisters' envious, sarcastic, bossy, and rude behavior; and have them mimic Cinderella's caring, cooperative, patient, and kind-hearted nature. Have them switch characterization, portraying Cinderella as a villain and her sisters as kind-hearted characters. Allow them to choose the traits that they would like to portray in re-enacting the story.

3. *"What If":* Have cooperative groups plan a dramatization in which the slipper breaks or is lost, stolen, or hidden. Allow them to dramatize and have the class discuss this new story twist.

ART AND WRITING

1. *Bridal Show:* In cooperative groups, have the students design Cinderella's bridal gown and the Prince's suit, using newspaper, scissors, tape and yarn. Have a fashion show to display the royal gowns and suits.

2. *Fashion Article:* Provide bride magazines and allow the students to view them freely. Have groups write fashion articles about the latest and most fashionable royal wedding gowns and suits.

3. *Paper-Plate Puppets:* Have students make Cinderella and prince puppets, using paper plates for the face and back of the heads, and paper-towel rolls as rods. They may use wallpaper or foil for crowns and construction paper for the facial features. Have them glue the features on the plate bottoms and insert the paper-towel rolls between the two plates (plate faces touching). Then have them staple and glue on the crowns. Have them write romantic or humorous dialogues that Cinderella and the prince might say to each other.

4. *Design Crown:* Have students make crowns using tagboard, sequins, foil paper, and tissue paper. Have them accordion-pleat pieces of 9" x 12" paper and cut out assorted shapes to create designs. Then have them staple the ends together and decorate the crowns by adding sequins, foil or tissue paper. While wearing their crowns, they may dramatize favorite stories about royalty.

5. *Scroll:* Have students make scrolls with announcements for the royal couple's forthcoming wedding. (Or use story characters from the Literature Input). Have them share their scrolls.

6. *Construct a Castle:* Have cooperative groups build castles using paper-towel rolls, cereal boxes, shoe boxes, and other assorted boxes. Allow them to write descriptions of the royal families that might move into their castles.

7. *Cinderella's Stepsisters:* Have students draw the funny-looking stepsisters. They may use yarn, construction paper, and noodles to create an imaginative picture. Let them pretend to be one of Cinderella's stepsisters and write descriptions of what life is like without Cinderella's maid service.

8. *Royalty Stand-Up Dolls:* Using Figure R (page 263), have children make royalty stand-up dolls. Have them color, cut out, and glue the figures onto the stand-up tabs. Have students imagine themselves as these royalty dolls and write essays describing «*Un día en mi vida como princesa o príncipe.*» ("A Day in My Life as a Princess or a Prince.") Allow them to use stand-up dolls to recreate dramatizations of the day's happenings. Use this activity to prompt writing in their literature logs.

9. *Self-Portrait:* Have students use a variety of craft items to create self-portraits as members of royalty. Have them use the caption «*Como me vestiría para el baile si yo fuera Cenicienta o el príncipe.*» ("How I would dress for the ball if I were Cinderella or the prince.") Have the students act as fashion critics, describing or critiquing, in writing, the princes' or princesses' attire.

10. *Thank-You Card:* Have the students take the roles of either Cinderella or the prince and design and write thank-you cards for Cinderella's fairy godmother.

11. *Fairytale Fun:* Have cooperative groups select their favorite fairytales about royalty to produce puppet shows for an audience. After they select the fairytales, have them plan skits, and make the necessary preparations. Using a long strip of butcher paper, have the students draw and cut out a window wide enough for a stage for the puppets to perform. Have them design scenery around the window and on the entire paper. Roll the ends of the paper around dowels or yardsticks. Hang the paper so that performers can get behind the hanging stage. Have them create paper-plate, paper-roll, stick, or rod puppets. Provide necessary materials for making the puppets.

SOCIAL STUDIES

1. *Family Relationships:* With students, discuss the fact that Cinderella is a member of a step-family in a fairy tale, but most real families try to establish positive family relationships. To focus on this concept, talk about the need for family members to share responsibilities and cooperate; to consider and respect the feelings of others; to be listened to; and to talk things through, especially when problems arise. Have them consider what happens when we fail to practice these necessary family behaviors. Allow them to role play the positive and the negative consequences back to back.

2. *Neglect:* Provide a bag with old and new items—an old worn book, stuffed animal, and slipper and a new toy, shoe, and doll. Without viewing the items, allow several students to pull out items and have observers discuss those that they think might be valued and why. Relate this activity to Cinderella who was made to feel like an old, neglected item even though she was really beautiful inside. With the students, discuss whether such a thing can happen in real life. Encourage students to write their thoughts about this experience in their personal journals.

POETRY

La golondrina

Ya esta el pájaro solo
puesto en la esquina,
puesto en la esquina,
esperando que salga
la golondrina,
la golondrina.

Folklore

El festín

En un gran país de abejas
vivía una reina y un rey
que pasaban todo el año
haciendo su rica miel.

Al llegar el año nuevo
todo el reino era invitado
a un gran baile y un festín
que el rey había preparado.

Concurrían muchas abejas
a bailar y festejar
y comían sus caramelos
todos rellenos de miel.

Al dar el reloj las doce
todos tenían que partir,
se despedían de la reina
y daban las gracias al rey.

Raquel C. Mireles

El postre real

En el castillo amarillo
se ha armado una gran confusión.

El rey Bombón
ordena un pastel de limón.

La reina Teresa
ordena uno de fresa.

La princesa Maravilla
prefiere uno de vainilla.

El príncipe, encaprichado,
llora porque él quería helado.

Y el cocinero don Ramón
grita desde la cocina:
«¡Si no toman una decisión,
comerán postre de sardina!»

Raquel C. Mireles

Figure Q: *Un castillo* / A Castle

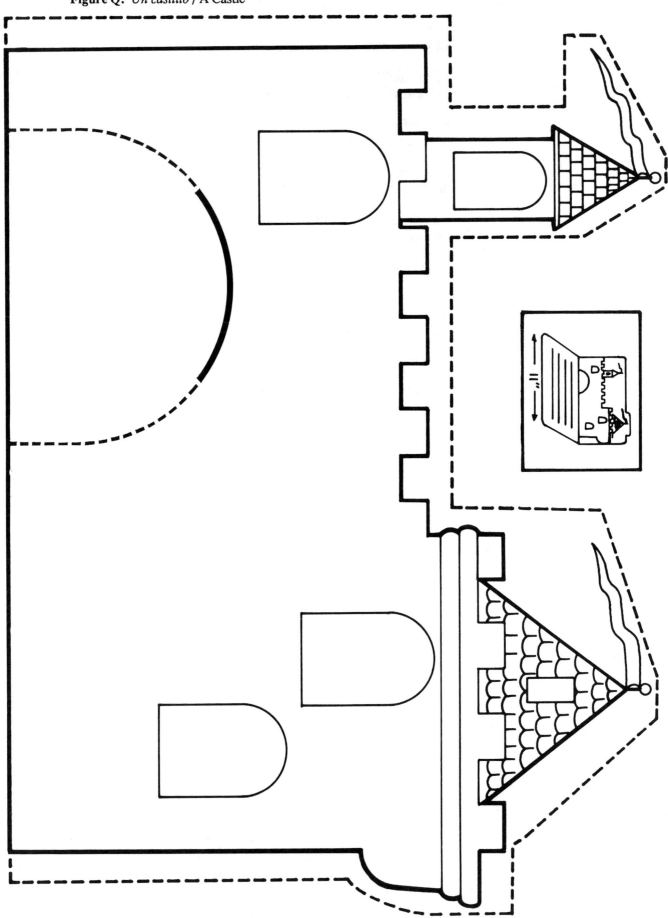

TAB

MY OWN CREATIVE TEACHING IDEAS FOR UNIT SIXTEEN

Books: _____

_____

_____

_____

_____

_____

Ideas: _____

_____

_____

_____

_____

_____

_____

_____

_____

_____

_____

_____

_____

_____

_____

_____

_____

UNIT SEVENTEEN

EL BUENO, EL MALO Y EL FEO

THE GOOD, THE BAD AND THE UGLY

Many folktales present obstacles which characters must overcome. Often, heroes or heroines are at odds with villainous giants, ogres, monsters, or witches. These villains may be challenged by clever, cunning characters who manage to outwit or overpower their antagonists, just as in *Hansel y Gretel*. In this folktale, a witch imprisons two innocent children who turn out not to be so helpless and powerless after all. However, not all giants, ogres, monsters, and witches are villains; sometimes they are friendly or even add enough humor to a story to become likeable, humorous, fun-loving characters. They are all interesting—good, bad and "ugly."

MAIN SELECTION

Before reading the Main Selection aloud, take your students through the Literature Input and Observation/Experience phases which follow.

Carreño, Mada.

Clásicos Trillas: Hansel y Gretel.
México: Editorial Trillas, S.A., 1986.

Because some children find the classic **Hansel and Gretel** to be a scary story, the authors have selected this refreshing and beautifully illustrated version in which the children's parents serve as positive role models.

I. LITERATURE INPUT: *Clásicos Trillas: Hansel y Gretel*

Select five or more titles from the following list to read aloud. Read at least one selection per day to the students. Make available and incorporate the suggested titles for voluntary independent reading. Titles marked with * are Spanish translations of the original English story; titles marked with + are recommended for more proficient listeners.

1. Alba, R.L. *Columpio-tobogán-noria-gigante.* Spain: Editors, S.A., 1984. In this tale a lonely giant seeks friendship from humans. As the title suggests, playful children find him invaluable as a slide, merry-go-round, swing, and climbing hill.

+2. Alcántara, Ricardo S. *La bruja que quiso matar al sol.* Spain: Ediciones Hymsa, 1983. Afkitán, the mean old witch, tries to destroy the sun. All the creatures are worried and devise a plan to stop her.

+3. Almodóvar, A.R. *Periquín y la bruja curuja.* Spain: Editorial Algaida, 1985. Periquín, an orphan, triumphs over a villainous witch with the help of his bird. His bravery wins him the king's daughter.

+*4. Bernadette. *Rapunzel.* Spain: Editorial Lumen, 1981. This classical fairytale is beautifully illustrated and retains much of the traditional story line, as when Rapunzel's teardrop restores her true love's sight.

5. *Blancanieves.* Spain: Editors, S.A., 1986. This interesting version of *Snow White* has the witch fall to her death when she crashes into a mountain.

6. Boada, Francesc. *El sastrecillo valiente.* Spain: Editorial La Galera, S.A., 1982. This classic tale is one of an extensive collection of popular tales from La Galera. The titles have colorful, appealing illustrations and are excellent for reading aloud.

+7. Bolliger, Max. *Enanos y gigantes.* Spain: Ediciones S.M., 1986. While the elders foretell the grim future of the dwarf society, it takes the younger generation of dwarves to liberate them from the slave-driving giants.

+8. Company, M., and R. Capdevila. *Las Tres Mellizas, Blancanieves y los siete enanitos.* Spain: Editorial Ariel, S.A., 1985. Nothing but surprises and humor take place when the three triplets are cast into the Snow White story.

+9. —. *Las Tres Mellizas y Barba Azul.* Spain: Editorial Ariel, S.A., 1985. When the three stir-crazy triplets meet Bluebeard's wife, they are, needless to say, a bad influence. What a heap of trouble they get into!

+10.   —. *Las Tres Mellizas y Pulgarcito*. Spain: Editorial Ariel, S.A., 1985. Leave it up to the three naughty triplets to ruin Pulgarcito's plan. Nevertheless, they whisk away with a souvenir—the magic boots!

11.   Capdevila, R., and E. Larreula. *La bruja aburrida y la mona*. Spain: Editorial Ariel, S.A., 1986. The popular character from the "Mellizas" series is with us again in a humorous adventure that takes her around the world in search of a companion—a monkey!

+12.   *Coleción cuéntame un cuento*. Spain: Ediciones Altea, 1986. These books, containing marvelous illustrations and easily comprehensible texts, include: *Blancanieves y los siete enanitos y otros cuentos, El libro de las brujas y otros cuentos,* and *El libro de los gigantes y otros cuentos.*

+13.   Freire de Matos, Isabel. *La brujita encantada y otros cuentos*. San Juan de Puerto Rico: Instituto de Cultura Puertorriqueña, 1979. This collection of short stories by a Puerto Rican writer is one that all Hispanic children will enjoy.

*14.   Gackenbach, Dick. *Harry y el terrible quiensabequé*. Scholastic Book Services, 1979. Harry overcomes his fear of a monster in the attic when he attempts to rescue his mother from a strange creature. His confidence increases as the creature diminishes in size.

+15.   García Sánchez, J.L. *El niño gigante*. Spain: Ediciones Altea, 1978. Only the town's children understand the injustice caused by the adults when a "child giant" is exploited and overworked. A child's right to childhood is the message in this tale.

+16.   Grimm, Wilhelm and Jacob. *Blancanieves y los siete enanos*. México: Promociones Editoriales Mexicanas, S.A., 1982. This beautifully illustrated Grimms' tale is told with enriching language and is available .

17.   Larreula, Eric. *El gigante pequeño*. Spain: Editorial Teide, 1984. Two giants give birth to the tiniest giant—a normal-sized child. All his gigantic toys make playing a wonderful experience for the "little giant" and all his friends.

+18.   Larreula, E., and R. Capdevila. *Las memorias de la bruja aburrida*. Spain: Editorial Ariel, S.A., 1986. Children will have to brace themselves for some serious laughter when they delve into this hilarious story recounting the Bruja's childhood.

19.   Pecanins, Ana María. *La bruja triste*. México: Editorial Trillas, S.A., 1986. An unhappy witch learns about the joy of children when they sympathetically cheer her up.

+20.   Postma, Lidia. *El jardín de la bruja*. Spain: Editorial Lumen, 1981. The neighborhood's witch is quite harmless. If fact, she invites all the children to her fantastic garden among the gnomes and elves.

21.   *Pulgarcito*. Spain: Editors, S.A., 1986. A variety of story twists occur in this tale— Pulgarcito frees the ogre's daughters, punishes the ogre, and is compensated by the king for his bravery.

22.   Rius, María. *El sastrecillo valiente*. Spain: Editorial Bruguera, 1980. The little tailor's fame for "slaying seven in one" prompts the king to request that he capture the giants that have been terrorizing the land. Luckily, the tailor's wit helps gain him a royal "reward."

+*23. Sendak, Maurice. *Donde viven los monstruos*. Spain: Editorial Alfaguara, 1986. Sendak's popular *Where the Wild Things Are* is just as exciting in Spanish as the power and magic of the imagination come to life!

24. *La sirenita*. Spain: Editors, S.A., 1986. This modified version of *The Little Mermaid* has envious witches who act as obstacles to the mermaid's dream—being loved by a real prince. When the mermaid is finally set free and rises to the water's surface, her voice attracts a real prince.

+25. Wilde, Oscar. *El gigante egoista*. Spain: Ediciones Altea, 1985. In Oscar Wilde's tale, *The Selfish Giant,* a remorseful giant discovers that his selfishness has created a cold, lonely, lifeless world. When he opens his garden and heart to children, he learns the true essence of love.

26. Wolf, Tony. *El bosque encantado y los gigantes*. Argentina: Editorial Sigmar, 1985. With the help of dwarves, wizards, and animals, we hear several delightful short stories about Barbarroja, the giant.

*27. Wylie, Joanne, and David Wylie. *¿Y tú crees que viste un monstruo?* Children's Press, Regensteiner Publishing Enterprises, 1986. A series of amusing books, told in verse, about a child's fantasy with monsters. Included among these titles are: *¿Sabes dónde está tu monstruo esta noche?* and *¿Has abrazado hoy a tu monstruo?*

28. Xandra. *¿Quién teme a . . . las brujas?* México: Fernández Editores, S.A., 1987. This is one of six delightful stories about the fears that children have, often stirred up by their imaginations. Children learn that they can have fun with seemingly scary characters.

The following selections should be read after the Main Selection has been presented. These supporting stories can be used for story comparisons, dramatization, or for writing about story variants; such activities are described in Experiences with Literature.

29. *Cuéntame un cuento: Mi casita de turrón y otros cuentos*. Spain: Editorial Altea, 1986. This Spanish version of *Hansel and Gretel* is colorfully illustrated and contains an enriching text.

+*30. Grimm, Wilhelm and Jacob. *Hansel y Gretel*. México: Promociones, Editoriales Mexicanas, S.A., 1982. This favorite children's classic contains beautiful illustrations and is available in hardback binding.

31. *Hansel y Gretel*. Spain: Editors, S.A., 1986. A modified version of *Hansel and Gretel,* this colorful hardback book has a witch planning a human feast for the witch community; she transforms into an eagle during Gretel's attempted escape.

RELATED TITLES IN ENGLISH FOR SECOND LANGUAGE ACQUISITION

Balian, Lorna. *Humbug Witch*. Tennessee: Abingdon Press, 1965.

Cameron, Ann. *Harry (the Monster)*. New York: Pantheon Books, 1980.

Crowe, Robert L. *Clyde Monster*. New York: E. P. Dutton and Company, 1976.

Galdone, Paul. *The Three Billy Goats Gruff*. New York: Clarion Books, 1973.

Kincaid, Lucy. *Jack and the Beanstalk*. Cambridge, England: Brimax Books, 1980.

Lobel, Arnold. Giant John. New York: Harper and Row, 1964.

II. OBSERVATION/EXPERIENCE: *Clásicos Trillas: Hansel y Gretel*
(Class Session One)

Guide students in the following observation/experience sequence to set the stage for reading the Main Selection.

Focus: In many folktales, good prevails over evil.

1. Have children play tug-of-war. Have one side (with fewer children than the other side) pretend to be witches, giants, and ogres. Have the opposite side (with more team players) be the children. Tell the children to tug the rope and see what happens.

2. Discuss the outcome and explain that often, in stories, little people or small children face struggles with seemingly powerful, intimidating characters such as giants and witches. However, in many of these tales, the villains are often outsmarted or overpowered by smaller or "weaker" characters.

3. Tell students that in a story titled **Hansel y Gretel,** two small children are placed in a terrible situation by a mean witch.

4. Have them predict what the situation is and how the children will get away from the witch. Following the story, discuss whether their predictions were correct.

III. READ AND DISCUSS THE MAIN SELECTION: *Clásicos Trillas: Hansel y Gretel*
(Class Session One)

Read the Main Selection from page 266 to the students. Highlight the unit's theme by relating this story to other selections from the Literature Input list on pages 266 - 268. Then, guide students in discussing some of the following questions.

1. *Cuando Hansel y Gretel se perdieron en el bosque, ¿qué plan hizo Hansel para regresar a la casa? Si ustedes estuvieran perdidos, ¿qué planes harían ustedes?* (When Hansel and Gretel become lost in the forest, what plan did Hansel make to return home? If you were lost, what plans would you make?)

2. *Describan la sorpresa que encontraron en el bosque.* (Describe the surprise they found in the forest.)

3. *¿Qué clase de personaje es la bruja? ¿Qué es lo que les dice a ustedes que es así?* (What type of character is the witch? What tells you that she is like this?)

4. *¿Qué clase de personajes creen ustedes que son Hansel y Gretel? ¿Qué es lo que les dice a ustedes que ellos son así?* (What types of characters would you consider Hansel and Gretel? What tells you that they are like this?)

5. *¿Cómo creen ustedes que se sentían los padres cuando supieron que se habían perdido los niños? ¿Qué parte del cuento indica que se sentían así?* (How do you think the parents felt when they learned their children were lost? What, in the story, shows that they felt this way?)

IV. "WHAT IF" STORY STRETCHER: *Clásicos Trillas: Hansel y Gretel*
(Class Session Two)

Next, re-read the Main Selection and choose one or more of the following questions to develop students' critical thinking skills. Story stretchers may also prompt discussion, drama or writing activities.

1. *Si Hansel y Gretel hubieran sido más precavidos y cuidadosos de no entrar a la casa de un desconocido, ¿cómo habría cambiado el cuento?* (If Hansel and Gretel had been more cautious about entering the stranger's house, how would the story have changed?)

2. *Si Gretel no hubiera engañado a la bruja, ¿cómo podrían haberse escapado ambos niños?* (If Gretel had not tricked the witch, how might both children have escaped?)

3. *Escojan alguna escena del cuento. Descríbanla y digan que habrían hecho distinto si ustedes fueran Hansel o Gretel.* (Think of a scene from the story. Describe it and tell what you would have done differently if you had been Hansel or Gretel.)

4. *¿Qué tal si la casa de la bruja hubiera sido hecha de gusanos, caracoles, y ajos? ¿Cómo habría cambiado el cuento?* (What if the witch's house had been made of worms, snails, and garlic? How would the story have been different?)

5. *¿Cómo cambiaría el cuento si la bruja en vez de ser mala, fuera buena?* (How would the story change if the witch were nice instead of wicked?)

V. INTEGRATING OTHER DISCIPLINES: *Clásicos Trillas: Hansel y Gretel*
(Class Session Three and Ongoing)

The following activities are designed to enhance children's response to literature and expand *beyond* the story and its theme. The variety of activities gives teachers and students an opportunity to choose those most appropriate.

CREATIVE DRAMATICS

1. *Story Dramatization:* Have groups dramatize the story in three parts: (1) the scene when the children realize that they are lost in the forest and Hansel's plan fails; (2) the scene when the children encounter the gingerbread house, the witch, and have a bad experience; and (3) the scene when Gretel gets rid of the witch, frees Hansel, stocks up on the witch's food, and finally, with her brother, rejoins her parents. Have each group practice a scene, then participate in the dramatization by re-enacting the entire story from beginning to end.

2. *Story Twist:* Have the students add story twists by having groups discuss and improvise what their own personal experiences might have been upon encountering the gingerbread house and meeting the witch.

3. *Silly Villains:* Instruct children to visualize and describe a silly witch. In a total group situation, have them become witches and perform appropriate actions—sneer, act, talk, laugh, fly—while you call out action words. The students may try the same activity as imaginary giants or monsters.

4. *Story Variant:* From among story variants in the Literature Input, have each group select one to re-enact and later compare the ending with the main story.

5. *Dramatization and Analysis:* Have cooperative groups re-enact a previously presented story from the Literature Input list. Following the dramatization, discuss whether the main characters were good, bad or "ugly" and why.

ART AND WRITING

1. *Gingerbread House:* Have students make gingerbread houses, using school milk cartons, graham crackers, gumdrops and assorted candy, colored frosting, colored marshmallows, glue, and ice cream sticks. Allow them to glue the items onto the milk cartons. Draw students' attention to the sensory features of the gingerbread houses. Have them write descriptions of the gingerbread houses and share their descriptive, sensory-focused writing samples.

2. *Changing Witch:* Using two copies of Figure S (page 275), have students color them, drawing in an evil expression on one witch and a different expression on the other. Then have the students cut out the two witches and staple them back to back. Have them create a change in the evil witch's character; e.g., friendly, silly, kind. On each witch, have them write predictions about all the different things each might do. Allow for group sharing.

3. *Watercolor Mosaic:* Using assorted sponges of assorted shapes and watercolors, have students make mosaics of the gingerbread house. Have them trace and cut out two identical houses, insert a lined sheet of paper, and staple them together. On the sheets of paper in the houses, have them write eyewitness accounts of what happened as if they were inside with Hansel and Gretel.

4. *Springy Witch:* Have children draw witches' faces on small paper plates. Allow them to trace and cut out bodies and hats from black paper. Have them draw the desired expressions on the faces—frightened, silly, happy, surprised. Have them fold accordion strips out of white paper and glue these to the bodies for arms and legs, and then have them add yarn for hair. Allow them to pretend to be the witch writing a letter of apology to Hansel and Gretel, expressing how ashamed she feels for her devious behavior. Let her explain how and why she has changed.

5. *Paper-Art Picture:* Have students create Hansel and Gretel, using small ripped construction paper pieces to give the pictures a mosaic effect. Allow them to use cereal to create the trail that Hansel made from his cottage to the forest. Have students write letters to Hansel and Gretel praising them for their bravery.

6. *Villain Fun:* We have all heard stories about witches, ogres, giants, and monsters. Have the students create villains on balloons or on large paper bags. For the design they may use rubber cement, construction paper scraps, tissue or crepe paper, permanent color markers, and yarn. Display them in a class parade. Using the following writing starter, have students write a story beginning: «*¡Cuidado con la/ el . . . !*» ("Watch out for the . . . !")

7. *Good, Bad and Ugly:* With the students, discuss how the terms "good," "bad" and "ugly" have different meanings for different people. Using characters from the Literature Input, discuss how such terms describe these characters. Have students draw pictures of the "best," "worst" or "ugliest" characters. Allow them to write

descriptions of their good, bad or ugly characters and tell about good, bad or scary things their characters do. Compile illustrations with captions written on them for a class book.

Tall Tale: Pair students and have them make up tall tales to tell a friend about the "best," "worst" or "scariest" thing that has ever happened to them.

8. *Sensational Headline:* Using a story from the Literature Input list, have students write sensational headlines that involve one of the characters; e.g., "TWENTY-FOOT-TALL GIANT SHAKES THE CITY." Have them write brief eyewitness accounts of the stories.

Tell the students that a major newspaper is interested in their stories. Have them rewrite the stories as feature stories, edit and revise them. Have them create accompanying illustrations for the feature stories. Lay the stories out as a class newspaper and distribute it to curious readers.

9. *Halloween Story:* Have students imagine that they have spent a Halloween night alone at home. Have them tell about the good, bad and ugly trick or treaters they saw and heard. Ask them to imagine how they managed until their parents got home. Have them write and illustrate their stories as part of a big book for the library corner.

SOCIAL STUDIES

1. *Make-Believe Characters:* Focus on the theme's characters as make-believe versus real characters, villains versus nice characters. Guide students in the following discussion:

   ¿Ustedes creen que los monstruos, ogros, gigantes, y brujas son verdaderos? (Do you believe that monsters, ogres, giants, and witches are real?)

   ¿Debemos tener miedo de todos ellos? ¿Por qué o por qué no? (Should we be afraid of all of them? Why or why not?)

   Allow the discussion to prompt personal journal writing.

2. *Problem Solving:* Using other versions of *Hansel and Gretel,* discuss variations about why Hansel and Gretel were alone in the forest. In cooperative groups, discuss whether or not this can happen in real life. If so, have them brainstorm and write about how they would solve the problems.

3. *"Good," "Bad" or "Ugly":* In advance, have students bring popular TV cartoon figures or pictures to class. With children, discuss how we often have misconceptions about the words "good," "bad" and "ugly," especially when "ugly" is equated with "bad." Write these words on the board and tell children that these words have different meanings for many of us. Display several figures among several cooperative groups and have them write word clusters to describe the characters. Allow them to share their word clusters and substantiate their ideas if "good," "bad" or "ugly" were given as descriptors.

SAFETY

1. *Unpleasant Strangers:* In the story the witch appeals to the children's taste for candy. Relate this to real-life situations when strangers may offer candy, toys, or money to children. Discuss how attractive things can entice us and blind us to danger. Have students role play some of these situations.

2. *Police Report:* Instruct students to take the roles of Hansel and Gretel and write reports to submit to the police describing "their" experiences with the witch and cautioning other children to be aware.

3. *Being Lost:* Hansel and Gretel were lost in the forest. Sometimes children face similar situations, but in different places such as crowded swap meets, stores or amusement parks. They can even stray off too far in their own neighborhoods. Brainstorm various situations in which children become lost and as a group write a list of some helpful tips for an "If you are ever lost" poster. For example,

   • Always wear an identification bracelet or a note with vital information indicating name, address, and telephone number.

   • Learn your telephone number and address so that it can help a helper locate your parents.

   • Know how to tell others your name, your parents', sisters', and brothers' names.

   • If you are the guest of a friend or family group, learn their names so that their names can be announced just in case you become separated from the group.

   • Stay where you became lost. Someone may return to that spot to look for you.

   • Tell a person who works at a place (or a mom) to help you because you are lost. Say, "I am lost. Please help me find my _____. My name is _____." Be prepared to give all vital information including names, telephone and address.

   • Do not panic because the person you were with is also looking for you. Just wait calmly and soon you will be found.

Engaños

La bruja muy lista
nos atrapó.
No nos perdió de vista
y así nos agarró.

Con dulces y mazapanes
ella nos engañó.
Se valió de varios planes
y a su casa nos llevó.

Hay que tener cuidado
y no dejarse engañar.
Hay desconocidos malos
que se tienen que evitar.

Raquel C. Mireles

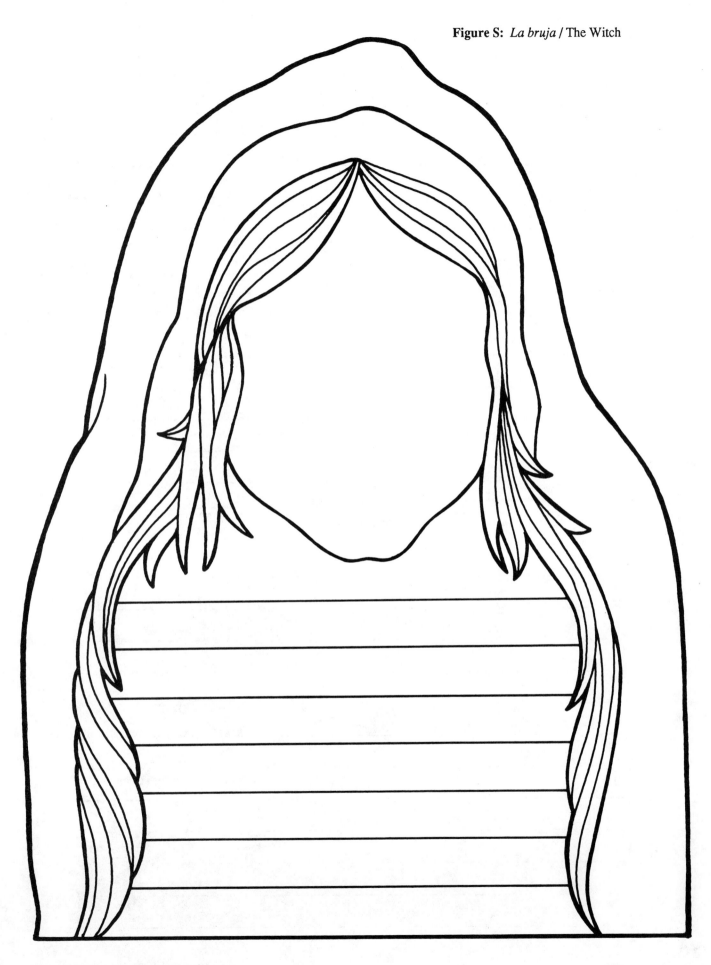

275

MY OWN CREATIVE TEACHING IDEAS FOR UNIT SEVENTEEN

Books: _____

_____

_____

_____

_____

_____

Ideas: _____

_____

_____

_____

_____

_____

_____

_____

_____

_____

_____

_____

_____

_____

_____

_____

_____

UNIT EIGHTEEN

LOS DUENDES Y LAS HADAS

ELVES AND FAIRIES

In folktales, fairies, dwarves, and elves are often sidekicks for the main character or supporting characters, who put the main character through a series of trials and tribulations. They often possess unique traits such as magical powers, wisdom, special gifts or talents. In some folktales, one of these magical creatures may be the main character and may display many human traits. This is the case in *Un cuento de enanos,* where the little dwarf, Gustavo, is endowed with a glorious gift of song and the wisdom to make a distinction between selfishness and selflessness—behaviors with which we sooner or later must come to terms.

MAIN SELECTION

Before reading the Main Selection aloud, take your students through the Literature Input and Observation/Experience phases which follow.

Bollinger, Max.

Un cuento de enanos.
Spain: Ediciones S.M., 1985.

A happy, gifted dwarf shares his beautiful, melodious voice with those who admire, love, and appreciate him. But when he begins to demand material goods as payment for his songs, he soon learns a valuable lesson about himself.

I.   LITERATURE INPUT: *Un cuento de enanos*

Select five or more titles from the following list to read aloud. Read at least one selection per day to the students. Make available and incorporate the suggested titles for voluntary independent reading. Titles marked with * are Spanish translations of the original English story; titles marked with + are recommended for more proficient listeners.

+1.   Andersen, Hans Christian. *Almendrita.* México: Promociones Editoriales Mexicanas, S.A., 1982. This hard cover Spanish version of *Thumbelina* contains wonderful illustrations and an enriching text.

2.   *Blancanieves.* Spain: Editors, S.A., 1986. In this classic tale, the villainous queen causes her own death and the poisoned princess is aided by a prince who later marries her.

+3.   Balzola, Ana. *El camisón bordado.* Spain: Editorial Miñón, S.A., 1982. When Margarita's mother falls ill, she takes over her mother's job washing laundry. Her beautiful embroidered gown is carried away by the river current and, upon following the gown, Margarita is taken on an adventure to the land of elves and fairies.

4.   Bolliger, Max. *Enanos y gigantes.* Spain: Ediciones S.M., 1986. Two giants invade the land of the dwarves, creating misery. The elderly dwarves foretell a grim future, but the young dwarves rebel against the giants to restore harmony in their land.

5.   Busquets, Carlos. *Pinocho.* Spain: Editorial Susaeta, 1980. The good fairy gives life to Pinocchio and is especially helpful when his little lies get him into trouble.

6.   —. *El zapatero y los duendes.* Spain: Editorial Susaeta, 1980. A shoemaker creates wooden elves as gifts for three little orphans. The elves are brought to life by a fairy so that they may fill the shoemaker's life-threatening shoe order. In so doing, they bring him wealth and pride.

7.   *La Cenicienta.* Spain: Editors, S.A., 1986. In this simplified and colorful version of *Cinderella,* some friendly birds and her fairy godmother make it possible for her to attend the royal ball.

8.   *Colección Topacio: Los tres enanitos.* Spain: Editorial Susaeta, S.A., 1973. Three dwarves test the goodwill of two sisters who receive just reward for their deeds. This collection includes short, simplified versions of many of the classical tales.

9. Company, Mercé. *Nana Bunilda come pesadillas*. Spain: Ediciones S.M., 1986. This is an interesting story about Bunilda, a good nana who takes nightmares away from children, cooks them, and makes delicious cupcakes.

10. *El enanito curioso*. Spain: Editorial Bruguera, 1982. A curious dwarf tests the worthiness of three orphaned brothers. The youngest brother is rewarded for his honesty while his brothers are punished for their insensitive, selfish ways.

11. *El enano saltarín*. Spain: Editors, S.A., 1986. This modified tale of *Rumplestiltskin* tells about a miller's daughter who, with the assistance of a dwarf, spins gold coins. Realizing that he cannot take her newborn baby, the dwarf returns as the baby's guardian.

+12. Company, M., and R. Capdevila. *Las Tres Mellizas, Blancanieves, y los siete enanitos*. Spain: Editorial Ariel, S.A., 1985. Nothing but surprises and humor take place when the three mischievous triplets join the cast in the Snow White story.

+13. —. *Las Tres Mellizas y Pulgarcito*. Spain: Editorial Ariel, S.A., 1985. Leave it up to the three naughty triplets to ruin Pulgarcito's plan. Nevertheless, they whisk away with a souvenir—the magic boots!

14. Fernández, Laura. *Luís y su genio*. México: Editorial Trillas, S.A., 1985. The shoe is on the other foot when Luís grants three wishes to his twin genie!

15. Garberi, Francisca. *Pituso*. Spain: Editorial La Galera, S.A., 1971. This is a humorous story about tiny Pituso, whose insistence upon being helpful gets him into an unusual predicament.

16. Gerson, Sara. *El hada Dalia*. México: Editorial Trillas, 1986. Feeling unneeded, the fairies are reassured by Dalia, the most outgoing among them, that children still love and believe in them. this is one of a series of small paperback books.

+17. Grimm, Wilhelm and Jacob. *Blancanieves y los siete enanos*. México: Promociones Editoriales Mexicanas, S.A., 1982. This beautifully illustrated Grimm's tale preserves the story's traditional elements as when the wicked step-mother is punished for her spiteful ways.

18. Guerrero García, J.J. *Las hadas*. Spain: Editorial Molino, 1983. A fairy's request for water from two sisters, brings results that are a reflection of their character.

+19. *La niña italiana*. Spain: Plaza Joven, S.A., 1985. The king sends gnomes to the black forest in search of magical, medicinal herbs for a stricken Italian princess. Thanks to their courage and wit, the little princess is cured.

20. Pecanins, Ana María. *La fiesta de cumpleaños*. México: Editorial Trillas, S.A., 1986. The town's children are treated to the best birthday party ever with the help of a friendly dwarf.

21. *Pulgarcito*. Spain: Editors, S.A., 1986. A variety of story twists occur in this simplified tale—Pulgarcito frees the ogre's daughters, punishes the ogre, and is rewarded by the king for his bravery.

*22. Suigne, M.C. *La Bella Durmiente del bosque*. Belgium: Ediciones HEMMA, 1981. This classic tale in hardback binding contains beautiful illustrations and an enriching text.

*23. —. *Cenicienta*. Belgium: Ediciones HEMMA, 1981. This wonderfully picturesque tale retains many of the elements of Perrault's classical *Cinderella*.

*24. —. *Pulgarcito*. Belgium: Ediciones HEMMA, 1986. Pulgarcito, the tiniest and bravest among seven brothers, triumphs over a villainous ogre, seizing his wondrous seven-league boots.

+25. Wolf, Tony. *El bosque encantado y los duendes*. Argentina: Editorial Sigmar, 1985. Children have several humorous experiences when they are invited into the enchanted world of dwarves.

+26. —. *El bosque encantado y los gnomos*. Argentina: Editorial Sigmar, 1985. Children will delight in the many experiences of the fun-loving gnomes.

+27. —. *El bosque encantado y las hadas*. Argentina: Editorial Sigmar, 1985. Six fairies take children on an adventure when they go vacationing in the land of the gnomes.

RELATED TITLES IN ENGLISH FOR SECOND LANGUAGE ACQUISITION

Birrel, William and Cynthia. *The Shoemaker and the Elves*. New York: Lothrop, Lee and Shepard Books, 1983.

+ Boden, Alice. *The Field of Buttercups*. New York: Henry Z. Walck, Inc., 1974.

Calhoun, Mary. *The Hungry Leprechaun*. New York: William Morrow and Company, 1962.

Darling, Kathy. *Jack Frost and the Magic Paint Brush*. Illinois: Garrard Publishing Company, 1977.

Kincaid, Lucy. *Now You Can Read: Snow White*. Cambridge, England: Brimax Books, 1980. (Additional title: *Elves and the Shoemaker*.)

II. OBSERVATION/EXPERIENCE: *Un cuento de enanos*
(Class Session One)

Guide students in the following observation/experience sequence to set the stage for reading the Main Selection.

Focus: Sometimes we need to examine our behavior when we forget to think about our friends.

1. Show students the book cover for **Un cuento de enanos.** Tell students that many of the stories about dwarves, elves and fairies teach us about how people behave; sometimes our behavior is good or shameful. We all have opinions about the behavior of other people, and we all know when our behavior is not appropriate.

2. Give each student a peanut. Ask if they would like another, but this time insist that they exchange a "valuable" as payment for the peanut. Pausing between questions to elicit their reaction, ask the following questions:

   • *¿Qué me darían por él? Solamente aceptaré cosas bellas.* (What would you give me for it? I'll only accept beautiful things.)

- *¿Qué piensan de mi idea?* (What do you think about my idea?)

- *¿Harían lo mismo con un buen amigo?* (Would you do this with a good friend?)

3. Have students think of a word that describes the modeled behavior (greedy, stingy, selfish). Tell them that in a story titled *Un cuento de enanos,* a dwarf named Gustavo behaves in the same manner.

4. Have them predict what Gustavo's behavior will be and what will happen to him for behaving in such a manner. Following the story, have students discuss whether their predictions were correct.

III. READ AND DISCUSS THE MAIN SELECTION: *Un cuento de enanos*
(Class Session One)

Read the Main Selection from page 278 to the students. Highlight the unit's theme by relating this story to other selections from the Literature Input list on pages 278 - 280. Then, guide students in discussing some of the following questions.

1. *¿Por qué era la vida del enanito tan agradable?* (Why was the dwarf's life so pleasant?)

2. *¿Por qué creen ustedes que los amigos de Gustavo no venían a visitarlo? ¿Creen que esto puede pasar en la vida real? ¿Cómo?* (Why do you suppose Gustavo's friends did not come to visit him anymore? Do you suppose that this could happen in real life? How?)

3. *¿Cómo se sentía Gustavo cuando los niños ya no venían a visitarlo? ¿Qué podría hacer para que ellos regresaran?* (How did Gustavo feel when the children no longer came to visit him? What might he do to bring them back?)

4. *¿Por qué creen que Gustavo decidió devolver el anillo, la corona, y la carroza? ¿Qué habrían hecho ustedes?* (Why do you suppose Gustavo decided to return the ring, crown, and chariot? What would you have done?)

5. *¿Qué aprendió Gustavo de esta experiencia? ¿Qué aprendieron ustedes de la experiencia de Gustavo?* (What did Gustavo learn from his experience? What did you learn from Gustavo's experience?)

IV. "WHAT IF" STORY STRETCHER: *Un cuento de enanos*
(Class Session Two)

Next, re-read the Main Selection and choose one or more of the following questions to develop students' critical thinking skills. Story stretchers may also prompt discussion, drama or writing activities.

1. *Si Gustavo se hubiera convertido en rey debido a sus posesiones nuevas, ¿qué clase de rey habría sido él?* (If Gustavo had become king with his new possessions, what type of king would he have been?)

2. *Si los niños hubieran hecho un plan para que Gustavo reconociera su actitud avariciosa, ¿qué habrían planeado?* (If the children had made a plan to make Gustavo realize his selfish behavior, what would they have planned?)

3. *Si ustedes tuvieran un talento como Gustavo, ¿qué clase de talento les gustaría tener? ¿Cómo lo usarían?* (If you could have a talent as Gustavo did, what talent would you like for yourselves? How would you use it?)

4. *Si ustedes fueran tan pequeños como Gustavo por un día, dígannos las cosas que harían y lo que les pasaría.* (If you could be as small as Gustavo for one day, tell us what things you would do and what things would happen to you.)

5. *Si Gustavo hubiera pensado solamente en sí mismo, olvidándose de sus amigos, describan como habrían sido sus días. ¿Qué tal si hubiera sido considerado y generoso?* (If Gustavo had thought only about himself, forgetting about his friends, describe what his days would have been like. What if he had been thoughtful and generous?)

V. INTEGRATING OTHER DISCIPLINES: *Un cuento de enanos*
(Class Session Three and Ongoing)

The following activities are designed to enhance children's response to literature and expand *beyond* the story and its theme. The variety of activities gives teachers and students an opportunity to choose those most appropriate.

CREATIVE DRAMATICS

1. *Story Dramatization:* Have groups re-enact the following scenes: (1) when Gustavo sings to his friends to show his appreciation for the modest gifts they gave him; (2) when he asks for the valuables as payment for his songs; (3) when he is lonely, returns the valuables, and regains his voice and friends. Have each group practice a scene and then dramatize the entire story from beginning to end.

2. *Story Twist:* Add a humorous twist to one of the scenes by adding an advice-giving fairy. Have cooperative groups plan, improvise and share with the class.

3. *Emotion Statue:* In four groups, have the children form emotion statues, displaying the emotions that the dwarf expressed—joy, sadness, loneliness, and greed. When the teacher calls out one of these words, the students will express this emotion by linking onto one another, forming a group statue.

4. *What If?:* Incorporate a "what if" story stretcher in a dramatization. Plan, dramatize, and evaluate.

5. *I'm a Fairy/Elf:* Brainstorm the limitless activities that a fairy might be able to perform—flying, floating, appearing, disappearing. To classical music, have students perform the actions in a circle. Teacher may prompt the actions.

ART AND WRITING

1. *Milk Carton Gustavo:* Have students decorate eight-ounce milk cartons, using construction paper, buttons and yarn. For props, they may draw, color and cut out Gustavo's ring, crown and chariot. In their literature logs, have the students write their thoughts about how these "things" were either good or bad for Gustavo and why.

2. *Fingerlings:* To represent Gustavo's friends, have the students make five construction paper finger rolls from paper strips. Have them cut strips, glue them together, and place on their fingers, adding features with marking pens. Then have the children retell the story using the milk carton Gustavo from #1 above and the fingerlings. Allow the children to write dialogues that the fingerling children might have with Gustavo. Share this activity among small groups.

3. *Friendship Tribute:* Have the students pretend to be Gustavo and write tributes to all of their little friends, acknowledging them as true friends. Have the students draw friends along the edges of the paper as borders.

4. *Gustavo Doll:* Using Figure T (page 285), have students color and cut out the ovals, triangles, and hands. Have them arrange and glue the features however they wish on paper plates to make the face. Next, have students glue hands and shoes on a sheet of lined paper to make the body. Staple the face at the top of the body. Yarn may be added to make hair. On the lined paper, have students write short songs that Gustavo might sing to his little friends.

5. *Remarkable Fairy/Dwarf:* Have the children paint pictures of favorite dwarves or fairies from the Literature Input. On large stars with lines, have them write about the remarkable traits—magical power, wisdom, talents, gifts—that their characters have and describe why the characters are so remarkable.

6. *Pop-Up Puppet:* Cut out individual sections from egg cartons, and provide paper cups, crayons, tape, yarn, glue, and straws or popsicle sticks. Have the students draw faces on the egg carton cups and attach hair. Poke a hole through each egg carton section; push a straw through the hole and securely tape it inside. Have the students poke another hole in each cup, insert a straw, and push it up and down. Have students write chants that Gustavo might recite to his friends. They may wish to examine Gustavo's many feelings to inspire the content of their chants. Allow them to recite the chants while using the pop-up puppets.

7. *Three Inches Tall:* Show the students a three-inch-long piece of yarn. Have them imagine being three inches tall. Instruct them to write about experiences they might have if they were that tiny. Have them edit their writing, then rewrite the stories in mini-books, drawing themselves as three-inch character in various situations.

8. *St. Patrick's Day Story:* Have students imagine that they are stopped by a leprechaun or elf on St. Patrick's Day. What does the leprechaun or elf want? Will the children do what was requested? How will they be rewarded? Have them write and illustrate their stories for a class big book publication.

9. *Three Trials:* Have students pretend to be fairies or elves. They really want to put someone they know through a test. Who is that person? What three trials must that person perform? Have them describe how this person performs each task. Allow them to write and illustrate their own publications.

10. *Flipbook:* Have students create flipbooks featuring one of their favorite dwarves or fairies by folding four 8-1/2" x 11 sheets of construction paper in half. Then have them staple the left side of each of the books. Have them draw and color their characters, posing them differently on each page. Holding the books in their left hands and beginning at the front, have them flip through the books, flipping with their right thumbs. They can see their "animated" characters move. Instruct them to write a brief caption on each page.

SOCIAL STUDIES

1. *Playing with Friends:* With students, discuss times when children have no one to play with and how when friends come to play, it enlivens their world. Allow this to prompt personal journal writing.

2. *Coping with Alienation:* As a consequence of Gustavo's behavior, he became alienated from those he loved. Have children brainstorm occasions when we all may feel alienated—being left out or when someone refuses to share toys, candy, or friends. In cooperative groups, brainstorm and suggest ways to cope with these problems. Allow the discussion to prompt personal journal writing.

3. *Contrasting Traits:* Form several groups and have children role-play the contrasting concepts of greediness and generosity. (From role-playing cards specify situations.) Let observers identify the concepts being displayed. Have children recall stories from the Literature Input and create their own stories, with illustrations, centered around these contrasting traits.

4. *Likes and Dislikes:* Gustavo's friends showed what they liked and disliked about his behavior. Have students brainstorm and discuss what they like and/or dislike about the behavior of characters from the Literature Input.

5. *Loneliness:* In the story Gustavo experiences loneliness. To emphasize this concept, show students a lifeless picture and have them imagine being in a place where there are no people, animals or flowers, just miles of sand, dirt or rocks. Have them orally describe a dark, dreary, lonely world; then allow each child to transform the scene by thinking of images that might enliven the world and orally describing them. Have them record their ideas. Allow cooperative groups to create murals that convey these concepts. Have them display and describe their murals.

POETRY

Zapatero remendón

Zapatero remendón,
esta bota hay que coser
clava bien este tacón
y a las tres yo volveré.

Zapatero, ¿está listo mi tacón?
No, porque no han llegado
los enanitos de San Simón.

Folklore

Los enanos

Ya los enanos
ya se enojaron
porque sus nanas
los regañaron.

Ya los enanos
ya están contentos
porque sus nanas
les cuentan cuentos.

Ya los enanos
ya están gozando
porque sus nanas
están cantando.

Canción popular

Figure T: *El enanito Gustavo* / Gustavo the Little Dwarf

285

MY OWN CREATIVE TEACHING IDEAS FOR UNIT EIGHTEEN

Books: _____

_____

_____

_____

_____

Ideas: _____

_____

_____

_____

_____

_____

_____

_____

_____

_____

_____

_____

_____

_____

_____

_____

UNIT NINETEEN

CUENTOS MULTICULTURALES

MULTICULTURAL TALES

Many ethnic tales, handed down from generation to generation, are used by wise adults to impart values and to deliver words of wisdom or advice to children. Through story animals and ethnic figures, children learn do's and don't's, universal truths, and problem-solving associated with real problems about real people. Today, Hispanic and other ethnic tales can still have an impact as many of these tales contribute to children's awareness and understanding of themselves and their cultural heritage as well as to an understanding of diverse cultures. In the Mexican tale *El pájaro Cú*, children learn a little "truth" about vanity. In the African tale *¿Por qué el conejo tiene las orejas tan largas?* they place themselves in a silly rabbit's predicament—taking a risk in order to belong to the "club" at all costs.

CHOOSE THE MAIN SELECTION

Before reading the Main Selection aloud, take your students through the Literature Input and Observation/Experience phases which follow.

Herrmann, Marjorie.

El pájaro Cú.
Illinois: National Textbook, 1983.

This Mexican folktale recounts the story of a homely, featherless bird that becomes an extraordinarily beautiful bird when all of the other birds from the community adorn him with their colorful feathers. Overtaken by his own vanity, the Cú bird abandons his friends. Determined to find that ungrateful Cú bird, the owl's search persists to this day.

If you choose *El pájaro Cú* as your selection, turn to page 292 to begin the Observation/Experience phase.

Vásquez, Zoraida, and Julieta Montelongo.

¿Por qué el conejo tiene las orejas tan largas?
México: Editorial Trillas, S.A., 1984.

This award-winning book is a delightful African tale about a rabbit. His eagerness to gain entrance into an exclusive party for horned animals gets him into a predicament that results in his appearance being permanently altered.

If you choose *¿Por qué el conejo tiene las orejas tan largas?* as your selection, turn to page 296 to begin the Observation/Experience phase.

I. LITERATURE INPUT: *Both Selections*

Select five or more titles from the following list to read aloud. Read at least one selection per day to the students. Make available and incorporate the suggested titles for voluntary independent reading. Titles marked with * are Spanish translations of the original English story; titles marked with + are recommended for more proficient listeners.

+1. Alcántara, S.R. *Guaraçú.* Spain: Editorial Hymsa, 1983. A young native boy longs to become friends with a remarkably beautiful blue bird that guides the child home after several lonely days of being lost in the forest.

+2. Alonso, Fernando. *El mandarín y los pájaros.* Spain: Santillana Publishing Company, 1976. A Chinese mandarin searches for the gifted musicians whose music so attracts him. Instead, he discovers that birds produce the melodious song.

+3. Andersen, Hans Christian. Translated by Rosanna Guarnieri. *El ruiseñor del emperador.* México: Fernández Editores S.A., 1983. This is the Spanish version of Andersen's tale, *The Nightingale,* in which an emperor is attracted to the song of an extraordinary bird.

+4. Armellada, Fray C. *El cocuyo y la mora.* Venezuela: Editorial Ekaré-Banco del Libro, 1983. This Venezuelan Indian tale is a love story that explains why the firefly has a light at the end of his tail and why he hovers around the mulberry during spring.

+5. —. *El rabipelado burlado.* Venezuela: Editorial Ekaré-Banco del Libro, 1983. A Venezuelan Indian fable relates how the opossum learned to eat plants rather than birds, thanks to the trick played on him.

+6. Arredonda, Inés. *Historia verdadera de una princesa*. México: S.E.P. CIDCLI, S.C., 1985. This wonderfully illustrated Mexican legend recounts La Malinche's childhood experience and romance with Hernán Cortés.

7. Barbot, Daniel. *Un diente se mueve*. Venezuela: Editorial Ekaré-Banco del Libro, 1981. In this Venezuelan story, a child loses a tooth and experiences a magical adventure. A tooth mouse takes Clarisse to his home in tooth-land to show her how children's teeth are used.

*8. Belpré, Pura. *Pérez y Martina*. New York: Fredrick Warne and Company, 1977. This is a delightful Puerto Rican folktale about Martina, the little ant. Several "gentlemen callers" try to win her heart, but instead, she reserves it for the charming and handsome mouse, Pérez.

9. Cardoso Onelio, Jorge. *Caballito blanco*. Cuba: Editorial Gente Nueva, 1980. This is a Cuban tale about a sick child's determination to walk when an encouraging carousel horse takes him on a fanciful adventure.

+10. Carreño, Mada. *Aladino y la lámpara mágica*. México: Editorial Trillas, 1986. This is the classic Arab tale about Aladdin and his magic lamp. This is one of fifteen beautifully illustrated tales from the *Clásicos Trillas* collection.

+11. —. *Los zapatos de Tamburi*. México: Editorial Trillas, S.A., 1986. Tamburi, the Egyptian, cannot destroy his "trouble-making" shoes no matter how hard he tries.

12. —. *Cheng y el grillo*. México: Editorial Trillas. 1987. In this Chinese tale, Cheng is concerned that his father will not be able to present the emperor with a strong, invincible grasshopper as commanded. This brings about a dream about being a valiant grasshopper.

+13. —. *El viaje del joven Matsua*. México: Editorial Trillas, 1987. A Mexican legend tells how Matsua journeys to the land of the swift-running Tarahumara Indians where, among them, he becomes a skillful runner.

14. Cruz Corzo, Hector F. *El caballito de siete colores*. Guatemala: Editorial Santa Piedra, 1984. In this Puerto Rican legend, a rainbow horse grants the farmer's youngest son any wish in return for its freedom.

+15. Darío, Rubén. *Margarita*. Venezuela: Editorial Arte, 1983. Rubén Darío's famous poem about a little princess, who literally reaches for the stars, is among the highest quality literary works.

+16. de la Rosa, Clarisa. *El perro del cerro y la rana de la sabana*. Venezuela: Ediciones Ekaré-Banco del Libro, 1986. A dog and a frog argue about which is braver in this Venezuelan tale. When a ferocious lion appears, they team up against adversity.

+17. Feliciano Mendoza, Ester. *Sinfonía de Puerto Rico*. San Juan de Puerto Rico: Instituto de Cultura Puertorriqueña, 1979. This is a collection of Puerto Rican legends recounting, in lyric vignettes, the origin of flowers, plants, birds, people, and instruments on the island.

18. Franca, Mary and Eliardo. *Rabo de gato*. Venezuela: Editorial Ekaré-Banco del Libro, 1983. In this Venezuelan tale, Toad is delighted when he tricks everyone into thinking that he is a cat, at least until he meets perceptive Miss Toad.

+19. Garrido, Felipe. *Tajín y los siete truenos*. México: Promociones Editoriales Mexicanas, 1982. This is a Mexican legend about Tajín, who tries to imitate the seven Thunder brothers by creating rain and thunder. This has adverse consequences for poor Tajín.

+*20. Goble, Paul. *El don del perro sagrado*. México: Promociones Editoriales Mexicanas, 1982. This legend tells how the nomadic American Indians came to call the indispensable, extraordinary horse "sacred dog."

+21. Ipuana, Ramón. *El conejo y el mapurite*. Venezuela: Editorial Ekaré-Banco del Libro, 1983. This Venezuelan tale explains why the rabbit twitches its nose. The rabbit tricks Mapurite, the skunk, out of all his cigars. The witty skunk then contrives a plan with some special cigars that cause the twitching nose.

+22. Jusayu, Miguel Angel. *Ni era vaca ni era caballo*. Venezuela: Ediciones Ekaré-Banco del Libro, 1984. In this Venezuelan Indian tale, a young shepherd is fascinated by a green truck and the gasoline that it needs. When he applies the same principle to his grandmother's mule, he learns that he has made a tragic mistake.

+*23. Kousel, D. and E. Thollander. *El premio del cuco*. New York: Doubleday, 1977. In this Mexican folktale, a beautiful and courageous bird loses his colorful feathers and his melodious voice during a valiant act. This is a story variant of *El pájaro Cú*.

+24. Kurtyez, Marcos. *De tigres y tlacuaches*. México: Editorial Novaro, 1981. Six Mexican tales about animals range from trickster tales to fables.

+25. Mistral, Silvia. *La Cenicienta china*. México: Editorial Trillas, S.A., 1986. Cinderella is a classic known the world over. Here it is beautifully told with a Chinese flavor and splendid illustrations.

+26. Pascuala, Corona. *Pita, pita, cedacero*. New York: Four Winds Press, 1979. These six Mexican fairytales are variants of classic stories including *Frastería,* a version of *Cinderella*. They contain charming illustrations and are in bold print.

27. Pettersson, Aline. *El papalote y el nopal*. México: CONAFE, CIDCLI, S.C., 1985. This is a Mexican tale about a cactus that succeeds in setting free an entangled kite.

+28. Porcel de Sastrías, Martha. *Cuentos de un martín pescador y su viaje por México*. México: Sitesa, S.A., 1988. Children are invited to see México through the eyes and cultural experiences of a little bird.

+*29. Okusuka, Yuzo. *Sujo y el caballo blanco*. México: Promociones Editoriales Mexicanas, 1982. This heart-warming Mongolian legend tells about the origin of the horse-head design on the Mongolian violin.

30. Reyes, Alfonso. *Ohia y los animales*. México: Fernández Editores, 1984. An African legend tells about a young man who knew the language of the animals. It was a secret that, if revealed, would cost him his life.

31. —. *Orfeo y Eurídice*. México: Fernández Editores, 1984. This is the Greek legend about Orpheus whose love for Euridice causes both her rescue and death.

32. —. *El rey Vikram*. México: Fernández Editores, 1984. This is an Indian legend about an extraordinary bird. Vikram was no ordinary parrot; he was a real king who played a clever trick on an infuriated dancer.

33. —. *Urashima el pescador*. México: Fernández Editores, 1984. In this Japanese legend, a fisherman had the good fortune of visiting the deep sea and the misfortune of aging because of it.

34. Rohmer, Harriet. *La montaña del alimento*. San Francisco: Children's Book Press, 1983. This is a Mexican legend about how a giant ant brought food into the world and how Quetzalcoatl protected it. This story was granted the American Book Award for outstanding achievement in multicultural literature.

35. Rohmer, Harriet, and Jesús Guerrero Rea. *Atariba and Niguayona*. San Francisco: Children's Book Press, 1988. A Puerto Rican legend tells how a young Taino saves the life of his ailing friend. He finds the tree whose fruit helps restore her health. This is one of a series of multicultural books written in both English and Spanish.

36. Rugeles, Ernesto F. *Águila Veloz*. Texas: Voluntad Publishers, 1978. A Native American hunter dreams that an eagle advises him where to hunt. When he awakens, the real eagle appears and leads him to a herd of buffalo. From that day on, the hunter is called Swift Eagle.

37. —. *El juego de pelota*. Texas: Voluntad Publishers, 1978. Grandfather tells his grandson a story about an Aztec sport which was a type of ball game. Ball games were important recreational activities even in pre-Columbian times.

+38. Uribe, Verónica. *El tigre y el cangrejo*. Venezuela: Ediciones Ekaré-Banco del Libro, 1985. This Venezuelan Indian tale explains how a tiger gets his yellow bright eyes. It is a beautifully illustrated story with a simple, yet enriching text. This is one of seven titles from the collection *Narraciones indígenas*.

39. Urrutia, Cristina. *El maíz*. México: Editorial Patria, 1984. This book from *Colección Piñata* is colorfully picturesque. It invites children to join in a rich cultural experience in rural México.

40. Zendrera, C. *Yaci y su muñeca*. Spain: Editorial Juventud, S.A., 1974. In this Brazilian tale, a little girl buries her special corn-husk doll and later discovers that something magical happens to it.

RELATED TITLES IN ENGLISH FOR SECOND LANGUAGE ACQUISITION

Addison-Wesley Big Book Program. *How the Moon Got in the Sky*. Reading, MA: Addison-Wesley, 1989.

—. *The Farmer and the Beet*. Reading, MA: Addison-Wesley, 1989.

—. *The Rabbit and the Turnip*. Reading, MA: Addison-Wesley, 1989.

+ Belpré, Pura. *Dance of the Animals*. New York: Frederick Warne and Company, 1972.

+ —. *The Rainbow-Colored Horse*. New York: Frederick Warne and Company, 1978.

Bishop, Claire H. *The Five Chinese Brothers*. New York: Putnam Publishers Group, 1938.

Bryan, Ashley. *The Dancing Granny*. New York: Macmillan, 1987.

Chandiet, Bernice. *Juan Bobo and the Pig*. New York: Walker and Company, 1973.

Dayrell, Elphinstone. *Why the Sun and the Moon Live in the Sky*. Boston: Houghton Mifflin, 1968.

Martel, Cruz. *Yagua Days*. New York: The Dial Press, 1976.

McDermott, Gerald. *Anansi the Spider*. New York: Holt, Rinehart and Winston, 1972.

—. *Tikki Tikki Tembo*. New York: Holt, Rinehart and Winston, 1968.

Mosel, Arlene. *The Funny Little Woman*. New York: E. P. Dutton and Company, 1972.

Politi, Leo. *The Nicest Gift*. New York: Charles Scribner's Sons, 1973.

—. *Song of the Swallows*. New York: Charles Scribner's Sons, 1978.

—. *Three Stalks of Corn*. New York: Charles Scribner's Sons, 1978.

Yashima, Taro. *Crow Boy*. New York: Puffin Books, 1984.

II. OBSERVATION/EXPERIENCE: *El pájaro Cú*
(Class Session One)

Guide students in the following observation/experience sequence to set the stage for reading the Main Selection.

Focus: Sometimes the actions of our friends disappoint us.

1. Display an empty nest or make one by crumpling a brown paper bag and adding twigs. Arouse the children's curiosity by having them observe. Ask students why they think the nest is empty. Have them share their ideas.

2. Tell students to imagine that it belongs to a bird named Cú, from the story *El pájaro Cú.*

3. Tell them that Cú left his friends without the courtesy of a goodbye.

4. Have them predict why Cú will leave and disappoint his friends. Following the story, have students discuss whether their predictions were correct.

III. READ AND DISCUSS THE MAIN SELECTION: *El pájaro Cú*
(Class Session One)

Read the Main Selection from page 288 to the students. Highlight the unit's theme by relating this story to other selections from the Literature Input list on pages 288 - 292. Then, guide students in discussing some of the following questions.

1. *Describan al pájaro Cú antes y después de haberlo adornado los otros pájaros.* (Describe the Cú bird before and after being adorned by the birds.)

2. *¿Cómo describirían ustedes al tecolote? ¿Fue culpa de él que el pájaro Cú se fuera? Explíquennos.* (How would you describe the owl? Was it his fault that the Cú bird left? Explain.)

3. *¿Por qué creen ustedes que todos los pájaros se enojaron tanto con el pájaro Cú? ¿Cómo se sentirían ustedes? ¿Por qué?* (Why do you suppose all of the birds became so angry with the Cú bird? How would you feel? Why?)

4. *¿Por qué creen ustedes que el pájaro Cú se fue?* (Why do you suppose the Cú bird left?)

5. *¿Cuáles fueron los personajes que más les gustaron en el cuento? ¿Y cuáles no les gustaron? ¿Por qué?* (Which were the characters that you liked the most in the story? Which did you like the least? Why?)

IV. "WHAT IF" STORY STRETCHER: *El pájaro Cú*
(Class Session Two)

Next, re-read the Main Selection and choose one or more of the following questions to develop students' critical thinking skills. Story stretchers may also prompt discussion, drama or writing activities.

1. *Si el pájaro Cú les invitara a ustedes a viajar con él, ¿a dónde irían y qué verían?* (If the Cú bird invited you to travel with him, where would you go and what would you see?)

2. *Si el pájaro Cú se hubiera encontrado con el patito feo, ¿qué le habría dicho?* (If the Cú bird had met up with the ugly duckling, what would he have said to him?)

3. *Si los pájaros no hubieran donado sus plumas al pájaro Cú, ¿cómo habría cambiado el cuento?* (If the birds had not donated their feathers to the Cú bird, how would the story have been different?)

4. *Si el pájaro Cú hubiera regresado a la comunidad de pájaros, ¿que le habrían dicho sus amigos a él?* (If the Cú bird had returned to the bird community, what would his friends have said to him?)

5. *Si el tecolote al fin encontrara al pájaro Cú, ¿que pasaría en el cuento?* (If the owl were finally to find the Cú bird, what would happen in the story?)

V. INTEGRATING OTHER DISCIPLINES: *El pájaro Cú*
(Class Session Three and Ongoing)

The following activities are designed to enhance children's response to literature and expand *beyond* the story and its theme. The variety of activities gives teachers and students an opportunity to choose those most appropriate.

CREATIVE DRAMATICS

1. *Creative Movement:* Using streamers in assorted colors, have students re-enact the scene when the birds adorn the Cú bird. Have the Cú bird fly away and hide. Next, have the students pretend to be the other birds, flying and moving as birds do. Have them fly together in a flock searching for the Cú bird.

2. *Reacting to a Character:* Have the students re-enact the scene when the birds become angry with the owl as he flies over the land seeking the Cú bird. During this scene, have the students add characters who will act as mediators, helpers, or instigators. Have groups plan, dramatize, and evaluate the outcome.

3. *Bird Improvisations:* Have students improvise being birds from the bird community—a flamingo, a stork, an owl, a crow. Have them form the birds' shapes with their bodies and imitate bird sounds. Allow observers to guess the birds being improvised.

4. *Blending Story Variants:* Have cooperative groups blend story elements from two Cú bird stories: *El pájaro Cú* and *El premio del cuco.* Provide planning, improvisation, and evaluation time.

ART AND WRITING

1. *Wanted Poster:* Have the students draw the Cú bird either as a peculiar-looking bird or as a beautiful bird on wanted posters. Have them write descriptions on the posters and offer rewards.

2. *Beauty Contest:* Have students paint pictures of the extraordinarily beautiful Cú bird to submit for a beauty contest. Have them write lists of ten beauty tips that all birds should know.

3. *Stuffed Owl:* Using lunch bags, have the children stuff them with newspapers, fold them down, and then staple them to create stuffed owls. Have them paint the owls and add paper features. Allow them to write questions to interview the owl regarding his quest for the Cú bird. Then have them feature the owl's interview in a class newspaper.

4. *Flying Cú Bird:* Using Figure U (page 302), have the students cut out the bird pattern. Have them trace the pattern on the folded edge of a sheet of construction paper and cut along the trace marks, taking special care to cut out the inner curved part of the pattern. Have them pull the rear panel of the pattern first under, then forward over the bird's head (see model). Allow the students to use crayons, markers, and yarn in assorted colors to create the bird's feathers. Have the students open the wings, punch a hole and tie a long string to the bird to make him fly! Then have them pretend to be the Cú bird and reveal the real reason why he left. They should write these deep secrets in their literature logs.

5. *Favorite Ethnic Tale:* Have the students create book jackets for their favorite ethnic tales. They may illustrate them using marking pens in assorted colors. Allow them to write synopses of the ethnic tales on the book jackets. Use these for book talks and display them on a literature bulletin board.

6. *Cultural Mural:* Have groups paint murals depicting their favorite Hispanic tales. Instruct the children to leave three-inch borders along the bottom of the long strips of butcher paper so that they can write descriptions of the murals indicating their cultural origins.

7. *Ethnic Crafts:* Have cooperative groups create varied ethnic crafts indigenous to specific Spanish-speaking countries.

8. *Flag Book:* Furnish pictures of flags and appropriate materials for making flags. Have each of the students staple two flag shapes together with a lined piece of paper inside to form a book. Have each student write specific facts about a Spanish-speaking country inside the flag book Display the crafts along with the flag books. Share them with other classes.

SCIENCE

1. *Bird Study:* The story presented a variety of birds. Present a mini-unit on different types of birds. Note how physical characteristics—beaks, bills, feet—are adapted to a variety of environments. Discuss migration pattern of birds; how and where birds build nests; what foods they eat. (Books, films, and science magazines can be used to expand information.) Have the students record facts in their science logs.

SOCIAL STUDIES

1. *Separation:* The Cú bird was separated from the bird community when he departed. Discuss how we are separated, at times, from people we love because of school, work, or other reasons. Emphasize how we can be with someone even though they are far away from us through phone calls, letters, messages and sharing when united. Have the children write letters to someone that they are separated from at the present time.

2. *Comparison:* Have the students compare the Cú bird and the ugly duckling stories. Have them focus on each bird's personal concept of self. Have students think about the way the other animals treated the two characters and how this made the characters feel. Ask if this can happen in real life. Have them write in their literature logs about the character they favored most and why.

3. *Being Blamed:* In the story, the owl was blamed for something that was not his fault. Have children brainstorm occasions when this may happen in real life and explore solutions to deal with the situations when they arise.

4. *Hispanic Cultural Awareness:* Use a favorite story from the Literature Input list as a motivator for developing a cultural unit about a Spanish-speaking country. Expose students to specific literary works associated with authors from a particular country or to tales about specific regions. Include children in planning what they would like to study about a specific Spanish-speaking country; e.g., literature, music, food, games, art, customs. Have them record facts that they know about Hispanic peoples.

   Invite guests from other countries to share information and experiences. With students, list the information and experiences on a chart.

I. LITERATURE INPUT: *¿Por qué el conejo tiene las orejas tan largas?*
See pages 288 - 292.

II. OBSERVATION/EXPERIENCE: *¿Por qué el conejo tiene las orejas tan largas?*
(Class Session One)

Guide students in the following observation/experience sequence to set the stage for reading the Main Selection.

Focus: Anything can happen when we try too hard to belong to the "club."

1. Using a large ball of clay, shape a peculiar-looking rabbit with some attribute from another animal, such as elephant ears, and then ask the children if they have ever wondered why a rabbit has a fluffy tail and elephant ears! Give several balls of clay to students, and have them create their own peculiar-looking rabbits. With each new attribute, have them ask a question such as, *¿Qué haría un conejo con un cuello de jirafa?* (What would a rabbit do with a giraffe's neck?) or *¿Qué haría un conejo con un cuerno de rinoceronte?* (What would a rabbit do with a rhinoceros' horn?)

2. Tell students that they will listen to an African tale titled, *¿Por qué el conejo tiene las orejas largas?,* to learn why the rabbit did something risky to belong to the "club."

3. Have students draw a picture of what they think a rabbit might have looked like without his long ears. Compare their illustrations with the book's pictures after reading the story to them.

4. Have them predict what the rabbit will do that causes his ears to grow long. Following the story, have the students discuss whether their predictions were correct.

III. READ AND DISCUSS THE MAIN SELECTION: *¿Por qué el conejo tiene las orejas tan largas?*
(Class Session One)

Read the Main Selection from page 288 to the students. Highlight the unit's theme by relating this story to other selections from the Literature Input list on pages 288 - 292. Then, guide students in discussing some of the following questions.

1. *¿Por qué el conejo no fue invitado a la fiesta de los venados?* (Why wasn't the rabbit invited to the deer's party?)

2. *¿Cómo describirían ustedes a los animales que fueron a la fiesta?* (How would you describe the animals that went to the party?)

3. *Después de ver lo que hizo el conejo, ¿qué dijeron y qué hicieron todos los otros animales? ¿Qué habrían hecho y qué habrían dicho ustedes? ¿Deberían haberlo castigado en esa forma? ¿Por que? ¿Por qué no?* (Seeing what the rabbit had done, what did the other animals say and do? What would you have said and done? Should they have punished him in this way? Why or why not?)

4. *¿Qué lección aprendió el conejo de esta experiencia?* (What lesson did the rabbit learn from this experience?)

5. *¿Qué clase de fiesta les gusta a ustedes más? Hay algunas reglas o requisitos para poder asistir a una fiesta?* (What type of party do you like best? Are there any special rules or requirements for attending a party?)

IV. "WHAT IF" STORY STRETCHER: *¿Por qué el conejo tiene las orejas tan largas?* (Class Session Two)

Next, re-read the Main Selection and choose one or more of the following questions to develop students' critical thinking skills. Story stretchers may also prompt discussion, drama or writing activities.

1. *Si el conejo no hubiera encontrado los cuernos, ¿cómo podría haberse disfrazado para entrar a la fiesta?* (If the rabbit had not found the horns, how might he have disguised himself to get into the party?)

2. *Si no hubiera sido un día tan caluroso, ¿cómo podrían haberle descubierto los cuernos postizos al conejo?* (If the day had not been so hot, how would the rabbit's fake horns have been discovered?)

3. *Si los venados hubieran defendido al conejo, ¿cómo habría sido diferente el cuento?* (If the deer had defended the rabbit, how would the story have been different?)

4. *Si los animales le hubieran dejado al conejo hablar antes de castigarlo, ¿qué podría haber dicho él para hacerles cambiar de parecer?* (If the animals had let the rabbit speak before punishing him, what might he have said to change their minds?)

5. *Si ustedes fueran el conejo, ¿sería muy importante para ustedes ir a la fiesta? ¿Por qué? Si no, ¿qué otras cosas podrían hacer en lugar de ir a la fiesta?* (If you were the rabbit, would going to the party be very important to you? Why? If not, what other things could you do instead of going to the party?)

V. INTEGRATING OTHER DISCIPLINES: *¿Por qué el conejo tiene las orejas tan largas?*
(Class Session Three and Ongoing)

The following activities are designed to enhance children's response to literature and expand *beyond* the story and its theme. The variety of activities gives teachers and students an opportunity to choose those most appropriate.

CREATIVE DRAMATICS

1. *Re-enact the Story:* Have groups re-enact the story in two parts: (1) the scene when the deer talks to the rabbit about the party, and then the rabbit makes a disguise; (2) the scene when the animals discover the rabbit's disguise and punish him for deceiving them. After practicing, allow students to dramatize the entire story from beginning to end. Following this, have cooperative groups create a different story ending. Allow them to plan, practice, and share the dramatization with the class. For fun, have some students wear horn headbands to represent animals at the party; another student can be the hot sun that melts the wax; and another can wear a hat with adjustable ears that grow when pulled to represent the rabbit. Have the children re-enact the entire story.

2. *Story Twist:* Have groups add another character to the story. How will this change the story? What will the character's role be? Allow them to plan the dramatization, act out the story and evaluate it.

3. *Be the Rabbit:* Have the children imitate the rabbit's expressions; e.g., curious, surprised, sad, happy, excited, disappointed, defeated, guilty. You may wish to call out descriptors and situations as students display the actions. Have the children visualize, describe the ambience of the party, and then re-enact the party scene.

4. *Pantomime Animals:* Have students pantomime movements of horned animals—running swiftly, grazing cautiously, leaping, bucking. Allow them to move in a circle as you direct their actions.

ART AND WRITING

1. *Horn Headbands:* Measure a cardboard strip to the circumference of each child's head. Have them staple or glue the ends together. Allow them to draw horns, cut them out, and glue them on the headbands. Also have them make rabbit ear headbands. Then allow them to use the headbands to dramatize the story.

2. *Rabbit Finger Puppet:* Furnish rabbit patterns and have students cut two holes above the eyes to insert two fingers. Have the students pretend to be the rabbit and show how the ears grow. Have them write complaints to the horned animals letting the animals know what they think about their long ears and the animals' rude behavior.

3. *Rabbit Illustration:* Using pastels, have students illustrate the rabbit in the story or another rabbit. Have them write letter to the rabbits inquiring about their ears. Distribute letters among the students to read. Later, they may write possible replies to the letters.

4. *Mural:* Paint a group mural depicting the party scene. Have students create and write party invitations to the animals and/or people of their choice. Allow them to plan the theme, activities and menu.

5. *Storytelling with Clay:* Pair students to retell the story. Have them shape rabbits with clay or playdough while telling the story. Instruct them to stretch out the ears when the narrators describe how the rabbits' ears grow. Allow them to use the same idea for different animals, inventing the story as they mold the animal shapes.

6. *Puppets:* Have each student use two 6" x 6" pieces of construction paper to make antlers. Have them trace around their hands and cut out the hand shapes. Have them glue the antlers to paper bags. Have them draw and cut out eyes, noses, and spots to glue on the deer. On 9" x 12" white construction paper, have them draw arches on the long sides and then cut along the arches. Have them roll these into tubes and glue the edges to create the bodies for the deer. Tell them to draw and cut out ears, arms, and feet. Have them glue these and other added features such as whiskers, carrots, baskets on the tubular bodies. Have students write dialogues that the deer puppet and the rabbit might say to each other.

7. *Protest Letter:* Have students pretend to be the rabbit and write letters protesting his treatment by members of the exclusive horned-animals club. The students may create protest signs.

8. *Before and After:* Have students imagine an animal's appearance being altered. Have them draw "before and after" pictures of the peculiar animals. Allow them to write captions describing the animals' peculiar, unique appearances.

9. *Changing Rabbit:* Using Figure V (page 303), have students color, cut out and fasten on ears or horns. On the rabbit's lined body, have students write a "way-out" story explaining why the rabbit's ears have grown or changed.

10. *Story Advertisement:* Have the students create wearable posters advertising their favorite multicultural tales. Have them write synopses, edit them, then write them on two posters. Attach both posters at the top ends and tie them with yarn so that the children can slip them on over their heads. Have the students wear their multicultural story advertisements and share with other classes.

SCIENCE

1. *Horns/Antlers:* Except for the rabbit, the other animals in the story are horned animals. Talk about varied shapes, sizes and types of horns and antlers and the process of shedding and regrowth. (Use picture books and science magazines.) Allow the children to record facts in their science logs. Discuss how the animals use their horns. Also discuss how people use animal horns.

2. *Rabbits:* After checking for allergies, bring in a real rabbit for students to touch gently. With the students, talk about and list the sensory descriptors. Brainstorm creative ideas to "explain" why the tail is so short, or the body so fluffy, and so on. Have language experience groups create silly group stories.

3. *Solids:* The rabbit used wax to fasten his fake horns. Under your supervision, have children watch a candle or wax crayon melt. Talk about the effect of heat on solids. Have students record facts in their science logs.

SOCIAL STUDIES

1. *Feeling Left Out:* In the story, the rabbit feels left out, at least until he crashes the party. Ask the children to imagine how the rabbit felt. Have cooperative groups role play some situations that demonstrate this point—not being chosen on a team, being excluded from a play group or club, not being invited to a party. Point out that sometimes we feel left out, but we should not dwell on these feelings; instead we should try to make the best of any situation. Brainstorm alternatives to help children cope with these situations—rechanneling activities, expanding interests, joining other play groups, sharing things of interest with others, and trying to smile more.

2. *Welcoming Committee:* Discuss how the rabbit was made to feel unwelcome by the horned animals. Have the children ever experienced a similar feeling? Which situations pose this problem? How could we be made to feel welcome in these situations? Brainstorm and record the children's ideas. With students, make a list of things that a class welcoming committee could do to welcome visitors—smile, greet them, read self-published books to them, show them interest centers.

3. *Brainstorm Rules:* In the story, the party rules were too rigid. Sometimes rules serve good purposes, and sometimes they serve useless purposes. Brainstorm rules of the classroom and discuss whether they are necessary. Then have cooperative groups create useful rules and list the purposes.

4. *Ethnic Diversity:* This tale and others from this unit are ethnic tales. Guide students in a discussion about the differences among people from different parts of the world. Brainstorm what some of those differences are—houses, clothes, foods, music, language, customs. Have them list ethnic groups that they have come in contact with and those that they have seen on television. Discuss groups they would like to learn more about and why. Allow them to write ideas about this topic in their personal journals.

   Have students prepare interview sheets to use with adults representing different cultures. (Use available school personnel, neighbors, or parents.) Share interviews with groups. Invite some of the interviewed adults to read ethnic tales representing their ethnic groups.

5. *Cultural Mural:* In groups, have the students use the information gained from the discussions and personal interviews to create murals that depicts our world as a more beautiful place because of the contributions offered by different cultures.

6. *Multicultural Party:* Have children bring musical recordings that represent their culture from home. (Provide additional varied recordings.) Have them learn "We Are the World" and/or "It's a Small World" (these are available in Spanish) as a culmination for the cultural music appreciation lesson. Children may also bring clothing, packaged food and artifacts representing their cultures. You may wish to have students contribute ingredients to prepare a multicultural treat in class. Multicultural games and stories can also be introduced.

POETRY

La mañana de San Juan

La mañana de San Juan
vuelan las palomas
del palomar.

Vuelan y van las palomas
la mañana de San Juan.
Llevan amor en el pico
y hacia la villa se van
las palomas
la mañana de San Juan.

Cancíon tradicional

El pájaro Cú

Pájaro Cú,
con plumaje de colores,
ya no alegras más
los árboles ni las flores.

Tu canto extrañamos
y te hemos buscado
por desiertos, bosques
y en muchos lugares.

Regresa Cú a tu hogar
rodeado de árboles y flores,
que queremos ya oir
tus hermosos cantares.

Raquel C. Mireles

El conejo

En la cueva hay un conejo
y el conejo ya se fue;
ha salido de mañana
y se fue pa Santa Fe.

En la cueva hay un conejo
y el conejo no está aquí;
ha salido de mañana
y a las doce ha de venir.

Y aquí está el conejo y aquí está.
Y aquí está el conejo y aquí está.

Folklore

Figure U: *El pájaro Cú* / The Cú Bird

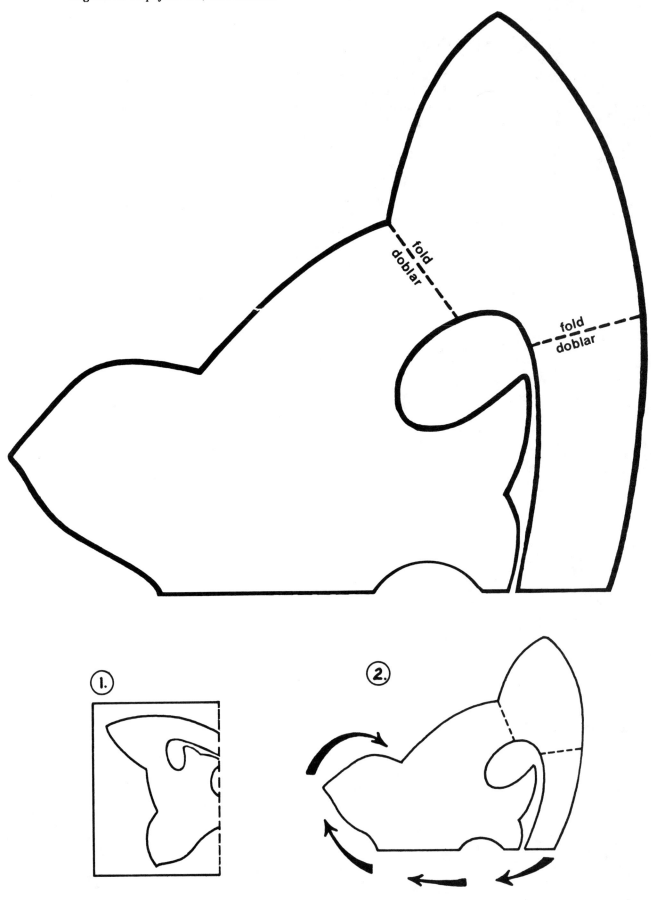

fold
doblar

fold
doblar

1.

2.

MY OWN CREATIVE TEACHING IDEAS FOR UNIT NINETEEN

Books: _____

_____

_____

_____

_____

_____

Ideas: _____

_____

_____

_____

_____

_____

_____

_____

_____

_____

_____

_____

_____

_____

_____

_____

UNIT TWENTY

MIS CUENTOS DE AMOR PREFERIDOS

MY FAVORITE LOVE STORIES

The theme of love and romance in many children's stories in Spanish entwines humor and real-life experiences, exposing children to a dimension of love outside the family. At a time when children are often saturated with unhealthy portrayals of love and romance in the media, this unit presents this theme in a simple, healthy way. *Pérez y Martina* and other stories from this unit allow children to find humor in make-believe experiences.

CONCEPTS AND VALUES

1. When we love someone, we do nice things for that person.
2. When we love someone, we want to spend time with that person.
3. When we love someone, we want to share our lives together.
4. In marriage, we experience happy and sad moments.
5. Though they may seem silly right now, love stories may not be silly when we grow up.

MAIN SELECTION

Before reading the Main Selection aloud, take your students through the Literature Input and Observation/Experience phases which follow.

Herrmann, Marjorie E.

Pérez y Martina.
Illinois: National Textbook Company, 1978.

Martina, the little ant, finds a penny and buys face powder to beautify herself. Several animals try to win her heart but she reserves it for a charming and handsome mouse named Pérez. Pérez and Martina get married and live very happily through both sad and happy moments.

I.   LITERATURE INPUT: *Pérez y Martina*

Select five or more titles from the following list to read aloud. Read at least one selection per day to the students. Make available and incorporate the suggested titles for voluntary independent reading. Titles marked with * are Spanish translations of the original English story; titles marked with + are recommended for more proficient listeners.

1.   Almendras, Herminio. *Había una vez . . . .* Cuba: Editorial Gente Nueva, 1982. This book contains an anthology of many of the classics and poems by Cuban authors. The selections represent this theme and a variety of other themes from this resource book.

+2.   Andersen, Hans Christian. *Almendrita.* México: Promociones Editoriales Mexicanas, S.A., 1982. This is the beautiful classical story of *Thumbelina.*

3.   —. *El soldadito de plomo.* México: Fernández Editores, S.A., 1984. This is another beautiful version of the classical *The Tin Soldier.*

+4.   —. *El valiente soldadito de plomo.* Spain: Alianza Editorial, S.A., 1985. This is a more advanced version of the classical romantic story of *The Tin Soldier.*

5.   —. *La princesa del guisante.* Spain: Editorial Lumen, 1986. This is a beautifully illustrated version of the classic *The Princess and the Pea.*

+6.   Armellada, Fray Cesáreo de. *El cocuyo y la mora.* Venezuela: Ekaré-Banco del Libro, 1978. A dry mulberry tree falls in love with a firefly and the most interesting situation develops.

+7.   Beaumont, L.P. Translated by Carmen Bravo Villasante. *La bella y la bestia.* Spain: Editorial Miñón, S.A., 1984. This version of the classic tale *Beauty and the Beast,* retains the traditional story line and contains handsome illustrations.

8.   Broger, Achim. *Historia de Dragolina.* Spain: Editorial Juventud, 1982. Dragolina, the last dragon on this planet, is the most adaptable and friendly creature in the land. She finds a home and meets her perfect mate to live happily ever after.

9.   Busquets, Carlos. *La cenicienta.* Spain: Editorial Susaeta, 1985. This is the classical story of *Cinderella.*

10.   —. *El soldadito de plomo.* Spain: Editorial Susaeta, 1985. This is the classical story of *The Tin Soldier.*

11. Claret, María. *La ratita Blasa*. Spain: Editorial Juventud, 1983. Blasa is a little rat looking for a mate. Every month she meets a different prospective husband until finally, she decides to marry the handsome December mouse.

+12. Gabán, Jesús. *El payaso y la princesa*. Spain: Ediciones Destino, 1983. In this romantic story about two puppets, a magic raindrop brings them to life in a most imaginative way. This book won the 1982 *Appel les Mestres* award in Europe.

+13. Garibay, Ricardo. *El humito del tren y el humito dormido*. México: CONAFE, CIDCLI, S.A., 1985. The smoke of passing trains meets the smoke from a chimney and every day is a day of romance.

+14. Grimm, Brothers. *Rapunzel*. Spain: Editorial Lumen, 1981. The classical fairytale is beautifully illustrated and retains much of the traditional story line as when Rapunzel's teardrop restores her love's sight.

15. Heuer, Margarita. *Carlitos el conejito*. México: Editorial Trillas, S.A., 1983. Carlitos tries to be fierce but never scares anyone. When he meets a female rabbit, he discovers he is happier as a rabbit.

16. Krahn, Fernando. *Hilderita y Maximiliano*. Spain: Editorial Juventud, 1979. This is a romance about two ladybugs that get married, fly to the moon, and live a happy life.

+17. Moodie, Fiona. *El pescador*. Spain: Ediciones S.M., 1984. Emma is magically transformed into a mermaid when she accidentally falls into the sea. She is freed from this enchantment when her husband recognizes her and devises a plan to rescue her.

18. Sennell, Joles. *El mejor novio del mundo*. Spain: Editorial La Galera, S.A., 1984. This story tells how the parents of the prettiest mouse search throughout their world to find the perfect husband for their daughter.

19. Torres, Daniel C., and Angelina R. de Torres. *Elotito y Mazorquita*. California: Blackstone Printing and Graphics, 1986. Elotito and Mazorquita fall in love, get married, and have a beautiful family. This story integrates science and nutrition so that children learn in a fun way.

+20. Turin, Adela. *Arturo y Clementina*. Spain: Editorial Lumen, 1976. Clementina, the turtle, is loved by her husband who never takes her seriously. She longs to see the world, and one day she finally decides to leave.

The following selections should be read after the Main Selection has been presented. These supporting stories can be used for story comparisons, dramatization, or for writing about story variants—such activities are described in Experiences with Literature.

*21. Belpré, Pura. *Pérez y Martina*. New York: Frederick Warne and Company, 1966. The classical fable of a little roach who seeks a husband. Several gentlemen callers visit her until she finally decides to marry Pérez.

22. Nazoa, Aquiles. *Fábula de la ratoncita presumida*. Spain: Editorial Europa-Ediexport, S.A., 1981. In this humorous new version of *Pérez y Martina*, proud Hortencia disdains the love of Alfredito while searching for a rich husband.

RELATED TITLES IN ENGLISH FOR SECOND LANGUAGE ACQUISITION

+   Anglund, J.W. *Love Is a Special Way of Feeling.* New York: Harcourt, Brace and World, 1960.

+   Cohen, Miriam. *"Be my Valentine!"* New York: Greenwillow Books, 1978.

Gross, Ruth Belov. *The Mouse's Wedding.* New York: Scholastic, 1972.

Marshall, James. *George and Martha.* Boston: Houghton Mifflin, 1973. (Other books in this collection include: *George and Martha Encore, George and Martha Back in Town, George and Martha Rise and Shine, George and Martha One Fine Day,* and *George and Martha Tons of Fun.*)

Sendak, Maurice. *A Kiss for Little Bear.* New York: Harper and Row, 1968.

II. OBSERVATION/EXPERIENCE: *Pérez y Martina*
(Class Session One)

Guide students in the following observation/experience sequence to set the stage for reading the Main Selection.

Focus: Love and marriage are a part of life's special experiences.

1. Provide an opportunity for children to share family wedding photos, if possible, or ones from a magazine.

2. Guide students in the following discussion:

   • *Platíquennos si han ido a alguna boda.* (Tell us about a wedding you have attended.)

   • *¿Por qué creen ustedes que se casan los adultos?* (Why do you suppose grown-ups get married?)

3. Tell students that you once thought falling in love was silly and that you would never get married. Now, as a grown-up, you have learned that marriage is filled with special moments. This was the experience of an ant and a mouse in a story titled *Pérez y Martina.*

4. Show the book cover and have the students predict what the special moments will be. Following the story, have students discuss whether their predictions were correct.

III. READ AND DISCUSS THE MAIN SELECTION: *Pérez y Martina*
(Class Session One)

Read the Main Selection from page 306 to the students. Highlight the unit's theme by relating this story to other selections from the Literature Input list on pages 306 - 308. Then, guide students in discussing some of the following questions.

1. *¿Por qué Martina prefirió a Pérez en lugar de los otros pretendientes?* (Why did Martina prefer Pérez over the other gentlemen callers?)

2. *¿Cómo celebraron Pérez y Martina su matrimonio? ¿Han ustedes asistido alguna vez a una boda? ¿Vieron algo igual a la boda del cuento?* (How did Pérez and Martina celebrate their marriage? Have you ever attended a wedding? Did you see something similar to the wedding in the story?)

3. *Cuando ustedes crezcan, ¿creen que se casarán? ¿Por qué? ¿Por qué no?* (When you grow up, do you think you will get married? Why? Why not?)

4. *¿Qué hizo Martina en la Navidad para mostrarle su amor a Pérez? ¿Que hacen ustedes para mostrarles su amor a otras personas? ¿Que hacen otras personas para mostrarles su amor a ustedes?* (What did Martina do during Christmas to show her love for Pérez? What do you do to show your love for others? What do others do to show their love for you?)

5. *¿Tuvieron Pérez y Martina momentos tristes y felices? Platíquennos. ¿Podría pasar esto en la vida real?* (Did Pérez and Martina experience sad and happy moments? Tell us about them. Could this happen in real life?)

IV. "WHAT IF" STORY STRETCHER: *Pérez y Martina*
(Class Session Two)

Next, re-read the Main Selection and choose one or more of the following questions to develop students' critical thinking skills. Story stretchers may also prompt discussion, drama or writing activities.

1. *Si Martina no hubiera escogido a Pérez, ¿cuál otro animal podría haber escogido ella para ser su esposo? ¿Por qué?* (If Martina had not chosen Pérez, which other animal might she have chosen for her husband? Why?)

2. *Si Pérez no hubiera sido tan bien educado, ¿por qué otra razón lo habría escogido Martina?* (If Pérez had not been so well-mannered, for what other reason would Martina have chosen him?)

3. *Si Pérez no hubiera sido tan curioso, ¿cómo habría cambiado el cuento?* (If Pérez had not been so curious, how would the story have changed?)

4. *Si ustedes fueran Pérez o Martina, ¿qué harían para ayudar a su esposo/a?* (If you were Pérez or Martina, what would you do to help your husband or wife?)

5. *Si Pérez se hubiera muerto, ¿que habría podido pasar a Martina? ¿Esto puede pasar en la vida real?* (If Pérez had died, what might have happened to Martina? Can this happen in real life?)

V. INTEGRATING OTHER DISCIPLINES: *Pérez y Martina*
(Class Session Three and Ongoing)

The following activities are designed to enhance children's response to literature and expand *beyond* the story and its theme. The variety of activities gives teachers and students an opportunity to choose those most appropriate.

CREATIVE DRAMATICS

1. *Mask Dramatization:* After the children have heard the story more than once, have them re-enact the entire story wearing animal masks or headbands.

2. *"What If" Dramatization:* Have small groups add twists to the story using the following "what if" story stretcher: *Si Martina no hubiera escogido a Pérez, ¿qué otro animal podría haber escogido ella para ser su esposo?* (If Martina had not chosen Pérez, which other animal might she have chosen to be her husband?) Students may use the new character and incorporate special moments.

3. *Reader's Theater:* Use the poem *"Las bodas de la mariposa"* (page 312) for a reader's theater. Divide the eight-stanza poem among eight students. Assign one character to each student. Have them read the entire poem, one stanza at a time.

4. *My Favorite Variant:* Read two supporting stories, *Pérez y Martina* by Pura Belpré and *Fábula de la ratita presumida* by Aquiles Nazoa. Discuss differences and similarities with reference to characters, setting, and plot. In cooperative groups, have children choose and dramatize one of their favorite story variants while observers guess which one is being presented.

ART AND WRITING

1. *Story Variant:* Have students choose story variants to write about and explain why they are their favorites. Let them draw accompanying illustrations.

2. *Animal Finger Puppets:* Using Figure W (page 313), have cooperative groups color and cut out the figures. Have the students size the figures to their fingers and glue the ends. Have partners retell the story or the variant they liked best.

3. *Big Book:* Using large sheets of butcher paper, have cooperative groups illustrate their choice of story events: finding the coin, meeting one of the gentlemen callers, meeting Pérez, getting married and celebrating, Pérez's accident, Pérez's funeral (one version), or Pérez's awakening (another version). Have them write the captions on separate sheets of paper, edit them, then write the revised captions on the illustrated sheets. Have the students place them in proper story sequence and staple them together. Allow them to read the big books in unison.

4. *Wedding Announcement/Invitation:* Have the students write engagement or wedding announcements or wedding invitations for Pérez and Martina. (For fun, the students may use the names of cartoon characters.) Have the students fold paper to make cards, print the information inside, and draw illustrations on the cover. They may share the cards.

5. *Class Newspaper:* Have students write news items in a class newspaper—a wedding announcement for the society section, an obituary report for the obituary section, an article cautioning others about kitchen-related accidents for the opinion section, and a report of Pérez's accident or fatality for the main headline. Have them draw accompanying illustrations. Circulate the completed newspaper among other classes.

6. *Valentine's Day Sweethearts:* Have students cut out two heart patterns. Allow them to draw Pérez, Martina, or another character from the Literature Input in the center of one of the hearts, and then staple them together at the top. Inside they may write Valentine messages that Pérez would write to Martina and vice versa or a message that any of the other characters would send.

7. *Story Sequel:* Have cooperative groups write and illustrate "happily ever after" stories as sequels to the story of Pérez and Martina. Let students brainstorm ideas, assign tasks, carry them out, and share story sequels with the class.

SCIENCE

1. *Real Versus Fictional Animals:* The animals in the story are fictional characters; so that children may distinguish the main characters from real animals, use resources (films, illustrations, or if possible, real animals) to display the physical characteristics and habitats of real ants, roaches, and mice. Allow the students to record their observations in their science logs.

2. *Cooking:* Supervise students in preparing vegetable soup as Martina did for her beloved Pérez. Have them tell what the ingredients are and write the soup's recipe. Have students share favorite soup recipes from home and swap them in small groups.

SAFETY

1. *Kitchen Hazards:* Poor Pérez was involved in a kitchen-related accident; have students brainstorm ideas to include in a safety bulletin cautioning children about kitchen-related hazards. Allow them to record their ideas on a safety chart and title it «*Seguridad en la cocina*» ("Safety in the Kitchen").

SOCIAL STUDIES

1. *Life's Events:* The Pérez and Martina story showed us some special events, some happy and some sad. Of all the events that occurred in the story, have students identify those that can actually occur in real family situations. Allow them to explain their answers. They may write about special family events.

POETRY

Se casa Benito

Mañana domingo
se casa Benito
con una hormiguita
que canta bonito.

¿Quién es la madrina?
Doña Catalina.

¿Quién es el padrino?
Don Juan el Ratón.
Comerán en la cocina y
bailarán en el salón.

Folklore

Las bodas de la mariposa

—Te vamos a casar,
mariposa de colores,
te vamos a casar;
tus madrinas serán las flores.

—¿Y por que me he de casar
sin hacerme de rogar?

—Yo, dice el caracol,
te daré una mansión,
amiga tornasol,
te daré mi habitación.

—Lo que da un amigo fiel
yo lo acepto siempre de él.

—Yo, dijo la hormiguita,
de mi rica provisión
te daré una migajita
y de granos un montón.

—¡Oh, que buena comidita,
oh, que gran comilitón!

La abeja de oro habló:
—Te daré mi mejor miel,
te regalo el postre yo.

—¡Gracias mil, abeja fiel!
¡Y que buena que es la miel!

—Yo—el grillo—iré a tu fiesta
para tocar mi guitarra.
—Completaré la orquesta,
dijo una cigarra.

—¡Gracias, grillo, no está mal!
Cigarrita, ¡está muy bien!

—Yo llevo mi timbal.
—Yo mi pífano también.
—Por ti voy a brillar,
el cucuyo prometió,
pues quiero iluminar
tus bodas sin cesar.

—Gracias a todos y a todas.
Serán soberbias mis bodas.
Me quiero ya casar.
No me hago de rogar.

Amado Nervo

MY OWN CREATIVE TEACHING IDEAS FOR UNIT TWENTY

Books: _____

_____

_____

_____

_____

Ideas: _____

_____

_____

_____

_____

_____

_____

_____

_____

_____

_____

_____

_____

_____

_____

_____

UNIT TWENTY-ONE

APRENDIENDO UNA LECCIONCITA

LEARNING A LITTLE LESSON

Fables are short tales which contain morals. Usually these tales are associated with the name Aesop and the Greek oral literature tradition. In fables, animal characters or key objects often speak and act as humans. Frequently, the animals are generalized or abstract symbols representing certain character types. Usually the story encompasses just a single, brief incident that focuses upon a direct or unwritten moral. Children enjoy fables, particularly when they relate, in some significant way, to their lives. *El asno y el perro* highlights the concept of forgiveness among friends, a significant experience in all of our lives.

MAIN SELECTION

Before reading the Main Selection aloud, take your students through the Literature Input and Observation/Experience phases which follow.

Valeri, Ma. Eulalia.

El asno y el perro.
Spain: Editorial La Galera, S.A., 1984.

True friendship between a donkey and a dog is demonstrated when a virtuous dog saves his friend from an attacking wolf. The story might have had a different ending if the dog had not been so forgiving of his inconsiderate, selfish friend; instead, this fable teaches the virtue of forgiveness.

I. LITERATURE INPUT: *El asno y el perro*

Select five or more titles from the following list to read aloud. Read at least one selection per day to the students. Make available and incorporate the suggested titles for voluntary independent reading. Titles marked with * are Spanish translations of the original English story; titles marked with + are recommended for more proficient listeners.

*1. Ada, Alma Flor. *El conejo y la tortuga.* Reading, MA: Addison-Wesley, 1989. This is a beautifully illustrated big book adaptation of the classic tale of the Hare and the Tortoise.

2. Belpré, Pura. *Pérez y Martina.* New York: Frederick Warne Company, 1977. In this amusing story of romance between an ant and a mouse, they marry and live through sad and happy moments.

*3. Bishop, Dorothy. *Chiquita y Pepita.* Illinois: National Textbook Company, 1978. This is the Spanish version of *The City Mouse and the Country Mouse.* The country mouse, Pepita, values and prefers her life-style over Chiquita's lavish city living. To each his own is the message in this fable.

*4. —. *Leonardo el león y Ramón el ratón.* Illinois: National Textbook Company, 1978. Ramón, the mouse, wins Leonardo's friendship when he gnaws a rope, ending the lion's captivity. Children learn that size is not a measure of one's ability.

*5. —. *Tina la tortuga y Carlos el conejo.* Illinois: National Textbook Company, 1978. Carlos, the hare, underestimates Tina's capacity to beat him in a race. Carlos' inflated confidence gets in the way of his goal while Tina's determination helps her accomplish her goal.

6. Boada, Francesc. *El grillo y el león.* Spain: Editorial La Galera, S.A., 1981. A lion that is a bully learns that he and his friends are no match for the cricket and his army of insects when a challenge to a duel results in his defeat.

7. —. *El lobo y el perro.* Spain: Editorial La Galera, S.A., 1981. A wolf envies a dog's life-style until he realizes that the dog must pay a price for his lavish lifestyle—his freedom.

8. Creus, Ricardo. *El perro y la golondrina.* Spain: Editorial La Galera, S.A., 1983. A dog believes that the world is round, and a swallow, with his perspective on the world, affirms the dog's belief.

*9. Herrmann, Marjorie. *Pérez y Martina*. Illinois: National Textbook Company, 1978. In this amusing tale of romance, Martina is admired by several animals that court her, but her heart belongs to Pérez.

*10. —. *El pájaro Cú*. Illinois: National Textbook Company, 1983. The featherless little Cú bird is helped by his friends in the bird community when each offers him a feather. Overtaken by his vanity, he abandons his friends. Since that time, the owl has continued his unending search for the Cú bird.

*11. —. *Las manchas del sapo*. Illinois: National Textbook Company, 1984. The frog's curiosity and adventurous spirit cause him some bumps and bruises when he crashes an exclusive party for birds.

*12. De Hoogh, Eugenia. *La lechera y su cubeta*. Illinois: National Textbook Company, 1979. The milkmaid "counts her chickens before they hatch" when she thinks about buying a dress before selling her milk. Stirred up with excitement, she spills the milk before she is able to sell it.

*13. —. *El muchacho que gritó—¡el lobo!* Illinois: National Textbook Company, 1979. A life-threatening incident is no joking matter, especially when Pablo comes face to face with the real wolf!

*14. —. *Poniendo el cascabel al gato*. Illinois: National Textbook Company, 1979. A family of mice make big plans to solve their biggest problem—the villainous cat. Grandfather points out, however, that "it is easier said than done."

15. Nazoa, Aquiles. *Fábula de la ratoncita presumida*. Spain: Editorial Europa-ediexport, S.A., 1981. In this humorous version of the popular favorite *La cucarachita Martina,* proud Hortensia disdains the love of humble Alfredito, desiring a rich husband instead.

16. Skutina, Vladimir. *Donde vive el tiempo*. Spain: Editorial S.M., 1986. Though this story is not a traditional fable, it points out a truth about our struggle with time and how haste may often affect our perception. A little girl helps her parents realize this concept.

17. Valeri, Ma. Eulalia. *La liebre y la tortuga*. Spain: Editorial La Galera, S.A., 1973. This adapted version of *The Tortoise and the Hare* tells about their race to reach a vegetable plant. The hare learns a valuable lesson about his underestimation of others.

18. —. *La paloma y la hormiga*. Spain: Editorial La Galera, S.A., 1973. A dove saves an ant from drowning in a stream, and later, in time of need, the favor is returned.

19. —. *La zorra y la cigüeña*. Spain: Editorial La Galera, S.A., 1973. A fox invites a stork to dinner and laughs when the stork is unable to eat his dinner. But the stork gets the last laugh, and manages to give the fox a taste of his own medicine.

20. —. *El ratón del campo y el de la ciudad*. Spain: Editorial La Galera, S.A., 1979. Little country mouse gets a taste of the luxurious city mouse's life-style when he spends a day in the city.

21. —. *El cuervo y la raposa*. Spain: Editorial La Galera, S.A., 1981. A fox tricks a raven out of a piece of cheese by playing upon his vanity.

22. —. *El león y el ratón*. Spain: Editorial La Galera, S.A., 1981. A small mouse gains a lion's respect when he helps the lion in time of need.

RELATED TITLES IN ENGLISH FOR SECOND LANGUAGE ACQUISITION

Addison-Wesley Big Book Program. *The Hare and the Tortoise.* Reading, MA: Addison-Wesley, 1989.

Alley, R. W. *Seven Fables from Aesop.* New York: Dodd, Mead and Company, 1986.

Buckley, Richard, and Eric Carle. *The Greedy Python.* Massachusetts: Picture Book Studio USA, 1985.

—. *The Foolish Tortoise.* Massachusetts: Picture Book Studio USA, 1985.

Carle, Eric. *Twelve Tales from Aesop.* New York: Philomel Books, 1980.

Evans, Katherine. *The Man, the Boy and the Donkey.* Chicago: Albert Whitman and Company, 1978.

Lionni, Leo. *It's Mine!* New York: Alfred A. Knopf, 1985.

Young, Ed. *The Lion and the Mouse.* New York: Doubleday and Company, 1979.

II. OBSERVATION/EXPERIENCE: *El asno y el perro*
(Class Session One)

Guide students in the following observation/experience sequence to set the stage for reading the Main Selection.

Focus: sometimes we think only of ourselves and not about others.

1. Show the book cover for ***El asno y el perro***, and tell students that fables always teach us something about our behavior. Instruct them to take a look at their behavior during an activity with a friend.

2. Pair students and guide them in the following discussion:

   ¿Han deseado que alguien les preste un juguete, pero él/ella no ha querido? (Have you ever wanted someone to share a toy, but he/she refused?)

   Pretendan que ustedes tienen un juguete que su amigo/a quiere; dejen que su amigo/a adivine que es cuando le dan dos claves. (Pretend that you have a toy that your friend wants; have your friend guess what it is by giving two hints.)

   Su amigo/a les pide el juguete imaginario, pero ustedes deciden si se lo prestan o no. (Your friend asks you for your imaginary toy, but you decide if you are going to share or not.)

   Have students act upon their decisions to share or not.

   Suban su dedo pulgar si se lo dieron y bájenlo si no se lo dieron. (Show me thumbs up if it was shared and thumbs down if it was not.)

   Supónganse que decidieron no compartir. ¿Cómo se sentiría su amigo? (Suppose you decided not to share. How would your friend feel?)

3. Tell them that a similar experience happened to a dog and a donkey in a story called *El asno y el perro*.

4. Have students predict what the dog will do when his friend the donkey only thinks about himself and refuses to share something that the dog wants. Following the story, have students discuss whether their predictions were correct.

III. READ AND DISCUSS THE MAIN SELECTION: *El asno y el perro*
(Class Session One)

Read the Main Selection from page 316 to the students. Highlight the unit's theme by relating this story to other selections from the Literature Input list on pages 316 - 318. Then, guide students in discussing some of the following questions.

1. *¿Cómo se portaba el asno con el perro? ¿Qué pasó en el cuento que les indica a ustedes esto?* (How did the donkey behave toward the dog? What events in the story tell you this?)

2. *¿Por qué creen que el asno se portaba así?* (Why do you suppose the donkey behaved as he did?)

3. *¿Cómo se portaba el perro? ¿Qué pasó en el cuento que les indica a ustedes esto?* (How did the dog behave? What events in the story tell you this?)

4. *¿Cómo se sentía el asno después de que su amigo le había salvado la vida? ¿Qué fue lo que él aprendió?* (How did the donkey feel after his friend had saved his life? What did he learn?)

5. *¿Pueden pensar en alguna vez cuando la gente se porta come el perro o el asno?* (Can you think of a time when people behave like the dog or the donkey?)

IV. "WHAT IF" STORY STRETCHER: *El asno y el perro*
(Class Session Two)

Next, re-read the Main Selection and choose one or more of the following questions to develop students' critical thinking skills. Story stretchers may also prompt discussion, drama or writing activities.

1. *Si el asno no hubiera sido tan desconsiderado o egoísta, ¿cómo habría cambiado el cuento?* (If the donkey had not been so inconsiderate or selfish, how would the story have been different?)

2. *Si ustedes fueran el perro, ¿cómo se portarían con el asno? ¿Por qué?* (If you were the dog, how would you act toward the donkey? Why?)

3. *Si el perro hubiera decidido ser terco cuando su amigo más lo necesitaba, ¿qué podría haber pasado en el cuento?* (If the dog had decided to be stubborn when his friend needed him the most, what might have happened in the story?)

4. *Si el perro no hubiera sobrevivido la pelea con el lobo, ¿cómo se habría sentido el asno? ¿Por qué?* (If the dog had not survived the fight with the wolf, how would the donkey have felt? Why?)

5. *Si ustedes se portaran mal, ¿cómo se sentirían? ¿Por qué? ¿Qué necesitan hacer para otra vez sentirse bien? ¿Qué hacen o qué dicen otros para mostrarles que les perdonan a ustedes?* (If you misbehaved, how would you feel? Why? What do you need to do to feel good again? What do others say or do to show that they forgive you?)

V. INTEGRATING OTHER DISCIPLINES: *El asno y el perro*
(Class Session Three and Ongoing)

The following activities are designed to enhance children's response to literature and expand *beyond* the story and its theme. The variety of activities gives teachers and students an opportunity to choose those most appropriate.

CREATIVE DRAMATICS

1. *Re-Enact the Story:* Have students re-enact the story, expressing the characters' emotions during each scene.

2. *Story Twist:* Have the students add a twist to the story by involving the farmer in any of the above scenes. How might he react? Would he show concern, take sides, or give advice?

3. *Create a Skit:* With students, cluster words describing each character's virtues and have cooperative groups create skits centered around the clustered words; e.g., the donkey—stubborn, inconsiderate, ashamed, selfish; the farmer—gentle, humble, hard-working; the dog—loyal, forgiving, brave, loving.

4. *Fruit Basket Game:* While half the class sits in the circle and participates in the activity, the other half observes. Instruct each child in turn to take an imaginary fruit from the donkey's basket, which is inside the circle. Tell the child to eat the fruit slowly while the observers guess what fruit is being eaten. Repeat with the other half of class.

5. *Favorite Fable:* Have students plan dramatizations featuring their favorite fables.

ART AND WRITING

1. *Stuffed-Bag Marionettes:* Have the students make dog and donkey marionettes using two stuffed bags for each body. They may draw ears, tails, eyes, and legs. Have the students cut them out and glue them onto the bags and tie the two bags together with string. Allow them to attach strings along the top of the animal bodies. Instruct them to make animal movements and sounds. Have students write friendship notes to the dog and donkey telling what they have learned about friendship from their example.

2. *Animal Face Masks:* Furnish dog and donkey face patterns (Figures X1 and X2, pages 324 - 325). Have the children trace, color, and cut out holes for their faces. Allow the children to re-enact the story or write dialogues that they might exchange.

3. *Thank-You Card:* Have the children illustrate thank-you cards for the dog and write heartfelt messages to him.

   Interactive Thank-You Note: Pair students and have one pretend to be the dog and one the donkey. Have the one acting as the donkey write a thank-you note to the other, and then let the other respond.

4. *Story Characters:* Have students paint their choice of unlikeable or likeable characters; or they may paint the farmer with his two domestic animals. Have the students develop a story from the farmer's point of view or from the dog's or donkey's viewpoint. Allow them to share written stories.

5. *Flip-Over Book:* In cooperative groups, have students illustrate four story scenes and tie the illustrations together with yarn to make flip-over scenery panels. Allow them to write captions for each panel.

6. *"Who Am I?" Mask:* Use Figures X1 and X2 (page 324 - 325). Have the students color and cut out the oval in the center of each. Allow them to draw the animal bodies on separate sheets. Have them glue the masks and bodies together. Pair students and have one hold a mask to her/his face without looking at its identity and ask *«¿Quién soy?»* ("Who am I?") while the other describes and writes several attributes about the character. When its identity is discovered, have them reverse roles. Students may also use the figure patterns to create any of the animal characters from previously presented fables.

7. *Shape Book:* Have students use Figures X1 and X2 (page 324 - 325) to trace shape books with front and back covers and one lined sheet of paper between. Allow them to write surprise endings for the fable or morals for the story.

8. *Big Book:* Have cooperative groups create big books titled *«Nuestras fábulas favoritas»* ("Our Favorite Fables"). Allow them to decide upon entries, art media, artists, writers, editors, and layout people. Allow them to do the artwork. Have them leave bottom six inches at the bottom of each page for a synopsis of the fable. Have them write the synopses of the fables, edit them, and rewrite them on the illustrated pages. Share books and circulate in a class library.

9. *Living Mural:* Have cooperative groups create living murals using scenes from favorite fables. Have them improvise the dialogues that might have occurred during the scenes. As they participate in the murals, allow them to invite the audience into their fables. Ask each group to describe why the fable is interesting and what lesson it teaches. Have viewers select fables to participate in, and later have them write the fables with twists. Share adapted fables.

10. *Fables Give Advice:* Have students fold long sheets of white construction paper in half. On the left half of the paper, have them draw pictures of favorite fables to include as photos for an advice column. On the right half, to go along with the "photo," have them write some advice for their readers. Distribute advice columns among the groups to read.

11. *Fable Mobile:* Have students create fable mobiles that consist of small replicas of their favorite fables and the characters in the fables. Have them put string on the figures and tie them onto small hangers. On strips of 14" x 3" paper, allow them to write words of wisdom about the fables. Have them put the strips across the hangers with another strip behind and staple the ends together. Display them in the classroom.

SCIENCE

1. *Domestic Animals:* Discuss the donkey and dog as domesticated animals: their value to people and the uses they serve. Brainstorm and record the value and uses of other domestic animals—rabbits, cows, cats, sheep, chickens, goats.

2. *Human Traits:* With students, brainstorm and record the human-like traits that some of the domestic animals from the Literature Input display; e.g., dog—loyal, resourceful, loving, and so on. Discuss whether or not real animals display these traits.

SOCIAL STUDIES

1. *Selfishness/Stubbornness:* To focus on the concepts of selfishness and stubbornness, discuss their meaning. Then have students role play situations that demonstrate these concepts—not sharing friends or things, always wanting to be first for everything, refusing to cooperate, hoarding everything, wanting to be the boss all of the time. Recalling undesirable traits of characters in the stories, have students write thoughts about these behaviors and how the characters might have behaved differently.

2. *Positive Traits:* To emphasize the concepts of love, friendship, and bravery, as demonstrated by the characters, have cooperative groups role play a variety of common experiences—ways friends can be helped, how we show love (verbally and non-verbally), rescuing others from life-threatening situations. Allow this to prompt personal journal writing.

3. *Positive Character Traits:* Have students brainstorm positive behaviors found among other characters in the Literature Input list and compare these characters and their behaviors to others which are totally opposite. Using their literature logs, have students write about the positive behaviors of one of their favorite characters from the Literature Input stories.

4. *Value Judgement:* Have pairs of children role play situations that will prompt a value judgement about selfishness. For example, pose a situation in which two friends go bicycling. One has a bag of candy and does not want to share. Overindulging in the candy while riding, the child falls off the bike. Instruct participants to role-play the situation and indicate whether the other friend should help or not. Have observers evaluate the situation and elaborate upon their opinions. Discuss how this situation relates to the story, *El asno y el perro*, in which the dog had to decide whether or not to help his selfish friend. Allow them to write about this experience in their personal journals.

HEALTH AND SAFETY

1. *Injury and Aid:* In the story the dog was injured. With the children, brainstorm common injuries that children may have. Have students role play several situations and have them include people that come to the victim's aid.

2. *911 Emergency Call:* An injury may constitute an emergency. Instruct students by using the following guide to indicate when and how 911 emergency calls should be made:

When to call:
• When someone has been hurt and needs help.
• If you smell smoke or see a fire.
• If you see someone stealing or hurting someone.
• If you need help quickly for any reason.

How to call:
- Stay calm.
- Say what is wrong.
- Give address where emergency is.
- Give telephone number and address where call is being made.
- Do not hang up until instructed to do so.

Have the students role play these procedures. With the class, brainstorm instances when it would not be appropriate to call 911.

POETRY

Arre, borriquito

Arre, borriquito,
vamos a Sanlúcar
a comer las peras
que están como azúcar.

Arre, borriquito,
vamos a Jerez,
a comer las uvas
que están como miel.

Arre, borriquito,
borriquito, arre;
arre, borriquito,
que llegamos tarde.

Folklore

Fábulas

Si vas a leer un libro,
te recomiendo las fábulas;
son cuentos de animales
todos ellos especiales:

Una ligera liebre y una lenta tortuga,
un agradecido asno y un fiel perro,
un gran león y un servicial ratón.

Todos son cuentos muy divertidos
y que además
te enseñan una buena lección.

Raquel C. Mireles

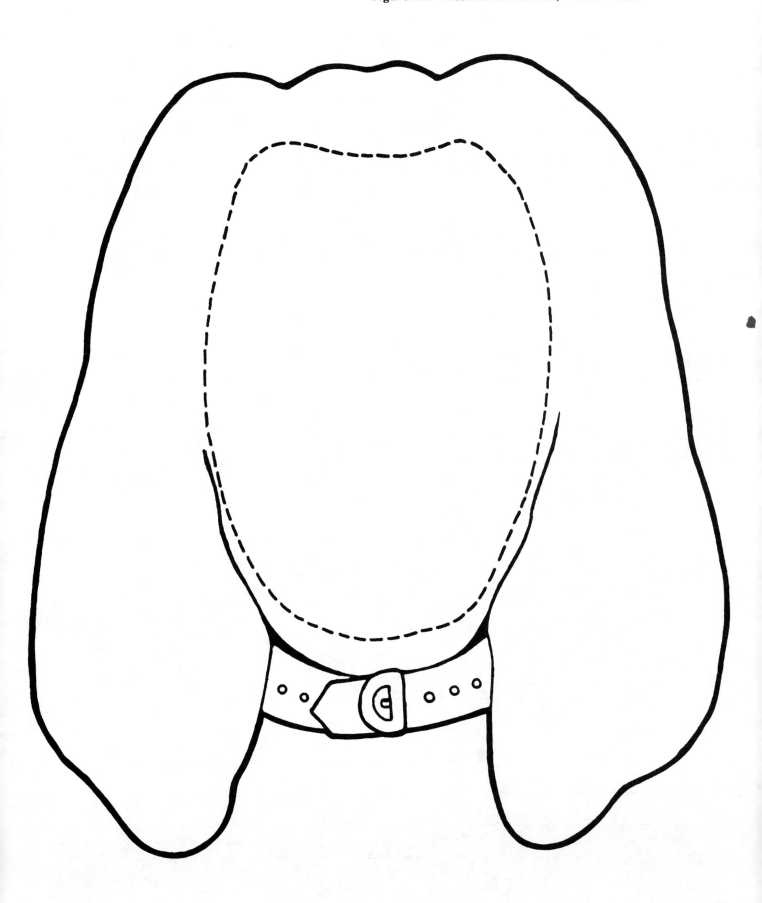

MY OWN CREATIVE TEACHING IDEAS FOR UNIT TWENTY-ONE

Books: _____

_____

_____

_____

_____

_____

Ideas: _____

_____

_____

_____

_____

_____

_____

_____

_____

_____

_____

_____

_____

_____

_____

_____

_____

_____

APPENDIXES

APPENDIX A

REPRODUCIBLE COVERS FOR LOGS AND JOURNAL

The following reproducible masters are intended for use as covers for these student logs:

Mi diario personal / My Personal Journal
Mi cuaderno de literatura / My Literature Log
Mi cuaderno de ciencia / My Science Log
Mi cuaderno de poesía / My Poetry Log

Children may color or otherwise decorate their log covers. The final master is lined paper for writing with a blank space for children's illustrations. It may be reproduced and used inside the logs.

Mi cuaderno de literatura
My Literature Log

Autor:
Author:

Autor:
Author:

Mi cuaderno de ciencia

My Science Log

Mi cuaderno de poesía

My Poetry Log

Los títeres encantados

Una princesita muy aburrida
con un payasito deseaba bailar.
¡Qué buena suerte tuvieron
cuando una gotita los vino a encantar!

Autor:
Author:

APPENDIX B

BRIDGING HOME-SCHOOL LITERACY

As teachers, how might we meet the challenge of bridging home and school literacy? An initial step toward meeting this challenge is to view ourselves as disseminators of information to Spanish-speaking parents, relating the importance of their role in providing books and reading experiences for their children.

Bridging home-school literacy requires coordinated support and an open line of communication among individual parents, school administrators, and classroom teachers; and it is a gradual process that requires sincere commitment.

Teachers may argue that the task of educating parents about the importance of books and the role parents play in the literacy development of their children is too great a challenge to take on, especially since teachers are already over-burdened; however, it is not an impossible task to recruit and inform parents regarding our mutual interest in their children. It is through outreach and communication between home and school that we will increasingly gain parent support and, as a result, extend our effectiveness in the classroom.

Involving parents in the school program requires patience and understanding on the part of teachers and administrators. Sometimes educators may misinterpret the parents' reluctance to become involved as a lack of interest. On the contrary, field studies and our own experience have indicated that the great majority of parents do want to participate in the education of their children.

An initial step toward this goal is to implement a well-planned, home-school read-aloud program that clearly outlines practical, motivating ways to extend literacy at home. A sincere effort to inform and involve Hispanic parents in a read-aloud program is crucial if we are to work towards our goal for meeting the challenge of creating truly literate children.

Guidance on how to work towards bridging an effective school-home reading program includes the following suggestions:

- To begin your school year, provide parent information on the importance of a school-home partnership in a read-aloud program.

- Inform parents of the importance of continuing the use of rich oral Spanish folklore in the home; this includes storytelling, riddles, nursery rhymes, popular sayings, and songs.

- Provide information relating the benefits of daily oral reading to children.

- Promote the use of the public and school libraries; provide addresses.

- Furnish a recommended list of suitable titles available from a local library.

- Let parents know what books you will be reading in class through periodic parent newsletters.

- Send a monthly home read-aloud contract so that the child, parent, or able reader may keep track of home reading.

- If available, send home book-club order forms that also contain Spanish titles.

- Stress to parents the value of books as gifts.

- Use every opportunity to promote the importance of home reading at parent conferences, open houses, parent meetings, and school programs. Encourage attendance at school site and district literature-related programs.

- Extend cordial invitations for literature-related presentations by students: readers theatre, drama, poetry reading, skits, story reading, creative writing, and content-area projects.

- Involve parents in assisting with literature-related extended activities.

- Offer a book loan to parents from your personal library. Stipulate that books be read aloud to children so that stories from home reading can be shared orally. The actual book or an illustration may be shared with the class.

- Coordinate public library card sign-ups. Invite public librarians to inform parents as to the location, privileges and responsibilities of card holders, children's programs, and stock of Spanish reading materials and other available resources. (At this time, have librarians provide library applications and, if possible, issue cards in class.)

- Involve parent volunteers and peer tutors, who feel comfortable reading aloud to small groups, in regular oral reading to children.

- Inform parents of their right to recommend to public and school library officials that the Spanish book collections be maintained and updated. Special children's programs such as storytime, story-related craft time, and project-oriented activities can also be requested.

- Get parents involved when organizing school book fairs.

- Get parents involved in literary guilds *(cafés literarios)*.

These practical suggestions are intended to help teachers extend literacy into the home environment and to include Hispanic parents in the educational process. Implementing many of these suggestions is a worthwhile benefit for students, parents, and teachers. Following through on all of them involves the concerted effort and active involvement of administrators, teachers, and parents who believe in the value of literature toward true literacy.

APPENDIX C

SUGGESTED RESOURCES FOR A PLANNED-LITERATURE PROGRAM

I. SOURCES FOR CREATING A LITERATURE PROGRAM

Allen, Adela A. *Library Services for Hispanic Children.* Phoenix, AZ: Oryx Press, 1987.

Bauer, Caroline F. *This Way to Books.* New York: H. W. Wilson Company, 1983.

Cullinan, Bernice E. *Children's Literature in the Reading Program.* Newark, DE: International Reading Association, 1987.

Cullinan, Bernice E., and Carolyn W. Carmichael. *Literature and Young Children.* Urbana, IL: National Council of Teachers of English, 1977.

Glazer, Joan I., and Gurney Williams. *Introduction to Children's Literature.* New York: McGraw-Hill, 1979.

Huck, Charlotte. *Children's Literature in the Elementary School.* New York: Holt, Rinehart and Winston, 1987.

Lamme, Linda L. *Learning to Love Literature.* Urbana, IL: National Council of Teachers of English, 1981.

Moss, Joy. *Focus Units in Literature: A Handbook for Elementary School Teachers.* Urbana, IL: National Council of Teachers of English, 1984.

Polingharn, Anney, and Catherine Toothey. *Creative Encounters: Activities to Expand Children's Responses to Literature.* Littleton, CO: Libraries Unlimited, 1983.

Rottger, Doris. *Reading Beyond the Basal: Using Children's Literature to Extend and Enrich the Basal Program.* Logan, IA: The Perfection Form Company, 1987.

Sharp, Peggy. *An ABC of Children's Book Activities.* Hagerstown, MD: Upstart, 1983.

Sloan, Glenna D. *The Child as Critic: Teaching Literature in Elementary School.* New York: Teachers College Press, 1984.

Stewig, John W. *Exploring Language Arts in the Elementary Classroom.* Urbana, IL: National Council of Teachers of English, 1980.

—. *Read to Write: Using Children's Literature as a Springboard.* Urbana, IL: National Council of Teachers of English, 1984.

II. DRAMA

Blatt, Gloria T., and Jean Cunningham. *It's Your Move*. New York: Teachers College Press, 1981.

Charters, Jill, and Anne Gately. *Drama Anytime*. Maryborough, Victoria: The Dominion Press-Hedge and Bell, 1986.

Cotrell, June. *Creative Drama in the Classroom*. (Grades 1-3) Lincolnwood, IL: National Textbook Company, 1987.

—. *Creative Drama in the Classroom*. (Grades 4-6) Lincolnwood, IL: National Textbook Company, 1987.

Fox, Menn. *Teaching Drama to Young Children*. Portsmouth, NH: Heinemann, 1987.

Lynch, Diane F. *Dancer Play, Creative Movement for Young Children*. New York: Walker and Company, 1982.

McCaslin, Nellie. *Creative Drama in the Classroom*. New York: Longman, 1984.

Rowan, Betty. *Learning through Movement Activities for the Preschool and Elementary Grades*. New York: Teachers College Press, 1982.

Stanch, Bob. *Sunflowering: Thinking, Feeling, Doing Activities for Creative Expression*. New York: Good Apple Publication, 1977.

Siks, Geraldine Brain. *Drama with Children*. New York: Harper and Row, 1983.

Stewig, John W. *Informal Drama in the Elementary Language Arts Program*. New York: Teachers College Press, 1983.

III. PUPPETRY / STORYTELLING / STORY KITS

Bauer, Caroline F. *Handbook for Storytellers*. Chicago: National Council of Teachers of English, 1981.

Brooks, Courtney. *Plays and Puppets Etcetera*. Claremont, CA: Belnice Books, 1981.

Champlin, Connie, and Nancy Renfro. *Storytelling with Puppets*. Chicago: American Library Association, 1985.

—. *Puppetry and Creative Dramatics*. Austin, TX: Nancy Renfro Studies, 1980.

Instructo, Judy. *Flannel Board Aid*. Minneapolis, MN.

Milton Bradley Company. *Milton Bradley Flannel Board Story Kits*. Baltimore, MD: Media Materials.

Philpott, Violet, and Mary Jean McNeil. *Como hacer y manejar marionetas*. Madrid, Spain: Publicaciones y Ediciones Lagos, S. A., 1981.

Renfro, Nancy. *A Puppet Corner in Every Library*. Austin, TX: Nancy Renfro Studies, 1978.

—. *Puppetry and the Art of Story Creation*. Austin, TX: Nancy Renfro Studies, 1979.

—. *Puppetry Media*. Austin, TX: Nancy Renfro Studies, 1980.

Renfro, Nancy, and Beverly Armstrong. *Making Amazing Puppets*. Austin, TX: Learning Works, 1980.

Rowland, Pleasant T. *Siempre felices / Happily Ever After*. Menlo Park, CA: Addison-Wesley, 1981.

IV. SOURCES FOR INTEGRATING OTHER AREAS OF THE CURRICULUM

Cantoni-Harvey, Gina. *Content-Area Language Instruction: Approaches and Strategies*. Reading, MA: Addison-Wesley, 1987.

Cole, Ann, and Carolyn Hass. *I Saw a Purple Cow*. Boston: Little, Brown and Company, 1985.

Curtain, Helena Anderson, and Carol Ann Pesola. *Languages and Children – Making the Match: Foreign Language Instruction in the Elementary School*. Reading, MA: Addison-Wesley, 1988.

Enright, D. Scott, and Mary Lou McCloskey. *Integrating English: Developing Language and Literacy in the Multilingual Classroom*. Reading, MA: Addison-Wesley, 1988.

Fortson, Laura R. *Integrating the Language Arts in the Elementary School*. Urbana, IL: National Council of Teachers of English, 1981.

Grubber, Barbara. *Instant Science Lessons*. Palos Verdes, CA: Frank Schaffer Publications, 1986.

Hall, Mary Ann, and Pat Hale. *Capture Them with Magic*. Rowayton, CT: New Plays, 1982.

List, Lynne K. *Music, Art, and Drama Experiences for the Elementary Curriculum*. New York: Teachers College Press, 1982.

Norton, Donna E. *Language Arts Activities for Children*. Columbus, OH: Charles E. Merrill Publishing, 1985.

Project AIMS. *Activities that Integrate Math and Science*. (Grades K-1). Fresno, CA: Fresno Pacific College, 1984.

Romberg, Jenean, and Miriam Rutz. *Art Today and Every Day*. West Nyack, NY: Parker Publishing Company, 1972.

V. AUDIO-VISUAL MATERIALS IN SPANISH AND ENGLISH

Ada, Alma Flor, and Jan Mayer, with Suni Paz. *SOL: Spanish Oral Language Enrichment Activities for Children*. Reading, MA: Addison-Wesley, 1989.

Children's All-Time Favorites: Classic Stories. Los Angeles, CA: Bilingual Educational Services, 1970.

Díaz, Mercedes Roig, and María Teresa Miaja. *Naranja dulce, limón partido*. México D.F.: El Colegio México, 1982.

Fábulas Bilingües. Lincolnwood, IL: National Textbook Company, 1980.

Famous Fable Series. Los Angeles, CA: Bilingual Educational Services, 1970.

VI. SPANISH POETRY AND ORAL FOLKLORE COLLECTIONS

(Titles marked with * are related to themes in this handbook.)

Aceves, Marianos. *Campanitas de plata*. México: CIDCLI, S.C., 1987.

Ada, Alma Flor, and María del Pilar de Olave. *Aserrín Aserrán*. Loveland, CO: Donars, 1979.

—. With Suni Paz. *Hagamos caminos*. Reading, MA: Addison-Wesley, 1986.

Almada, Pat. *Rimas para Marisa*. Pico Rivera, CA: Education in Motion Press, 1983.

Bayley, Nicola. *El gato oso polar. El gato loro. El gato araña. El gato cangrejo. El gato elefante*. Spain: Editorial Lumen, 1987.

Beisner, Monika. *El libro de las adivinanzas*. Spain: Editorial Lumen, 1986.

Bravo-Villasante, Carmen. *El libro de las fábulas*. Spain: Editorial Aguilar, 1982.

—. *Al corro de la patata, cantaremos ensalada*. Madrid, Spain: Editorial Escuela Española, 1984.

Cadilla de Ruibal, Carmen Alicia. *Alfabeto del sueño*. Puerto Rico: Editorial de Departamento de Instrucción Pública, 1970.

*Conafe. *Costal de versos y cuentos*. México, D.F.: Consejo Nacional de Fomento Educativo, 1984.

*—. *Cuantos cuentos cuentan*. México, D.F.: Consejo Nacional de Fomento Educativo, 1984.

Díaz, Andres M. *Poemas para niños*. San Juan, PR: Editorial Sendero, 1979.

Díaz, Gloria C. *Un mundo de poesía*. Bogotá, Colombia: Voluntad Publishers, 1980.

Feliciano, Ester. *Nanas*. Puerto Rico: Editorial Universitaria, 1970.

Feliciano, Ester M., and Felix B. Rodríguez. *Ala y Trino*. Puerto Rico: Editorial Universitaria, 1980.

Fernández, Laura. *De tin marín*. México, D.F.: Editorial Trillas, S.A., 1983.

—. *Pío, pío*. México, D.F.: Editorial Trillas, S.A., 1983.

*Figuera, Angela A. *Canciones para todo el año*. México, D.F.: Editorial Trillas, S.A., 1984.

—. *Cuentos tontos para niños listos*. México, D.F.: Editorial Trillas, S.A., 1985.

Fort Worth Independent School District. *Resource Materials for Bilingual Education: Poetry Handbook*. Fort Worth, TX: 1978.

Florit, Eugenio, and José O. Jiménez. *La poesía Hispano-Americana desde el Modernísmo*. Englewood Cliffs, NJ: Prentice-Hall, 1968.

Freire de Matos, Isabel. *Poesía menuda*. Rio Piedras, PR: Hastas Para Niños, 1965.

—. *ABC de Puerto Rico*. Connecticut: Sharon Troutman, 1968.

Fuentes, Gloria. *El dragón tragón. El hada acaramelada. El libro loco de todo un poco. Yo contenta tu contenta, que biem me sale la cuenta*. Spain: Escuela Española, S.A., 1983.

*Galarza, Ernesto. *Rimas tontas*. U.S.A.: Editorial Almaden, 1971.

Granados, Antonio. *Versos de dulce y de sal*. México: Editorial Amaquemecan, 1986.

Griego, Margot, and Gilbert K. Bucks. *Tortillitas para Mamá*. New York: Holt, Rinehart and Winston, 1982.

Guillen, Nicolas. *Por el mar de las Antillas anda un barco de papel*. Spain: Editorial Loguez, 1984.

Lisson, Asunción, and María Eulalia Valerie. *Pito Pito Colorito*. Barcelona, Spain: 1979.

Lorca, Federico G. *Canciones y poemas para niños*. Spain: Editorial Labor, 1986.

*Medina, Arturo. *El silbo del aire: Antología lírica 1 y 2 infantil*. Spain: Visena-Basica, S.A., 1985.

Mendoza, Esther Feliciano. *Arco iris. Coqui. Nanas de adolescencia. Nanas de la Navidad. Literatura infantil Puertorriqueña*. Puerto Rico: Editorial del Departamento de Instrucción Pública, 1956.

Mercedes, Saenz. *Lectura para los niños de mi tierra*. Puerto Rico: Instituto de Cultura Puertorriqueña, 1979.

Nisten, Ernest. *Estampas Infantilas*. Bogotá, Colombia: Editorial Carvajal, S.A., 1980.

*Olave, María del Pilar de, and Alma Flor Ada. *Poesía pequeña*. Lima, Peru: Editorial Arica, S.A., 1972.

Perera, Hilda. *Cuentos para chicos y grandes*. Spain: Editorial Miñón, S.A., 1985.

Rivera, Flor Piniero de. *Literatura infantil Caribeña: Puerto Rico, Republica Dominicana y Cuba*. Dominican Republic: Boriken Libros, 1983.

Romero, Marina. *Alegrias, poemas para niños*. Spain: Editorial Escuela Española, S.A., 1980.

*Salvat. *El mundo de los niños: Poesías y canciones*. Barcelona, Spain: Salvat Editores, S.A., 1973.

Schneider, Esther S. *Desde chiquito. . . .* Argentina: Editorial Guadalupe, 1969.

*Schon, Isabel. *Doña Blanca and Other Hispanic Nursery Rhymes and Games*. Minneapolis, MN: T.S. Denison and Company, 1985.

*Serradell, Luz María R. *La alegria de los niños*. México, D. F.: Editorial Avante; S.A., 1983.

*Secretaria de Educación Pública. *Apuntes de literatura infantil*. La Trinidad, Tlaxcala, México: 1986.

*Uzcanga, Alicia María Lavalle. *Poesías para la infancia*. México, D.F.: EDAMEX, 1986.

*Walsh, María Elena. *Zoo loco*. Buenos Aires: Editorial Sudamericana, S.A., 1977.

*—. *Tutu maramba*. Buenos Aires: Editorial Sudamericana, S.A., 1984.

*—. *La foca loca. La reina batata. Manuelita. Palomita de la puna*. Argentina: Editorial Sudamericana, S.A., 1987.

*Zuluaga, Mariela, and Eutiquio Leal. *Ronda de hadas*. Bogotá, Colombia: Voluntad Publishers, 1978.

VII. PARENT INVOLVEMENT IN LITERACY

Huber, William T., Jr. *Helpbook: Helping Energetic Learning Parents in Primary Grades*. Franklin, PA: Franklin Area Public Schools, 1978. (ED 167 965)

Kentucky State Department of Education. *Parents are Reading Teachers Too!* Frankfort, KY: Kentucky State Department of Education, Division of Program Development, 1976. (ED 169 517)

New York State Department of Education. *Language Experience for Your Preschooler. Part I: Activities at Home*. Albany, NY: New York State Department of Education, Bureau of Continuing Education Curriculum Development, 1974. (ED 095 987)

Oklahoma State Department of Education. *Reading: Parents, Kids, Teachers, Inc. A Resource Guide for Teachers Interested in Parent Involvement*. Oklahoma City: Oklahoma State Department of Education, 1982. (ED 221 843)

Ransbury, Molly Kayes. *How Can I Encourage My Primary-Grade Child to Read?* Bloomington, IN: ERIC Clearinghouse on Reading, 1972. (ED 112 358)

Simons, Jenny. *Learning to Read: Parents Can Help.* Watson, Australia: Australia Early Childhood Association, 1981. (ED 212 350)

Teale, W. H. "Parents Reading to Their Children: What We Need to Know." *Language Arts* 58 (1981): 901-912.

—. "Preschoolers and Literacy: Some Insights from Research." *Australian Journal of Reading* (1982): 153-161.

—. "Toward a Theory of How Children Learn to Read and Write Naturally." *Language Arts* 59 (1982): 555-570.

Micromonographs are available from the International Reading Association.

APPENDIX D

DISTRIBUTOR INFORMATION

The major distributors that carry many of the titles contained in this handbook are listed as follows:

* Bilingual Educational Services, Inc.
  2514 South Grand Avenue
  Los Angeles, CA 90007 (213) 749-6213

* Bilingual Publications Company
  1966 Broadway
  New York, NY 10023 (213) 873-2607

* Hamel-Spanish Book Corporation
  10977 Santa Monica Boulevard
  Los Angeles, CA 90025 (213) 475-0453

  Iaconi Book Imports
  300 Pennsylvania Avenue
  San Francisco, CA 91407 (415) 285-7393

* Libería el Día
  R. Sánchez Taboada 61-A
  Tijuana, Baja California Telephone: 84-09-08

  Lectorum Publications, Inc.
  137 West 14th Street
  New York, NY 10011 (212) 929-2833

* These distributors have furnished books referred to in this handbook.

APPENDIX E

REFERENCES

Ada, A.F., and M. de Olave. *Hagamos caminos*. Teacher's Edition. Reading, MA: Addison-Wesley, 1986.

Canella, G.S. "Providing Exploration Activities in Beginning Reading Instruction." *The Reading Teacher* (December 1985): 284-289.

Chomsky, C. "Stages in Language Development and Reading Exposure." *Harvard Educational Review* 42 (1972): 33.

Cummins, J. *Schooling and Language Minority Students: A Theoretical Framework*. Los Angeles, CA: California State University; Evaluation, Dissemination and Assessment Center, 1981.

—. *Bilingualism and Special Education: Issues in Assessment and Pedagogy*. Clevedon, Avon, England: Multilingual Matters, 1984.

Elbow, P. *Writing Without Teachers*. New York: Oxford University Press, 1972.

Goodman, K. *Language and Thinking in School*. New York: Holt, Rinehart and Winston, 1976.

—. *Language and Literacy*. London, England: Routledge and Kegan Paul, 1982.

—. *What's Whole in Whole Language?* Portsmouth, NH: Heinemann Educational Books, 1986.

Goodman, K., and Y. Goodman with B. Flores. *Reading in the Bilingual Classroom: Literacy and Biliteracy*. Rosslyn, VA: National Clearing House for Bilingual Education, 1984.

Goodman, Y., and C. Burke. *Reading Strategies: Focus on Comprehension*. New York: Holt, Rinehart and Winston, 1980.

Halliday, M.A.K. *Explorations in the Study of Languages*. London, England: Edward Arnold, 1981.

Holdaway, D. *Foundations of Literacy*. Sydney, Australia: Ashton Scholastic, 1979.

Huck, C. "Literature for All Reasons." *Language Arts* 56 (1975): 283.

—. *Children's Literature in the Elementary School*. New York: Holt, Rinehart and Winston, 1979.

Huck, C., and J. Hickman. *Children's Literature in The Elementary School*. New York: Holt, Rinehart and Winston, 1987.

Krashen, S.D. "The Power of Reading." In *Inquiries and Insights: Essays in Language Teaching, Bilingual Education, and Literacy*. Hayward, CA: Alemany Press, 1985.

Krashen, S., and D. Biber. *On Course: Bilingual Education's Success in California.* Sacramento, CA: California Association for Bilingual Education, 1988.

Langer, J., and A. Applebee. *How Writing Shapes Thinking.* NCTE Research Report No. 22. Urbana, IL: National Council of Teachers of English, 1987.

Martínez, M., and N. Rosner. "Read It Again: The Value of Repeated Readings During Storytime." *The Reading Teacher* (April 1985): 782-786.

McClure, A.H. "Integrating Children's Fiction and Informational Literature in a Primary Reading Curriculum." *The Reading Teacher* 35 (1982): 784-788.

Purves, A.C. "Research in the Teaching of Literature." *Elementary English* 52 (1975): 462-466.

Sloan, G.D. *The Child as Critic: Teaching Literature in Elementary School.* New York: Teachers College Press, 1984.

Smith, F. *Reading Without Nonsense.* New York: Teachers College Press, 1979.

—. *Understanding Reading.* Third Edition. Hillside, NJ: Erlbaum, 1982.

—. *Joining the Literacy Club.* Portsmouth, NH: Heinemann, 1988.

Snow, C.E. "Literacy and Language: Relationships During the Preschool Years." *Harvard Educational Review* 53 (1983): 1-33.

Stewig, J.W. *Read to Write: Using Children's Literature as a Spring for Teaching Writing.* Urbana, IL: National Council of Teachers of English, 1984.

Teale, W.H. "Preschoolers and Literacy: Some Insights from Research." *Australian Journal of Reading* 3 (1982): 152.

Trealease, J. In H.E. Groff. *Once Upon a Time.* New York: Crowell-Collier, 1987.

Wells, G. *Learning Through Interaction: The Study of Language Development.* Cambridge, MA: Cambridge University Press, 1981.

—. *The Meaning Makers.* Portsmouth, NH: Heinemann, 1985.

INDEX

NOTES

NOTES

NOTES

NOTES

NOTES

NOTES

NOTES

NOTES